CONSTITUTIONAL PARADIGMS AND THE STABILITY OF STATES

To the members of the Faculty of Law of the University of Cambridge and to the President, Fellows and other members of Wolfson College, Cambridge, in whose company the writing of this book was commenced, and to Katy, whose support, patience and understanding are always appreciated.

Constitutional Paradigms and the Stability of States

NOEL COX,
Aberystwyth University, Wales

ASHGATE

Published by

Ashgate Publishing Limited
Wey Court East
Union Road
Farnham
Surrey, GU9 7PT
England

Ashgate Publishing Company
Suite 420
101 Cherry Street
Burlington
VT 05401-4405
USA

www.ashgate.com

British Library Cataloguing in Publication Data
Cox, Noel, 1965–
Constitutional paradigms and the stability of states.
1. Constitutional law--Philosophy. 2. Constitutional history.
3. State, The. 4. Political science--History.
I. Title
342'.02-dc23

Library of Congress Cataloging-in-Publication Data
Cox, Noel, 1965-
Constitutional paradigms and the stability of states / by Noel Cox.
p. cm.
Includes bibliographical references and index.
ISBN 978-0-7546-7920-2 (hardback : alk. paper) -- ISBN 978-0-7546-9818-0 (ebook)
1. Constitutional law. 2. Constitutional history. 3. Security, International. 4. Globalization.
5. Failed states. I. Title.

K3165.C695 2011
342--dc23

2011040765

ISBN 9780754679202 (hbk)
ISBN 9780754698180 (ebk)

FSC www.fsc.org MIX Paper from responsible sources FSC® C018575

Printed and bound in Great Britain by the MPG Books Group, UK.

Contents

Preface

In broad terms this book examines the influence of constitutional legal paradigms upon the political stability and viability of states. The 'legal paradigms', in this sense, is to be understood relatively broadly, not as covering the specific constitutional rules which may apply to any given situation, or even the framework of institutions, powers and responsibilities within a constitution. Rather it should be understood to refer to the driving ethos, or *Grundnorm*, which underpins the whole constitutional system; the principles upon which the system operates. Nor is this *Grundnorm* to be seen as simply the economic imperative that drives a regime, though this may be a major element in a socialist or communist system (or indeed, in a pure capitalist system, if such a system exists in the real world). In these systems, the economic and the political imperative, cannot be easily separated – may be deliberately conflated – and the economic model may bear close resemblance to, or be indistinguishable from, the constitutional *Grundnorm*. But the *Grundnorm* also includes the historical, social and political principles which influence a constitution, including the degree to which the constitution may be classified as entrenched, flexible or normative. Thus constitutional legal paradigms refer to the underlying political theory, ethos and practice of a given state.

Success and stability are also terms that defy precise definition, and no attempt will be made here to construct a precise definition, even if this were possible or desirable. The success and stability of the state will be measured by comparison with other states with which the subject states have direct contact, or with which they may otherwise be compared. Thus only the broadest conclusions, if any, can be drawn from these empirical comparisons, and from the theoretical modelling which accompanies this. The more valuable contribution may indeed be to examine those states where there has been a fundamental change in *Grundnorm*. However, essentially this book is an exercise in analysing theoretical principles rather than practice, though from the theory practice may indeed follow.

The political viability of states is also to be understood, for the purposes of this study, in a limited, and special, sense. This is the on-going viability of a state, measured by internal and external factors, to successfully exist and compete with other states, as a state, rather than as a loose collection of individuals and communities. The state is more than simply a collection; it is greater than the sum of the components, or it would scarcely qualify, sociologically or politically, as a state. Here, too, the term 'state' is used in its broadest sense. No attempt has been made to exclude those states whose separate existence is not recognized by other states, for the existence of a state is determined by both reality and recognition. Nor is a distinction to be drawn between those states that have a fully developed jurisprudence of the state, those where notions of public law are less systematically developed, and where the very notion of the 'state' may be looked upon with suspicion, or if not indeed regarded as an alien concept.

The viability of the state – and the viability of any human institution – may depend upon an apparently infinite number of variables. It may well be impossible to separate each of these from the others, or to distinguish what is truly the determining factor in any one given situation. These factors may include such divergent elements as the physical geography of the country, the composition – or the size, distribution and density – of the population. Nor is it possible to use a control group, a selection of countries whose variables are known, to identify the variables of other states.

In order to limit what might otherwise be an impossibly broad study, the book will examine one element only. It will consider the degree to which constitutional flexibility, rather than broader societal and environmental factors, appears to have contributed to stability, and thus led to the rise of 'successful' states and to the decline of 'unsuccessful' states. This will include some case studies, but this book is in no sense an empirical work. Rather, the emphasis is upon identifying the elements of state success and failure – if any – that may be ascribed to the underlying nature of the constitution.

Essentially this book is an exercise in discovering how the one element of the character or ethos of a legal system has influenced economic, social and political success. In part this is a consideration of the contribution of law, widely defined, to the success of states. Using primarily jurisprudential tools and lens, though not constrained by these, it applies a historical institutionalism to the identification of key dynamics in legal, political and economic history. It is necessarily a broad sweep, covering socialist and capitalist models, the rise and fall of empires, the growth and decline of the nation-state in Europe, and the emergence of the post-modern state.

This book began as a research project undertaken while I was in residence as a visiting fellow at Wolfson College, Cambridge and as a Visitor to the Faculty of Law of the University of Cambridge during Michaelmas Term, 2006. I wish particularly to acknowledge the assistance and support of the President, Fellows, and staff of Wolfson College, as well as that of the graduates and undergraduates of the College, and of various visiting fellows and scholars.

I would also like to thank the Faculty of Law of the University of Cambridge, in particular Professor David Feldman, BCL MA *Oxford* FBA FRSA (Downing College), quondam Chairman of the Faculty Board of Law. Special thanks are also due to Sir Derek Oulton, MA PhD *Cambridge* GCB QC (Magdalene College). My thanks are further due to many others, who must remain unnamed, who have contributed in one way or another during the gestation of this work.

The remainder of the work for this book was undertaken at the School of Law of the Auckland University of Technology, New Zealand, which has a particular interest in the implications of the interaction of law and economy, and the Department of Law and Criminology, Aberystwyth University.

I would also like to thank the other scholars, commentators, reviewers and myriad other people who are inevitably involved to some degree in the production of any work of this sort. As always, any errors and omissions remain mine alone.

Noel Cox

Note on the Author

Noel Cox was born in Auckland, New Zealand. After attending grammar school in Takapuna, he took up the study of law at the University of Auckland. After graduation with an LLB he was admitted and enrolled as a Barrister and Solicitor of the High Court of New Zealand. He later undertook an LLM at the same university, and received the Fowlds Memorial Prize as most distinguished student in the Faculty of Law. He subsequently undertook a PhD. His doctoral research was under the supervision of Associate Professor Raymond Miller, and was on the topic of the 'The Evolution of the New Zealand Monarchy: The Recognition of an Autochthonous Polity'. He also obtained a Certificate in Tertiary Teaching (CertTertTchg) and a Graduate Diploma in Tertiary Teaching (GradDipTertTchg), both from the Auckland University of Technology.

He also holds an MA of the Archbishop of Canterbury's Examination in Theology, for a thesis entitled 'An exploration of the basis of legal authority of the Anglican Church in New Zealand', and a Licence in Theology (LTh) from the University of Wales Lampeter. He completed an MTheol at the University of Auckland, in the field of systematic theology, on the topic, 'The meaning of catholicity with respect to ordained ministry in the Anglican Communion: An examination of the ecclesiology implicit in the validity of orders debate'.

Noel Cox holds the position of Head of the Department of Law and Criminology at Aberystwyth University. He was Professor of Constitutional Law at the Auckland University of Technology to 2010, and was Head of the Department of Law 2004–2008. He received the Vice-Chancellor's Excellence Award for Research, in 2002. He spent the summer of 2003–2004 as a Visiting Fellow, Faculty of Law, The Australian National University, Canberra, and the latter part of 2006 at Wolfson College, the University of Cambridge. He was elected a Visiting Fellow at St Edmund's College, the University of Cambridge, in 2009, though he was not able to take this up as he then accepted appointment to Aberystwyth University.

Apart from New Zealand, he is also admitted to practice law in England and Wales, the Australian Capital Territory, New South Wales, the Northern Territory, Queensland, South Australia, Tasmania and Victoria.

His previous books include *The catholicity of ordained ministry in the Anglican Communion* (Verlag Dr. Müller, Saarbrücken, 2009), *Church and State in the Post-Colonial Era* (Polygraphia Ltd, Auckland, 2008), *A Constitutional History of the New Zealand Monarchy* (Verlag Dr. Müller, Saarbrücken, 2008), and *Technology and Legal Systems* (Ashgate Publishing Ltd, Aldershot, 2006).

He was formerly Chairman of Monarchy New Zealand (previously The Monarchist League of New Zealand), and a member of the Council of the Auckland District Law Society. He is a Fellow of the Royal Historical Society.

Introduction

The question of why some parts of the world have advanced politically, economically and technologically, while others have remained relatively less developed, is one which has interested historians, economists, social scientists (and to a lesser extent lawyers) for generations. What has been called the 'Great Question' is nothing less than an attempt to explain the rise of one civilization when others are in decline or stagnation, though the narrower phenomenon of state failure is relatively under-researched.[1] Needham, one of the leading early commentators on this question, asked 'why, then, did modern science, as opposed to mediæval and ancient science (with all that modern science implied in terms of political dominance), develop only in the Western world?'[2] His answer, at least with respect to China – which has long been a staple subject for comparison – was the failure of the development of the merchant class,[3] which was pivotal in the West in its fostering of novel ideas. But he also ascribed to China a degree of innovation that has been questioned by others,[4] and thus, although his writings contain much of undoubted value, the application of his theoretical approach may not always have been sufficiently careful. We must be careful, lest our generalizations rob our hypotheses of any meaningfulness. It is also true that a great deal has already been written on this subject, and any writer should be wary of adding to this literature without some certainty that their contribution will be worthwhile. The particular contribution in this study is the focus upon constitutional modelling, and the influence of legal systems on political stability. While the latter in particular is not wholly original, nonetheless, it is rare for the influence to be considered holistically in this manner.

We will commence with a review of some of the main themes in the literature of the 'Great Question'.

In a chapter in Marciano and Josselin's *Law and the State: A Political Economy approach*,[5] Dudley considered the great increase in European wealth *vis-à-vis* that of Asia during the period 1700–1870. In a brief review of literature in the field,

---

1 Robert I. Rotberg (ed.), *State Failure and State Weakness in a Time of Terror* (Washington, 2003), p. 2.

2 Joseph Needham, *The Great Titration: Science and Society in East and West* (London, 1969), p. 11.

3 Ibid, and *Science and civilisation in China* (Cambridge, 1954-95).

4 David Cosandey, *Le Secret de l'Occident* (Paris, 1997).

5 Leonard Dudley, 'Explaining the great divergence: Medium and message on the Eurasian land mass 1700–1850', in Alain Marciano and Jean-Michel Josselin (ed.), *Law and the State: A Political Economy Approach* (Cheltenham, 2005), pp. 100–120.

two major camps emerged. One emphasized geography as the primary influence which led to this rapid growth in one region and comparative stagnation in others. The other group emphasized economic institutions as the primary influence. While there is something to be said in favour of each argument, it is possible to identify slightly more complex influences than geography, or economic institutions alone, at work.

Dudley, in assessing the physical and human environment, argued that Europe, more especially Western Europe, was the only one of the four major cultural regions that comprised Eurasia to have both a standardized medium and a non-standardized message. [6] By this he meant a common language – in each state rather than across the region (yet with a *lingua franca* to allow the free exchange of ideas) – and a diversity of scientific, cultural, religious and political ideas. Between 1700 and 1850, per-capita income effectively doubled in Europe. Over the same time period it was falling, at least in real terms, in the rest of the greater continent of Eurasia. Largely this is the result of political stability – or lack of it. Neither geography nor economic institutions alone can explain this relatively sudden divergence.

The result of both the advent of a free exchange of ideas, and a diversity of scientific, cultural, religious or political ideas, was a dramatic increase in the development of innovation, due to the reduction in the difficulties hitherto faced. Meanwhile, elsewhere in Eurasia, a reduced standardization of the medium – through political and ethnic rivalry and subdivision – inhibited, rather than fostered, innovation. The tendency at this time for common ideas to be enforced, rather than divergent views promoted, led to a concurrent tendency to conformity. Put simply, diversity of ideas in an environment where communications allowed the free (or relatively free) exchange of these ideas, was more beneficial than a uniformity of ideas and limited communications.

While this theory may be more finely nuanced than that offered by the geography versus institutions argument, it does not specifically consider the role played by the character or ethos of a legal system, and the ways in which this has influenced economic and political success. It is not necessarily true that the conditions that existed in Europe were markedly different from those in, for instance, the Roman Empire at its height. This was, for a considerable time, successful across much of Europe and parts of North Africa and Asia. It may be said, however, that the Roman empire was successful because it too allowed a diversity of ideas to be freely exchanged. It was, indeed, successful for a considerable period of time, but ultimately collapsed due to a variety of factors – factors that might have led to the eventual collapse of any civilization, however constituted.

It is possible, indeed desirable, to consider the question of human and natural environmental influences on economic growth. But this book is intended to both

6 Leonard Dudley, 'Explaining the great divergence: Medium and message on the Eurasian land mass 1700–1850', in Alain Marciano and Jean-Michel Josselin (ed.), *Law and the State: A Political Economy Approach* (Cheltenham, 2005), p. 120.

narrow the study and to alter its focus. Dudley's focus was on ideas; the focus of the book will be narrower – the idea of the constitution.

We will consider the degree to which constitutional flexibility, rather than broader societal and environmental factors, may have led to the rise of 'successful' states, and to the decline of 'unsuccessful' states, by promoting stability. Economic growth is one, but not necessarily the sole, criteria of success. The 'Great Question' may be based upon a yet more profound 'grand question' (as Cosandey calls it):[7] why do civilizations rise and fall? Answering that question is beyond the scope of this or of any single work or author. But it is the underlying hypothesis of this book that the constitutional paradigm of a country has a prime influence upon that country's success or failure, and that this principle can be extended to regions and continents also. Thus, although environment, broadly defined, is often a crucial element – for a country totally devoid of natural resources is scarcely likely to prosper – the model of constitution, or shape of the body politic, is critical to its viability and stability.

The model of the constitution is not necessarily confined to any particular form of government, democratic, parliamentary, presidential, monarchical, or any other form that may be imagined, but rather the underlying nature of the constitution. Is it rigid or flexible, can it adapt, or is it too flexible that it lacks coherency? These questions are important in influencing the success or failure of a state – or rather, since in the modern age states rarely fail (though examples have occurred however, such as Newfoundland,[8] and more disastrously for its people, Somalia[9]), the degree of success.

Of necessity this study is both historical and theoretical. As Mokyr has observed (in the context of a discussion of European pre-eminence, though his reasoning has general application here), 'Western technological superiority has deep historical roots, and can only be understood – if at all – by an analysis that

7 David Cosandey, *Le Secret de l'Occident* (Paris, 1997).

8 Newfoundland, a dominion of the British Empire and Commonwealth, voluntarily surrendered its independence and joined the Dominion of Canada in 1949, after a transitional period as a British colony, as a consequence of financial collapse brought about by the depression of 1929–30; *Report of the Royal Commission on Newfoundland Finances* (London, 1933).

9 Somalia is commonly, and perhaps fairly, regarded as a failed state (a term introduced by G.B. Helman and S.R. Ratner, 'Saving Failed States', *Foreign Policy*, 89 (1992–93): 3–20), after a decade without an effective central government – or without any central government at all for some years. Whether this can be regarded as a failed state, or whether this is simply an interregnum, or period without effective leadership pending the establishment of a new (probably dictatorial or military-backed) regime is uncertain. But the effective secession of Somaliland (formerly British Somaliland), a part of the country only since independence, probably indicates that the old Somalia is not a viable state; see Noam Chomsky, *Failed States: The abuse of power and the assault on democracy* (Crows Nest, 2006).

is willing to look back centuries, even millennia'.[10] The constitutional heritage of states cannot be understood out of the context from which it grew. For this reason there is some validity in the argument some have made that Western notions of democracy are alien to other parts of the world. They may be unfamiliar, even alien, but they may still be worthwhile. However the body's immune system has an unfortunate habit of rejecting alien implants. An alien concept will only add to the viability of a state if it is consistent with the constitutional ethos of the recipient state, and transplantable onto it.

Constitutional flexibility, in the sense of the hard or the soft constitution, is distinct from the narrower question of democracy, and is therefore foreseeable in any constitutional model. States have been successful in the past when democracy was rare or non-existent. Equally, today some states that might not be regarded as democratic – such as China – are apparently successful despite this absence of democracy. But in a soft constitution, where there is a degree of flexibility, societal pressures encourage and indeed depend on accountability, and in time this leads to democratic processes being created, and then instinctively followed. Democracy may not, *per se*, be essential to economic success, but its absence may prevent the long-term preservation of that success, in an environment where other states are democratic. It may also be that democracy develops as a necessary accessory to a maturing liberal state, as that state develops and grows. Perhaps, too, democracy is a phase through which states pass; is there a post-democratic future awaiting us? As yet there is little, if any, evidence for this, though the tendency towards voter apathy in much of the West could point towards this direction. If this does arise, then perhaps it will be a sign that the era of the dominance of the West is at an end, for the West's pre-eminence draws some of its strength from its liberal democratic ethos.

Part I of the book, 'Legal Paradigms', considers the theories that have been advanced in an attempt to explain the rise and fall of civilizations. Some of these are valuable in general, while others contribute to an understanding of the process by which these variables can be isolated and studied. The focus is then changed, in the second and third chapters of the first part, to look at individual states, and the factors that appear to have led to their success and failure. Finally, the concept of the hard and soft constitutions will be introduced and explained. This concept is based on the notion that the formal constitutional flexibility of states is a major factor in determining their success and failure.

In Part II, 'The Viability of States', we will apply this concept to different types of state models. These types include authoritarian, doctrinaire liberal, empires and supra-national entities, and mixed models. None are exclusively of the soft or the hard constitution type. Still, some have been markedly less successful than others, and we will examine the performance of these state models, with the purpose of ascertaining whether it may be the flexibility of the underlying constitutional

10 Joel Mokyr, *The Lever of Riches: Technological creativity and economic progress* (Oxford, 1990), pp. 209–18.

paradigm, rather than the form or type of the model itself, that helps influence state stability and viability.

This part comprises a series of case studies, looking at particular states at specific points in time. In doing so, the scale of the study is made more manageable, yet its validity remains essentially unimpaired. As noted in the Preface, using jurisprudential tools and lens, but not constrained by these, it applies an historical institutionalism to the identification of key dynamics in legal, political and economic history. Through these case studies we may identify at least some of the elements common to the hard and the soft constitution, and the correlation between these and the stability of the regimes. The case studies include, among others, Ireland and New Zealand in the twentieth century, and eastern Europe in the late twentieth century. In these and other examples the focus is upon the responsiveness of the constitution to changing circumstances.

PART I
Legal Paradigms

From Gibbons's *Decline and Fall of the Roman Empire*, onwards – and even earlier – there have been various attempts to explain the apparent mystery of why some civilizations rose and fell without reason, or at least without reasons that were clearly evident to the later observer (or to the contemporary spectator). Some of these studies have sought to identify key political or military influences – or the advent of a new technology – as affecting success or failure. Others have emphasized structural elements, such as the existence or absence of critical environmental factors. In a comparatively simple and small state such factors may be crucial. For ancient Sparta, to use an example, the form of the body politic, with its inherent and systematic militarism, was a key element to the success of that state during its heyday from the seventh to the fourth centuries BC. Similarly, the presence of the Nile, the comparatively fertile lands of the Indus valley, and the golden crescent in Mesopotamia, led to the early development of civilizations in these regions.

In some instances the success and failure of a city state – perhaps the most simple, or least complex, form of state that we have known (or at least of which surviving records, literary and archaeological, tell) – has been largely due to the existence of trade routes, and to a plentiful and reliable supply of water. The disruption of one or other of these has been catastrophic for the states concerned. Parts of Asia are liberally sprinkled with the desiccated remains of cities, whose days of glory passed as rapidly as their wells grew dry. For many of these cities, important enough in their own day, we do not even know their names.

We are left to speculate on the thoughts and sensations that passed through the minds of the last generations of City Fathers, as they saw their glory depart from them, unable to stay the seemingly inescapable advance of death. For us, now, there is often little more than the 'two great trunks' of stone, in Shelley's sonnet 'Ozymandias' (published in 1818). Although written of Egypt, whose glory did not altogether pass from the knowledge of mankind, this can describe many lost and now almost entirely forgotten civilizations of the past.

There is something tragic in viewing the surviving tangible evidence of the death throes of a civilization, whether it be great or small. For those most intimately concerned – the dwellers in that civilization – the end may, however, have been neither recognized nor understood. Perhaps it was blamed upon the enmity of the Gods – as indeed it must have seemed to the people of a great city, when they saw the enemy at the gates – whether that be human or environmental. The human enemy will only reach the gates of the city when its internal strength is sapped in some manner. A successful state, a viable one, as it were, will only suffer the ignominy of the enemy battering at the gates if its own essential vitality is lost (unless it suffers a series of unfortunate strategic disasters). The terrible drawn-out fate of the Roman Empire is a case in point. In its dying days the empire based on Constantinople, ultimately reduced to the city of New Rome itself, and little more, suffered the crushing humiliation of invasion from both Christian and Muslim powers. Both were ravening upon the still warm corpse of a once great civilization, whose decline must have seemed both inexplicable and inexorable to many of its leaders and people. It is scarcely surprising that many later Roman Emperors and their consorts turned to the consolation of religion.

The rise and fall of civilizations, and of states, is comparatively slow. Ultimately the great complexity of states – and especially of the modern state compared to the city state of antiquity – renders any attempt to identify the key cause of rise or decline difficult if not impossible (if there is a 'key' cause at all). We should be loath to follow those writers of the past who ascribed the decline and fall of the Roman Empire solely to the sins and the follies of their emperors, or to the pernicious effects of a decaying paganism. Yet it may be that there is some wisdom amid the folly, some wheat amid the chaff.

Among some more visionary, or more foolhardy, commentators, the study of the rise and decline of civilizations has continued to attract interest. Perhaps this is through a desire to understand some of the most poignant times in human history, or perhaps because it may be a means of identifying some of the worst follies of the past so that we may guard ourselves against repeating them. One particular focus of much work in the twentieth century was on the rise of Western Europe, especially from the Scientific Revolution, but generally from the end of the Dark Ages and the beginning of the Renaissance in the twelfth century.

The Scientific Revolution, and the Industrial Revolution which followed it, saw the rise of enormous wealth and power in parts of Europe. Whether this was due to the benign influence of the Reformation, the Age of Reason, the racial superiority of Western Europeans, the direct intervention of the Almighty (all of which have been postulated by one writer or another), or to some other cause or causes, the difference in the situation in Europe and most of the rest of the contemporary world was striking and undeniable.

But recognizing that differences existed, does not render the task of understanding those differences – and critically, the reasons for the differences – any easier. We must, for instance, guard against the excessive use of generalization, yet at the same time this is necessary in order to identify underlying principles. Equally we must be alert to the fact that the rise of Western Europe, remarkable as it may appear to be, indeed, as it was, it was neither the first, nor will it likely be the last, instance of the rise of a civilization contemporaneous with the decline or stagnation of others. China, with which many comparisons have been made, is an example.

In this first section of the book, Part I, 'Legal Paradigms', we will look at some of the theories that have been posited to help explain the rise and fall of civilizations and states. Building upon this more general foundation, the focus will then turn to individual states, which may be seen either as civilizations in their own right, or as sub-sets of them. We will examine theories that seek to explain the particular dynamics of state success and failure. We then will introduce and consider the underlying hypothesis that this book proposes. This is the concept of the hard and soft constitution, and the effects this has upon state viability. Briefly, this is the principle that the flexibility of the constitution – its liberality – has a direct effect upon the success or failure of the state. The more flexible (or soft) the constitution the greater is the likelihood of success, as flexibility requires the development of shared power, dynamic tension, yet an overall cohesion that brings much needed political, social and economic stability.

Chapter 1
The Rise and Fall of States

1.1 Introduction

The question of what may be the key elements that determine the success or failure of a state is an extremely challenging one, fraught with danger to the wary and unwary alike. Any institution, whether it is large or small, is influenced by a range of factors. The greater the number of variables, the less likely is the identification of a credible hypothesis to explain the development of that institution. This is especially so with states, which are not only complex, but also rarely homogeneous to any significant degree. It is often all but impossible to identify the casual influences that were dominant at any given time.

The definition of success is also problematic, given that success is determined as much by the cultural context, so is not wholly objective. It is partly for this reason that the focus of the book is on the possible influence of constitutional flexibility upon the stability of a state, and hence its success. It should be observed at this point that the term 'state' is used throughout the book in preference to the term 'country', or 'nation'. The state is a legal, political and social entity, and countries and nations may lack one or other of these attributes – though they may have others unique to themselves. The success (or the stability) of nations, which may be classified according to racial, ethnic or other identifying features, may be less readily ascribed to the institutional arrangements of that nation, as there is generally a degree of homogeneity present in the nation (or nation-state) that may not be present in the state.

A state is a much more complex entity than any other human institution, though it is not incapable of being understood as an institution. In practice one state might have a distinct political and religious history from its neighbouring state or states, perhaps as the result of conquest long ago.[1] For instance we might have a region of the world in which there is one dominant ethnic group that is divided politically into two contiguous – and possibly even hostile – states. The separation may be simply political, perchance due to some historical incident or agreement of the past. It might be religious or cultural, the direct result of the imposition of an alien culture on a conquered people, or of its preservation in the non-conquered state. In our example, one state might be Muslim, the other Christian, or one Orthodox Christian, the other Roman Catholic.[2]

1 This example can of course be seen as loosely based on the example of the Balkans, though there are equivalent situations elsewhere.

2 See the situation in the former Yugoslavia, and indeed in the Balkans generally.

If we were to measure the respective degrees of success or failure of these states (however that might be done), it may be possible to draw some conclusions from this with respect to the influence of this one variable – religion. In other words, did this one significant variable contribute to the success or failure of the state?

But this seems to presuppose that there are no other variables, or at least to assume that they were less significant than the more obvious difference between the two states. It could be that one state is oil or mineral-rich, and the other destitute of valuable natural resources. Still, one common element is better than none at all, and makes the task of the would-be comparer of the respective states slightly easier, with at least one element that may be discounted – or partially accounted for. A strict application of Ockham's Razor[3] would doubtless reduce the variables still further, for the *lex parsimoniae* (law of succinctness) argues in favour of economy.[4]

It will be immediately apparent that comparing and contrasting states in this way will never be an exact science, due to the subjectivity inherent in identifying and selecting variables, and the sheer number of variables. However, it may nevertheless have some advantages as a tool in identifying key elements for state sector reform.

Despite the inherent difficulties involved, or perhaps because of them, the study of the rise and fall of states, and civilizations, has proven a popular subject – especially among those inclined to speculate on the history (and the future) of humanity. For a relatively early work that sought to explain, and describe, the course of history, we have the magisterial example of Gibbons's *Decline and Fall of the Roman Empire*.[5] Though this is now superseded as a work of scholarship, it was unsurpassed in its influence. There are many other relevant works, both before and since that magnum opus was published.

Some early histories, such as Raleigh's *History of the World*,[6] were inevitably limited in their coverage, temporally and geographically, and were scarcely

3 *Numquam ponenda est pluralitas sine necessitate* ('Never posit pluralities without necessity); *Quaestiones et decisiones in quattuor libros Sententiarum Petri Lombardi* ('Sentences of Peter Lombard') Editione Lugdunensi (Lyon, 1495), i, dist. 27, qu. 2, K. In his *Summa Totius Logicae*, i. 12, William Kneale and Martha Kneale (eds), *The Development of Logic* (London, 1962), p. 243, Ockham cites the principle of economy, *Frustra fit per plura quod potest fieri per pauciora* ('there is no value in using more when less will suffice').

4 Inferring that 'simpler theories are, other things being equal, generally better than more complex ones' is just one way of many, and only seems more plausible to us because we are already assuming the razor to be true; see for instance Richard Swinburne, *Simplicity as Evidence for Truth* (Milwaukee, 1997). We are left with the choice of either accepting Ockham's Razor as an article of faith based on pragmatist considerations or opting to attempt justifying it deductively rather than inductively.

5 Edward Gibbon, *The Decline and Fall of the Roman Empire* (London, 1994).

6 This was written while he was in prison in the Tower of London. It was published in 1614, in five volumes, but the content only reached as far as the Second Macedonian War in 130 BC.

'world' histories as we would understand that term today. They also tended to be Euro-centric – for the simple reason that the majority of authors of such works were more familiar with Europe than they were with other continents and regions.

With a greater knowledge of the rest of the world, and especially after the late nineteenth century explosion of European colonial activity around the world, came a greater interest in, and awareness of lost civilizations, decayed empires and the forces that shaped them. There were, for instance, important anthropological surveys undertaken in India during the nineteenth century, in an attempt to understand the complexity of that country.[7] Rather than to generate theoretical concepts, those surveys aimed to improve the efficiency of colonial administration. But much of this work was still irremediably and inevitably Euro-centric.

In the twentieth century the focus tended to broaden to encompass the history and cultures of the world beyond the shores of Europe, European colonies and ex-colonies, and those lands contiguous to these. Even within empires greater attention was paid to the pre-European histories of the various cultures concerned. The economic, social and political decline of India and China, relative to Western Europe, was a popular subject of study. Some of these works, while worthwhile for their own sake – for the furthering of genuine knowledge is rarely entirely profitless, whatever the direct benefits may be – came to be discredited. They were suspected of harbouring, or encouraging, notions of racial superiority. This, particularly after the Second World War, tended to have a stifling effect upon the more radical thinkers, possibility to the detriment of human society as a whole.

There is much to be said for the argument that 'I disapprove of what you say, but I will defend to the death your right to say it.'[8] But an argument that one race is superior to another is as difficult to prove as many other variables in the success and failure of states – and probably less useful than most. A state is more than a collection of individuals, good, bad and indifferent, or it would not be a state. It is the community, the unity of the whole, which is critically important. Some races may have been less well adapted to life in a modern or post-modern commercial world, because of their cultural heritage, or levels of education, than others. But nevertheless, as human beings all naturally adhere to a state (as we understand states in the post-1648 Westphalian sense), and all are capable of contributing to the success or failure of the state. It has yet to be shown whether the range of innate ability between races is statistically any more significant than the range within races. Probably it is not, and therefore adds little to our understanding of the dynamics of states, except insofar as the homogeneity of a state may be important.

---

7 The Survey of India dates from 1767, the Geological Survey from 1851, and the Archaeological Survey from 1861.

8 Voltaire probably never said these exact words. They were written in 1906 by Evelyn Beatrice Hall (pseudonym S.G. Tallentyre) in the biography *The Friends of Voltaire* (London, 1906). The authoress did not attribute the words to Voltaire, but used them to sum up Voltaire's attitude.

One undoubted variable, when comparing and contrasting state with state, or region with region, is the ethnic composition of the population. Just as natural resources vary from state to state, both in quantity and quality, so the populations of states differ. But while the size, distribution, and educational attainments might legitimately be compared, any suggestion that one race was superior – or another inferior – was rapidly dismissed as racist, and not worthy of serious consideration. If racial characteristics are thorny problems for the investigator, so too are the political and economic, though for different reasons.

In this chapter we will commence with a review of some of the literature in the debate as to why some civilizations rise, while others decline or stagnate. As outlined in the Introduction, these arguments may be seen to fall broadly into the environmental or the institutional camps, though there is a degree of overlap, the emphasis varies among theorists. We will then narrow and refine the focus of the study on to the state, which may be a whole civilization, or a sub-set of it. This will involve consideration of the theoretical modelling that has been proposed for civilizations, but with stress upon that which is most immediately applicable to the state, as distinct from the civilization. The difference here being that the civilization is political, social and economic, while the state has a particularly strong political aspect.

1.2 The rise and fall of civilizations – some theoretical explanations

Let us return briefly to the consideration of environmental factors upon the economic growth of civilizations. That group of scholars which emphasized the pivotal influence of geography may be typified by McNeill.[9] He argued that the West's growth was due to its resource base and to political competition that encouraged innovation. The latter variable may be seen as institutional – at least to some degree – but the former is explicitly environmental. In a similar vein Jones noted that the mountain chains and marshes of Europe formed barriers that prevented a single dominant state from evolving.[10] In the absence of this dominance, a dynamic tension was created between relatively evenly matched states, which encouraged the creation and dissemination of ideas and competition (both state and individual, with all levels between).[11]

Diamond also emphasized geography, especially the abundant rainfall and the favourable effects of an indented coastline and high mountains on political

9 William McNeill, *The Rise of the West* (Chicago, 1963), p. 114.

10 Eric L. Jones, *The European Miracle: Environments, Economies, and Geopolitics in the History of Europe and Asia* (2nd edn, Cambridge, 1987), p. 226; *The Record of Global Economic Development* (Cheltenham, 2002).

11 It might, however, be countered here that Rome grew beyond the barriers and was, for a time, a successful state.

evolution.[12] The rainfall allowed and encouraged stable, reliable settled agriculture, which in turn led to the establishment of settled communities. The coastline provided numerous opportunities for the establishment of cities and towns based upon commerce. The high mountains created natural barriers, carving up the continent into conveniently-sized pieces, each of which evolved into a stable political entity. It might be argued that the rainfall and coastline argument goes some way to explaining the development of civilization in its earliest stages, but that it does not go far enough to explaining the modern success of the European states. It could however be argued that the agricultural stability and coastal trade allowed the states that had developed between the mountain chains to maintain and preserve their independence into modern times, and so allowed them to benefit from the dynamic tension of the intellectual revolutions from the twelfth century onwards.

Landes also laid much emphasis upon Europe's temperate climate, which allowed the population to accumulate a surplus above a subsistence level.[13] In contrast China's environmental conditions allowed a generally stable peasant agriculture that was characterized by plenty in good times, but destructive and destabilizing famine in bad years. That did not encourage the pursuit of surplus and so the development of a strong middle class. He also promoted a cultural hypothesis, which might be characterized as a belief that the defining element in Western growth and development was a more dynamic European culture.[14]

This 'environmental' argument assumed that one culture might be more dynamic than another. This situation could be explained as being the result of a permanent state of imbalance (dynamic tension), or it might reflect the greater dynamism of an evolving culture – such as Europe's was from the end of the Dark Ages. This latter argument would help explain why the Crusades from the twelfth century onwards proved to be of such a lasting benefit to Europe. Not only was lost classical and all but lost Greek knowledge re-acquired, along with the newer Islamic learning, but the innovation and rapid growth that this engendered led to an intellectual blossoming in Western Europe, and a challenging of received knowledge generally. The evolution of modern states was brought about in large measure by the political and military aspects of the Crusades.

To Landes, and others who emphasized environmental factors, this dynamic evolution was due, at least in part, to the physical environment of Europe. However, the existence of plentiful and reliable rainfall could scarcely be enough to be considered the key element that led to the development of this region, for

12 Jared Diamond, *Guns, Germs and Steel: The Fates of Human Societies* (London, 1997), pp. 409–12.

13 David S. Landes, *The wealth and poverty of Nations: why some are so rich and some so poor* (New York, 1998).

14 David S. Landes, *The Unbound Prometheus: Technological Change and Industrial Development in Western Europe from 1750 to the Present* (Cambridge, 1969); *Revolution in Time – Clocks and the Making of the Modern World* (New York, 1983).

parts of the tropics enjoyed much higher rainfall, but rarely developed significant lasting civilizations. To the environmentalist this too could be accounted for, being the result of excessively high temperatures (with an enervating effect on the human inhabitants, and the discouragement of complex clothing- and house-making), or an over-abundance of natural resources (with a similar effect).

Water is an important element in the human condition, as is the shape of the coastline (allowing safe harbours for ships), and the existence of rivers, allowing for inland navigation, irrigation, or providing a reliable water supply. It also provides a sewerage system. Water was especially important in the thinking of Wittfogel. His hydraulic hypothesis contended that despotic governments often arose around rivers, as in ancient Egypt, China, and Mesopotamia. For him the presence – or absence – of water was the single most important element in the development of the state. He developed the theory that the state arose when villages joined together to develop common irrigation projects (not necessarily due to free choice, but rather out of necessity, due to the physical environment). This co-operation, in Wittfogel's model, greatly improved the productivity of agriculture.[15] But the next step, according to Wittfogel, was less beneficial. Once the state came into being as a means of developing irrigation (and it might be questioned whether the co-operation of a group of villages can constitute a state), it soon applied its bureaucracy to oppressive purposes.[16] In fact, according to Wittfogel,[17] what he termed an hydraulic state will cease appropriating only when the marginal cost of further administrative control begins to exceed the marginal revenue to those

15 He wrote that:

> In a landscape characterised by full aridity permanent agriculture becomes possible only if and when coordinated human action transfers a plentiful and accessible water supply from its original location to a potentially fertile soil. When this is done, government-led hydraulic enterprise is identical with the creation of agricultural life. This first and crucial moment may therefore be designated as the 'administrative creation point'.

– Karl A. Wittfogel, *Oriental Despotism: A Comparative Study of Total Power* (New Haven, 1957), p. 109.

16 Ibid., pp. 126–36.

17 Wittfogel wrote that:

> The power of the hydraulic despotism is unchecked ('total'), but it does not operate everywhere. The life of most individuals is far from being completely controlled by the state; and there are many villages and other corporate units that are not totally controlled either.
>
> What keeps despotic power from asserting its authority in spheres of life? Modifying a key formula of classical economics, we may say that the representatives of the hydraulic regime act (or refrain from acting) in response to the law of diminishing administrative returns.

benefiting from state action. This is fundamentally a technology-driven model of the state.[18]

While this model might be of particular relevance to more primordial and less sophisticated states than are found today, it nevertheless illustrates the dependence of states on their physical environment.[19] Wittfogel identified, correctly it would seem, centralized bureaucratic empire in China as inhibiting Chinese science, technology and economic development. But his central premise perhaps did not give sufficient weight to the fact that Chinese water management was mostly small-scale and local. Nor can this hypothesis explain the recent relative backwardness of Eastern Europe, or the success (albeit relatively short-term), of the Hittite empire, whose capital Hattusa was largely devoid of natural water.[20] But he correctly saw Latin America and Russia as failing due to the existence of large landowners or the concentration of land ownership, the tradition of authoritarian governments, and the failure of the merchant class to develop fully. He did not, however, explore the underlying causes of these factors.

Finally, in a small selection of advocates for this approach, Pomeranz focused upon the stocks of coal, and access to the resources of the Americas.[21] For him, the economic explosion in Europe from the fifteenth century onwards was due to the availability of these new resources. This however fails to explain the subsequent development of intellectual ideas and industrialization in the United Kingdom, which did not obtain this type of resources until relatively late, and the relative decline of Spain and Portugal, which did. The latter has, of course, been blamed on the sheer richness of the new continent – Spain collapsed amid an embarrassment of riches. But it has also been ascribed to the political or religious conditions of the Iberian peninsula.

The second group among the rising/declining civilizations theorists gave pre-eminence to institutions, particularly what they saw as economic institutions. North argued that the structure of a society's political and economic institutions determines the performance of its economy and its rate of technological change. This is because institutions define the degree to which property rights are protected and contracts enforced – the cost of transactions, or the transactional cost.[22] This can be seen as primarily an economic model.

– Ibid., pp. 108–9. In Roman times whole districts were laid waste by the depredation of the tax collectors. See, generally, Jean Andreau, *Banking and business in the Roman world*, trans. Janet Lloyd (Cambridge, 1999).

18 For more on this argument, see Noel Cox, *Technology and Legal Systems* (Aldershot, 2006).

19 Karl A. Wittfogel, *Oriental Despotism: A Comparative Study of Total Power* (New Haven, 1957).

20 O.R. Gurney, *The Hittites* (2nd edn, Harmondsworth, 1990).

21 Kenneth Pomeranz, *The Great Divergence: Europe, China and the making of the modern World Economy* (Princeton, 2000).

22 Douglass C. North, *Structure and Change in Economic History* (London, 1981), p. 171; Douglass C. North, *Institutions, institutional change and economic performance*

Josselin and Marciano suggested that by constraining the growth of the public sector, a country's legal system can and probably will have a considerable impact on its development.[23] This could be described as the 'arteriosclerosis' argument, though the constraint is not necessarily unconscious; it may be the result of deliberate and conscious choice. However, the greater the degree of freedom of choice, the greater the likelihood that this choice will lead to innovations. Conversely, if little choice is offered, as a result of a stifling legal code, or archaic and inefficient administrative procedures or political apparatus, there is little incentive for innovation. Innovation might indeed be positively discouraged, for political, religious or cultural reasons. In the late eighteenth century the negative Chinese imperial reply to the tentative overtures of a British trade commission led by Earl Macartney was that 'Our empire possesses all things in prolific abundance.'[24] In such an ideological environment innovation is unlikely to prosper. But focusing primarily upon the growth of the public sector undervalues the positive consequences of a bureaucracy, in guarding against the acquisition of property or ideas from others.

Lal took a different approach, arguing that the West's success was due to cultural factors. These included cosmological beliefs, political decentralization and what he called 'the inquisitive Greek mind'.[25] For him the structure of governmental institutions was a consequence of underlying cultural factors, and not in themselves a cause.

Huff examined the cultural – religious, legal, philosophical, and institutional – contexts within which science was practised in the disparate cultures of Islam, China, and the West. He found in the history of (European) law and the European cultural revolution of the twelfth and thirteenth centuries what he saw as major clues as to why the ethos of science arose in the West, permitting the breakthrough to modern science that did not occur elsewhere. It might be countered that any argument based on the preconception that 'modern science' is predominantly Western, or that it is inherently different to pre-modern science, is skewed.

(Cambridge, 1990), p. 27.

23 Jean-Michel Josselin and Alain Marciano, 'The Paradox of Leviathan: how to develop and contain the future European state', *European Journal of Law and Economics*, 4 (1997): 5–21.

24 In 1793 Macartney was followed by 600 packages of presents, borne by 3,000 coolies. But his refusal to go down on both knees to the Chinese emperor ('kowtow', or *kòu tóu*) meant that his request for permission to open Chinese ports to British trade was turned down; See Sir George Staunton, *An account of Macartney's embassy to China* (London, 1797); Sir John Barrow, *Some Account of the Public Life, and a Selection from the Unpublished Writings, of the Earl of Macartney* (London, 1807); Helen Macartney Robbins, *Our First Ambassador to China: An Account of the Life of George, Earl of Macartney* (London, 1908). See also, for later initiatives, G. Melancon, 'Peaceful Intentions: The First British Trade Commission in China, 1833–5', *Historical Research*, 73(180) (2000): 33–47.

25 Deepak Lal, *Unintended consequences: the impact of factor endowments, culture, and politics on long run economic performance* (Cambridge, 1998), p. 173.

However, Huff's line of inquiry leads to novel ideas about the centrality of the legal concept of corporation, which is unique to the West (at least as the 'corporation' is understood in the modern West). This concept gave rise, according to Huff, to the concepts of neutral space and free inquiry.[26]

For Huff, free inquiry was limited in Islam due to the educational system which that religion engendered. Madrassas[27] were aimed at teaching two classes of science, and legal systems (or jurisprudence with associated logic, analysis and metaphysics). There were 'prophetic sciences' and 'foreign sciences'. The former was actually based on logic systems whose boundaries were very clearly drawn: the prophetic sciences were in line with the concept of upholding 'divinity' as revealed by the *Quran*. The foreign sciences, on the other hand, was that analytical body of knowledge that was at odds with the Quranic traditions and the theological propositions:

> It was even essential to Islam, …, because the method was part and parcel of the Islamic orthodox process for determining orthodoxy. Where it failed was in the creation of a set of objective standards of law, against which all other laws and principles could be judged. Since the legal principles of Islamic law had been given once and for all, in the *Quran* and the sunna, and in the principles of fiqh worked out by al-Shafi'i, the only task left was to use logic in the narrow sense, to uncover faulty reasoning and thus preserve the doctrinal status quo …[28]

In this cultural tradition innovation could not prosper, yet in the tenth century Baghdad was the centre of a great Islamic civilization – one that was based on ancient principles of science and knowledge.

Rosenberg[29] and Birdzell[30] argue that standard growth models can only provide the proximate causes of growth. Innovation and accumulation of capital, labour and natural resources is growth, but it does not explain growth. For them, the fundamental causes of growth lie in favourable institutions and freedom from political restrictions – more specifically, secure property rights and the freedom

---

26 Toby Huff, *The rise of early modern science: Islam, China, and the West* (2nd edn, Cambridge, 2003).

27 Madrasah (Arabic ةسردم) is the Arabic word for school. It is variously transliterated as *madrasah*, *madrash*, *medresa*, *madreseh*, *madrassa*, or *madressa*. It refers especially to an Islamic religious school. The word also exists in many Arabic-influenced languages such as Urdu, Hindi, Farsi, Turkish, Kurdish, Indonesian, Malaysian and Bosnian. The Hebrew word *midrasha* also means a place of learning.

28 Toby Huff, *The rise of early modern science: Islam, China, and the West* (2nd edn, Cambridge, 2003), p. 158.

29 Nathan Rosenberg, *Exploring the black box: technology, economics, and history* (Cambridge, 1994); Nathan Rosenberg and Walter G. Vincenti, *The Britannia Bridge: the generation and diffusion of technological knowledge* (Cambridge, 1978).

30 Nathan Rosenberg and E.E. Birdzell, *How the west grew rich: the economic transformation of the industrial world* (London, 1986).

to engage in (almost) any line of business and to acquire and sell goods at an unregulated price. This meant that the process of innovation was delegated to private firms and that individuals themselves were forced to bear full responsibility for their failures and reap the full benefits of their successes; a *laissez-faire* model.

According to Rosenberg and Birdzell these favourable institutions and political and economic freedoms arose in the West because of political fragmentation and competition between different territories in Europe. Investments and the merchant class were drawn to areas where property rights were respected and where they could carry out their business without too much political interference. There was no single empire in Europe, and therefore merchants could move from state to state as circumstances changed. Even within the Holy Roman Empire the imperial free cities existed to encourage just this sort of movement. The growth of markets – especially that of cities and long-distance trade – further spurred this development.

Dudley rightly observed that favourable geographic conditions are a necessary prerequisite for economic progress; but that this is not alone sufficient explanation.[31] China arguably had the highest rate of innovation over two millennia before the modern era,[32] yet its economic progress – at least until very recently – was, according to Dudley, markedly inferior to that in the West. Both geography and institutions are important.[33] Dudley's approach was to look at communications, using Innis's[34] model, as modified by Kuznats.[35] The latter asked why over certain periods have income levels risen more rapidly in some societies than in others.[36]

Other approaches exist also, such as Cosandey's 'rich state system theory'.[37] In his view, internalist explanations of this sort all suffer from two serious inherent defects. First, Eastern Europe remains backward, despite ostensibly largely sharing the same environmental advantages supposedly enjoyed by the West. Second, because leadership fluctuations occurred among civilizations, such as in China, India, the Middle East, while at the height of their wealth, inherent

31 Leonard Dudley, 'Explaining the great divergence: Medium and message on the Eurasian land mass 1700–1850', in Alain Marciano and Jean-Michel Josselin (eds), *Law and the State: A Political Economy Approach* (Cheltenham, 2005), p. 101.

32 Joel Mokyr, *The Lever of Riches: Technological creativity and economic progress* (Oxford, 1990), pp. 209–18.

33 Leonard Dudley, 'Explaining the great divergence: Medium and message on the Eurasian land mass 1700–1850', in Alain Marciano and Jean-Michel Josselin (eds), *Law and the State: A Political Economy Approach* (Cheltenham, 2005), p. 101.

34 Harold A. Innis, *Empire and Communication* (Oxford, 1950); *The Bias of Communication* (Toronto, 1951).

35 Simon Kuznats, *Modern Economic Growth: Rate, Structure and Spread* (New Haven, 1966).

36 See also Angus Maddison, *The World Economy: a millennial perspective* (Paris, 2001).

37 David Cosandey, *Le Secret de l'Occident* (Paris, 1997).

superiority cannot be a sufficient explanation.[38] Cosandey favours a mixed model, with environment being also an important factor.

Lang studied sociological and ecological aspects of Asian societies, religions and science. He identified stable political divisions to be a factor in scientific progress – China was more productive when it was divided politically. He also saw that the different coastline profiles of Europe and China was a major element in the development of different political models in the two regions.[39]

Sardar saw the present relative backwardness of many non-European countries as due mainly to their past colonization by Europeans.[40] Non-Western cultures are not, *per se*, obstacles to science, but science needs money to advance. The comparative backwardness of science in the Third World is due – according to Sardar – to the lack of financial means, which he ascribed to the intervention of the West. While he would appear to be correct in some aspects of his views (such as the need for money to advance science), it must be questioned whether the West was primarily responsible for the weakness of non-European science. The great ages of Chinese innovation ended in around 1300, in the Arab world in about 1050, and in India as early as 700 AD. Some of this could be ascribed to the invasions of foes, but internal divisions – often through internecine fighting, but also motivated by religious or other differences – seem to have played a larger role.

Nor is it certain that financial means were lacking in all of Africa in the post-colonial era; yet the majority of states on that continent suffered repeated economic, political and social crises, and many today are in a markedly worse situation relatively to that in which they were at the time of the granting of independence. The explanation may owe more to the constitutional arrangements of these states than to their innate resources. But Zimbabwe collapsed, or was on the verge of collapse, economically and politically, yet its constitutional arrangements were apparently sound. There were, however, certain difficulties, derived in part from the political dominance of one party, which in turn led to constitutional reforms which benefitted that party.[41]

In a similar manner to that just suggested – namely that progress and retardation was influenced more by a state of mind or institutional arrangements than by natural resources, Weber contended that religion was a prime catalyst for growth in Europe. In this theory a stern doctrine of Lutheranism and Calvinism promoted capital accumulation and economic development as a relentless commitment

38 Ibid.

39 Graeme Lang, 'Structural factors in the origins of modern science: a comparison of China and Europe' in Steven Tötösy de Zepetnek and Jennifer Jay, *East Asian Cultural and Historical Perspectives* (Edmonton, 1997), pp. 71–96.

40 Ziauddin Sardar, *Science, Technology and Development in the Muslim World* (London, 1977).

41 For the situation in Zimbabwe see Jacob Chikuhwa, *A crisis of governance: Zimbabwe* (New York, 2004).

to one's earthly calling and in avoidance of trivial pleasures.[42] He derived the idea of religious inspiration for capitalism from the seventeenth century English economist Sir William Petty,[43] the founder of the modern science of demography, and considered by Marx to be the founder of classical political economy.

Weber argued that behavioural change alone could not bring about modern capitalism, as it required an 'appropriate set of conditions' in the economic sphere. It was also driven by an underlying cultural (specifically religious) ethos. However, it may be questioned whether people are motivated by abstract ideas as much as Weber argued; Petty had relied on abstract ideas rather less, and cited many examples in order to prove that religious heterodoxy and trade go together. Perhaps more seriously, it was in the Catholic but Reformed England (though also perhaps in the Calvinist Scotland), rather than the Calvinist parts of Europe, that the scientific revolution primarily originated, though there were instances of it appearing elsewhere. The role of religion cannot be ignored however, and there may be some truth in the comment by Kojève, that 'Europe owed its success to Christianity'.[44] The implications of the advent of a post-religious Europe on its economic standing – if any – remain to be seen.

It is important to observe that the advance of science and technology requires a thriving economy and a stable political balance; not necessarily a concentration of power –this would probably not promote innovation – but rather a dynamic tension between and among stable competitor states and within those states. If one is too dominant there could be a serious imbalance. This could result in instability in the weaker states, and eventually to the decline of the state, as its markets and sources of raw materials become weaker. Balance – and the resultant tension of comparatively equal players – is crucial.

Baechler, developing a nascent state systems theory, concluded that Western Europe enjoyed a stable state system which was instrumental in the economic development of the region (what he called the 'growth of capitalism').[45] For him the existence of political stability was a necessary pre-condition for growth, and this pre-condition could only be brought about by the existence of stable states.

Taking a step back, to look at some of the possible reasons why stable states promoted growth, Blamont argued that government support for science and technology was motivated by a desire to foster prestige and thus increase power. Science was pursued as well, if not mostly, to satisfy the princely will for power

42 Max Weber, *The Protestant Ethic and the Spirit of Capitalism*, trans. Talcott Parsons (London, 1992).

43 Sir William Petty, *The Collected Works of William Petty*, ed. T.W. Hutchison (London, 1997).

44 Alexandre Kojève, Александр Владимирович Кожевников, Aleksandr Vladimirovič Koževnikov. See Shadia B. Drury, *Alexandre Kojève: The Roots of Postmodern Politics* (Basingstoke, 1994).

45 Jean Baechler, *Les Origines du Capitalisme* (Paris, 1971).

and domination.[46] This domination might be internal or external – but it required a competitor to the prince, so the latter provided the most stable circumstances for innovation.

Braudel classified many decisive economic and political factors. He identified in particular the crucial role of sea-borne trade in the development of economic power. But he also emphasized the importance of multipolarity and the ultimately harmful effect of what he saw as a unique (without significant internal dynamic tensions) empire for China and the Muslim world. While this may have been overly simplistic, Braudel also recognized the importance of the causal relation between economic prosperity and the progress of science and technology.[47]

Jones, though advancing an environmental argument, considered many possible views, but was essentially what we might describe as an externalist. He also stressed the gradual 'taming' of governments as pivotal in the development of economies.[48] He sought mechanistic reasons – social, political, economic – for the rise of the West, and finally identified the state system as the decisive factor in the ascendance of Western Europe and Japan.[49]

Many of these theorists were concerned with the particular problem of China. That country was for many centuries marked by scientific and technological innovation, and it enjoyed considerable natural resources. Why then did it fail to grow, in the eighteenth to the twentieth centuries, at a rate comparable with that of Europe? There must logically be some explanation, however difficult it might be to identify. While China differed in many respects from Europe, this did not mean that it should not be equally successful economically. One aspect in which it differed, and which may have had an effect, was in its constitutional ethos or paradigm. Intellectual and economic freedom was not merely tolerated in Europe, but encouraged (at least after the Reformation, and in many fields well before this). This process began to have an obvious effect in the United Kingdom, the first of the liberal democracies, though it can be traced back many centuries. While it would, in Chapter 1, be precipitant to suggest that democracy is the explanation, it may be worthwhile to set this aside for later consideration.

Diamond suggested that the mountain chains and marshes of Europe formed barriers which prevented a single dominant state from evolving. But would these physical barriers actually foster – or hinder – economic growth? The Roman Empire extended across large tracts of Europe and North Africa despite these boundaries, and it was, for some centuries, economically and politically successful by any reasonable measure. Success may have been due to factors independent of

---

46 Jacques Blamont, *Le Chiffre et Le Songe: Histoire politique de la découverte* (Paris, 1993).

47 Fernand Braudel, *Civilization and Capitalism, 15th–18th century* (London, 1985).

48 Eric L. Jones, *The European Miracle: Environments, Economies, and Geopolitics in the History of Europe and Asia* (2nd edn, Cambridge, 1987).

49 Eric L. Jones, *The Record of Global Economic Development* (Cheltenham, 2002).

the physical environment, features that allowed success (or at least some measure of success) despite the hurdles the empire faced.

Mokyr concentrated his attention very largely on Western Europe and China, neglecting almost entirely the Middle East, India and other East Asian countries.[50] Further (like many before him, and many after), he tended to over-simplify the degree of unity displayed in China, and as a consequence did not fully recognize that the degree of progressiveness of the Chinese governments was directly linked to the macro-political situation in which it was placed.

It has been observed that progressiveness was evident when China was divided but stable, and non-existent or even negative when it was united.[51] However, it might also be observed that the current cycle of Chinese industrialization and economic growth appears to contradict this hypothesis. But it can be countered that the primary catalysts for this expansion has been the existence of the Hong Kong Special Administrative Region, and to the fact that in mainland China, though provinces are theoretically subservient to the central government of the People's Republic of China, in practice provincial officials have a large amount of discretion with regard to economic policy. It may also be observed that the relative prosperity of China today is largely the result, not of political liberalization, but of economic deregulation.

It is the constitutional tension offered by the division of the country into relatively stable but competing units that led to progress. It might almost be said that Orson Welles's memorable line from the film *The Third Man*, was prescient in anticipating later theorists: 'In Italy for thirty years under the Borgias they had warfare, terror, murder, bloodshed – they produced Michelangelo, Leonardo da Vinci, and the Renaissance. In Switzerland they had brotherly love, five hundred years of democracy and peace, and what did they produce? The cuckoo clock.'[52] This may be a gross over-simplification, but dynamic tension has its advantages, as the role played by biodiversity in evolutionary biology illustrates.[53]

Europe itself was to undergo a long Dark Age, from c.300 AD to 1100 AD, that was caused by a variety of forces, not least of which was the mass migration of peoples from the east.[54] This was so despite the resources of the continent, both human and natural. Pomeranz argued that stocks of coal, and access to the resources of the Americas, aided European economic growth. But China had much coal, and furthermore, the gold from South and Central America helped to ruin the economy of Spain, and condemn it to centuries of relative economic and political oblivion.

---

50 Joel Mokyr, *The Lever of Riches: Technological creativity and economic progress* (Oxford, 1990).

51 David Cosandey, *Le Secret de l'Occident* (Paris, 1997), pp. 209–64.

52 See the novel of the film, by its scriptwriter Graham Greene, published 1950.

53 Kevin J. Gaston and John I. Spicer, *Biodiversity: an introduction* (2nd edn, London, 2004).

54 Ferdinand Lot, *The End of the Ancient World and the beginnings of the Middle Ages* (London, 1953).

Baechler, Blamont, Cesandey, Diamond, Needham and others offer us a variety of political and economic theories for the success, and failure, of states. Whilst they have some similarities there are also aspects in which they are divergent. The institutional theories from Huff, Rosenberg and Birdzell also reflect these difficulties. But from our perspective the greatest problem is that they are attempting to describe the success and failure of whole states and multi-state regions. Such exercises inevitably involve complexities that threaten to reduce them to idle speculation. We will therefore attempt to narrow the focus, firstly by looking at the structural influences upon the success of individual states that may be ascribed to statehood itself.

1.3 The success of individual states

The concept of failure in states is a notion that presents an immediate difficulty. Legal formalism may be in decline in respect of domestic law, but has strengthened its hold on international law.[55] A failed state (however a 'failure' may be measured) is still a state in international law, though sociologically or economically it may not be one. A state is distinct from a civilization because it is a political entity, which a civilization need not necessarily be (though it very often is, and the state and the civilization may be one and the same). The existence of the legal structure or entity called the state, distinct from the communities that comprise it, is an important element. The state itself, as an entity, has its own inherent dynamism or tenacity.

This dichotomy – the tension between the state entity and the community or civilization of which it is a part – allows the survival of many states whose viability is marginal, at best, and may itself actually contribute to the decline of such states.[56] This is especially so if they comprise ill-matches geographical and ethnic components – though whether this is a good or a bad thing is another question. In other cases the mere legal and conceptual existence of the state may also contribute to its survival as a community, though ultimately even here the normative effect of statehood has its limits. In recent years the collapse of Somalia may be seen as one example of the failure of a state. The efforts of foreign powers, and domestic political, religious, tribal and military leaders to hold it together have not yet proven successful, though it is perhaps premature to entirely dismiss that state as failed. But there is a limit to the extent to which the notion of the state can contribute to the actual existence of that putative state.

The extent to which the notional existence of the state is crucial is subject to an important qualification. The notion of the state has subtly different meanings

55 Gerard Kreijen, *State failure, sovereignty and effectiveness: Legal lessons from the decolonisation of Sub-Saharan Africa* (Leiden, 2004), p. 98.

56 Ibid; Georg Sørensen, *Changes in Statehood: The Transformation of International Relations* (Basingstoke, 2001).

depending upon whether we are considering the state as an entity in international law, or from the internal perspective of the inhabitants. Although these two notions tend to be conflated – and the distinction is increasingly ignored in practice – it is nevertheless important. Let us begin with the notion of the state in international law.

The Montevideo Convention of 1933 is generally regarded as formally articulating for the first time the modern requirements for statehood. According to this Convention (strictly binding only on the party states, but generally accepted since then as representative of customary international law), a state must meet certain conditions to be a state in international law. It must have a permanent population – a settled population, rather than a merely transitory population, though numbers are not specified. It must have a defined territory (again, size is not specified, though presumably a *de minimis* condition applies). It must have an established government – though this need not be a democratic one, nor comply with any other preconditions as to nature or form. Lastly, it must have the legal capacity to enter into diplomatic relations.[57] Although since the early 1930s there has been some consideration given to the minimum standards for governments – arguments that played a particularly important role during the prelude to the Balkans wars in the 1990s,[58] and the invasion of Iraq in 2003[59] – these conditions listed remain the only ones generally accepted at this time.

No other entity could be regarded as a state, whatever *de facto* power it may have – or purport to have – although a case has been unpersuasively made on behalf the Sovereign Military Order of Malta.[60] Leaderless and displaced populations, or distinct ethnic groups within states, generally lacked sovereign status and, accordingly, the recognition and protection of public international law, though there is some movement towards the recognition of indigenous populations. These groups may be fluid with respect to physical geographic boundaries, but do normally comprise a distinct political entity, at least in domestic law. The formal recognition of them in international law, on the other hand, would have potentially

---

57 *Montevideo Convention on the Rights and Duties of States*, 26 December 1933, 49 Stat 3097; USA Treaty Series 881, entered into force 26 December 1934, in *International Legislation*, ed. M.O. Hudson (6 vols, Washington, 1931–50), vol. 6, p. 620; Ian Brownlie, *Principles of Public International Law* (5th edn, New York, 1998), ch. 5. Although the application of the Convention is confined to Latin America, it is regarded as declaratory of customary international law. See also *Island of Palmas Arbitration Case* (1928) No. xix (2) Reports of International Arbitral Awards 829; (1928) 22 American Journal of International Law 986; 4 Arbitration Decisions 3.

58 Noel Cox, 'Developments in the Laws of War: NATO attacks on Yugoslavia and the use of force to achieve humanitarian objectives', *New Zealand Armed Forces Law Review* (2002): 13–24.

59 Noel Cox, 'The Consequences for the World Legal Order of the War on Iraq', *New Zealand Armed Forces Law Review* (2003): 11–17.

60 See Noel Cox, 'The Continuing question of sovereignty and the Sovereign Military Order of Jerusalem, of Rhodes and of Malta', *Australian International Law Journal*, 13 (2006): 211–32.

significant implications for the concept of state sovereignty, consequences as far-reaching as those that followed the Treaty of Westphalia in 1648.

Once we have identified a given political entity as constituting a state, much yet remains unsettled. It may be a far from easy task to identify a given political entity as constituting a state, despite the apparent simplicity of the Montevideo requirements.[61] Much remains unsettled primarily because there are few, if any, internationally valid norms of domestic law with respect to statehood. In other words, though a sovereign state may appear much the same externally, from within there are marked internal structural differences discernable between one state and another.

The precise nature of the authority of a state within its own territory is not within the scope of international law, and is heavily influenced by the particular constitutional, political, historical, social and economic heritage of individual states. It is therefore difficult to generalize about the nature and form of government. However, there are certain common elements, at least among the modern legalistic entities which we call states. In earlier times, that is before the advent of modern juridical states, there was a greater element of flexibility and consequently a lesser degree of similarity in statehood. The universality of international law, however fluid it may be, has had an influence upon the development of the notion of the state domestically.

The spread of European colonial empires across much of the world, and especially in the nineteenth century – at the height of the notion of the sovereign state in international law – also had important implications domestically. Whereas in a state like Somalia institutional government was weak, and the 'state' depended upon internal checks and balances; post-colonial states sought to emulate the strong government models of the West – whether or not these were suited to their own particular circumstances. The world community generally also sought to impose certain standards domestically, such as democracy and the rule of law, again irrespective of the applicability of such concepts, which were assumed to be ubiquitous.

With the growing dominance of democratic concepts of government[62] – though not necessarily the spread of democracy – it might be thought that if the people believe that a governmental institution is appropriate, then it is also legitimate.[63] But this scheme omits important substantive questions about the justice or even

61 C. Hillgruber, 'The Admission of New States to the International Community', *European Journal of International Law*, 9 (1998): 491–509.

62 Initially in western liberal democracies, and by extension, particularly through such institutions as the Commonwealth, throughout most of the world; See 'The Harare Commonwealth Declaration, 1991' (Issued by Heads of Government in Harare, Zimbabwe, 20 October 1991) available at <http://www.thecommonwealth.org/-gender/htm/commonwealth/about/declares/harare.htm> (as at 6 December 2003).

63 Penelope Brook Cowen, 'Neo Liberalism', in Raymond Miller (ed.), *New Zealand Politics in Transition* (Auckland, 1997), p. 341.

the role of the state and the protection it offers the individuals and communities who belong to it.[64] It is generally more usual for commentators to maintain that a state's legitimacy depends upon its upholding certain human rights.[65] This may be seen in the use of such terms as freedom, democracy, the rule of law, and tolerance, to be found even in the constitutions of many totalitarian dictatorships.[66] Truly democratic states scarcely need to assert such principles, since they comprise the foundations of the constitution, formally or practically, yet they are rarely absent from modern constitutions.[67] But the state is as much an economic as it is a social or legal construct,[68] and it is important for its legitimacy and viability that the constitution remains broadly consistent with economic, and technological, realities. The internal dynamics of states are dependent on many factors.

Economic and technological changes eventually alter constitutions, because they change society, which constitutions reflect to a greater or lesser degree.[69] These changes need not necessarily be in the formal written Constitution, where these exist. They may be – and are indeed more likely to be – in the understanding, operation, or perception of the constitution. They are likely to be in the nature of the fundamental relationship between individuals and the state, between communities or society as a whole and the state, and between state and state. Yet because of their nature they may be only dimly perceived, and then possibly only with the incontestable advantage of hindsight.

Constitutional reform may itself be revolutionary yet preserve apparent formal continuity.[70] Changes need not be revolutionary in a strict legal sense, yet its effect may be revolutionary – as may be its *Grundnorm*. The formalist approach of Kelsen maintains that if the constitution is changed according to its own provisions then

---

64 This is illustrated by the study of the application of the model to Mummar Qadhafi's Libya; See Saleh Al Namlah, 'Political legitimacy in Libya since 1969' (1992) Syracuse University PhD thesis.

65 See John Rawls, *Political Liberalism* (New York, 1993); Ted Honderich (ed.), *The Oxford Companion to Philosophy* (Oxford, 1995), p. 477; Matthew Swanson, 'The social extract tradition and the question of political legitimacy' (1995) University of Missouri-Columbia PhD thesis.

66 Such as the 1977 Constitution of the Soviet Union; Constitution of the Union of Soviet Socialist Republics, 7 October 1977.

67 The Constitution of the European Union also states that the Union is founded on the values of 'respect for human dignity, freedom, democracy, equality, the rule of law, and respect for human rights …' in a society in which 'pluralism, non-discrimination, tolerance, justice, solidarity and equality between women and men prevail' (Article 1–2).

68 See, for instance, John Locke; Martyn P. Thompson, *Ideas of contract in English political thought in the age of John Locke* (New York, 1987).

69 See, generally, J. Woodford Howard Jr., 'Constitution and society in comparative perspective', *Judicature*, 71 (1987): 211–15.

70 See Peter Paczolay, 'Constitutional Transition and Legal Continuity', *Connecticut Journal of International Law*, 8 (1993): 559–74; Ralf Dahrendorf, 'Transitions: Politics, Economics, and Liberty', *Washington Quarterly*, 13 (1990): 133–42.

the state and its legal order remain the same.[71] In this view it does not matter how fundamental the changes in the substance of the legal norms may be. If they are performed in conformity with the provisions of the (formal) constitution, continuity of the legal system will not be interrupted.[72] Thus, even though the nature of the relationship between individual and state – or between state and state – may have been profoundly altered, there is no revolutionary change to the constitution.[73] As an illustration, when the former republics of the Soviet Union declared their independence in 1991–92,[74] the provisions of the former Constitution of the Soviet Union (under which the constituent republics supposedly enjoyed considerable autonomy) meant that the revolutionary nature of the dismemberment of the union was more real than apparent. Thus the formal structures of the post-Soviet states often closely resembled – at least during the transitional phase – their Soviet forms, yet their actual operation was quite distinct. However this understanding appears to minimize the real effect of constitutional change. Constitutions both reflect and influence governmental and societal behaviour, and fundamental changes in constitutions, however achieved, are likely to have significant medium- and long-term implications.

Nor does apparent continuity mean that there is real continuity. Ross emphasizes the necessary discontinuity of a new constitutional order which has replaced an earlier one.[75] According to Ross, the legitimacy of a constitutional order goes beyond the legal system. If the political ideology changes at a time of constitutional change, so the legal continuity is disrupted.[76] In other words, if there is a profound social, political, or economic change, any resulting constitutional change may well be revolutionary in nature.[77] In this model, the post-Soviet states were truly revolutionary in nature, since they rejected the social, economic and political model of communism – although their formal constitutional structures survived for a time. But it must be recalled that a constitution is far more than a statement of a formal power structure – it includes the ways in which that power structure actually operates.

Bearing this in mind it may be seen that there are profound constitutional changes occurring even when the formal constitution remains essentially unchanged. This may also be observed even in those countries which have not undergone a

71 Hans Kelsen, *General Theory of Law and State*, trans. Anders Wedberg (Cambridge, 1945), pp. 117–18.

72 Ibid., p. 119.

73 And therefore the knowledge revolution would be economic and social, but not political.

74 Edward W. Walker, *Dissolution: sovereignty and the break-up of the Soviet Union* (Lanham, 2003).

75 See Alf Ross, *On Law and Justice* (London, 1958).

76 Ibid.

77 See, for instance F.M. Brookfield, *Waitangi and indigenous rights: revolution, law, and legitimation* (Auckland, 1999).

revolutionary change of political or economic *Grundnorm*. The United States of America is far more centralized politically than it was when it was established a little over two hundred years ago. But the formal constitutional division of responsibilities between the states and the federal government remain largely unaltered. Profound constitutional changes have occurred, but not revolutionary ones – provided one discounts the American civil war and its aftermath, which may be seen, at least in principle, as revolutionary in effect.

The importance of this distinction between the legitimacy of a continuous legal order (however great the changes in the underlying norms may be), and the discontinuity of a new order, is profound. For although superficially the constitutional order remains unchanged, in one model legitimacy is preserved, in the other it is undermined. It might well be wondered how this could be so, unless the notion of legitimacy is unrelated to any practical social application. Surely, it could be argued, the people of a given country know whether their governing regime is legitimate or not? It should not be a matter for political theorists to advise them, but should rather be an instinctive reaction to the regime which controls the state, the (non-political) apparatus of the state, and the role of the state.

This would again appear to be an illustration of the political discourse of legitimacy being controlled by the academic writers, and having comparatively little impact upon the general population. The model of legitimacy envisaged by some of these writers is not always strongly grounded upon sociological and political reality. This may be seen in the development of popular uprisings, mass protests and similar manifestations of popular discontent however the formal legitimacy of the state may be maintained. Ross would appear to more accurately reflect the political reality, which might be put simply thus: a government, however great its military or bureaucratic stranglehold on a country, cannot survive long if it does not have the support or at least the acquiescence of a sizable proportion of the population – though it may lengthen this hold through judicious manipulation of education and communications. This acquiescence may be the result of complacency, fear or more positive emotions.

It is also important to consider the role and purpose of the state – though this has been a fundamental problem of all theories of the state since Aristotle[78] and doubtless will remain so. Legitimacy of government has its social, political and economic aspects. As Hobbes maintained, government was a product of consensual alliance, and whilst it was generally for the common good, its primary purpose was to further the interests of the individual.[79] These interests are economic, in that the state should be able to ensure that the majority of its people have sufficient

78 He maintained that 'all associations are instituted for the purpose of attaining some good'; *The Politics of Aristotle*, trans. Ernest Barker (London, 1958), p. 1, cited by Hermann Heller, 'The Decline of the Nation State and its Effect on Constitutional and International Economic Law', *Cardozo Law Review*, 18 (1996): 1139.

79 See, generally, works on sixteenth- and seventeenth-century political economy; Gerald Aylmer, *The struggle for the constitution, 1603–1689: England in the seventeenth*

resources to live with some degree of comfort. They are also political, with the population having certain expectations of involvement in decision-making, or at least some degree of consultation over matters which concern them. Social aspects include the element of belonging, a feeling of community with others of the nation-state.

Grady and McGuire have considered the nature of constitutions from an economic perspective. They have concluded that constitutions are not the product of consensual choice, but rather the result of weaker humans banding together to resist forceful appropriations from more dominant humans.[80] This conception may fit one economic model, but it does not necessarily assist us greatly when we consider the constitutional implications of the knowledge revolution, or any other external tensions. Nor may it be particularly helpful when we consider that government in any modern state – or even any pre-modern state – is more than simply a tribal alliance such as they conceive it to be. That is not to say that this model does not adequately describe the origins of tribal and pre-city government, and many have some broader application.

The revolutionary potential of the knowledge revolution involves the empowerment of smaller and smaller groups, almost until one reaches the nadir, the wholly empowered individual. It is possibly true that no true Lockean constitution (where state and society are in a true compact[81]) exists today.[82] However consent – through acquiescence and participation – is found in most governmental systems.[83] It may just be that the level at which consent occurs – and the means of obtaining consent – are in the process of changing.

Let us begin with a review of four theories of the origin of the state, courtesy of Grady and McGuire.[84] These are the Hobbes–Buchanan contractarian theory, Karl Wittfogel's hydraulic despotism theory, Robert Carneiro's circumscription theory, and Mancur Olson's stationary bandit theory.[85] We will examine each of these in turn.

---

century (4th edn, London, 1975); John Pocock, *The ancient constitution and the feudal law: a study of English historical thought in the seventeenth century* (Cambridge, 1987).

80 Mark F. Grady and Michael T. McGuire, 'The Nature of Constitutions', *Journal of Bioeconomics*, 1 (1999): 227–40.

81 See Martyn P. Thompson, *Ideas of contract in English political thought in the age of John Locke* (New York, 1987).

82 If, that is, it ever did.

83 See Noel Cox, *A Constitutional History of the New Zealand Monarchy: The evolution of the New Zealand monarchy and the recognition of an autochthonous polity* (Saarbrücken, 2008), chapter 2.

84 Grady and McGuire, 'The Nature of Constitutions'.

85 Thomas Hobbes, *Leviathan*, ed. Edwin Curley (Indianapolis 1994, first published 1688); James Buchanan, *The Limits of Liberty: Between anarchy and Leviathan* (Chicago, 1975); Karl A. Wittfogel, *Oriental Despotism: A Comparative Study of Total Power* (New Haven, 1957); Robert L. Carneiro, 'A Theory of the Origin of the State', *Science*, 169

Thomas Hobbes began his analysis of the state with a consideration of the state of nature, for he saw the one as dependent upon the other. He assumed that before formal governments existed people were reasonably equal in endowments[86] – an assumption that might perhaps be subject to challenge, but which is nonetheless an appropriate starting point. Each individual, with approximately equal mental, physical and moral attributes, had an equal hope of acquiring the same ends, which were scarce (food, shelter and similar necessaries of life, as well as the rarer 'luxuries'). Each individual depended on their own efforts for his or her livelihood, and those of their family.[87] As a consequence, individuals were in direct and indirect competition with each other. This resulted in the 'war of every man against every man'.[88] In such a state of being, opportunities for production, investment, learning, and exchange were limited, because each individual possessed 'continual fear and danger of violent death'.[89] Life was, or could very easily be, 'nasty, brutish and short'.[90] This created an incentive to seek improvement, though not necessarily the opportunity.

To escape from this ongoing cycle of conflict, individuals have an incentive to organize themselves into a commonwealth. This, in Hobbes's model, is a hierarchy that 'tie[s] them by fear of punishment to the performance of their covenants and observation of th[e] laws of nature ...'[91] They institute this commonwealth by giving a monarch or an assembly the right to represent them.[92] Government, then, was a product of self-interested consensual alliance. Whilst it was, in practice,

(1970): 733–8; Mancur Olson, 'Dictatorship, Democracy, and Development', *American Political Science Review*, 87 (1993): 567–76.

86 He wrote that:

> Nature hath made men so equal in the faculties of body and mind as that, though there be found one man sometimes manifestly stronger in body or of quicker mind than another, yet when all is reckoned together the difference between man and man is not so considerable as that one man can thereupon claim to himself any benefit to which another may not pretend as well as he.

– Hobbes, p. 74.

87 See J. Desmond Clark, *The common heritage: the significance of hunter-gatherer societies for human evolution* (Canberra, 1990).

88 Hobbes, p. 76. For Hobbes, war did not consist only of actual battles, but also threats of battle ('For War consisteth not in battle only, or the act of fighting, but in a tract of time wherein the will to contend by battle is sufficiently known').

89 Hobbes, p. 76.

90 'No arts; no letters; no society; and which is worst of all, continual fear and danger of violent death; and the life of man, solitary, poor, nasty, brutish, and short'; Hobbes, part 1, ch. xviii.

91 Ibid., p. 106.

92 Ibid., p. 110.

generally for the common good, its primary purpose was to further the interests of the individual.[93]

This model, which may be described as a contract theory of government, was especially popular during the seventeenth century, when the tensions of a post-mediæval monarchy and early-modern society came to the fore in England. At a time of dynamic tension it is common to seek for answers in the writings of theorists, though rarer to find the answers therein. The importance of the contract theory lay not in its perspicuous author's foresight, but rather in its universality and applicability at once to a traditional early modern society and a modern post-industrial state. Whereas in earlier societies the relative immobility of individuals led to a greater sense of community – which would allow the development of commonwealths – modern technological substitutes for the community provide equivalent mechanisms.

The new social and political structures potentially facilitated by advances in information technology offer the possibility of something very much like a constitutional contract,[94] though not necessarily with existing states or forms of states.[95] All existing states may however be much more complex constitutional structures than the Hobbesian constitution would appear to suggest.

In Grady and McGuire's view,[96] Hobbes and Buchanan[97] have not fully addressed the problem of what they termed sovereign appropriation. Hobbes assumed that the sovereign would behave benevolently. This assumption may only be correct if the sovereign is deemed to be rational, and even then they may not necessarily be benevolent, notwithstanding Platonic arguments to the contrary.[98]

---

93 See, generally, works on sixteenth- and seventeenth-century political economy; See Gerald Aylmer, *The struggle for the constitution, 1603–1689: England in the seventeenth century* (4th edn, London, 1975); John Pocock, *The ancient constitution and the feudal law: a study of English historical thought in the seventeenth century* (Cambridge, 1987).

94 For an example, see Ronald M. Peters, Jr., *The Massachusetts constitution of 1780: a social compact* (Amherst, 1978).

95 See, for instance, the arguments of the 'cyberspace'; John Perry Barlow, co-founder of the Electronic Frontier Foundation (EFF), made the seminal statement to this effect:

> Governments of the Industrial World, you weary giants of flesh and steel, I come from Cyberspace, the new home of the Mind. On behalf of the future, I ask you of the past to leave us alone. You are not welcome among us. You have no sovereignty where we gather.

– John Perry Barlow, 'A Declaration of the Independence of Cyberspace', at <http://www.eff.org/pub/Publications/-John_Perry_Barlow/barlow_0296.declaration> (as at 6 December 2003).

96 Grady and McGuire, 'The Nature of Constitutions'.

97 Buchanan.

98 *The Republic*, ed. G.R.F. Ferrari and trans. Tom Griffith (Cambridge, 2000).

Nevertheless, with a monopoly of force over a particular geographic area, a sovereign possesses a private incentive – or at the least the opportunity – to appropriate from his or her subjects,[99] without inhibition. This however, is unlikely to happen because the sovereign, whether individual, oligarchy, or party, will wish to retain power. When over-reaching occurs, revolution (formally or simply constitutional shifts in the balance of power or authority) will occasionally restore the balance[100] – though they will not necessarily do so rapidly.

Because of the greater mobility of people and assets that it brings,[101] the networked economy reduces the ability of sovereigns to appropriate, because their subjects can more easily exit over-reaching regimes.[102] This assumes the networked economy is independent of state control to the extent that the state does not restrict, in part or in whole, this movement. The reduction in transaction costs created by the Internet and other information technologies, generally creates the possibility of competing Hobbesian commonwealths, each constituted by customers and dependent upon their continuing loyalty. This view was widely held in the halcyon early days of Internet growth in the 1990s,[103] but has since fallen out of favour,[104] as the reality of the Internet was seen to be not as independent or as robust as many observers had hoped and expected it would be. But, whilst the Hobbesian state was a social construct, its nature – even its existence – was determined by the technological limitations of its makers.

---

99 Grady and McGuire, 'The Nature of Constitutions'.

100 Formerly great theologians of the Church like St Thomas Aquinas [*Summa theologiæ*, ed. John A. Oesterle (Englewood Cliffs, 1964), vol. II–II, Q. xlii, a.2], Francisco Suarez ['Defensio fidei', book VI, ch. iv, p. 15, in *Selections from three works: De legibus, ac deo legislators, 1612, Defensio fidei catholicae, et apostolicae adversus anglicanae sectae errores, 1613, De triplici virtute theologica, fide, spe, et charitate, 1621*, trans. Gladys L. Williams, Ammi Brown and John Waldron (Oxford, 1944)], and Domingo Bañez, O.P. [*De justitia et jure*, Q. lxiv, a. 3], permitted rebellion against oppressive rulers when the tyranny had become extreme and when no other means of safety were available. This carried to its logical conclusion the doctrine of the Middle Ages that the supreme ruling authority comes from God through the people for the public good. As the people immediately give sovereignty to the ruler, so the people can deprive him of his sovereignty when he has used his power oppressively (mediæval rulers were seldom women).

101 It has been said that a global economy is largely replacing and overwhelming national and regional economies; Louis Henkin, 'That 'S.' Words: Sovereignty, and Globalization, and Human Rights, Et Cetera', *Ford Law Review*, 68 (1999): 1–14, 5–6.

102 See, for instance, Noel Cox, 'Tax and regulatory avoidance through non-traditional alternatives to tax havens', *New Zealand Journal of Taxation Law and Policy*, 9 (2003): 305–27.

103 See David R. Johnson and David G. Post, 'Law and Borders: The Rise of Law in Cyberspace', *Stanford Law Review*, 48 (1996): 1367–402.

104 See Jonathan B. Wolf, 'War games meets the Internet: Chasing 21st century cybercriminals with old laws and little money', *American Journal of Criminal Law*, 28 (2000): 95–117.

If this is so, fundamental changes in technology may – and perhaps should – result in changes to the constitution itself. If the individual's need for protection, assistance, or supervision, is reduced (or disappears), so the role of the state changes.[105] A specific example of this is the tendency of the Internet, and modern electronic telecommunications in general, to reduce the degree of reliance upon formal contact with governmental agencies – such as educational institutions – for information and knowledge. This both tends to break down the dependence upon the state and also allow greater interaction with the state at the user's choice. This may result in a centralization of government agencies, and a gradual decline in the importance of regional, provincial, state and municipal agencies.

The second theory of the state to be considered is that of Karl Wittfogel. Wittfogel argued that despotic governments often arose around rivers, as in ancient Egypt, China, and Mesopotamia.[106] He theorized that the state arose when villages banded together to develop common irrigation projects, which vastly improved the productivity of agriculture.[107] Nevertheless, once the state came into being as a means of developing irrigation, it soon turned its bureaucracy to what he described as oppressive purposes.[108] This is fundamentally a technology-driven model of the state.[109] While this model might be of particular relevance to more primitive and less sophisticated states than are found today (or even in mediæval times), it nevertheless illustrates the dependence of states on their physical environment.

Carneiro, an anthropologist, theorized that states began in areas of environmental or social circumscription.[110] These were areas where the physical environment imposed some limitation upon geographical growth, or where linguistic, cultural or other social circumstances restricted the spread of populations. He looked at the

---

105 The converse is true also. In the course of the Industrial Revolution the scale and complexity of the state grew enormously, in part as a consequence of the technological change, and as a result of the social changes which these wrought. See, for instance, Steven Puro, 'Technology, politics and the new Industrial Revolution', *Public Law Forum*, 4 (1985): 387–98.

106 *Oriental Despotism: A Comparative Study of Total Power* (New Haven, 1957).

107 He wrote that:

> In a landscape characterised by full aridity permanent agriculture becomes possible only if and when coordinated human action transfers a plentiful and accessible water supply from its original location to a potentially fertile soil. When this is done, government-led hydraulic enterprise is identical with the creation of agricultural life. This first and crucial moment may therefore be designated as the 'administrative creation point'.

– Wittfogel, p. 109.

108 Ibid., pp. 126–36.

109 Remembering the definition of technology as processes and things people create for the purpose of using them to alter their lifestyle or their surroundings.

110 Carneiro, p. 738.

places where states first arose (as far as our imperfect knowledge of human pre-history can tell us). These were areas such as the Nile, Tigris–Euphrates, and Indus valleys in the Old World and the Valley of Mexico and the mountain and coastal valleys of Peru in the New World. These were all areas where water, or arable land, was present, but to a severely limited extent.

He concluded that all were areas of 'circumscribed agricultural land'.[111] In his words, '[e]ach of them is set off by mountains, seas, or deserts, and these environmental features sharply delimit the area that simple farming peoples could occupy and cultivate'.[112] He contrasted these 'environmentally circumscribed' areas to areas in which states did not arise as early, for instance, the Amazon basin and the eastern woodlands of North America.[113] From this we might conclude that states arose when competition for scarce resources – with limited or no room for expansion – reached a critical level. The necessity of economic survival led to the development of settled states.[114] It was the degree of technological development which determined when this critical level which led to state development would occur.[115] Settled agriculture – as distinct from the hunter-gatherer culture – was a more technologically advanced economic structure,[116] that led to a more advanced constitution.

In the fourth and last of the models of the state considered by Grady and McGuire,[117] Mancur Olson has argued that the state can be equated to a 'stationary bandit', who robs the people within his or her jurisdiction (through taxation and the like) and protects them from roving bandits[118] – competitors. These quasi-parasitical arrangements are similar to the 'manors' of the criminal underworld in many nineteenth- and twentieth-century western cities. Olson argues that ruled people prefer a stationary bandit to roving bandits because the stationary bandit has an incentive to invest in public goods that increase the people's wealth and therefore the tax revenues that can be extracted from them.[119] Thus, a 'bandit' will wish to provide services to his or her subject people, because of the direct and indirect benefits they will thereby receive.

111 Ibid., p. 734. The degree of circumscription varied considerably.

112 Ibid., pp. 734–5.

113 Ibid., p. 735. It might be countered that the Amazonian jungle provided a commensurate degree of circumscription – and even the woodlands of North America may have done so.

114 See Anthony Molho, Kurt Raaflaub and Julia Emlen, *City states in classical antiquity and Mediæval Italy* (Ann Arbor, c.1991).

115 The processes used to alter their lifestyles being settled agriculture – including animal husbandry.

116 See Max Weber, *The agrarian sociology of ancient civilizations*, trans. R.I. Frank (London, 1976).

117 Mark F. Grady and Michael T. McGuire, 'A Theory of the Origin of Natural Law', *Journal of Contemporary Legal Issues*, 8 (1997): 87–129.

118 See Olson, 'Dictatorship, Democracy, and Development', pp. 568–70.

119 Ibid., p. 569.

This theory is very similar to a more general theory developed independently by Grady and McGuire to explain primate, including human, political structures.[120] In some respects it is an economic model of society, but it is, like Hobbes's model, based on self-interest rather more than the physical environment. It also has strong parallels with the feudal system of allegiance and service, which was primarily based on the idea of reciprocal obligations.[121]

The basic idea common to both Grady and McGuire's theory and that of Olson is that the sovereign[122] is effectively the residual claimant of the group he or she (or more usually, 'it', since the sovereign is likely to be corporate) rules.[123] When the group creates a surplus of resources, the sovereign is in a position to appropriate that surplus, though it will not inevitably do so. Olson stressed that the sovereign's position of residual claimant – or what we might call holder of an eminent domain – could induce the sovereign to create public goods, such as irrigation projects (to use Wittfogel's example). The sovereign could then appropriate the surplus from these investments.[124]

The sovereign would have an incentive to keep peace within the group and even to enforce efficient private law because these types of legal rules would increase the surplus from group activities and therefore create a greater possibility for sovereign appropriations.[125] The surplus, as in ancient Egypt, was then at the disposal of the state, which might use it to undertake further public works or to feed the population in times of need.[126] The 'surplus' model may be correct – but it was very often the existence of a technological system which enabled this surplus to be achieved in the first place.[127] It is also a mechanistic model, which presupposes conscious or unconscious self-interest as the predominant motivation for state action.

Each of these models for the origins of states is, in effect, an attempt to explain not merely why states come into existence, but also why they survive – at least for

---

120 See Grady and McGuire, 'A Theory of the Origin of Natural Law'.

121 See Francois Ganshof, *Feudalism*, trans. Philip Grierson (London, 1952).

122 Meaning the holder of authority in a state, not necessarily limited to hereditary monarchs of traditional form.

123 The Crown, in British law and practice remains the residual landlord, and entitled to the assets of those who die without any heirs, under the doctrine of *bona vacantia*; Chris Ryan, '"The Crown" and corporate bona vacantia', *Kingston Law Review*, 12 (1982): 75–87.

124 See Olson, 'Dictatorship, Democracy, and Development', pp. 569–71.

125 See Grady and McGuire, 'A Theory of the Origin of Natural Law', pp. 118–20.

126 For Egyptian administration generally, see Klaus Baer, *Rank and title in the Old Kingdom; the structure of the Egyptian administration in the fifth and sixth dynasties* (Chicago, 1960); Naguib Kanawati, *The Egyptian administration in the Old Kingdom: evidence on its economic decline* (Warminster, 1977). See also Joseph G. Manning, *Land and power in Ptolemaic Egypt: the structure of land tenure* (Cambridge, 2003).

127 This may be governmental technology, or human resource management, rather than mechanical technology (though even this latter played a part).

a time. It is thus an explanation of a principal aspect of the states' legitimacy – that derived from continuity and (perhaps more importantly) the functional efficiency of the state – what might be called its utility. Without this utility the state ceases to have a reason for existence. Changes in the expectations of its people through new technologies and greater capabilities – economic, educational and otherwise – place potential pressures upon the legitimacy of the state, as they challenge the underlying reason for the existence of the state.

The state is more than simply a collection of individuals, however powerful; it is a system. This system may be described in accordance with the specific constitution of that state. Whichever theoretical model of state is preferred – and it may well be that none are adequate to describe the complex modern state – all are attempts to explain the functional rationale for the existence of the state, and for the particular power structures which they contain. As the physical environment – including human expectations and requirements – which gave rise to the state change, so the constitution changes, though this may be less rapid than might be desirable.

The state is very resilient, both internally and externally, as an institutional entity, and as a concept in international law. However, the late twentieth century was marked by the development of new types and new hierarchies of state, as understood in international law. Partly this was the result of the ending of the Cold War, and partly of independent long-term political and economic developments, such as globalization, and colonial and post-colonial legacies. Transnational organized crime is also said to threaten the viability of societies.[128] These developments brought challenges to the Westphalian model of the exclusivity and equality of states, especially since the co-operation of states, that had become more sophisticated during the nineteenth century, and into the twentieth, fractured under the pressure of an increasing number of states.

Several studies have shown that the so-called 'post-modern' state may have matured (or be in the process of maturing) in the West. In these, the state confines itself – or is confined – to guarding and improving the free market conditions through which wealth is generated. It is in Second and Third World countries (perhaps more the former than the latter) that the strong state is still sought.[129] Whether this continues, in light of economic upheavals in 2008, is however uncertain. But it is clear that the role of states may be changing.

In *The Breaking of Nations*,[130] Cooper denies what he calls the universality of international society. In effect, this is a rejection of the mid- to late-twentieth-century acceptance of the equality of states – an idea that was not necessarily

128 Neil Boister, 'The Trend to Universal Extradition over Subsidiary Universal Jurisdiction in the Suppression of Transnational Crime', *Acta Juridica* (1993): 287–313.

129 Robert I. Rotberg (ed.), *State Failure and State Weakness in a Time of Terror* (Washington, 2003), pp. 3–4.

130 Robert Cooper, *Breaking of Nations: Order and Chaos in the Twenty-First Century* (revd. edn, London, 2004).

accepted in earlier centuries, though rarely enunciated formally. He divides states into three types (or rather, the world into three parts, since not all the world is necessarily comprised of states): the pre-modern, the modern and the post-modern. The pre-modern world covers an expanding area of the world where the state has lost the monopoly of the legitimate use of force (which is an essential attribute of *de facto* or *de jure* statehood), and which is without fully functioning or notional states. The modern state is primarily concerned with the notion of territorial sovereignty (its creation, preservation, and, at times, its expansion), and national interest (which may be more inward-looking). In the post-modern state foreign and domestic policy are inextricably linked, and tools of governance are shared. Security is no longer based on control over territory or the balance of power (as in Europe for much of the nineteenth and twentieth centuries). Cooper writes that:

> we have, for the first time since the 19th Century, a terra nullius … And where the state is too weak to be dangerous, non-state actors may become too strong. If they become too dangerous for established states to tolerate, it is possible to imagine a defensive imperialism. If non-state actors, notably drug, crime or terrorist syndicates take to using non-state (that is pre-modern) bases for attacks on the more orderly parts of the world, then the organised states will eventually have to respond. This is what we have seen in Colombia, in Afghanistan and in part in Israel's forays into the Occupied Territories.[131]

Arguably the 'war on terror' is a manifestation of this reaction.

Among the pre-modern parts – or states – of the world are the failed states.[132] These have included Somalia, Afghanistan and Liberia,[133] and other states and former states where chaos rather than order has prevailed. Many of these are post-colonial states. The failure in these states might not necessarily be irreversible – indeed in some cases apparently terminal decline has been reversed, usually through the intervention of other states. In the cases where no revival has yet occurred the state no longer fulfils Max Weber's criterion of having a legitimate monopoly on the use of force. Cooper develops this notion with respect to Sierra Leone.[134] That country's collapse taught three lessons (as Carty paraphrased Cooper), firstly:

> Chaos spreads (in this case to Liberia, as the chaos in Rwanda spread to the Congo). Secondly, as the state collapses, crime takes over. As the law loses

131 Ibid, pp. 17–18.

132 A term introduced by G.B. Helman and S.R. Ratner, 'Saving Failed States', *Foreign Policy*, 89 (1992–93): 3–20.

133 Anthony Carty, 'The Iraq Invasion as a Recent United Kingdom "Contribution to International Law"', *European Journal of International Law*, 16 (2005): 143.

134 Robert Cooper, *Breaking of Nations: Order and Chaos in the Twenty-First Century* (revd. edn, London, 2004), pp. 66–9.

> force, privatised violence comes in. It then spreads to the West, where the profits are to be made. The third lesson is that chaos as such will spread, so that it cannot go unwatched in critical parts of the world.[135]

To Cooper, the United Nations is an expression of the modern, while failed states come largely within the ambit of the pre-modern. The United Nations Charter is simply conceptually inapplicable.[136] The modernity of the United Nations is that it rests upon state sovereignty and that, in turn, rests upon the separation of domestic and foreign affairs.[137]

Cooper describes the European Union as advancing a policy of replacing balance of power diplomacy with a diplomacy enmeshed in law and linked through economics – the epitome of the post-modern, stability not being based on the traditional search for security. Whether this is correct remains uncertain, but to distinguish between the state-based and the post-state (or sub-state focused) European Union does have some attractions.

The pre-modern, the modern and the post-modern division may also be seen as linked to state success or viability. The pre-modern can rarely compete with the modern and post-modern. It is yet to be seen whether the modern can compete with the post-modern, but in terms purely of industrial production the former is generally successful, if only because of sheer volumes of production, and a (generally) lower wage structure. They cannot necessarily compete in the high-technology, high skills fields – although the development of the so-called 'knowledge economy' is by no means confined to the post-modern world.

Studies have shown that there are several strong indicators of a high risk of state failure.[138] In one report these were described as being when a state favoured a closed economic system (such as when openness to international trade was low or non-existent); when infant mortality was high; and when they were undemocratic.[139] Lack of democracy fed on itself,[140] and led to other social and economic ills. A state in the early stages of modernity may suffer especially seriously from these symptoms, as they have a developed authority and a degree of centralization, but are otherwise in some respects undeveloped. However, infant mortality, for instance, does not necessarily have a direct correlation with state

135 Anthony Carty, 'The Iraq Invasion as a Recent United Kingdom "Contribution to International Law"', *European Journal of International Law* 16 (2005): 143.

136 Robert Cooper, *Breaking of Nations: Order and Chaos in the Twenty-First Century* (revd. edn, London, 2004), pp. 16–37.

137 Ibid, pp. 22–6.

138 Daniel C. Esty, J. Goldstone, T.R. Gurr, P.T. Surko and A.N. Unger, 'State Failure Task Force Report', in Robert I. Rotberg (ed.), *State Failure and State Weakness in a Time of Terror* (Washington, 2003).

139 Ibid.

140 Robert I. Rotberg (ed.), *State Failure and State Weakness in a Time of Terror* (Washington, 2003), p. 9.

failure, though it may indicate generally weak social and economic conditions. It might also be said that these three primary factors were also present in pre-modern states, many of which did not fail, though perhaps, over the centuries, most did.

It has been observed by Rotberg that some states fail because they are 'convulsed by internal violence and can no longer deliver positive political goods to their inhabitants'.[141] In *State Failure and State Weakness in a Time of Terror*, a book he edited, contemporary cases of nation-state collapse and failure are examined. Perhaps more importantly, Rotberg establishes clear criteria for distinguishing collapse and failure from generic weakness or apparent distress, and collapse from failure.[142] This may be applied generally.

Clarke and Gosende examine how Somalia, a nation-state with an apparently strongly cohesive cultural tradition, a common language, a common religion, and a modern 'shared history of nationalism', could fail. They suggested that it could be due to Somalia having never been a single coherent territory.[143] In Cooper's model and taxonomy, Somalia would be a pre-modern state. As such, it would be vulnerable to the pressures of the state-centred modern world.

Crucially, Somalia had existed with a finely balanced anarchical tribal order, based on the Xeer, a self-regulating set of rules and norms, which balanced economic and political life, in which one sector was prevented from dominating others.[144] European-style centralized governmental institutions, based on hierarchical notions of sovereignty, were alien,[145] and the subsequent endeavours of the post-colonial regime to develop a merchant and middle class seemed to merely exacerbate the problem.[146]

The advent of the modern state (to again use Cooper's proposed structure) was not necessarily the solution, because the country was naturally at the pre-modern stage, and the imposition of a new model, whether from within or without, led to apparently insolvable tensions. Some of these tensions were based on the domestic concept of a state – a concept that evolved in Europe over a period of centuries, during which time the notions best suited to that continent – and to the various states within it. One of these concepts was democracy (though for much of Europe

---

141 Ibid, p. 1.

142 Ibid, p. 1.

143 Walter Clarke and Robert Gosende, 'Somalia: Can a Collapsed State Reconstitute Itself?', in Robert I. Rotberg (ed.), *State Failure and State Weakness in a Time of Terror* (Washington, 2003).

144 I.M. Lewis, *A Pastoral Democracy: a study of pastoralism and politics among the Northern Somali of the Horn of Africa* (Oxford, 1982); *A Modern History of Somalia: nation and state in the Horn of Africa* (4th edn, Oxford, 1988); J. Chopra, 'Achilles' Heel in Somalia: Learning from a Conceptual Failure', *Texas International Law Journal*, 31 (1996): 495–525.

145 Gerard Kreijen, *State failure, sovereignty and effectiveness: Legal lessons from the decolonisation of Sub-Saharan Africa* (Leiden, 2004), p. 66.

146 A.I. Sarnatar, 'Destruction of State and Society in Somalia: Beyond the Tribal Convention', *Journal of Modern African Studies*, 30 (1992): 625.

this arose only in the past century or two), and another was legitimacy, at least as understood on that continent.

Davenport asked, in a paper on the evolution of segregation in South Africa, 'can liberal doctrines be applied in states whose citizens are backward'?[147] This is daring, but does raise the question of whether or what degree of political sophistication of the electorate (or the elite for a non-democracy) is needed for the effective operation of a state. Even J.S. Mill, in the introduction to his essay 'On Liberty' (1859), argued that:

> Despotism is a legitimate mode of government in dealing with barbarians, provided the end be their improvement, and the means justified by actually effecting that end. Liberty, as a principle, has no application to any state of things anterior to the time when mankind have become capable of being improved by free and equal discussion.[148]

Indeed, Hobhouse observed that 'A specious extension of the white mans' rights to the black may be the best way of ruining the black.'[149] Though these may be relatively extreme views, their message is clear – we may have a consistent and ubiquitous notion of the state in international law, but the state domestically may not be so uniform, and we impose or expect uniformity at the risk of de-stabilizing the state.

1.4 Conclusion

The rise and fall of civilizations and of states has been variously ascribed to institutional and environmental factors. Attempts to develop rational and systematic explanations have not however necessarily avoided the perils of generalization, and many theories (at least partially) contradict each other. However it would seem that changes in intellectual attitudes have been as significant as any environmental elements, though these may perhaps be ascribed, in part, to environmental factors. But change implies some catalyst. Technological discoveries may themselves prove catalysts for further developments, but the greatest catalyst would appear to be the intellectual quest, which is driven by religious, political, and philosophical ideas. Perhaps Lal was not altogether wrong in his assessment of the pivotal role of the 'the inquisitive Greek mind'[150] in the development of the West.

---

147 T.R.H. Davenport, 'Civil Rights in South Africa, 1910–1960', *Acta Juridica*, (1960): 11–28, 27.

148 *Utilitarianism* (London, 1910), p. 73.

149 L.T. Hobhouse, *Liberalism* (London, 1911), pp. 43–4.

150 Deepak Lal, *Unintended consequences: the impact of factor endowments, culture, and politics on long run economic performance* (Cambridge, 1998), p. 173.

Weber's *The Protestant Ethic and the Spirit of Capitalism*[151] has been described as 'a polemic that links the Protestant Revolution (the Reformation) and the Industrial Revolution, in particular, Calvinism and the rise of entrepreneurial capitalism'.[152] In this model a paradigm shift away from religious conceptions which had shaped the European world for over a thousand years brought with it a renewed interest in the physical world – and a new approach to observing and understanding it. This was more than a more revolution; it was a new approach to life, a change as profound as that which punctuated the end of the classical world and the beginning of the modern world.[153] The Reformation led at once to new governmental structures and to new innovations in technologies. A revolution changes political systems and governments; the Reformation changed almost every aspect of western European society, including religion, government, scholarship, education, and business.[154]

McGready has argued that the advent of the personal computer (PC), the Internet (and the World Wide Web – often included in the term Internet) is causing a reformation rather than a revolution.[155] He argues that the changes being wrought by the knowledge revolution will be as far-reaching as those of the Reformation.[156] Like the Reformation, it will be a series of revolutions, and not simply a single discrete change. Whilst this view is not shared by all – it may be seen as radical by the Internet realists – nevertheless it is worth careful consideration.

One reason for this profound change, according to McGready, is that the new rights which aim to respond to opportunities and risks arising from new information and communication technologies, biotechnological or other technology-based industrial development, are not grounded in the nation-state. Generally, established

---

151 Max Weber, *The Protestant Ethic and the Spirit of Capitalism*, trans. Talcott Parsons (London, 1992).

152 Steven McGready, 'The Digital Reformation: Total Freedom, Risk, and Responsibility', *Harvard Journal of Law and Technology*, 10 (1996): 148. Even those theorists who dispute Harvey's Marxist accounts of the origins of social and economic acceleration generally accept his observation that 'the history of capitalism has been characterised by a speed-up in the pace of life'; David Harvey, *The Condition of Postmodernity* (London, 1989), p. 240.

153 See Ferdinand Lot, *The end of the ancient world and the beginnings of the Middle Ages* (London, 1953).

154 See Norman Jones, *The English Reformation: religion and cultural adaptation* (Oxford, 2002); Ethan H. Shagan, *Popular politics and the English Reformation* (Cambridge, 2003); Elmore Herbison, *The Christian scholar in the age of the Reformation* (New York, 1956); Lewis W. Spitz, *The Reformation: education and history* (Aldershot, 1997); and Joseph Loewenstein, *The author's due: printing and the prehistory of copyright* (Chicago, 2002) respectively.

155 McGready, 'The Digital Reformation', p. 139.

156 Ibid.

civil, economic, social and political rights,[157] were predicated upon the existence of the nation-state, and were constructed within the framework of the nation-state.[158] Globalization, and a concurrent individualization (or the enfranchisement of the individual) has led to additional rights, desires and pressures.[159] These threaten the state, not to its very existence,[160] but in its relationship with its people and with other states. The economic turbulence of the early years of the twenty-first century suggests financial interdependence is having an equally significant affect on the future of the state.

The concept of the state is not unassailable, as has been seen in the few modern examples we have of supra-national political entities. Indeed, the concept of the autonomous sovereign state is a relatively modern one. The state's potential loss of power and autonomy to regulate economic and social activity, as well as to protect individual rights, has been accepted by the member states of the European Union. They have voluntarily relinquished some of their sovereignty – and will gradually lose more of it, some powers passing to the Union, and some being delegated to regional authorities.[161]

The creation of this supra-national entity is the result of a process that, to a certain degree, anticipated contemporary global tendencies,[162] but which is so far the best (if not the only) example of a modern multi-national quasi-state. The members of the European Union enjoyed certain shared heritage, including significant cultural, historical and legal links – though Christianity was rejected as a core principle.[163] Such common elements are not found throughout the

157 See, for instance, the Universal Declaration of Human Rights, as passed and proclaimed by the General Assembly of the United Nations on the tenth day of December 1948 (Wellington, 1951).

158 See Maria Eduarda Goncalves, 'Technological change, Globalization and the Europeanization of rights', *International Review of Law, Computers and Technology*, 16 (2002): 301–16.

159 Such as raised economic and political expectations in poorer and less democratic countries.

160 See Martin Wolf, 'Will the nation-state survive Globalization?', *Foreign Affairs*, 80 (2001): 178–90.

161 See Nick Bernard, *Multilevel Governance in the European Union* (The Hague, 2002).

162 See Goncalves, 'Technological change, Globalization and the Europeanization of rights'.

163 The Constitution states that the Union is founded on the values of 'respect for human dignity, freedom, democracy, equality, the rule of law, and respect for human rights …' in a society in which 'pluralism, non-discrimination, tolerance, justice, solidarity and equality between women and men prevail' (Article 1–2). It fails to mention Christianity, which is the conceptual basis for these principles, though the preamble does say that the signatories to the Constitution draw inspiration from the 'cultural, religious and humanist inheritance of Europe, from which has developed the universal values of the inviolable and unalienable rights of the human person, freedom, democracy, equality and the rule of law'.

world, thus making truly global government rather more complex a proposition. Economic and cultural globalization will continue regardless, but it will have an uncertain effect on states.

In 1996 Khan argued that the evolution of a world without borders seemed unavoidable.[164] He postulated a theory of a Free State, relying on Hugo Grotius, most particularly in *The Law of War and Peace*.[165] Khan argued that the globalizing tendencies of the late twentieth century, when he was writing, rendered the state effectively obsolete, as it was no longer the efficient player which justified its creation.

Yet it is possibly premature to consign the nation-state to the scrapheap of history.[166] This is not least because, despite continued falls in the costs of transport and communications in the first half of the twentieth century, integration actually reversed course – for predominantly political and related sociological reasons.[167] But it may well be necessary to re-examine the place of the state in the new world technological order.[168] It is information, not transportation, that is crucial to globalization, and the biggest potential threat to the state.

Cortada examined the historical, cultural, and (to some degree) legal aspects of interaction between society and information.[169] He maintained that the information age is not really a new phenomenon, but rather is the most recent manifestation of a long-standing process of historical evolution.[170] This would seem both logical and correct – so far as it goes. As McGready might argue, this is a reformation, a series of revolutions, and so the apparent continuity is masking a deeper, more profound, underlying change.

Lessig suggests that the historical evolution of the information society is a foundational preamble for what he characterizes as one of the most critical

---

164 L. Ali Khan, *The Extinction of Nation-States: A World without Borders* (The Hague, 1996), p. 1.

165 *De jure belli ac pacis*, ed. F.W. Kelsey (New York, 1964, reprint of 1925 edn).

166 Wolf, for instance, argues that the nation-state is not endangered by globalization. His reasons are that the ability of a society to take advantage of the opportunities offered by international economic integration depends on the quality of public goods; the state normally defines identity; and International governance rests on the ability of individual states to provide and guarantee stability; Wolf, 'Will the nation-state survive Globalization?'.

167 Ibid.

168 The term 'new world order' has been much used in the context of the global security system, but it arguably has greater relevance in the economic sphere, where it is more clearly developing. See Laura Yavitz, 'The WTO and the environment: the Shrimp case that created a new world', *Journal of Natural Resources and Environmental Law*, 16 (2001): 203–55, cf Ernest Easterly, III, 'The rule of law and the new world order', *Southern University Law Review*, 22 (1995): 161–83.

169 James W. Cortada, *Making the Information Society: Experience, Consequences and Possibilities* (Paramus, 2001).

170 Ibid.

battles of our time – the battle for the future of the Internet.[171] Both views may be correct, for while the knowledge technology may be grounded in an earlier Industrial Revolution, so evolution has its periods of stagnation, and its periods of fundamental change.[172] We may be entering just such a latter phase now.

The challenge for governments is to respond to this ongoing – and possibly long-term[173] – revolution,[174] and not become victims of it.[175] The more inflexible the state is – or the more dogmatic – the greater the risk of failure.[176] Failure by governments to respond fully and effectively to changing paradigms[177] can result in a loss of competitive advantage[178] – or even the existence of that state (through the loss of economic viability).[179] This ability to respond is not merely political,

171 Lawrence Lessig, *The Future of Ideas: The Fate of the Commons in a Connected World* (New York, 2001).

172 See later sections.

173 It is, of course, impossible to predict what further developments are likely to occur, which makes it necessary that the legal system – and the constitution – is sufficiently flexible so as to allow this development, and yet restrict or prohibit developments which are deemed unsuitable.

174 See Ilene K. Grossman, 'The new Industrial Revolution: meeting the challenge', *Public Law Forum*, 4 (1985): 419–26; Rudin, 'State involvement in the "new Industrial Revolution"'.

175 See Maurice Pearton, *The knowledge state: diplomacy, war, and technology since 1830* (London, 1982).

176 See Bruce Parrott, 'Technology and the Soviet polity: the problem of industrial innovation, 1928 to 1973' (1976) Columbia University PhD thesis; Rensselaer W. Lee, 'The politics of technology in Communist China' (1973) Stanford University PhD thesis.

177 A paradigmatic is a technical concept derived from linguistics and semiotics, used in anthropological theories of meaning, to denote the stable, rule-governed aspect of communication (opposite of syntagmatic, that which flows and moves in time). The concept is often used more loosely about basic premises underlying communication (as grammar underlies language). 'Paradigmatic shifts' should thus be understood as fundamental changes in the premises of communication; Thomas Kuhn, *The Structure of Scientific Revolutions* (Chicago, 1962).

178 For example, see House of Representatives Standing Committee for Long Term Strategies, *Government response: Australia as an information society: grasping new paradigms* (Canberra, c.1992); Nick Moore and Jane Steele, *Information-intensive Britain: an analysis of the policy issues* (London, 1991), where the emphasis of both is upon information technology. See also James Botkin, Dan Dimancescu, Ray Stata and John McClellan, *Global stakes: the future of high technology in America* (Cambridge, c.1982); Thomas L. Friedman, *The Lexus and the Olive Tree* (London, 2000), p. 9.

179 Response does not mean single-issue responses, but refers rather to the matching of constitution and society.

social or economic. It is also constitutional. The challenge – or threat – of techno-globalism to sovereign states[180] has profound implications for jurisprudence.[181]

The difficulty with understanding the nature of the information revolution is that we are all part of it – though that is perhaps not a dissimilar difficulty to that presented by evaluating any contemporary political, social or technological change. We do not have the luxury of being an interested (or disinterested) bystander,[182] nor do we enjoy the benefits of hindsight. We are also constrained by our own cultural traditions, which tend to inhibit our appreciation of cross-disciplinary changes. All writing on the constitution – in whatever way this may be defined – is underpinned by some theoretical perspective, however dimly perceived or narrowly conceived.[183] Legal and constitutional history cannot be left to the lawyers alone, or to historians.[184] Neither can the analysis of the contemporary constitution by political scientists exclude consideration of its legal and historical, as well as its political, aspects. Constitutional lawyers are concerned particularly with legal validity. They may not be especially interested in the normative standing of the power arrangements that the law validates. None of these approaches are especially sensitive to technology. A multi-disciplinary approach is needed.

---

180 See Sylvia Ostry and Richard R. Nelson, *Techno-nationalism and techno-globalism: conflict and cooperation* (Washington, 1995).

181 See Catherine Dauvergne (ed.), *Jurisprudence for an interconnected globe* (Aldershot, 2003); Richard Warren Perry and Bill Maurer (eds), *Globalization under construction: governmentality, law, and identity* (Minneapolis, 2003); Jean Stefancic and Richard Delgado, 'Outsider jurisprudence and the electronic revolution: Will technology help or hinder the cause of law reform?', *Ohio State Law Journal*, 52 (1991): 847–58.

182 Though classical communism would claim that it possesses the tools to achieve this.

183 Martin Partington, 'The Reform of Public Law in Britain,' in Patrick McAuslan and John McEldowney (eds), *Law, Legitimacy and the Constitution: Essays Marking the Centenary of Dicey 's Law of the Constitution* (London, 1985), pp. 191–211, 192.

184 F.M. Brookfield, *The Constitution in 1985: The Search for Legitimacy* (Auckland, 1985), p. 1.

Chapter 2
The Influence of Constitutional Paradigms

2.1 Introduction

In the first chapter we have considered some of the theoretical discourse concerning the rise and fall of states. Although this is divided essentially into two major camps – based on environmentalist and institutionalist[1] theories respectively – nevertheless there is much to be learnt from the consideration of both approaches. This is perhaps scarcely to be wondered at. The forces that shape the human world include both human and natural aspects,[2] and an attempt to explain the relative success or failure of a state or a civilization without considering both aspects is bound to be inadequate. It was suggested that the institutionalist argument may be the stronger of the two, and that the normative influence of the state itself was also important, especially in the international context. This gives it a degree of resilience as an institution, but does not, of itself, explain why some states are more stable, or more successful than others. This may in part be due to the constitutional structure of the state – in particular the degree of flexibility and adaptability which it exhibits. This will be explored in Chapter 3.

This chapter will develop further the idea of the normative influence of constitutional structures, exploring the influence of constitutional paradigms, particularly through the influence of the state. The emphasis will be upon the notion of the state, how it developed, and the influence it may have had upon the evolution of civilization. We will commence with a consideration of the notion of the state, and its evolution.

The state has had an important normative influence internally and externally. Thus, the mere existence of a universally-recognized international entity imposes certain constraints upon nations and regions, and encourages certain forms of governance. Externally, the state offers a degree of permanence and elasticity to a political entity that it might not otherwise enjoy.

From consideration of the normative influence of the state we proceed to examine some of the challenges to the notion of the state. These include the twin developments of technology and globalization. Although both, it will be argued,

1 'Institutionalist' is not being used here in the formal sense applied to the political science methodology by that name, but rather more loosely; Stephen Krasner, 'Sovereignty: an institutional perspective', *Comparative Political Studies*, 21 (1988): 66–94. The same observation may be made with respect to environmentalism.

2 Excluding consideration of the supernatural or the divine, which might be included in the broad category of the 'natural'.

are not new elements, the speed of evolution today is markedly greater than in any prior period of human history.

As we proceed through this historical review so we will pause from time to time to consider the contemporary effect of constitutional thought upon political, social and economic stability, and the strength of the state. This is introduced by considering one example of the unwritten, instructive and therefore ill-understood, constitutional *Grundnorm* or guiding ethos. This is especially significant where, in the case of the United Kingdom, New Zealand, and Israel, the constitution is 'indeterminate, indistinct and unentrenched'.[3]

2.2 The State

If the constitution is seen as comprised of the rules and procedures through which a state is governed, to understand the constitution it is first necessary to consider the nature of the state. The constitution may be seen to be the result of a formal process of development or adoption, or it may be as a result of evolutionary or revolutionary development (and in many cases a combination of the three forces). However, although the form and content of the constitution will vary considerably, due to the internal and external influences which have shaped it, including the specific history, politics, culture, geography and so on of the country concerned, the nature of the state itself is seen more readily as being generic. This is in part because it is a simpler or less multifaceted concept. This is also, externally at least, because it is an artificial product of the evolution of international law – though it is a concept which may have much to commend it in principle. Since the development of the modern nation-state the concept of the state has dominated international law, but it has always been present, in one form or another, from the creation of the first city-states, tribal federations and complex social alliances of like nature.[4]

The modern state as generally understood today evolved in Europe in the wake of the decline of the classical world. This was especially under the impetus of the crusades against Islamic aggression in Europe[5] and to recover the Holy Land of

3 S.E. Finer, Vernon Bogdanor and Bernard Rudden, *Comparing Constitutions* (Oxford, 1995), p. 41.

4 M.I. Finley, *Authority and legitimacy in the classical city-state* (København, 1982); Mason Hammond, *City-State and world state in Greek and Roman political theory until Augustus* (Cambridge, 1951). See also Charles Keith, 'The origins of settlement, agriculture and the city-state in Mesopotamia' (1984) University of Edinburgh PhD thesis.

5 See, for Iberia, Simon Barton and Peter Linehan (eds), *Cross, crescent and conversion: studies on medieval Spain and christendom in memory of Richard Fletcher* (Leiden, 2008).

Palestine and its contiguous regions.[6] It gained encouragement from the growth of trade and commerce, and from the rediscovery of Roman laws and classical learning, in the years after the final long-drawn out and painful collapse of the Eastern Empire based on the city of Constantinople.[7] Following the advent of the modern nation-state in the later middle ages, political and legal theory tended to exalt the state as the pinnacle of authority – though this was disputed both by the Church,[8] and, at times, by mesne feudal lords, burghers and other communities of interest and power.

During what might be termed the classical period of statehood[9] – from the Treaty of Westphalia 1648 to the Treaty of Versailles 1919 – the study of politics tended to centre on the state. But for much of the twentieth century it had focused on political behaviour and policy-making, with governmental decisions explained as a response to societal forces. In part this has been due to a growth in awareness of the limitations of studies based on political events which might themselves be the product of underlying stresses and dynamics. It also suited the increased emphasis in Western debate upon countries outside Europe and North America and those countries within their direct and indirect spheres of influence of these regions.

This change in emphasis to focus on political behaviour and policy-making can be seen in the growth of behaviouralism, which sought to escape from what has been described as an 'anaemic mixture of law, philosophy, and history',[10] to a more empirical, quantitative, interdisciplinary approach to the study of politics. This was justified on the basis that traditional studies were said to be essentially non-comparative, descriptive, legalistic, and static.[11] It was argued that the state, rather than being a discrete entity whose structure, form and very existence influenced political, social and economic developments, was lacking in autonomy, and largely reflected the concerns, ideology and interests of the power players.

---

6 Depending upon definitions – which have been fluid over the past three millennia – this includes parts of Syria, Lebanon, the Gaza strip, the West Bank (Judea and Samaria), the Sinai Peninsula, and Jordan. Attempts were also made to recover, or protect, parts of North Africa and the Mediterranean Sea (such as Egypt and Libya, Cyprus and Rhodes); Daniel H. Weiss and Lisa Mahoney (eds), *France and the Holy Land: Frankish culture at the end of the crusades* (Baltimore, 2004).

7 Cecil Stewart, *Byzantine legacy* (London, 1947).

8 See Hyginus Eugene Cardinale, *The Holy See and the international order* (Toronto, 1976); Walter Ullmann, *The growth of papal government in the Middle Ages: a study in the ideological relation of clerical to lay power* (2nd edn, London, 1965).

9 Though there is no generally accepted and satisfactory modern legal definition of statehood: James Crawford, *The Creation of States in international law* (Oxford, 1979), p. 31.

10 Bernard Susser (ed.), *Approaches to the Study of Politics* (New York, 1992), p. 4.

11 For the criticism of the traditional study of political science, see Roy Macridis, 'Major Characteristics of the Traditional Approach', in Bernard Susser (ed.), *Approaches to the Study of Politics* (New York, 1992), pp. 16–21.

Behaviouralism, generally, is an approach which seeks 'hard data'. Analysis of such mysteries as 'the state' did not come readily to it.[12] In an environment in which political behaviour was assessed through such a lens it might be doubted whether the constitutional paradigm of a country would be a likely subject of study.

But the notion of the state is far from dead, or even moribund. In recent decades state-centred theorists have sought to bring the state back into the forefront of research, arguing that it is more autonomous than society-centred theorists (such as neo-liberals[13]) have suggested. They have argued that the state is an independent player, with interests of its own, independent of those of the state's leadership. The recent growth of a 'new institutionalism' has placed the state at the very centre of political science, ironically at a time when the state has arguable become less involved in society,[14] at least in many countries of the industrialized world due to policies of economic liberalization. Whether this will change, however, is unclear. Recent turmoil in financial markets suggests a new resurgence of state management may be occurring – or be about to occur – in the West.

Hall and Taylor suggest that the 'insights of one approach might be used to supplement or strengthen those of another'.[15] For example, one might benefit from examining the possibility that actors are motivated in a 'calculus' manner, pursuing their own goals, but are at the same time constrained within their cultural environment.[16] Historical Institutionalism can serve as a meeting-point, as it recognizes the importance of several institutionalist approaches.[17] Furthermore, it adds a unique dimension not addressed by the other institutionalisms. The passage of time and the consideration of large periods of history are integral to this perspective.[18] This appreciation for evolution over time allows historical institutionalists to examine more case studies, to consider slow, incremental or sequential changes, and the oft-overlooked variable of historical knowledge and experience gained.

---

12 Bernard Susser (ed.), *Approaches to the Study of Politics* (New York, 1992), p. 180. As Bogdanor found, it is necessary to range across law, politics and history to understand a historic constitution; Vernon Bogdanor, *The Monarchy and the Constitution* (Oxford, 1995).

13 For definitions of the different perspectives of the State see Shaun Goldfinch, 'The State', in Raymond Miller (ed.), *New Zealand Government and Politics* (Melbourne, 2003), pp. 511–20, 512.

14 See, for example, Jane Kelsey, *Rolling Back the State*: *Privatisation of Power in Aotearoa/New Zealand* (Wellington, 1993).

15 Peter Hall and Rosemary Taylor, 'Political Science and the Three New Institutionalisms', *Political Studies*, 44(4) (1996): 936–57, 957.

16 Ibid.

17 Ibid., p. 944.

18 Pierson, Paul and Theda Skocpol, 'Historical Institutionalism in Contemporary Political Science' in Ira Katznelson and Helen V. Milner (eds), *Political Science: State of the Discipline* (New York: Norton, 2002) 693–721, 698.

There are limitations to a conceptual lens which emphasizes the autonomy of the state, just as much as there are in approaches which emphasize the role of the political actors through which the state operates. Both are in danger of underestimating the importance of external influences; for the behaviouralist, the structure and existence of the state, and for the new institutionalist, the political actors, their electorates and personal interests. There are equally limitations to purely legal understandings of the concept of the state.

The traditional understanding of public law (and especially the more narrowly defined constitutional law) emphasized particular ideas of power that are associated with territory, sovereignty, and law. These are all concepts about which there is often uncertainty – though some legal systems tend to imply a form of permanence, even akin to Platonic forms.[19] The ideas of the state, and state power expressed through law, however remain central to understanding government.[20]

It has been argued, by Morison amongst others, that the nature of public power, and practices of government, have changed so far beyond the public law framework that a new approach is needed. This is because – similar to the behaviouralists approach emphasizing the participants' individual motivations – government is seen to not be autonomous, nor the monopoly of the 'formal' government. Governmentality, which has its origins in the later writings of Michel Foucault[21] and subsequent criticism of his work,[22] has been offered as an important way of understanding how power is arranged in society and how government can be conceptualized.[23]

Government, for Foucault, was not so much the political or administrative structures of the modern state as 'the way in which the conduct of individuals or of groups might be directed: the government of children, of souls, of communities,

---

19 Forms, or ideas, see *The Republic*, ed. G.R.F. Ferrari and trans. Tom Griffith (Cambridge, 2000), pp. 476d–80a; R.M. Dancy, *Plato's introduction of forms* (Cambridge, 2004).

20 John Morison, 'Modernising Government and the E-Government Revolution: Technologies of Government and Technologies of Democracy', in Nicholas Bamford and Peter Leyland (eds), *Public Law in a Multilayered Constitution* (Oxford, 2003), pp. 157–88, 157–8.

21 In particular, see Michel Foucault, 'Governmentality', in J.D. Faubion (ed.), *Michel Foucault, Power: The Essential Works* (3 vols., London, 2000), vol. 3; L. Martin, H. Gutman and P. Hutton (eds), *Technologies of the Self: A Seminar with Michel Foucault* (London, 1998); and P. Rabinow (ed.), *Michel Foucault: Ethics* (London, 1997).

22 See Graham Burchell, Colin Gordon and Peter Miller (eds), *The Foucault Effect: Studies in Governmentality* (London, 1991); A. Barry, T. Osbourne and Nicolas Rose (eds), *Foucault and Political Reason: Liberalism, Neo-Liberalism and Rationalities of Government* (London, 1996); Nicolas Rose, *Powers of Freedom: Reframing Political Thought* (Cambridge, 1999); M. Dean, *Governmentality: Power and Rule in Modern Society* (London, 1999); A. Hunt and G. Wickham, *Foucault and Law: Towards a Sociology of Law and Governance* (London, 1994).

23 Morison, 'Modernising Government and the E-Government Revolution', p. 158.

of families, of the sick … To govern, in this sense, is to structure the possible field of action of others.'[24]

In Foucault's later work he stressed the importance of the active subject as the entity through which, and by means of which, power is actually exercised. Emphasis is placed on the way in which certain attitudes and behaviours came to be. Foucault observed that 'Political theory has never ceased to be obsessed with the person of the sovereign',[25] in effect, concerned with the legitimation of power.

Governmentality is a term that has been used to describe centralization and increased government power, though these two concepts are not necessarily inherently conjoined. This government power utilizes what have been termed 'rituals of truth'. In so doing it creates a particular style of subjectivity with which one conforms to or resists. According to Foucault, power as a social structure resides in the discourse itself.[26] The rules of the discourse prescribe which arguments can legitimately be used by the participants.[27] Because the individuals are taken into this subjectivity they become part of the normalizing force. Governmentality also includes that knowledge that presents itself as 'scientific', and which contributes to the power of governmentality;[28] the growth of the technocracy.

The notion of governmentality emphasizes the creation and deployment of a whole range of technologies connecting multiple centres of power within an exercise of government. It avoids, though does not ignore, particular ideas of power associated with territory, sovereignty and law (arguably the greatest single weakness of the traditional – pre-behaviouralist – approach to constitutional law, sovereignty and politics).

Like behaviouralism, governmentality places less weight upon the organs of government, and stresses the importance of the active subject as the entity through which, and by means of which, power is actually exercised beyond traditional state boundaries. This approach adapts itself readily to an environment in which one of the globalizing tendencies – and itself a result of globalization – is the trans-national corporation. Power (not simply political, or legal power, but power

24 *The Foucault Effects: Studies in Governmentality*, ed. Graham Burchell, Colin Gordon and Peter Miller (London, 1991).

25 Michel Foucault, *Power/Knowledge: Selected Interviews and Other Writings 1972–1977*, ed. Colin Gordon (New York, 1980), p. 121.

26 An authoritative way of describing. Discourses are propagated by specific institutions and divide up the world in specific ways.

27 Michel Foucault, *Dispositive der Macht* (Berlin, 1978); Michel Foucault, 'Politics and the Study of Discourse', in *The Foucault Effects: Studies in Governmentality*, ed. Graham Burchell, Colin Gordon and Peter Miller (London, 1991).

28 The 'Governmentality' was introduced in Michel Foucault, *Resume des cours* (Paris, 1989), and illustrated in other articles 'Governmentality', *Ideology and Consciousness*, 6 (Summer 1986): 5–21; 'Omnes et Singulatim: Toward a Criticism of "Political Reason"' in *The Tanner Lectures of Human Values. II* (Salt Lake City, 1981), pp. 223–54; and 'Space, Knowledge and Power', in Paul Rabinow (ed.), *The Foucault Reader* (New York, 1984), pp. 239–56.

more broadly conceived) is diffused.[29] It is influence rather than control which is dominant,[30] though it might be argued that the distinction between influence and control is not great in that context.

The emphasis of Foucault's governmentality, unlike behaviouralism or new institutionalism, is less upon the state or the single political entity than it is upon the discourse itself. The recognition of the fluidity or multi-directional nature of power relations is one of the strengths of an approach which minimizes the formalism of many of the earlier approaches. This is particularly crucial when we consider that government exists at multiple levels and that at the level of the state there are also dynamic relations with other states to consider. The normative effect of the existence of the state may be seen as important with respect to both internal perceptions and actions, and also external actions. The relationship between states is formally governed by international law, though it might be observed that even here there is a distinction between public international law, which governs the relations of states with one another, and private international law, or conflict of laws, which is concerned with the laws involved in the settlement of private disputes and relationships.[31]

International law is more fluid and less certain than the domestic legal systems of most, if not all, states. This is perhaps inevitable for a system which has evolved largely through state practice over a considerable period of time – and which has lacked a truly effective enforcement or sanction system such as was almost indispensable for domestic state legal systems. It is derived from written and unwritten rules, treaties, agreements and customary law. Custom is general state practice accepted as law. The elements of custom are a generalized repetition of similar acts by competent state authorities and a sentiment that such acts are juridically necessary to maintain and develop international relations.[32]

---

29 See particularly, Nicolas Rose, 'Government and Control', *British Journal of Criminology*, 40 (2000): 321–39, 323.

30 See P. Beaumont, C. Lyons and Neil Walker (eds), *Convergence and Divergence in European Public Law* (Oxford, 2002).

31 Sir Peter North and J.J. Fawcett, *Cheshire and North's private international law* (13th edn, London, 1999).

32 *Lotus Case (France v Turkey)* 1927 PCIJ ser A No 10 (Judgment of 7 September); *Asylum Case (Colombia v Peru)* 1950 ICJ 266 at 276 (Judgment of 20 November); *Delimitation of the Maritime Boundary in the Gulf of Maine Area (Canada v United States)* 1950 ICJ 266 at 299–300 (Judgment of 12 October); *Fisheries Case (UK v Norway)* 1951 ICJ 116 (Judgment of 18 December); *Military and Paramilitary Activities in and against Nicaragua (Nicaragua v United States)*, 1969 ICJ 3 at 97–98 (Judgment of 27 June). See also *North Sea Continental Shelf Cases (Federal Republic of Germany v Denmark; Federal Republic of Germany v The Netherlands)* 1969 ICJ 3 at 43–5 (Judgment of 20 February) in which the International Court of Justice emphasized the importance of *opinio juris* even in the face of inconsistent state practice in *Nicaragua v United States*. *Opinio juris* may be determined from resolutions of international organizations, notably the General Assembly.

The existence of custom, unlike treaty-law, depends upon general agreement, not deliberate consent.[33] This requires time to develop, and is often uncertain.

The development of public international law and indeed of law in general, never truly ceases; like all living things, it evolves. There are times when important, profound, changes occur, or milestones are reached – such as the establishment of the League of Nations, or of the Nuremberg and Tokyo war crimes tribunals.[34] These events may be important in themselves, or because of the example which they present for the future – though the latter may not always be perceived at the time as being especially significant. At other times there may appear to be little or no progress, neither improvements nor retrograde changes.[35] But, as Foucault would maintain, formal stasis – if such a thing can be found in international law – does not mean that the discourse has ceased or the power relations are unchanging.

Change there may well be, for international law is intensely political and dynamic, as any law must be; such is the distillation of the hopes, needs and desires of some two hundred sovereign states.[36] Nor is it immutable by nature, though international laws may evolve more slowly than the domestic laws of some, though not necessarily all, countries.[37] Law itself, as a human artefact, is also inseparable from history and from culture.[38] This is especially true of public international law, which is formed and developed through the interactions of numerous sovereign states, but dominated by concepts derived from Roman law and the laws and practices of European states, principally during the period of European commercial and later colonial expansion.

---

33 Gerhard von Glahn, *Law Among Nations: An Introduction to Public International Law* (7th edn, Boston, 1996).

34 See Charles Howard-Ellis, *The origin structure and working of the League of Nations* (Union, 2003); Geoffrey Best, *Nuremberg and after: the continuing history of war crimes and crimes against humanity* (Reading, 1984).

35 What may be perceived initially as a retrograde step may, of course, ultimately prove beneficial for the future development of public international law, by proving an example or lesson for others to learn from.

36 The UN has 191 members; and the United States, for example, recognizes 192 countries – including the Vatican City State, or Holy See, which is not a member of the UN; 'Basics facts about the UN', DPI, 2000, Sales No. E.00.I.21; Fact Sheet, Office of The Geographer and Global Issues, Bureau of Intelligence and Research, United States Department of State, Washington, DC, 7 February 2003. There are a number of other territories which meet most if not all of the requirements for recognition as a sovereign state, such as Taiwan. There are also dozens of dependencies, territories and colonies, many of which are self-governing, and some of which have a significant international profile; see Harvey W. Armstrong and Robert Read, 'Comparing the economic performance of dependent territories and sovereign microstates', *Economic Development and Cultural Change*, 48(2) (2000): 285.

37 Principally through the absence of a single law-making body, the large number of participants involved, the bi-lateral and multi-lateral negotiations, and the gradual evolution of customary law through state practice.

38 Ali Khan, *The Extinction of Nation-States*, p. 1.

Throughout the twentieth century, and for much longer, the sovereign state had seemed to be one of the relatively few abiding constants in international law[39] – though sovereignty is not a necessary feature of a domestic legal system.[40]

The concept of the sovereign state, though one of comparatively ancient origin,[41] has not continued completely unquestioned – nor has it continued unchanged.[42] Its place in the global political and legal system is not absolute, for the sovereign state belongs in a world in which interdependence (whether acknowledged or not) is inescapable.[43] Governmentality would recognize that it is in the discourse, rather than the formal structure (though this informs the discourse), that the real power may be seen.

In the latter years of the twentieth century and the first years of the twenty-first century several important developments in particular have had the effect of encouraging the reconsideration of the nature of the sovereign state, and of the limitations upon it. The first was technological in nature; the second may be termed geo-political. Each will be considered in turn.

2.2.1 Global technological environment

Technology[44] can have important implications for law, because it can challenge the existing legal norms of any society.[45] We have seen this occurring most recently

39 Though often dated from 1648, the modern state system is very much older. See Benno Teschke, *The myth of 1648: class, geopolitics, and the making of modern international relations* (London, 2003).

40 Norman Barry, 'Sovereignty, the Rule of Recognition and constitutional stability in Britain' in Hume Institute, *In search of new constitutions* (Edinburgh, 1994), vol. 2 no. 1, Hume Papers on Pubic Policy, pp. 10–27, 15.

41 An international system of sovereign states such as we would recognize today did not exist in mediæval times, which were characterized by a system based on strongly hierarchical and parallel religious or secular concepts of subordination and dependence; see, for example, Christopher Schreuer, 'The Waning of the Sovereign State: Towards a New Paradigm for International Law', *European Journal of International Law*, 4 (1993): 447–71. Non-European states were not so influential in the development of the international system.

42 As Schreuer has said, '[a] look at history … tells us that conceptions of world order have by no means always been shaped by the model of sovereign co-equal actors with a territorial basis'; Ibid.

43 One might even say of the state, as did the English poet John Donne of the individual, that 'No man is an island, entire of itself'; 'Meditation XVII', from *Devotions Upon Emergent Occasions* ed. Anthony Raspa (Montreal, 1975, first published 1624).

44 Here again 'technology' is defined broadly, as those processes and things people create for the purpose of using them to alter their lifestyle or their surroundings.

45 See, for example, Nasheri Hedieh, 'The Intersection of technology crimes and cyberspace in Europe: The Case of Hungary', *Information and Communications Technology Law*, 12 (2003): 25–48.

with respect to developments in the bio-technology field especially.[46] The advent of the new telecommunications technologies and of the World Wide Web and the Internet,[47] in particular, has caused some commentators to question the relevance, or even the survival, of the sovereign state. It might seem to be rather surprising that the future of the state, with which we are so familiar and which seems such a permanent feature of the political landscape, should be questioned in this way. The reason, however, is because the Internet's globalizing potential[48] has been seen as possibly weakening, if not destroying, the rational justification for the state. Efficiency, or a form of political Darwinianism,[49] might lead thence to the demise of the inefficient state.

This revolutionary view of the Internet and of the future of the state is not one which is readily acceptable to the realist or the less ideologically-obsessed observer (or probably even the less technologically perspicacious). Indeed, though it may have been popular in the untroubled days of Internet growth in the 1990s,[50] this radical view of the effect that the Internet is having or is likely to have on the state has since largely fallen out of favour.[51] It is easier to accept that the Internet has caused some practical and possibly conceptual difficulties for state sovereignty,[52] and may have greater long-term effects. In fact Lessig has written that the battle for the future of the Internet is the most critical battle of our time[53] – whatever

46 See Christine C. Vito; Organization for Economic Co-operation and Development, *Bio technology and the changing role of government* (Paris, 1988); Elliott, 'The Genome and the law'.

47 The architecture of the Internet or World Wide Web was developed by British physicist and computer scientist Sir Timothy Berners-Lee as a project within the European Centre for Nuclear Energy Research (CERN, now the European Laboratory for Particle Physics) in Geneva. Berners-Lee first began working with hypertext in the early 1980s. His implementation of the Web became operational at CERN in 1989, and it quickly spread to universities in the rest of the world through the high-energy physics community of scholars. It is now ubiquitous; World Wide Web Consortium, <http://www.w3.org/People/Berners-Lee/> at 29 October 2009.

48 See Emanuele Giovannetti, Mitsuhiro Kagami and Masatsugu Tsuji (eds), *The Internet revolution: a global perspective* (Cambridge, 2003); Tunstall; Kahin and Nesson.

49 From Darwin's theory of evolution through natural selection – the survival of the fittest; Charles Darwin, *On the origin of species by means of natural selection*, ed. Joseph Carroll (Peterborough, 2003, first published 1859).

50 See David R. Johnson and David G. Post, 'Law and Borders: The Rise of Law in Cyberspace', *Stanford Law Review*, 48 (1996): 1367–402.

51 See Jonathan B. Wolf, 'War games meets the Internet: Chasing 21st century cybercriminals with old laws and little money', *American Journal of Criminal Law*, 28 (2000): 95–117.

52 Remembering that globalization, though perhaps accelerated, is not an unprecedented development; Giovanni Arrighi, 'Globalization, State Sovereignty, and the "Endless Accumulation of Capital"', Paper presented at the Conference on 'States and Sovereignty in the World Economy', University of California, Irvine, 21–23 February 1997.

53 Lessig, *The Future of Ideas*.

the eventual outcome may be. Time alone will tell whether this is so and if it is, what the shape of the new society will be like. It is clear that this technological evolution – or revolution[54] – will have an effect upon public international law which is as significant as that it is having upon private international law, and upon the domestic laws of sovereign states. This effect may well differ depending upon the constitutional structure and laws of each state, and will thus not be uniform.

Public international law is not immune from this influence. Modern state institutions,[55] and the principal western models of state structures themselves, were established or consolidated during the fifteenth- to early twentieth-century era of European nation-state building.[56] That time also was a revolutionary one in its own way, for it saw the decline of the Middle Ages (itself the product of cultural, social, economic and political change and crisis at the end of the classical period of history) and the growth of the modern era. The present technological revolution raises questions about the nature of the state, just as earlier technological, economic, social and political revolutions have done.[57]

Changes in technology which affect states in their relations with one another may be thought to be comparatively rare, but they actually are many and varied. They include all those innovations which enable one state or civilization to impose its will on another (both directly and indirectly), and well as a plethora of less dramatic examples.

2.2.2 Global geo-political environment

Some of these geo-political developments which have also encouraged a re-evaluation of the nature and role of the state have been the recent use of force by great powers and a superpower and the attitudes and assumptions which these actions reflect.[58] In Yugoslavia this was in the name of humanitarian

54 McGready claims that the advent of the personal computer (PC) and the Internet is causing a reformation rather than a revolution. A revolution changes political systems and governments; the Reformation changed almost every aspect of western European society, including religion, government, scholarship, education, and business. He argues that the changes being wrought by the knowledge revolution will be as far-reaching as those of the Reformation; McGready, 'The Digital Reformation', p. 139; See Jones; Shagan.

55 At least those of the European model, non-European models have largely not survived at the level of the sovereign state, though there are some exceptions, particularly in the Middle East, and some hybrid states, such as Samoa.

56 Philip Cooke, 'Globalization of economic organization and the emergence of regional interstate partnerships', in Colin H. Williams (ed.), *The Political Geography of the New World Order* (London, 1993), pp. 46–58, 47.

57 For example, Max Weber, *The Protestant Ethic and the Spirit of Capitalism*, links the Protestant Revolution (the Reformation) and the Industrial Revolution, in particular, Calvinism and the rise of entrepreneurial capitalism. Ibid., p. 138.

58 The collapse of the Soviet block, and the dismemberment of the eastern European Communist empire, have left the United States as the sole superpower. Though it has been

intervention,[59] and in Iraq it was on the basis of pre-emptive self-defence.[60] The Iraq war in particular has served to highlight structural weaknesses in the fabric of the international security framework,[61] since it was widely (though far from universally) condemned as illegal, yet little could be done to prevent it, even if this were politically and diplomatically desirable. At the same time, it is possible to be cautiously optimistic. At the forefront of much of the discourse from the allies in both wars was the perceived need for their actions to be justified in international law.[62] These cases illustrate the dynamic effect of both power projection and technology – of a military and political sort – upon the relationships between states. Formal political equality may exist, but that is relatively meaningless when the political will exists to ignore or disregard that equality and impose (or attempt to impose) the will of one nation – or a coalition of states – on another.

These recent wars, relatively small though they may have been in historical terms, have served to draw both popular and academic attention to the evolution of, and recent challenges to, the laws of armed conflict – or laws of war as they were formerly known.[63] These laws have long had the effect of imposing limitations upon the freedom of states to levy war without the support of the international community and without 'just' or lawful cause.[64] Precisely what constituted a just cause (or just war) was never entirely certain. However, like the equally vague concept of the rule of law, the notion of the 'just war' served to impose some limitations on freedom of state action – by operating in a form of Foucaultian discourse among the politicians and rulers who decided national policy. But such

---

predicted that China may one day reach a similar strategic level to that enjoyed alone today by the United States, there are a number of counties whose military, economic or political influence and capabilities qualify them for the lesser, though nonetheless exalted style, of great power. This term, which had been somewhat neglected, has enjoyed a resurgence, though the term major power still seems more prevalent; See David Shambaugh (ed.), *Greater China: the next superpower?* (Oxford, 1995).

59 See Noel Cox, 'Developments in the Laws of War: NATO attacks on Yugoslavia and the use of force to achieve humanitarian objectives', *New Zealand Armed Forces Law Review* (2002): 13–24.

60 See Noel Cox, 'The Consequences for the World Legal Order of the War on Iraq', *New Zealand Armed Forces Law Review* (2003): 11–17.

61 For a view of the inherent weakness in the international security system, see Joseph P. Lorenz, *Peace, power, and the United Nations: a security system for the twenty-first century* (Boulder, 1999).

62 For example, for an attempt to justify the 2003 war against Iraq, see 'War and law: Attorney General statement', *The Times* (London), 17 March 2003.

63 Strictly, the laws of war might be said to cover a narrower field than the laws of armed conflict.

64 See Michael Walzer, *Just and Unjust Wars* (3rd edn, Plymouth, 2000).

limitations on state sovereignty have been challenged by these wars, which were conducted despite lacking clear justification in public international law.[65]

Regretfully, it would appear that the precise legal limits upon the levying of war, perhaps the most ancient and fundamental of a state's responsibilities towards its people,[66] are now more uncertain than they have been for fifty years. Both these wars have also raised important questions about the legal justification for state or international intervention in another state's internal affairs, on humanitarian grounds, or to depose a tyrannical regime.[67]

The geo-political environment is concerned with the strategic balance, and relations between states. This is affected by the law of armed conflict and other formal legal limitations which are imposed upon state sovereignty. These can be, and often are, challenged by the strategic balance, by wars and by the threat of the use of force by states. It is also affected by changes of an ostensibly more benign – or less obviously malignant – form, such as telecommunications, transportation, agricultural improvements, and so on.

2.2.3 The global environment

The period between the late twentieth century and early twenty-first century is an appropriate time to re-evaluate the concept of sovereignty. The sovereign state must evolve or have its nature re-assessed, as its environment changes. The world is very different today than how it was in the zenith of state sovereignty, the nineteenth century.[68] The notion that all states are legally equal,[69] whilst perhaps laudable in principle, has also been shown more than once to be subject to important practical qualifications.[70] Nor, indeed, is the notion of equality of particularly great antiquity.[71] The freedom of action of states can at times be severely restricted, both

65 St Thomas Aquinas, '*Summa theologica*', *Secunda secundae*, *Quaestio XL* (*de bello*), quoted in John Eppstein, *The Catholic Tradition of the Law of Nations* (London, 1935), 83.

66 Whether there is a duty to levy offensive war might be questioned, though sometimes attack is the best form of defence.

67 Both grounds were used, at times, along with self-defence, to justify the United States-led invasion of Iraq in 2003; see Noel Cox, 'The Consequences for the World Legal Order of the War on Iraq'.

68 See Hayward R. Alker, Thomas J. Biersteker and Takashi Inoguchi, 'From Imperial Power Balancing to People's Wars: Searching for Order in the Twentieth Century', in James Der Derian and Michael J. Shapiro (eds), *International/Intertextual Relations: Postmodern Readings of World Politics* (Lexington, 1989), pp. 135–62.

69 Schreuer, 'The Waning of the Sovereign State'.

70 For the origins of state sovereignty, the peace of 1648 was influential, see Leo Gross, 'The Peace of Westphalia, 1648–1948', *American Journal of International Law*, 42 (1948): 20–41. See also Teschke.

71 The year 1648 is also usually given as the decisive date for the transition from the vertical imperial to the horizontal inter-state model; see Richard Falk, 'The Interplay

legally, and practically,[72] by strategic considerations, by international law, and by economic factors. The increasingly pivotal role of international economic law is also having a significant effect.[73]

As a consequence of these developments, and others, the relationship between national law and international law, and the concept of state sovereignty, are arguably more uncertain today than they were one hundred years ago. It is therefore an opportune time for investigation and exploration, albeit one which is narrowly focused.

2.3 Dark Ages and mediæval Europe

This section moves from considering the state from the outside to considering it from within. This commences with an historical review. The so-called Dark Ages after the collapse of the Roman empire in the west, and the Middle Ages which followed, were times when the weakness of communications contributed to the division of states, and to feudalism.[74] Feudalism was a political, social and economic system founded upon the conditions of the time – including physical and technological limitations (especially transportation and communications).[75] Government was limited in scope and breadth by environmental factors – and primarily by the limited communications systems. It has been said that the roads of England were not to regain the height of efficiency that they enjoyed in Roman times until the nineteenth century, and this is broadly true also for much of continental Europe. Feudalism, as a constitutional system, relied upon a

of Westphalia and Charter Conceptions of International Legal Order', in Cyril E. Black and Richard A. Falk (eds), *The Future of the International Legal Order* (2 vols., Princeton, 1969), vol. 1, pp. 32, 43.

72 Not all states follow the same model, either. It was observed (before the collapse of organized Communism) that at least five world orders – Soviet Socialism, Capitalist Power Balancing, Authoritarian Corporatism, Maoist agrarian Communalism and Islamic Transnationalism – could be found within all world regions; Hayward R. Alker, 'Dialectical Foundations of Global Disparities', *International Studies Quarterly*, 25 (1981): 69–98, 81–5.

73 See Joost Pauwelyn, *Conflict of norms in public international law: how WTO law relates to other rules of international law* (Cambridge, 2003); Robert W. Cox, *Production, Power, and World Order: Social Forces in the Making of History* (New York, 1987), p. 107.

74 See Frank M. Stenton, *The first century of English feudalism* (Oxford, 1961); J.M.W. Bean, *The decline of English feudalism, 1215–1540* (Manchester, 1968); Jerome Blum, *The end of the old order in rural Europe* (Princeton, 1978).

75 See, for instance, Ferdinand Lot, *The end of the ancient world and the beginnings of the Middle Ages* (London, 1953); Stenton; J.M.W. Bean, *The decline of English feudalism, 1215–1540* (Manchester, 1968); Blum.

hierarchical structure of political, social and economic obligations.[76] It might be said to be a type of Lockean constitution, with individuals and communities linked for mutual protection.[77] This had implications for the success of states.

The limitations of technology, physical and personnel, meant that the constitutional arrangements were restricted in scope, and decentralization was common in this era. This was true even for a state such as England, which generally lacked the over-mighty baronage more common on the continent of Europe,[78] and which enjoyed an unusually sophisticated centralized fiscal system from late Saxon times.[79] There were of course important influences upon the constitution, and upon society in general, including the gradually increasing rate of literacy, and the consequent spread of new political and religious ideas.[80] These were eventually to lead to a profound religious and political revolution – and to technological and constitutional change. While the state remained largely confined to the geographic entity that could be governed by a relatively simply central regime, its size and complexity were limited. Transmarine states were uncommon.[81]

The European Middle Ages might have been distinguished by a conceptual world-view markedly different to that of classical Rome, but its environment was in many ways not so dissimilar. The attacks of the Muslims from Arabia replaced the invading Germanic hordes which the later Roman empire faced. Feudalism, which had started as a response to the exigencies of the time, became a permanent feature of life in the West, though now imbued with a Christian perspective which changed it considerably from its pagan origins. This was to become especially significant as knowledge of Roman law became more widespread, and Roman notions of property and of state authority were grafted onto the feudal structures.

---

76 See Brian Tierney, *Religion, law, and the growth of constitutional thought, 1150–1650* (Cambridge, 1982); Kenneth Pennington, *The Prince and the Law, 1200–1600: Sovereignty and rights in the Western legal tradition* (Berkeley, 1993); Thomas Ertman, *Birth of the leviathan: building states and regimes in mediæval and early modern Europe* (Cambridge, 1997); Heinrich Mittels, *The state in the middle ages: a comparative constitutional history of feudal Europe*, trans. H.F. Orton (Amsterdam, 1975).

77 See John Hudson, *Land, law, and lordship in Anglo-Norman England* (Oxford, 1994). There were however signs of a more complex form of constitution emerging; See Arthur P. Monahan, *Consent, coercion, and limit: the mediæval origins of parliamentary democracy* (Leiden, 1987).

78 See Jonathan Dewald, *The European nobility, 1400–1800* (Cambridge, 1996). See also Richard Gorski, *The fourteenth-century sheriff: English local administration in the late Middle Ages* (Woodbridge, 2003).

79 See Henry Loyn, *The governance of Anglo-Saxon England, 500–1087* (London, 1984).

80 See Jean Gimpel, *The Mediæval Machine: the industrial revolution of the Middle Ages* (London, 1977); Steven Justice, *Writing and rebellion: England in 1381* (Berkeley, 1994).

81 See Michael Lawson, *Cnut: England's Viking king* (2nd edn, Stroud 2004).

The Christian notion of the Prince was also important in legitimating existing regimes, and influenced the way in which governments operated.

The definition of feudalism itself is disputed. A wide definition is favoured by French and German historians generally[82] and a narrow by historians of the Norman Conquest.[83] The wide definition assumed the existence of peasantry who had little or no political, social or economic independence. This subservience was implemented and maintained through the widespread use of the concept of 'feudal' service, such as serjeanty, socage, and ties of obedience and protection which bound man to man. There was also an elite martial class. This concept of feudalism embraced all mediæval European societies between the ninth and twelfth centuries, as its advocates intended. In this model, late Anglo-Saxon society in England was broadly feudal. Maitland would agree,[84] but not so Stenton, in whose view service must be exactly defined in order to be feudal.[85] This definition is at once legalistic and moralistic, with a strong Christian aspect, but perhaps out of keeping with the context of the time.

A wide definition links the mediæval feudalism more closely with its classical origins. One especially important distinction lies, however, in its juristic nature, one which emphasized legal rights and responsibilities. To some degree, the most influential technology of the Middle Ages was not the surviving road or aqueduct of the Roman world, but the quill pen and the parchment of the lawyer-cleric. This is seen most clearly in the development of formal feudalism as a political, economic and social system throughout most of western Europe, and elsewhere – including the Latin kingdoms and principalities of the Holy Land, Cyprus, Armenia and other parts of the Near and Middle East.[86]

The nature of feudalism depended upon land ownership, but its defining characteristic was obligation. In the early Carolingian empire the protective relationship set up by one free man over another was called *patrocinium*.[87] One placed oneself in this position by an act of commendation.[88] The obligation of serving and respecting the vassal's superior was therefore created,[89] but only so far as compatible with the maintenance of the vassal's status as a free man. In his turn the lord was to aid and support his vassal, in the manner of food and clothing.

82 The wide definition may be taken from Marc Bloch, *Feudal Society* (Chicago, 1961).

83 Stenton.

84 Frederic Maitland, *Domesday Book and Beyond – three essays on the early history of England* (New York, 1966, first published 1897).

85 M.T. Clanchy, *England and its Rulers, 1066–1272: Foreign Lordship and National Identity* (London, 1983), p. 83.

86 States in these regions included the kingdoms of Jerusalem, Cyprus and the Armenian kingdom of Cilicia, and numerous principalities, duchies, counties and lordships.

87 In Latinized German *mundium* or *mundeburdis*.

88 *Commendatio*.

89 *Dominus*.

Although the various obligations became more specialized, this was essentially a formal contractual arrangement.[90]

Feudalism prevented the break-up of the Carolingian state in tenth-century France, because although the supremacy of the king was purely theoretical, vassalage remained a real practical bond, as well as a technical one.[91] Until late in the twelfth century the French king could only exercise power outside the royal domain in a feudal capacity. Monarchical sovereignty was only clearly recognized by a few, and most reliance was placed on the feudal authority of lord-vassal.

Feudalism played a similar role in Germany.[92] The basis of royal power in Germany was not however vassalage,[93] but the surviving organization of the Carolingian state, and the use of the Church until the struggle with the Pope over investiture in the second half of the eleventh century weakened the political role of the Church. Emperor Frederick Barbarossa tried to reform the state on a feudal basis in the second half of the twelfth century, and from the re-grant of the lands of Henry the Lion (Duke of Saxony and Bavaria) all imperial grants were of fiefs directly held of the emperor.[94] But this approach did not give the empire the strength it needed, because fiefs which escheated had to be re-granted, effectively preventing the formation of any considerable royal domain.[95] The structure of the Holy Roman Empire – which, for most of its long life was primarily confined to the German-speaking lands – was legalist and theoretical or conceptual, rather than bound by force of arms, or a complex communications system. The notion of the empire as the descendant of the Roman Empire of old, with the added authority of the Church, contributed symbolic strength to what was otherwise a comparatively weak edifice. The conceptual strength of the empire cannot be underestimated at a time in human history when ideas, and especially those of

---

90 Francois Ganshof, *Feudalism*, trans. Philip Grierson (London, 1952, first published 1944), pp. 5–8.

91 Commendation, by which men assumed the reciprocal obligations of service and protection, grew out of the needs of the later Roman Empire. While the services owed by a vassal might be domestic, economic, military or all three, where the land he owned was allodial land, the new lord would normally receive the land and grant it back to the new tenant. In this way, the greater part of western Europe passed into the lands of the baronage, and in Germany at least, prepared the way for their political independence as well.

Yet it was in England, where the remaining allodial land passed to the Crown under William the Conqueror, that the central authority grew most at the expense of the baronage, and the reasons must lie in part in the feudal structure which he imposed: G.W. Hinde, D.W. McMorland and P.B.A. Sim, *Land Law* (Wellington, 1978), vol. 1, pp. 7–8. Feudalism, by farming out Crown lands, was necessary to raise revenues, as well as military service: G.C. Cheshire, *Modern Law of Real Property*, ed. E.H. Burn (13th edn, London, 1982), p. 10.

92 Ganshof, pp. 55–6.

93 Although this was common.

94 The imperial princes or *Reichsfürsten*.

95 Ganshof, pp. 145–9.

an esoteric, mystical or metaphysical nature, held considerable sway over the popular mind – and often over those of their leaders too. But ultimately it proved insufficient to survive the stresses of the late eighteenth- and early nineteenth-century wars with revolutionary France.

One of the principal parts of Europe which never rejoined the revived Roman empire (for such it was, at least on one level), was England. Physically isolated by the English Channel, it enjoyed protection from most invaders, but was also subject to the insularity, emotional and practical, which can arise from the absence of unrestricted and regular contact with other peoples. England was never immune from political and intellectual developments on the Continent, both before and after the Norman Conquest of England in 1066. The Norman kings of England were potentially far stronger than their Saxon predecessors. This was in part due to their position as conquerors, which, in mediæval theory, demonstrated that God had shown them His favour; this left them fully in command of a unified military, social and political structure.[96] It was also because, with the advent of the formal feudal system of land tenure and its associated social structure, the king became far more the apex of society than he had been to the Saxons. The relationship of king and subject extended not just to the great tenants-in-chief but to everyone possessed of an interest in land. The eleventh- and twelfth-century renaissance across Europe, and the accompanying economic expansion also benefited the Normans,[97] in England and elsewhere. Kings eventually also benefited from civil wars (especially the War of the Roses), which dispersed the lands of potentially over-mighty barons.

The development of feudalism and the state in England had a number of peculiar features, and was in some respects the converse of what took place in Germany. The pre-Conquest thegnage was similar to vassalage, but royal thegns had allodial land (that is, not held of any lord or superior), not conditional tenure,[98] and true feudalism, in the narrower definition of Stenton, was only introduced by the Normans.

Every estate was held directly or indirectly of the king, and to avoid sub-vassals from being used by tenants-in-chief against the king, an oath of fealty or allegiance was occasionally demanded, as at Salisbury in 1086. By the

96 The redistribution of land in 1066 led to an enormous increase in the resources of the Crown, especially in the demesne lands of the king: John Cannon and Ralph Griffiths, *The Oxford Illustrated History of the British Monarchy* (Oxford, 1988), p. 160. The Conqueror allowed all Englishmen who recognized him as king to redeem, by money payments, the estates which by right of conquest had momentarily passed to him: Cheshire, p. 12.

97 Sir William Anson, *The Law and Custom of the Constitution*, ed. A.B. Keith (5th edn, Oxford, 1922; 3rd edn, 1907), vol. 2, Part 1, pp. 8–9.

98 Tenure by frankalmoign ('free alms'), which elsewhere was regarded as allodial, was in England after the Conquest regarded as a feudal tenure carrying with it an obligation of prayer.

Salisbury Oath all freemen were bound to swear allegiance directly to the king instead of to the immediate lord from whom they held their lands.[99] This method was used especially to designate the heir and obtain promises of support, as for William Rufus in 1087, and King Henry I in 1100. All those swearing allegiance became liegemen of the king. The obligations of vassals were now fixed in relation to the needs of the royal army. From Henry I onwards the ordinary oath of vassalage included a reservation of fealty to the Crown, and no holder of a normal fief enjoyed powers of jurisdiction or administrative functions comprised in the mediæval concept of *justicia*. The growth in the use of scutage and the replacement of military service by payment made the Crown more independent of the feudal levy.[100] The great census now known as the Doomsday Book aided this process by strengthening the economic independence of the King. Fiscal exemptions, such as were common on the continent – where they weakened and even impoverished central governments – were rare and comparatively insignificant in England.[101] There a clear and comprehensive inventory showed the true economic – and hence political – fabric of the country.

Feudalism made the king the supreme landowner and invested the relation of king and subject with a contractual character, rights to service and protection. The association of land ownership and the rights of the Crown tended to assimilate the descent of the Crown to the descent of an estate in land, and inevitably increased the hereditary at the expense of the elective character of kingship.[102] The obligation on the king's part, however, of providing good government, remained. The *Witan* of the Saxon kings gave way to the *Commune Concilium* of the Normans, a body which was much more dominated by the landed interest, because land-ownership was the principal source of wealth and a sign of importance far more to the Norman than to the Saxon.[103]

Had the Norman dynasty lasted, the earliest wave of French settlers might have been assimilated in time without radically affecting the broad lines of indigenous development. But with the death of William's grandson William the Ætheling in the *White Ship*, the Crown went to a count of Boulogne, a member of the House of Blois, and then a count of Anjou. With the sons and descendants of King Henry II, the influence of Aquitaine on England was profound.[104] The political

99 Cheshire, p. 13.

100 Ganshof, pp. 149–51.

101 Palatine jurisdiction, where some elements of royal authority are vested in a delegate, entrusted with what might be categorized as a form of mediæval provincial self-government, derives its name from the counts palatine. A county palatine was a county whose lord held particular rights, in lieu of the king or emperor, such as pardoning treasons and murders.

102 See Noel Cox, 'The Law of Succession to the Crown in New Zealand', *Waikato Law Review*, 7 (1999): 49–72.

103 Anson, *The Law and Custom of the Constitution*, pp. 8–9.

104 Frank Barlow, *The Feudal Kingdom of England, 1042–1216* (2nd edn, London, 1961, first published 1955), p. 108.

development of England became more closely aligned to that on the Continent, and yet subtly different. The concept of Saxon kingship was merged with that of Norman feudalism.

The juristic theory of territorial sovereignty, with the king being supreme ruler within the confines of his kingdom, was originally two distinct conceptions. The king acknowledged no superior in temporal matters, and within his kingdom the king was emperor.[105] The emperor had legal supremacy, or he did not. If the former, theories of the sovereignty of kings were not needed, as they swayed merely *de facto* power. Sovereignty remained essentially *de jure* authority.[106] Bartolus and Baldus led the way towards recognition of a legal sovereignty of kings. The emperor had a genuine *de jure* sovereignty within the *terrae imperii*. Other powers could obtain true sovereignty on a purely *de facto* basis. This was not merely power without legitimacy.[107]

In the later Middle Ages, it was believed that England was an independent sovereign monarchy answerable only to God: in mediæval parlance an empire, self-contained and sovereign.[108] The focusing of the Crown's activities almost exclusively on the realm of England after 1216 encouraged such thinking. Sir John Fortescue remarked that 'from of old English kings have reigned independently, and acknowledged no superior on earth in things temporal'. This was a fundamental feature of English monarchy by the fifteenth century, based on precepts of Roman law.[109] They rejected a Holy Roman Empire that had been narrowly German for

105 Walter Ullmann, 'This Realm of England is an Empire', *Journal of Ecclesiastical History*, 30 (1979): 175–203.

106 J.P. Canning, 'Law, sovereignty and corporation theory, 1300–1450' in J.H. Burns (ed.), *The Cambridge History of Mediæval Political Thought c.350–c.1450* (Cambridge, 1988), pp. 465–7.

107 Ibid., pp. 467–71.

108 In 1485 Chief Justice Huse observed that the king was superior to the pope within his realm, and answerable directly to God: YB Hil 1 Hen VII fol. 10 pl. 10. Appeals to the papal courts, which were only abolished by the Ecclesiastical Appeals Act 1532 (24 Hen VIII c 12) (Eng.) and s 4 of the Submission of the Clergy Act 1533 (25 Hen VIII c 19) (Eng.), were prohibited, otherwise than with the royal assent, by the Constitutions of Clarendon 1164 (Eng.). The Ecclesiastical Appeals Act 1532 itself did not expressly confer a *potestas ordinis* (authority for certain purposes which only the possession of holy orders could confer). It was only a *potestas jurisdictionis*, but such a jurisdiction could be pushed far beyond questions of property, of discipline, and of morality.

109 Majesty, the sense of awe-inspiring greatness, in particular, the attribute of divine or sovereign power, was part of the legacy of Rome. The *maiestas* of the Republic or the people of Rome had become that of the emperor, the *maiestas augustalis*. The crime against the majesty of the republic, *crimeri laesae*, became the crime against the emperor, the later *lèse-majesté* or treason. Western emperors were frequently called 'majesty' after the letter of Q. Aurelius Symnachus to Theodosius I. Eastern emperors were styled 'megaleiotes''. The Holy Roman emperors were 'majesty' from the time of Louis the Pious.

Kings (such as Henry II of England), popes, cardinals and archbishops were occasionally to enjoy the style. Hugh, Count of Champagne, was so styled by his own clerks in a letter

several centuries, and the temporal authority of the Pope. The French had asserted their own empire for very similar reasons by 1200.

King Henry V especially emphasized his legal status as an emperor in his kingdom. His son Henry VI was occasionally called 'Most Imperial Majesty', and he was the first to wear a new imperial Crown of state: a closed or arched Crown with four curved hoops meeting in the centre above the diadem itself, and surmounted by a cross.[110]

The fact remains, however, that although the mediæval English king always had, as one of his principal functions, the granting of laws to his subjects, he was never in any way above the law. These kings did not have exclusive legislative authority either, but kings were relatively free from formal and permanent limitations on their powers and freedom of action. When the nobility felt that kings had gone too far they occasionally sought to restrain them. Earthly pressures,[111] including rebellion, were used against kings on six occasions from 1327 to 1485.[112] The feudal theories which were the basis of the right of counsel found in chapter 14 of Magna Carta, were only put forward when feudalism as a method of government was already in decay.[113]

Monarchy was not the only system of government the twelfth- and thirteenth-century jurists knew, but it was the only one they treated seriously and extensively. Ruler, nobility, clergy, and people were part of a mediæval constitutionalism, a *societas Christiana* that encompassed all of Christian Europe.[114]

---

to the monks of Saint-Remi in 1114, as was Philip the Good, Duke of Burgundy, in a letter from the citizens of Ghent in 1453. Most of these were however instances of a superior being addressed by an inferior, and so did not establish a precedent.

The emperor Charles V allowed the style to King Francis I of France in 1544, though it was qualified by the addition of 'Royal' while Charles styled himself 'Caesarean Majesty'. This technique was adopted generally in subsequent centuries, though not immediately in Spain, whose king was styled 'Majesty', as Charles V was both king and emperor. However, in the eighteenth century the style used was borrowed from that used by the papacy in addressing sovereigns. Thus the French monarch, styled by the Popes the 'Most Christian King', became 'His Most Christian Majesty'. The Spanish king became 'His Catholic Majesty', while the King of Portugal was 'His Most Faithful Majesty'.

The Holy Roman Emperor, and his successor the Austrian emperor, was the 'Imperial and Apostolic' emperor, the 'Apostolic' coming from the Kingdom of Hungary. In the United Kingdom, the style of the Sovereign is 'His (or Her) Britannic Majesty'. 'His Majesty' is usually enough for use within a sovereign's own realms, but may be amplified, in British usage, 'His Most Gracious Majesty', 'His Most Excellent Majesty', or 'His Sacred Majesty', the latter being common in the sixteenth and seventeenth centuries, the others still used occasionally in certain formal instruments.

110 Cannon and Griffiths, p. 203.

111 At great risk to the perpetrators in Heaven and on earth.

112 Cannon and Griffiths, p. 205.

113 Frank Barlow, *The Feudal Kingdom of England*, pp. 112–13.

114 Kenneth Pennington, 'Law, Legislative authority and theories of government, 1150–1300' in Burns, *The Cambridge History of Mediæval Political Thought c.350–c.1450*,

The canonists' corporate theory explained the relationship between the head of a *universitas* and its members.[115] In the thirteenth century this led to a new theory of government, based in part on Aristotle's mixed constitution.[116] Aquinas also 'discovered' this system in ancient Israel.[117] At the beginning of the fourteenth century John of Paris combined the corporate theory and Aquinas's mixed constitution, and applied it to the government of the Church.[118]

Kingship conferred a coercive jurisdiction, with the king a dispenser of justice, and repressor of evil. But a king could also be a guide to the end for which the state was ordained. In this, the king disposed of moral authority which could command obedience. Belief in this second attribute of kingship was revived under the influence of Aristotelian teleology.[119] There was philosophical support for monarchy in Aristotle.[120]

King Henry II abandoned the old fiscal system, as well as the *renovatio monetae*, in 1158, and the last *danegeld* was levied in 1162.[121] Nearly the whole of England was organized into shires and hundreds in 1066, and almost all land was assessed in hides and the like, for the purposes of taxation and service. This allowed a uniquely (for the era and continent) high degree of fiscal mobilization.[122] In the eleventh century the aristocratic landholding of England twice refashioned. The refashioning which occurred in the period on either side of Canute's accession weakened the king, whilst that occurring in the two decades after the Battle of Hastings empowered him.[123]

Sub-tenancies were less formal in Saxon times than they were under the feudal system of the Normans, but the patterns of land occupation at the lowest levels changed much less markedly.[124] The barons required the permission of the king to embark on foreign voyages, to build castles, alienate land, marry or arrange the marriage of a child or other dependent. The wide range of economic resources

p. 443.

115 Very Rev'd Rashdall Hastings, *The Universities of Europe in the Middle Ages*, ed. F.M. Powicke and A.B. Emden (Oxford, 1936).

116 A mixture of monarchy, aristocracy, and democracy.

117 St Thomas Aquinas, *Summa theologiæ* (London, 1963), 1.2 q. 1051.

118 John of Paris, *De potestate regia et papali, Johannes Quidort von Paris Über Königliche under päpstliche Gewalt*, ed. F. Bleienstein (Stuttgart, 1969), ch. 19.

119 Jean Dunbabin, 'Government', in Burns, *The Cambridge History of Mediæval Political Thought c.350–c.1450*, pp. 482–3.

120 'Monarchy is the best form of government': Aristotle, *Ethica Nicomachea*, ed. R.A. Gauthier and E.J. Brill (Rotterdam, 1972–74), viii, 10, 1160b.

121 James Campbell, *Essays in Anglo-Saxon History* (London, 1986), p. 167.

122 Ibid., pp. 171–2.

123 The dissolution of the monasteries caused a revolution in land ownership comparable with 1066: Cannon and Griffiths, p. 324.

124 Robin Fleming, *Kings and Lords in Conquered England* (Cambridge, 1991), p. 216.

in the hands of the king remained.[125] The higher nobility were at once the king's main potential enemy and the principal ally of central government. Yet even under William II, England was a more centralized country than France, although similarly composed of largely self-governing lordships[126] – these were rarely formally so, as they were in France.[127]

Because Henry II successfully reversed the tendencies of Stephen's reign, England never developed formal nobility with powers of life and death over their subjects, and neither did the privileges of noble birth extend equally to all members of a family. There were to be no more hereditary sheriffs, so the nobility did not acquire the measure of independence they enjoyed in France and Germany.[128]

By 1377, Parliaments were in England an almost annual occurrence, and the monarchy was regularly dependent upon the commons for financial aid, though in theory the king was to continue for a long time to rely upon his own hereditary revenues, perquisites, and large, expensive borrowings.[129] The King was both a beneficiary of the advanced taxation system which he oversaw, and a victim of it. By the time of the 'Good Parliament' of 1376 it had become possible for the commons to organize and launch a far-reaching attack on the conduct and policies of the government, and yet still be allowed to remain in session for more than two months.[130] Richard II tried to revive the personal monarchy which had been on the decline since the last years of his grandfather Edward III.[131] The steady decline

125 This distribution of financial obligations across the entire kingdom allowed a much more efficient royal economy than was available in France or Germany. The ransom for King Richard I was raised 1193–94 by the justiciar using the whole range of feudal and more ancient levies. Levied were a scuttage at 20 s, the knights' fee, a tallage on the royal demesne, and a quarter of a man's movable goods and revenues (or a fine instead). More was required, and a *geld* at 2 s, the year's crop of wool from the Cistercians and Gilbertines, and the treasure from the churches were taken. All in fact were fairly apportioned, and reflected the obligation on a vassal to redeem their captive lord: Frank Barlow, *The Feudal Kingdom of England*, p. 389.

126 Ibid., pp. 185–6.

127 Under King William I there were four counties palatine in England; Chester, Durham, Kent, and Shropshire. Pembroke followed later (these latter three were only palatinates for a short time). Other palatine counties, which only retained their exceptional position for a short time, were the Isle of Ely, and Hexhamshire in Northumbria. In Ireland there were palatine districts, and the seven original earldoms of Scotland occupied positions somewhat analogous to that of the English palatine counties. The duchies of Cornwall, Lancaster, the principalities of Wales, Scotland (not to be confused with the Kingdom of Scotland), and the county of Carrick, were others of the various independent jurisdictions at various times in the countries of the United Kingdom. There were also palatine jurisdictions further afield, including North America.

128 M.T. Clanchy, *England and its Rulers*, p. 121.

129 Hereditary revenues survive even now in the United Kingdom.

130 Stanley Chrimes, *Lancastrians, Yorkists and Henry VII* (2nd edn, London, 1966), p. 4.

131 Ibid., p. 32.

in prestige and resources of the monarchy since the end of the fourteenth century brought disaster and decadence in government, and had made civil war not only possible but inevitable.

Fifteenth century England was a limited monarchy; one which was limited by the reliance of the king on laws made by the king-in-Parliament.[132] The king could do no wrong, and his ministers took the blame for decisions even in the fifteenth century.[133] The extreme weakness of the office of king under Henry VI had gravely jeopardized law and justice, administration, and economic development; it had reduced to a low ebb the position of England on the Continent. It was necessary for the monarchy to be restored, set along more efficient and vigorous lines than Lancaster had achieved. The only alternative was some kind of magnate conciliar government, with all its accompanying corruption, dissension, and administrative anarchy, as found in the time of Henry VI.

The first attempt to wrest actual control over the direction of affairs from the king is found in the Provisions of Oxford, though the council established under it lasted only 18 months.[134] King Henry IV achieved the remedy to the assertion of authority by the barons – by the end of the reign there were no over-mighty subjects left.[135] From 1471, Edward IV had found the solution to the problem of the Crown. He succeeded in reviving and arresting the decline of the kingship and improved markedly the working of government. Henry VII took over the Yorkist monarchy, used its methods and institutions, extended and improved them, and made them more efficient.[136] Continual wars led to the need for working arrangements between king and subjects in Parliament.[137] Kings came to rely more and more on their councillors.[138]

Although mediæval and early modern constitutions were to develop in rather different directions in England and elsewhere in Europe, the prevailing influence was the evolving body of laws. There were not merely individual laws, but one could speak of 'the law' as an entity in its own right. In much of Europe this was to be heavily influenced by the reception of the laws of ancient Rome, and everywhere they were strongly affected by the laws and beliefs of the Church. When knowledge of Roman law was 'rediscovered', especially from the twelfth century, contemporary ideas of governance were reinterpreted in the light of Roman principles. This led at once to the growth of centralized royal administration and to the exultation of the papacy. The kingship under Henry III was strengthened in no

132 Stanley Chrimes, C.D. Ross and R.A. Griffiths (eds), *Fifteenth-century England 1399–1509* (Manchester, 1972), p. 30.

133 Ibid., p. 32.

134 Cannon and Griffiths, p. 208.

135 Stanley Chrimes, *Lancastrians, Yorkists and Henry VII*, pp. 124–5.

136 Ibid., p. 178.

137 Cannon and Griffiths, p. 211.

138 Ibid., p. 213.

small part by the work of those educated in the newly fashionable civil law.[139] As the state evolved as an institutional entity separate from the nation or the king – even in France – so it began to exhibit signs of independent existence. In particular it became increasingly bureaucratic and legalistic. This strengthened it and made the state more able to utilize the resources of the country. Checks and balances, and dependence upon the law, became the norm.

2.4 The Reformation

The importance of the internal and external normative influence of the state may be seen particularly in the period known, somewhat loosely, as the Reformation. This era, in contrast to much of the preceding Middle Ages,[140] was a time of significant constitutional and technological change. In part this was caused by specific inventions such as the printing press,[141] but it was also a result of increased trade

139 Robin Frame, *The Political Development of the British Isles 1100–1400* (Oxford, 1990), pp. 101–2. From the time of Edward I the influence of the civil law on the development of the common law declined. But the legacy of Roman law was still felt in equity. All Chancellors till Wolsey, with one or two exceptions, were clerics as well as statesmen, and consequently learned in canon and civil law rather than the common law. It was therefore to the Roman system that they would naturally turn for a reason, if it could be found, when it was necessary to 'abate the rigour of the common law'. The law merchant (especially that part relating to maritime law) not only had its origin in Roman law, but was developed by civilians in the Admiralty Courts.

As a result of the Renaissance there was a heated controversy over whether there should be a general reception of Roman law. This was fought by scholars, in favour of reception, and the common lawyers, who were opposed. The common lawyers won, but the Church courts survived the Reformation, and preserved their jurisdiction over wills and matrimonial causes. Since they had virtually adopted a civil law procedure, as well as many rules of Roman jurisprudence, advocates in the Church courts were civilians of Doctors' Commons, and could plead only as doctors of the civil law.

After the renaissance, the common law was too mature to be much influenced by external sources, with the exception of the law merchant. Equity was now more inclined to rely on invention, rather than borrow from the principles of the civil law. The law merchant itself is still developing, but is more influenced by the customs of the modern commercial world than by the considered ideas of the Roman world. The same holds true for admiralty law. See George Squibb, *Doctors' Commons: a history of the College of Advocates and Doctors of Law* (Oxford, 1977).

140 There were, of course, many advances at times, especially during the renaissance of the eleventh and twelfth centuries.

141 See John Man, *The Gutenberg revolution: the story of a genius and an invention that changed the world* (London, 2002). For a slightly later period see David Zaret, *Origins of democratic culture: printing, petitions, and the public sphere in early-modern England* (Princeton, 2000); Alexandra Halasz, *The marketplace of print: pamphlets and the public sphere in early modern England* (Cambridge, 1997).

with the east,[142] and the importation of new ideas (including from the classical world, and the Islam-dominated Near and Middle East), beginning as early as the time of the first crusade.[143] These developments led to changing perceptions of the role of the state, including the rise in a belief in a social compact between state and individual, or state and community.[144] These developments were themselves also, at least partly, a consequence of the long-term influence of the notion of the state, and of law and government more broadly, as these had developed in Europe.

The centuries leading to the Reformation also led to an increased awareness of the differences between the peoples of different states of Europe. Though the westerners might have been categorized as 'Franks' by the Saracens (another generalization), they were far from homogeneous. It is not clear that these changes were a result of social and technological changes, or whether the social and technological changes led to social changes, which in turn led to constitutional changes.[145] Yet the example of the Reformation shows us that even in relatively complex societies constitutions may be affected by technology. Technology itself continued to develop, particularly where constitutions, and societies, were more liberal,[146] and where received wisdom was systematically challenged. As an example, medical science was greatly advanced by the use of dissection, which had been largely proscribed, in most of Europe for religious reasons, throughout the Middle Ages. Muslims, Jews and other non-Christians were, however, able to engage in such practices and passed much of their knowledge on to Christian physicians in due course.

---

142 Including with Byzantium, the heart of the eastern empire; See Deno John Geanakoplos, *Constantinople and the West: essays on the late Byzantine (Palaeologan) and Italian Renaissances and the Byzantine and Roman churches* (Madison, c.1989); Krijnie N. Ciggaar, *Western travellers to Constantinople: the West and Byzantium, 962–1204: cultural and political relations* (Leiden, 1996).

143 See Aziz Suryal Atiya, *Crusade, commerce and culture* (Bloomington, 1962); Vladimir P. Goss and Christine Verzair Bornstein (eds), *The Meeting of two worlds: cultural exchange between East and West during the period of the Crusades* (Kalamazoo, 1986).

144 See David Boucher and Paul Kelly (eds), *The social contract from Hobbes to Rawls* (London, 1994); Patrick Riley, *Will and political legitimacy: a critical exposition of social contract theory in Hobbes, Locke, Rousseau, Kant, and Hegel* (Cambridge, 1982); Martyn P. Thompson, *Ideas of contract in English political thought in the age of John Locke* (New York, 1987).

145 It is probably both working together. The spread of knowledge led to greater awareness, and greater demands. But it is also true that these tools were also utilized by the state, and this subtly changed the ways in which it operated. For instance, the increased administrative efficiency of central government encouraged centralization. See, for example, the decline of the offices of sheriff and coroner; Judith A. Green, *English sheriffs to 1154* (London, 1990); Richard Gorski, *The fourteenth-century sheriff: English local administration in the late Middle Ages* (Woodbridge, 2003); R.F. Hunnisett, *The mediæval coroner* (Cambridge, 1961).

146 As generally in England, and the Protestant parts of Europe.

The advent of the printing press meant that for the first time it was possible to transmit, preserve, and utilize large quantities of information. This was soon used by government bureaucracies, which sought to record as much information as they could – initially often for taxation purposes – but later for other purposes also, as the scope of government and the complexity of the constitution grew.[147] While taxation and other records from the ancient near east and elsewhere were at times voluminous, the printing press allowed and encouraged record keeping an order of magnitude greater – with profound consequences.

The invention of the printing press encouraged the circulation of information, which in turn encouraged the development of common politics beyond the immediate community.[148] This spreading of knowledge was to have a major role in German, and somewhat later, Italian re-unification.[149] The modern territorial state was unknown to antiquity and to the Middle Ages, except in those cities which alone saw sufficient division of labour and concentration in a confined area.[150] The Roman empire was a partial example, but even there it remained in many ways a city state to the end, with the relationship between the eternal city and the provinces always uncertain.

The particular constitutional structures – at a level beneath the state – had a significant influence upon the nature and form of development. Partly because of the centralization of government, and the highly developed but evolutionary legal system, the Reformation in England may be characterized as relentlessly juridical in nature.[151] It both rebelled against the perceived legalism of the papacy, but also grafted onto the now headless church a new head. Legalism, in St Paul's eyes, is dangerous because it focuses the mind on human achievement rather than on the inevitable inadequacy of that achievement in God's sight.[152] Yet even today much of the law governing the Church is to be found in secular statutes and the decisions

147 See M.T. Clanchy, *From memory to written record, England 1066–1307* (Oxford, 1993).

148 See Joseph Loewenstein, *The author's due: printing and the prehistory of copyright* (Chicago, 2002).

149 McGinnis, p. 6; Detlev F. Vagts, 'State Succession: The Codifiers View', *Virginia Journal of International Law*, 33 (1993): 275–97.

150 Hermann Heller, 'The Decline of the Nation State and its Effect on Constitutional and International Economic Law', *Cardozo Law Review*, 18 (1996): 1139, 1142.

151 This was, of course, an ironic development given that papal authority had been extended and reinforced throughout Western Christendom through the work of the great lawyer-popes and the canonists and civilians; see, for example, Brian Tierney, *Church law and constitutional thought in the Middle Ages* (London, 1979).

152 Brash, Anthony, 'Ecclesiastical Law and the Law of God in Scripture', *Ecclesiastical Law Journal*, 5(22) (1998): 7, 10; see Heikki Räisänen, *Paul and the Law* (Tubingen, 1983).

of secular courts, in accordance with the relationship between church and State[153] as this has developed since the Reformation in England.

The Reformation did not, of course, affect countries equally, even within Europe, and it was confined to that continent, though its effects were felt further afield. It passed through various stages – including the Counter-Reformation – which also saw a blossoming of constitutional theory,[154] driven by political and religious forces.

The modern territorial nation-state arose in the years prior to the Reformation. It was largely a product of the new learning that had come to dominate in the West. The ancient and mediæval state was limited in its ability to impose ideas upon the people, but was equally unable to defend them against usurpers, tyrants and petty thievery – which are a few of the most fundamental functions of any government. This of course also limited the extent to which it could promote, regulate or discourage commerce and industry, or the dissemination of ideas. But the tendency since the Renaissance of the twelfth century had been for the gradual expansion of knowledge. It is perhaps not a coincidence that the university evolved almost simultaneously in several countries of Western Europe during the twelfth and thirteenth centuries.[155] The growth of the new knowledge both encouraged constitutional change and was a consequence of that change.

2.5 The Industrial Revolution

At a somewhat later period in the development of European civilization the physical technologies began to evolve at an especially rapid rate. This era has been called the Industrial Revolution. It was a time which saw the true advent of mass manufacture, and which led to greater population size (through the elimination of many diseases and the increased availability of employment for individuals rather than family units as formerly), higher productivity and rapid economic growth.[156] Social theorists tend to agree that the ascent of industrial capitalism in the nineteenth century unleashed a particularly intense period of social and

153 The term 'State' is used throughout this discussion for convenience, though in the English constitutional tradition it is by no means certain that such an entity exists; see Noel Cox, 'The Theory of Sovereignty and the Importance of the Crown in the Realms of The Queen', *Oxford University Commonwealth Law Journal*, 2(2) (2002): 237–55.

154 See Michael A. Mullett, *The Catholic Reformation* (London, 1999); Nicholas S. Davidson, *The Counter-Reformation* (Oxford, 1987).

155 Very Rev'd Rashdall Hastings, *The Universities of Europe in the Middle Ages*, ed. F.M. Powicke and A.B. Emden (Oxford, 1936).

156 See Sidney Pollard, *Essays on the industrial revolution in Britain*, ed. Colin Holmes (Aldershot, 2000); Margaret C. Jacob, *Scientific culture and the making of the industrial West* (New York, 1997).

economic acceleration.[157] This led to more taxation revenue for governments, but also to more social and economic problems,[158] and so to enlarged opportunities and requirements for government intervention.[159] This in turn led to greater demands for democracy, such as was manifested by the chartists and the electoral reformers in the United Kingdom during the early nineteenth century.[160] But domestic economic policies in that country remained largely *laissez-faire*, which encouraged further development.[161]

It may well be true that it was economic and social changes, wrought by technological advances, which resulted in constitutional changes during the Industrial Revolution – domestically at least.[162] The development of colonial empires by European states in the course of the nineteenth century seems to have been due, at least in part, to the direct effect of technology. Naval and military technology enabled colonial powers to build empires in places previously beyond their reach.[163] The very needs of those naval forces led to further expansion, as, for example, in the building of coaling stations across the globe.[164] Each of these had to be administered, and might become colonies, then self-governing dependencies, and later (depending upon the whim, inclination or weakness of the colonial power) independent, as the need for such stations declined, or the circumstances of the colonial power allowed. At the same time the constitutional structures in place

157 William E. Scheuerman, 'Constitutionalism in an age of speed', *Constitutional Commentary*, 19 (2002): 353–90, 357–8. Koselleck highlights key aspects of early modern history, including innovations in transportation and communications inspired by mercantilism, as motivating forces behind much of this development; Reinhart Koselleck, *Zeitschichten* (Frankfurt, 2000), pp. 157–8.

158 See Paul Slack, *The English poor law, 1531–1782* (New York, 1995).

159 See Arthur J. Taylor, *Laissez-faire and state intervention in nineteenth-century Britain* (London, 1972); Sir Norman Chester, *The English administrative system, 1780–1870* (Oxford, 1981). See also Roy MacLeod (ed.), *Government and expertise: specialists, administrators, and professionals, 1860–1919* (Cambridge, 1988); Bernard S. Silberman, *Cages of reason: the rise of the rational state in France, Japan, the United States, and Great Britain* (Chicago, 1993).

160 See Nancy D. LoPatin, *Political unions, popular politics and the great Reform Act of 1832* (New York, 1999); John Charlton, *The Chartists: the first national workers' movement* (London, 1997).

161 See Arthur J. Taylor, *Laissez-faire and state intervention in nineteenth-century Britain* (London, 1972).

162 Though it could equally be said that it was the social changes which led to constitutional changes – particularly the growth in disparity between those places represented in Parliament, and those which had the largest populations; See John K. Walton, *The Second Reform Act* (London, 1987).

163 See Woodruff D. Smith, *European imperialism in the nineteenth and twentieth centuries* (Chicago, c.1982).

164 For an illustration of these, see Adam Kirkaldy, *British shipping: its history, organization and importance, with a map of main routes and coaling stations and full appendices* (London, 1914).

either encouraged – as in the United Kingdom – or discouraged – as arguably in the case of the Iberian peninsula countries – this colonial evolution. In other instances the constitutional systems may have been ambivalent to outward expansion – as in the case of the United States of America (where internal expansion was fostered) – and there private enterprise often prevailed.

Like the much earlier Roman Empire, these new empires relied heavily upon communications. As the empires spread well beyond the narrow confines of Europe – indeed the comparatively long-settled political boundaries and sophisticated societies there rendered the acquisition of new territory difficult, as Napoleon Bonaparte and later Adolf Hitler were to find to their cost – so more complex long-distance communications were required. The invention of an effective chronometer, and the invention of the principle of longitude, did much to open up the world's oceans in the eighteenth century,[165] and the principal countries of Europe soon took advantage of this. The telegraph,[166] seabed cables and fast shipping, meant that an empire could encompass the globe, and yet be administered without too much difficulty from the imperial heartland.[167] There was a considerable degree of de-centralization, which was to increase as colonial territories developed more fully.[168] But the oversight of territories changed the nature of domestic political structures – for example, in the British experience, the notion and role of the Crown – considerably.[169]

The Industrial Revolution gave economic power to those counties in which it began – particularly the United Kingdom, but it also gave them technological advantages (especially in respect of communications, mass production, and military and naval force – power projection) which meant that they enjoyed significant

165 Dava Sobel, *Longitude: the true story of a lone genius who solved the greatest scientific problem of his time* (New York, 1995).

166 See Tom Standage, *The Victorian Internet: the remarkable story of the telegraph and the nineteenth century's online pioneers* (London, 1999).

167 See Alpheus H Snow, *The administration of dependencies: a study of the evolution of the federal empire, with special reference to American colonial problems* (New York, 1902); *Analysis of the system of government throughout the British Empire* (London, 1912); John W. Cell, *British colonial administration in the mid-nineteenth century: the policy-making process* (New Haven, 1970); Cedric Lowe, *The reluctant imperialists: British foreign policy, 1878–1902* (London, 1967).

168 See, for instance, Noel Cox, 'The control of advice to the Crown and the development of executive independence in New Zealand', *Bond Law Review*, 13 (2001): 166–89.

169 See George Winterton, 'The evolution of a separate Australian crown', *Monash University Law Review*, 19 (1993): 1–22; Noel Cox, 'The control of advice to the Crown and the development of executive independence in New Zealand'. The office of secretary of state also evolved over time, partly as a consequence of greater emphasis upon external affairs; David Kynaston, *The Secretary of State* (Lavenham, 1978).

political advantages.[170] These resulted in constitutional changes, primarily including a focus on empire, a rapid development in social and educational policies, the scope and reach of government generally, and greater democracy.[171]

2.6 Constitutional paradigms

The existence of the concept of the state (as distinct from the mere existence of the state) has a normative influence both internally and externally. But with almost all nations or country states in a formal sense, this offers little or no guidance with respect to the stability or success of the state. However, when we consider the internal aspects of the state we are reminded that as institutional entities they differ. In particular they have differing constitutional arrangements. There is a considerable difference between the constitutions of countries, and that all assert the status of a sovereign state has little bearing on the internal arrangements of the states. It may well be that a state appears more effective externally – by the mere fact of its existence – than it actually is internally.[172]

These internal differences have an important normative effect. It is also important to emphasize that these differences may be either formal or informal. Some aspects of the constitutional ethos of a state are found solely in custom, historical tradition, and the unwritten rules of conduct strengthened and legitimated by time. Others may be primarily or exclusively formal rules entrenched in written and codified constitutions. Both have an effect on the way in which the constitution operates and upon the way in which the state sees itself – and is perceived by others external to it.

One of the aspects of early twenty-first-century Western culture which is most remarkable is the intellectual dominance of secularism. This is in marked contrast to the situation in parts of Africa and Asia, and especially the Middle East and North Africa. Society is undergoing – in the West at least – a rapid and seemingly irreversible secularization. This evolution has not been without its effects on the constitution of states despite the oft-quoted principle of the separation of church and state.[173] A state is not without some elements of an ethos, or an underlying philosophical or moral identity. A widespread disillusionment with liberal democratic models of government, with capitalism, and with materialism, has left

170 As exemplified in the era of 'gunboat diplomacy', for instance, Miriam Hood, *Gunboat diplomacy, 1895–1905: great power pressure in Venezuela* (London, 1975).

171 See, for instance, the 1848 revolutions on the European continent; See Rudolf Stadelmann, *Social and political history of the German 1848 revolution*, trans. J.G. Chastain (Athens, 1975).

172 Gerard Kreijen, *State failure, sovereignty and effectiveness: Legal lessons from the decolonisation of Sub-Saharan Africa* (Leiden, 2004).

173 See Noel Cox, *Church and State in the Post-Colonial Era: The Anglican Church and the Constitution in New Zealand* (Auckland, 2008).

the state, in many societies, unable to provide the degree of conceptual unity of focus which it might be expected to do.

This has been exacerbated by declining homogeneity and increased political, social, cultural and economic polarization and marginalization. Increased diversity in a pluralist society is said to bring strength, but it cannot do so if it means there is little or no common identity to the state. Only when diversity becomes the underlying principle of the state – as arguably it has in several countries including the United Kingdom and the United States of America – can it strengthen the state.

Constitutional paradigms also influence the basic forms of government. Monarchy is amongst the more ancient, if not the most ancient, forms of government. It is found in biblical and pre-biblical times, was the prevailing form of government until the twentieth century, and remains a leading form of political organization into the twenty-first century.

Monarchy, as found in classical and ancient times, was the most stable form of government. It comprised centralization of authority and certainty of succession with moderation of rule. The King was always, or nearly always, subject to the limitation of conciliar government. He needed to govern with the advice and consent of a council, or at least was subject to some ghostly or spiritual authority. The early Saxon monarchy, whether found in the wilds of northern Germany, or in sub-Roman Britain of the Dark Ages, depended upon these limitations.

But in England the King also sought to appeal to higher notions than mere consensus, so Saxon monarchs appealed, as did their Continental cousins, to mythical descent from Woden, the Saxon god of war, or other dread ancestors, from whom they claimed descent.

The traditional date of the Saxon settlement of Sussex is 477, and of Wessex 495 – with Kent somewhat earlier. From the fifth century, as the new separate kingdoms of Britain merged and divided, sometimes in war, sometimes by dynastic alliances, Christianity became an important additional element.

Cerdic, son of Elesa, was King of Wessex (or West Saxons) 519–34, and is the earliest clearly recognizable ancestor of Elizabeth II, Queen of the United Kingdom. He was a pagan, like his people. Doubtless many of the Britons still fleeing to the west to escape the invading Saxons were also pagan, though Christianity had been adopted as the official religion of the Roman Empire in 310. But in 597, St Augustine arrived in Kent, and began the re-Christianization of Britain. Success was swift. King Edwin of Northumbria was converted in 627, and King Cynegils of Wessex followed in 635. In both cases their subjects followed their example – sometimes through policy and persuasion, but often through conviction.

In 959 Edgar, King of Wessex, became King of England after the last pagan Norse king of York was deposed, and received the submission of British princes at his coronation in 973. The country was united for the first time in some 500 years – and once again as a Christian country. This had enormous implications for the nature of the mediæval and modern monarchy. Unlike the Saxon monarchies, which began as a form of tribal chiefship, and Celtic kingship, which had a similar origin, this was national – it was not mere vanity that led Edgar to style himself *Albionis Imperator Augustus* (literally Emperor of England).

The Christian nature of the monarchy was reflected in the coronation service, and the strong ongoing relationship between what we would now call church and state. St Dunstan, archbishop of Canterbury 961–88, who anointed and crowned three kings (Edgar 973, St Edward the Martyr 975, and Ethelred the Unready 978), saw anointing as being a sacrament (or sacramental) on the same level as baptism and confirmation. Just as the early Church used oil in baptism and confirmation, so the Church also used oil for anointing Christian kings – and kings, like priests and bishops, used chrism.

This owed much to the Old Testament of the *Bible*. The anthem 'Zadok the Priest' has for centuries been sung at coronations during the anointing, since long before the glorious setting by Handel was arranged. The biblical precedent was deliberately followed:

> And Zadok the priest and Nathan the prophet have anointed him king in Gihon: and they are come up from thence rejoicing, so that the city rang again. This is the noise that ye have heard.[174]

The anointing invoked the descent of the Holy Spirit on the candidate for kingship, making him a new man, transmitting through the anointing the divine grace by which alone he would be able to fulfil his royal *ministerium* as defender of the Church. Kingship became an office within the Church without bestowing on it any priestly status. This did not change markedly over time – even the Reformation did not alter this, in England at least. The coronation services there remained replete with pre-Reformation ritual, though performed in the vernacular, with the blessing, censing and prayers to the saints alone deleted. A second crowning was possible, but not a second anointing; though King Henry III obtained a papal dispensation for this in 1220.

In the tenth and eleventh centuries the coronation robes were deliberately priestly in character – though whether this was in emulation of Byzantium or whether (in England) it was for indigenous reasons is not clear. Kings were dressed in choir (not eucharistic) dress like bishops, as the priest kings of the Old Testament.

There were two rulers in mediæval European society, the King and the Pope. Thomas Aquinas, in *On Kingship* (1260–65) wrote how a good king avoided tyranny.[175] Both the King and the Pope had religious sanction.

Pope Gelasius I, in a letter to the Eastern Roman Emperor Anastasius I in 494, wrote that 'two there are, august emperor, by which this world is chiefly ruled, the sacred authority of the priesthood and the royal power'. Though the former may be

---

174 1 Kings 1:45.

175 St Thomas Aquinas, *On Kingship to the King of Cyprus*, trans. G.B. Phelan and I.T. Eschmann (Toronto, 1949), pp. 3–7, 22–34.

weaker, at least in the West, the latter is now pre-eminent (though today the 'royal power' is more likely than not to be wielded by an elected or appointed politician of one sort or another). As we are told, we should 'Render therefore unto Caesar the things which be Caesar's, and unto God the things which be God's'.[176] St Peter adds 'Honour all men. Love the brotherhood. Fear God. Honour the king.'[177]

But the early mediæval times rulers were cast as *Christus Domini* (literally as though they were Christ on earth). 'Let every soul be subject unto the higher powers. For there is no power but of God: the powers that be are ordained of God.'[178]

This theocratic conception of monarchy – common to most of the West – was seen as a potential threat to the papacy in the eleventh century, so royal unction was declared to not be a sacrament, and anointing with chrism was for a time ended. Despite this break, it was back again by the fourteenth century. Today the anointing survives only in the United Kingdom, the remaining European monarchies having either never been granted the privilege of using holy oil, or having abandoned the rite, usually due to revolution (as in Spain) or a desire to modernize (in Scandinavia). However, modernizing is dangerous if it means abandoning an element which was once seen as an integral part of establishing a royal title. Indeed, the desire to deny the Sovereign any religious or historical mandate was behind most moves to 'modernize'. This amounted to a drive to remove any basis for legitimacy not derived from popular mandate – or a formal constitution.[179]

Yet the hallowing of the Sovereign remains vital. St Augustine of Hippo, Doctor of the Church, wrote at the beginning of the fifth century, during the first great wave of barbarian incursions into the Western empire. He described (in *The City of God*) two societies, of the spirit and of the world. Despite Christianity's designation as the official religion of the empire from the beginning of the fourth century, Augustine declared its message to be spiritual rather than political. Christianity, he argued, should be primarily concerned with the mystical, heavenly City of Jerusalem rather than with Earthly politics.

Augustine's book presents the span of human history as being a conflict between what Augustine calls the City of God and the City of Man. This conflict is destined to end in victory for the former, not simply because of God's omnipotence, but because the City of God was inherently stronger. It is marked by the presence of people who chose to forego earthly pleasure, and to dedicate their lives to the promotion of Christian values. The City of Man, on the other hand, consisted of people who had strayed from the City of God. The coronation is the hallowing of the Sovereign to be a kind of bridge between the two cities. While

176 Luke 20:25, and Matthew 22:21.

177 1 Peter 2:17.

178 Romans 13:1.

179 See Ian Bradley, *God Save the Queen: The Spiritual Dimension of Monarchy* (London, 2002).

this might be dismissed as religious 'mumbo-jumbo' by many – especially in an age of dissent, and opinion-stifling political correctness – but still of importance to many others. Most critically, any abandonment of the key ritual of king-making threatens to undermine the legitimacy of the monarchy. This may also occur with the abandonment or radical reform of the coronation oath.

The idea that the Sovereign of the United Kingdom is above politics – which can be traced to *The Patriot King*, a 1714 essay by the statesman and philosopher Henry St John Viscount Bolingbroke[180] – does not render the oath any less important. It becomes, like the anointing, part of the hallowing and dedication of the Sovereign as a national figure.

While the Christian beliefs of Queen Elizabeth II is well known, that of the Prince of Wales is perhaps misunderstood. Yet he is remarkable as a philosopher-prince, a Christian King in waiting, who genuinely strives to bring some sense to the place of religion in society. This role is as relevant to the athiest and agnostic as it is to the believer.

Surprisingly perhaps in what is often seen as a post-Christian era, there is no inherent inconsistency with Christianity remaining at the heart of the political system, despite the long-established principle of freedom of religion. Freedom for individuals to choose does not mean that the state must be athiest or agnostic – for that is adopting a stance on – or rather against – religion. If a Sovereign reflects and adheres to a religious belief system it gives them a sense of moral purpose which is often lacking in political figures.

At a time when the West has been said to be at war with a conflicting belief system – radical Islam – abandonment of our own beliefs might serve only to strengthen the disdain which many Muslims hold for what they see as the godless West.

Saladin, whose struggles with the Crusaders and especially his relationship with Richard Coeur de Lion (King Richard I of England) are justly famous, was a chivalrous Muslim leader of the late twelfth century. He understood the position of his Christian foes, and dealt fairly with them by the standards of the time. But he could not tolerate the godless and those who lacked moral or religious principles – or whose principles were flexible.[181]

Religion and monarchy may not be mainstream concerns for the majority of the people, even in countries where the two are (even partially) linked. But they nevertheless exercise a significant influence on constitutional thought and practice. A post-modern political ethos has challenged both; but there are signs that this tendency is being countered. Dr Rowan Williams, Archbishop of Canterbury, noted in 2005 that:

---

180 Henry St John Viscount Bolingbroke, *The Idea of a Patriot King: With respect to the Constitution of Great Britain* (London, 1740).

181 James Reston, Jr., *Warriors of God: Richard the Lionheart and Saladin in the Third Crusade* (New York, 2001).

> Europe is, historically speaking, an unusual experiment. It is a cultural and political community which has developed steadily towards a situation in which power is understood and exercised in a 'secular' framework; but that secular framework exists because of a set of religious and theological foundations, sometimes acknowledged, sometimes not.
>
> …
>
> But the history of Europe is the history of a culture in which, because religious authority has always remained distinct in principle from state authority, the ideal of a politics of questioning and creative adjustment and change has slowly taken shape. Political arrangements have never been beyond question. The way this has developed, especially during and since the Enlightenment, has taken a shape which often looks deeply hostile to religious faith; but the paradox which the secularist fails to see is that this vision of a free and self-determining political life, this classical liberal vision, is what it is primarily because of the particular religious faith that moulded Europe.
>
> …
>
> Europe's distinctive identity, then, is a 'liberal' identity, in the broadest meaning of the word: a political identity which assumes that argument and negotiation, plural claims adjudicated by law, suspicion of 'positivist' notions of political power, are all natural, necessary features of a viable and legitimate communal life in society. But the crucial point for the Christian is the conviction that this 'liberal' identity is threatened if it does not have, or is unaware of, that perpetual partner which reminds it that it is under a higher judgement. Unless the liberal state is engaged in a continuing dialogue with the religious community, it loses its essential liberalism. It becomes simply dogmatically secular, insisting that religious faith be publicly invisible; or it becomes chaotically pluralist, with no proper account of its legitimacy except a positivist one (the state is the agency that happens to have the monopoly of force).
>
> The Christian sense of what matters about European identity, then, is not about some mythical unity between the faith and the historic culture of Europe, a 'Christendom' picture. Nor is it to insist that what is now politically defined as Europe cannot expand beyond the boundaries of what were once the Christian nations of the continent.[182]

Archbishop Williams is ascribing to the Christian ethos much of the credit for the particular path political and social evolution took in Europe – a position which is relatively non-contentious. More interesting, perhaps, is his belief that this influence continues.

The state is a concept in international law, and a convenient term for describing the domestic constitutional or institutional entity. Still, this tells us little or nothing

182 Dr Rowan Williams, Archbishop of Canterbury, 'Forum debate: Is Europe at its end?', Sant'Egidio International Meeting of Prayer for Peace, Palais de Congress, Lyons, 12 September 2005.

of the principles upon this this entity is based. These must be discovered by examining the workings of the state. The growth in plurality render this task of discovery more difficult.

Internally, the basic rules that determine the structure of government – democracy, separation of powers and others – may be readily perceived. The reasons for these rules and the underlying principles upon which they are based are much less easily identified. It may matter little on a short time frame what these principles are – indeed it may matter not at all. Over the longer term it may matter. This is because the closer the constitution is to accurately reflecting the societal nature of the state, the greater is the prospect that this harmony brings stability and success. Modern notions of plurality, diversity and inclusiveness are not necessarily the most efficient principles upon which to construct a state, though we may be too early in this phase of societal development to be sure of this. Where a consensus arose and was followed, as in most pre-modern states and nations, plurality worked for the good of the political entity. This could be through the harnessing of political factions, who could be 'played off' one against the other by the prince. Democracy, with its majoritarian rule principle, has weakened this approach, and the need for consensus has eroded.

The normative influence of constitutional principles remains important, but its precise role is less clear where there is little discernible consensus as to the nature of the polity. Unanimity is scarcely required, but some degree of acceptance of an underlying ethos helps to ensure that constitutional principles are consistent. Many western constitutional principles can be traced to concepts of natural law that can be seen as grounded or at least influenced by Christianity. The common abandonment of Christianity as a justification for constitutional rules – or even as a factor that influences the development of constitutional rules – means that there is probably a less homogeneous approach to constitutional reform in the West in the twentieth and twenty-first centuries than for the past five hundred years. Given that this corresponds with a reappraisal of the nature of statehood in international law, the element of conceptual continuity is endangered. Whether this would have the effect of rendering constitutions less stable is uncertain, but it may well make them more flexible.

2.7 Conclusion

The state has an important normative role, in its conceptual foundations. This is so both internally and externally. This is scarcely sufficient of itself to explain why some states are more successful than others, unless we argue that there different types of state, or dismiss altogether the argument that the nature of the state can affect the success of a country. This explanation (that the state has a normative role) was obscured during the classic period of the sovereign state in the nineteenth century, due to the contemporary balance of power in Europe. It was also complicated by a marked contrast between state theory as understood in

Europe, and the nature of governance elsewhere in the world, whether colonial territories or independent states.

In the latter part of the twentieth century, and especially in response to the failure of states in many of those parts of the world that were formerly colonized by European powers, the concept of a hierarchy of states has been revived. This was revived because prior to 1648 such a graduation was a practical reality that was acknowledged by the political theory of the time. Today we are compelled to revisit this. It should not be seen simply as a hierarchy of states. That is an international law perspective, which shows a seeming reluctance to look at the domestic constitutional arrangements of states – which are in many if not most cases the primary cause of the raising or lowering of states' positions in the hierarchy.

The existence of statehood partially masks the reality of state viability, and bolsters some weak states by giving them an external credibility that the domestic reality does not justify. The more fundamental concern would appear to be with the internal perception of the state, and, critically, the constitutional ethos of the state. How does it operate as an entity? Does this add to or detract from state viability? The answer may vary from state to state.

Equally important, however, is the constitutional paradigm on which the state is based. For most of Europe, and all of Western Europe, this was historically (though not today) strongly influenced by Christianity. In 2006 the Rt Rev'd Michael James Nazir-Ali, Pakistan-born Bishop of Rochester, noted that:

> Whether we like it or not, characteristic British values arise out of the Christian faith and its vision of personal and common good. These were clarified by the Enlightenment and became the bed-rock of our modern political arrangements. The Enlightenment, however, by consigning Christianity to the private sphere, also removed the basis and justification for these values in the public sphere.
>
> It is this basis and justification that needs to be recovered if our values are to be secure, and if they are to help inculcate the virtues of generosity, loyalty, moderation and love that lead to personal fulfilment and social wellbeing.[183]

The following chapter will introduce the concept of the flexibility of constitutions as a determining factor in the stability of states. It will be argued that the greater the degree of flexibility of a constitution, the greater the stability of the regime, and hence the greater the likelihood that it will qualify externally and internally as a successful state. It must be added at once that a constitution can potentially be too flexible, for a degree of certainty is required. But the ability of the constitution to respond to the changing needs of the state is of fundamental importance. Above all, it must be consistent with the political, cultural and historical customs of the state, or the prospect of rejection or inapplicability is raised.

183 Dr Michael Nazir-Ali, Bishop of Rochester, 'Multiculturalism is to blame for perverting young Muslims', *The Daily Telegraph* (London), 15 August 2006.

Chapter 3
Hard and Soft Constitutions

3.1 Introduction

In the preceding chapters we have considered two important questions related to the central theme of this book. The first was what has been called the 'Great Question'; the explanation of why some civilizations and states have proven more successful than others – or more particularly, why the Industrial Revolution occurred in some states and apparently not in others. Specifically, this question has concentrated on finding an explanation of why the West, in particular, underwent a significant period of economic expansion through the later mediæval period and subsequently, and into the twentieth century of the Christian era, and why parallel developments of a similar magnitude did not occur elsewhere.

Two principal emphasizes emerged in the discourse. One may be broadly termed environmental, and the other institutional. It could be argued though that the physical and human environments are interlinked, and that there is no state in which the natural environment is without influence upon the institutional arrangements of the state. This might suggest that a more holistic approach would be appropriate, but the discourse has generally been seen as favouring two distinct approaches. The institutional approach would appear to be the preferred of the two principal models, for it is more appropriate to explain what seems to have been largely a manifestation of human endeavour, although the effects of environmental factors are important.

Positing then that artificial human structures have affected economic development as much, if not more than, the presence of a benign or malign natural physical environment, and the presence or absence of key ('strategic') resources, the question became how this process might have operated. In the second chapter we concentrated on normative influences, specifically that of the state. The existence of the state in the modern international law system has a certain influence, principally that of rigidity – the *status quo* is not as fluid as it would be if states formed, reformed and disappeared as readily as natural (or even other human) organisms.

At the same time the internal – or domestic – normative influence of the state remains important. It as an independent player, and not merely as a shadowy manifestation of power, or as a conduit through which other forces work (though there may be an element of these roles present as well). The modern concept of the state arose in Europe as a consequence of an ongoing process of evolution in law, politics, religion and governmental theory and practice.

The second question to be asked was this: 'have institutional structures at the highest level – such as the concept of the state itself – affected the success of states?' It does seem that there has been a normative effect, though the exact consequence of this is unclear. There may possibly be a link between the development of the modern concept of the state in the West, and the economic and technological development of that region.[1] We might have seen the development of an industrialized West without the existence of the state, and the existence of the state might not be a condition precedent to the evolution of a technologically advanced economy. It would be more worthwhile, perhaps, to ask whether there are any aspects of the state, domestic or external, that contribute to development; aspects that may indeed be present even where the state, as a distinct entity, does not exist. In other words, some regions, parts of states, and continents, may manifest certain state-like attributes which contribute materially to their success or failure as entities.

This chapter takes the last point further, and introduces the central proposition of this book. If the development of the state did have the beneficial effect suggested – assuming for the purposes of the exercise that economic development is beneficial for humanity (and this proposition would not necessarily go unchallenged) – then it must be more than simply the concept of the state which had this effect, although the concept itself led to the establishment of semi-permanent political boundaries in Europe. This is because the state now exists across the world, but only in certain parts of the world are there signs of constant or near-constant vigorous development over time.

According to theorists such as Diamond,[2] the mere existence of states would have an important role in promoting effective competition and thus economic and technological development. However political boundaries have been established on a similar pattern across the world in the past century, and the performance of states has become more variable, not less. We should look, therefore, further into the constitutional paradigms of these states, to see if there is anything that can be identified as an important influence on the viability, or the stability of states. The existence of states has an important role with respect to the international political, legal and economic system, but it does not solely explain the wide range in the levels of performance of states as entities in their own right. In other words, the internal normative affect of the state would appear more important than the

1 As elsewhere in this work, the term 'west' is used to refer to Western Europe, and those regions of the world, principally North America and Australasia, which are predominantly settled by populations from Western Europe, adopted the political and economic models of the region, and partook of the technological, economic and political advance of that region. It is not therefore a purely geographical expression, but neither does it encompass those states, such as Japan, that underwent marked development without the direct inherited or transplanted legacy of Western Europe.

2 Jared Diamond, *Guns, Germs and Steel: The Fates of Human Societies* (London, 1997), pp. 409–12.

external, in relation to the performance of states. This is influenced primarily by the particular details of the constitution, and the nature and form of the polity – including its ethos or *Grundnorm*.

In this chapter we will narrow the focus of the inquiry to the effect of the constitution on the operation of the state. Any state constitution, of whatever form or type, describes not only the formal rules by which the state operates; it also reflects, to a greater or lesser extent, the nature of the state. This nature is a product of the historical evolution of the state; a state is primarily a product of evolution, even where it is ostensibly the outcome of immediate political expediency, chance, or colonial (or other) arbitrariness. The degree to which the constitution accurately reflects the nature of the country – to discard for a moment the legal construct of the state – may be an important element. Indeed, it is the thesis of this book that there is a direct correlation between the flexibility of the constitution (and hence its responsiveness) and the stability – and ultimately the viability – of the state.

To express this more simplistically, we will examine the hypothesis that the advance of the West from the Middle Ages onwards was a consequence of the flexibility of the constitutional models which were developing. They were not too fluid that no rules prevailed – some rigidity is necessary to provide a degree of certainty (and much of this was provided in Western Europe by Christianity) – but they were sufficiently responsive to changing societal demands that they were able to evolve to respond to the needs of the developing community.

We commence this chapter with a discussion of the relationship between law and government. This is important because constitutional laws are a sub-set of general laws, and not inherently distinct – despite growth in the concept of 'public law' as a separate category of laws.

We then proceed with a discussion of the rule of law, the concept (hard to define, but often cited) that underpins western constitutions and which is often said to be fundamental to a successful modern society. If decisions must be made in a particular way, and government actions require authorization in some legal form, then the constitution, as the set of rules through which these sub-sets of rules are framed, is fundamentally important. As Finer observed, there is 'a tendency to dismiss the constitutional texts themselves as highly incomplete, if not misleading, guides to actual practice'.[3] This of course raises questions about the definition of a constitution, and the distinctions between entrenched and unentrenched, or written and unwritten constitutions – not all of which distinctions are necessarily fruitful. Since this chapter is intended to concentrate upon the influence of the constitution on the state, the emphasis here will be on the way in which the rule of law, as a constitutional principle, affects the state.

Finally, we consider the concept of inflexibility and what might be termed 'constitutional arteriosclerosis' – the lack of flexibility leading to state illness. If the constitutional rules are so important, what are the consequences if the constitution

3 S.E. Finer, Vernon Bogdanor and Bernard Rudden, *Comparing Constitutions* (Oxford, 1995), p. 1.

itself is inflexible, incapable of development, or worse, is (or is perceived as) an alien imposition? This notion of the flexibility or inflexibility of a constitution is what is meant by the concept of the hard or soft constitution.

3.2 The relationship between law and government

We may now ask 'what is the relationship between law and government?' To answer, in essence this may be categorized as regulatory. To Machiavelli the state was an organized force, supreme in its own territory, and pursuing a conscious policy of aggrandizement in its relations with other states.[4] The distinction could be drawn by European theorists between the state in the exercise of its legal functions and the state in the exercise of activities carried out by or in common with its subjects. In the latter case, the state, having entered into competition with private citizens, is deemed to waive the advantages of its public character, something which the Crown, in the British tradition, and many if not most of those legal systems derived from it, does not generally do.[5] This may result in apparent injustices, as for example with the Crown's presumed legal priority over debts. However, this is a natural consequence of the historical origin of the Crown, and it may also be seen as a logical result of a developing concept of legal positivism. To correct these perceived injustices – for, to a legal positivist, they are not injustices inasmuch as law and justice are not inextricably linked – there has been a significant move towards the development of public law, and an awareness of civil law principles and their reception, in common law jurisdictions. Government operates through law, and it is the latter which is therefore supreme.

The supremacy of the law is an idea we owe, in the European legal tradition, to the early Middle Ages.[6] There was then no concept of the sovereign state, at least in part because everyone had a different lord to whom they owed allegiance.[7] This was true even for those parts of the continent of Europe and adjoining lands where the economic, social and political system of feudalism had not been fully accepted. Relationships were essential to orderly life, and these relationships were

---

4 Niccolo Machiavelli, *The Prince*, ed. Quentin Skinner and Russell Price (Cambridge, 1988).

5 See, for instance, the Crown Proceedings Act 1950 (NZ).

6 In England, Reginald Peacock and John Fortescue, and on the Continent, Pierre D'Ailly, Nicholas of Cusa; Reginald Peacock, *The Donet of Reginald Peacock*, ed. Elsie Vaughan Hitchcock (London, 1921, repr. 1971), p. 76; Sir John Fortescue, *In Praise of the laws of England (De Laudibus Legum Angliæ)*, ed. Stanley Chrimes (Cambridge, 1942), c. 36, p. 87; Sir Robert Carlyle and A.J. Carlyle, *A History of Mediæval Political Theory in the West* (6 vols, Edinburgh, 1928–36), vol. 6, pp. 138, 141.

7 Frederic Maitland and Sir Frederick Pollock, *History of English Law before the Times of Edward I* (2nd edn, Cambridge, 1895), vol. 1, p. 182.

clothed in legal – and also often religious – form. In all cases the law prevailed, and formed the basis for relationships.

The law was distinct and universal. It was distinct from the relationships themselves and from the parties, however exalted. It was universal in that this was the era of the dominance of belief in the notion of the natural law (*jus naturale*),[8] a view of law not now finding favour with the majority of jurists. Laws exist independently of the positive law of a given political order, society or state, since it is not dependent upon the behaviour of humanity, individually or collectively. Rights are assumed, explicitly or implicitly, as being inherent, immanent and inalienable. St Thomas Aquinas, whose development of Aristotelian concepts did much to shape natural law theory for the next eight hundred years, argued that natural law could approach but not fully comprehend the eternal law.[9] Natural law was, with its emphasis upon the discovery or finding of the law, rather than its creation, particularly important in the development of the common law.[10]

Finnis drew on both Oxonian and Roman Catholic Thomistic philosophical traditions. His *Natural law and natural rights* (1980)[11] is a natural law challenge to what he saw as the dominant Anglo-American positivist approach to legal philosophy taken by Austin and Hart. He focuses on seven basic goods, which he regarded as intrinsically valuable: life, knowledge, play, aesthetic experience (or beauty), sociability (or friendship), practical reasonableness and religion. Like the Platonic forms, they are intrinsically distinct and immutable, and don't have a hierarchy. This concept also forms part of Finnis's critique of utilitarian (proportionalist philosophies, as he calls them).

According to Finnis, the main responsibility of the ruler is to further the common good. A ruler's exercise of power is weakened if a ruler exploits his opportunities by making stipulations intended by him not for the common good but for his own or his friends' advantage, or out of malice against some person or group. Except in 'emergency' circumstances, in which the law (or even the constitution) should be bypassed, an office-holder who acts beyond his authority is guilty of an abuse of power and an injustice to those treated as subject to it;[12] the tort of misfeasance of public office is thus appropriate. The exercise of authority in conformity with the Rule of Law is for the common good.

8 John Finnis, *Natural law and natural rights* (Oxford, 1980).

9 St. Thomas Aquinas, *Summa theologiæ* (London, 1963).

10 For the discovery of the law see Bruno Leoni, *Freedom and the Law* (Princeton, 1961).

11 *Natural law and natural rights* (Oxford, 1980).

12 The tort of misfeasance in public office is designed to target 'the deliberate and dishonest abuse of power'. Public officers are not liable merely because a *bona fide* administrative act is later found to be unlawful. There is a misfeasance in public office if a person suffers loss or damage as a result of administrative action known to be unlawful by those persons taking it, and those persons knew that the claimant would suffer loss or were recklessly indifferent as to whether the claimant would suffer loss; *Three Rivers District Council* v *Governor and Company of The Bank of England* [2000] 2 WLR 1220 (HL).

The social contracts of Hobbes, Locke and Rousseau were also based on principles of natural law and natural rights. These rights were, however, transferred from individual subjects to a sovereign state.

In the natural law tradition, especially as understood in England during the seventeenth century, the law itself was the true sovereign. With the Reformation, a fuller theory of sovereignty became possible, because of the vast increase in the powers and activities of the legislature. Later, and especially after the Enlightenment, judges, as professors of the law, claimed for it supreme authority, though Coke had asserted this at the beginning of the century.[13] Had this been admitted, they (the judges) would have been the ultimate authority in the state,[14] as they are today in the United States of America, where the Supreme Court is the final arbiter of the law.[15]

Legal positivism (particularly as described by Austin[16]) asserts the dominance of the sovereign authority – the state; from Holmes' American vantage point, the decisions of the courts were the final source of the law.[17] For the natural law adherent, the law always was pre-eminent; basic human goods, such as human life, are self-evident and intrinsically worthwhile.[18]

Hart's *The Concept of Law* (1961) contained a critique of John Austin's[19] theory that law is the command of the sovereign, backed by the threat of punishment. He also drew a distinction between primary and secondary legal rules, where a primary rule governs conduct and a secondary rule allows for the creation, alteration, or extinction of primary rules. A distinction was also made between the internal and external points of view of law and rules, close to (and influenced by) Max Weber's distinction between the sociological and the legal perspectives of law.[20] Hart also criticized the idea of the rule of recognition, a social rule that differentiated between those norms that have the authority of law and those that do not. Hart viewed the concept of rule of recognition as an evolution from Kelsen's *Grundnorm*.[21]

---

13 *Dr Bonham's Case* (1610) 8 Co Rep 114, 118; *The Prince's Case* (1606) 8 Co Rep 1a; 77 ER 481.

14 Figgis, p. 230.

15 Constitutional rather than parliamentary sovereignty leaves courts in charge, though they themselves are subject to the law, which they are tasked to interpret.

16 John Austin, *The Province of Jurisprudence Determined*, W. Rumble (ed.) (Cambridge, 1995); *Lectures on Jurisprudence, or The Philosophy of Positive Law*, R. Campbell (ed.) (4th edn, rev'd., London, 1879).

17 Oliver Wendell Holmes, *The Common Law*, ed. Mark DeWolfe Howe (Cambridge, 1963).

18 See John Finnis, *Natural law and natural rights* (Oxford, 1980).

19 John Austin, *Sense and sensibilia* (Oxford, 1959).

20 *Weber: Political Writings*, trans. Peter Lassman and Ronald Speirs (Cambridge, 1994).

21 Hans Kelsen, *General Theory of Law and State*, trans. Anders Wedberg (Cambridge, 1945).

Hart rejected two distinctive features of Kelsen's positivism: the idea that law necessarily requires sanctions; and the neo-Kantian idea that a normative social phenomenon could not be explained purely in terms of social facts.

Raz has been important in continuing Hart's arguments of legal positivism since the latter's death. Raz's most recent work has dealt less with legal theory proper and more with political philosophy and practical reasoning. In political philosophy, Raz is a proponent of a Perfectionist Liberalism.[22]

Dworkin disagreed with Hart and Raz's legal positivism. He sets forth the fullest statement of his critique in his book *Law's Empire* (1986). Dworkin's theory is what has been described as 'interpretive'. According to this, the law is whatever follows from a constructive interpretation of the institutional history of the legal system. In order to discover and apply these principles, courts interpret the legal information that is available to them, in the form of legislation and judgements. They develop an interpretation which best explains and justifies past legal practice.

Out of the idea that law is 'interpretive', Dworkin argues that in every situation where people's legal rights are controversial, the best interpretation involves the right answer thesis. Dworkin opposes the notion that judges have such discretion in difficult cases (though it is also observed that difficult cases make bad law).

Dworkin's model of legal principles is also connected with Hart's notion of the Rule of Recognition. Dworkin rejects Hart's conception of a master rule in every legal system that identifies valid laws, on the basis that this would mean that the process of identifying law must be uncontroversial, whereas (Dworkin argues) people have legal rights even in cases where the correct legal outcome is open to reasonable dispute.

While Dworkin moves away from positivism's separation of law and morality, his concept suggests that the two are related in an epistemic rather than the ontological sense as posited by traditional natural law.

To the positivist, legal validity has no essential connection with morality or justice,[23] and positivist law is changeable law – it is neither immutable nor immanent. Similarly in the legal realism school, popular in the United States of America and Scandinavia, all law is made by mankind and is therefore inherently flawed. Legal realism emphasizes the indeterminancy of law, and legal instrumentalism.[24]

Legal interpretivism, which has been suggested as a *via media* between natural law and legal positivism, argues that law is not a set of given data. Instead, it is the construct of the lawyer. There is therefore no separation between law and morality, although there are distinctions between the two, as law may be moral, immoral or

---

22 *The concept of a legal system; an introduction to the theory of legal system* (Oxford, 1970).

23 Though Fuller argued that law has its own internal morality; Lon F. Fuller, *The Morality of the Law* (New Haven, 1964).

24 See Alf Ross, *On Law and Justice* (London, 1958).

amoral. Law is not immanent in nature and nor do principles of law exist outside the legal system itself.[25] In this model of the law there is no room for a natural law.

Fuller's *The Morality of the Law* (1964) sees the inner morality of law as a 'model of law as a body of general, clear, stable, and proscriptive rules, capable of obedience, and faithfully applied by judges and other public officers'.[26]

Whichever view of law is preferred – and certain approaches find greater favour in some states than in others – we can see how this can have a practical application when we consider the political and legal discourse that preceded the civil wars in seventeenth century England,[27] and indeed the period up until the so-called Glorious Revolution in 1688. This latter event was the deposition of a King, whose religious and political principles and policies were anathema to the political elite (and to many of his subjects), and saw the victory of parliamentary government, ostensibly in the name of the ancient laws and liberties of the land,[28] the latter notion reflecting a tradition in England since at least the time of Bracton.

But this discourse was still some way off when the English civil wars offered one of the more important occasions when differing legal theories led to direct political and ultimately military conflict. Generally, all parties in the key seventeenth-century British constitutional disputes united to respect law, but differed as to the nature of law and sovereignty. Whigs saw law as the product of custom, and ancient statute little removed from custom (in what may be seen as a rather ahistorical approach to the constitution). Tories, in contrast, reasoned that in no state could there be law without a lawgiver, so deduced the necessity for a true legal Sovereign.[29]

Throughout the debates and struggles of the Middle Ages, the Reformation, the Renaissance and later years, the law alone remained permanent and ever-present, in a way similar to the later conceptualization (in England) of the Crown. It did not remain unchanging, however, though the speed of change may have been markedly less than it is today.

The mere immanence of law does not offer guidance as to the function of that law, nor its origins. Oresme argued that legislative power was vested in the people as a whole, since they alone could judge the common good.[30] This view was roughly compatible with the English constitutional position in the latter Middle Ages, when Parliament was regarded as the indispensable forum for the production of statute law.[31] Fortescue came to a similar conclusion, albeit one

25 Ronald Dworkin, *Law's Empire* (Cambridge, 1986).

26 *The Morality of the Law* (New Haven, 1964), p. 61.

27 See Gerald Aylmer, *The struggle for the constitution, 1603–1689* (4th edn, 1975).

28 Ibid.

29 Ibid., p. 245.

30 Nicole Oresme, *Le livres de Politiques d' Aristotle*, ed. A.D. Menut (1970) Transactions of the American Philosophical Society 137–8.

31 He followed Masilius, drawing on Roman law and Aristotelian utility; Jean Dunbabin, 'Government', in J.H. Burns (ed.), *The Cambridge History of Mediæval Political*

arrived at by a very different route. This was a result of his experience in the English law courts, where he concluded that:

> The statutes of England … are made, not only by the Prince's will, but also by the assent of whole realm, so they cannot be injurious to the people nor fail to secure their advantage.[32]

Fortescue's doctrine of English kingship was that it was *dominium politicum et regale*, in contrast with the French *dominium regale*.[33] Continental princes ruled on the basis of the civil law of their stronger Roman legal heritage.[34] They relied especially on the maxim *quod principi placuit legis habet vigorem* ('what hath pleased the prince has the force of law').[35] According to the chancellor in Fortescue's fictitious disputation which comprises the basis of *De Laudibus Legum Anglia*,[36] English kingship was superior because the monarchy was limited by the requirement for the assent of Parliament. This was despite the fact that the power of kings was everywhere the same in Fortescue's conception of the constitution, but authority differed because of differences in their origins. The laws of England were more venerable, and must therefore be deemed to be the best obtainable. This was because they were not enacted at the sole behest of the prince, but by the prudence of three hundred members of Parliament.[37] Whether this reasoning is seen as sound possibly depends upon one's view of the motives and actions of politicians, but there is little doubt that the active involvement of Members

---

Thought c.350–c.1450 (Cambridge, 1988), p. 507.

32 *Sed non sic Angliae statuta oriri possunt, dum nedum principis voluntate sed et totius regni assensu ipsa conduntur, quo populi laesuram illam efficere requeunt vel non corum commodum procurare.* – Fortescue, *In Praise of the laws of England*, p. 41.

33 A limited monarchy, in contrast to an absolute monarchy; Sir John Fortescue, *The Governance of England*, notes by Charles Plummer (Westport, 1979).

34 The extent to which the common law resisted the reception of Roman law has been much disputed, though recent research suggests that the mediæval common law, though surviving in an organic sense, actually underwent a substantial reformation in the Renaissance period, especially from the 1490s to the 1540s; See the introduction to *The Reports of Sir John Spelman* (2 vols, London, 1978), vol. 2 Seldon Society vol. 94; Sir John Baker, 'English Law and the Renaissance', *Cambridge Law Journal* (1985): 46.

35 '*Sed e quod principi placuit, legis habet vigorem, cum lege regia, quae de imperio eius lata est, populous eiet in eum onme suum imperium et potestatem concessit*'; Inst. 1. 2. 6; G.I. 5; Dig. I. 4. 31. Ulpians's original formulation probably was '*quod principi placuit legis habet vicem, utpote cum lege quae de imperio eius lata est populous et hanc potestatem conferat*"; F. Schulz, "Bracton on Kingship' (1945) 60 English Historical Review 136–76.

36 Sir John Fortescue, *In Praise of the laws of England (De Laudibus Legum Angliæ)* ed S.B. Chrimes (London, 1942).

37 *In Praise of the laws of England*, vols 12–98.

of Parliament did mean that the law was less the result of regal choice and more clearly the product of conciliar deliberation.[38]

The aims of the late mediæval and early modern state were negative and disciplinary. The extreme emphasis on property rights carried with it an emphasis on law – a lawyer's rather than a politician's view of government. By Fortescue's time, if not earlier, men felt that strong monarchy upheld their rights (a mass of technical rules and practices), more so than did Parliament.[39]

De Laudibus Legum Angliæ,[40] written 1468–71, was one of the first coherent exercises in comparative law. It was strongly influenced by the French experience of Sir John Fortescue. It had a direct effect on the constitutional thinkers of the seventeenth century. Fortescue's successors in that century argued more precisely that the ancient constitution was Anglo-Saxon – and that the royal prerogative was the right of conquest of William the Conqueror.[41]

Fortescue supported the doctrine of constitutional monarchy found in St Thomas, but more correctly his support was derived from his own liberal sentiments and the experience of England,[42] as he saw it.

The Reformation Parliament settled the conventional view of the English constitution so clearly expounded in Sir Thomas Smith's *De Republica Anglorum* (1565)[43] and so hard to find even obscurely stated before the 1530s.[44] As a result of the Reformation the doctrine of parliamentary supremacy was developed.[45] Nonetheless, a long fight was waged by King Charles I in defence of his prerogative. He was committed to the traditional symbiosis of prerogative and law, rather than any new theory of the state.[46] He fought a losing fight against the new conception of the constitution – one founded on the liberty of the individual, as constituted by the Members of Parliament.

In the course of time the King-in-Parliament, the legislature, became supreme over the law. On the Continent the lawyers and courts were antagonistic to

38 Jeffrey Goldsworthy, *The sovereignty of parliament: history and philosophy* (Oxford: 1999).

39 J.R. Lander, *The Limitations of English Monarchy in the Later Middle Ages* (Toronto, 1989), pp. 4–6.

40 *In Praise of the laws of England.*

41 Robert Brady argued that Parliament and the common law were not part of an ancient and immemorial constitution, but traceable instead to the Conquest and the institution of feudalism; J.G.A. Pocock, *The Ancient Constitution and the Feudal Law; A Study of English Historical Thought in the Seventeenth Century* (2nd edn, Cambridge, 1987), pp. 3–8.

42 Fortescue, *The Governance of England*, p. 172.

43 Sir Thomas Smith, *De Republica Anglorum* (New York: 1979).

44 Sir Thomas Smith was a civil lawyer who stood analytically outside the constraints of the common law tradition.

45 Sir Geoffrey Elton, *Reform and Reformation, 1509–1558* (London, 1979), pp. 199–200.

46 Kevin Sharpe, *The Personal Rule of Charles I* (New Haven, 1992), p. 930.

representative assemblies. Courts persisted in maintaining the pre-eminence of the law over the authority of such assemblies, and so encouraged the growth of legal absolutism. In England, after 1688 no claim was made that any rule of the common law was too fundamental to admit of change.[47] The course of our constitutional and legal development would have been profoundly different had it been otherwise.[48] It is unclear when parliamentary sovereignty triumphed over the supremacy of the Crown, but Parliament took control of the succession in 1689 and asserted it in 1701.[49]

The law remained supreme over all organs of government as well as people, and legislative power (properly expressed) extended over the whole field of law.[50] In this lay the origins of the rule of law.

The growth of the territorial state brought about the need for one supreme authority. As a consequence a more modern doctrine, a doctrine embodying a conception that was widely held, was developed. This was the supremacy of the Crown as the mystical holder of the sovereignty of the state. Continental Europe found in kingship the state's source of unity and power. This was to remain the lynch-pin of constitutional theory until modern times.

The early mediæval legal thinkers had to reconcile three distinct systems of thought – Roman, Christian, and Germanic. Perhaps the most difficult task was to accommodate a conception of kingship that rested on divine foundations, derived in part from Roman thought, from Christian thought and from Germanic and feudal kingship, which based its claim to legitimacy on the relationship of the King to his barons and people.

German custom subjected the King to the law, and limited his authority to govern without the consent of his subjects.[51] Christian thought and classical jurisprudence and philosophy stressed the divine origins of kingship and the sacral nature of political authority. This tension led the lawyers to distinguish between the prince's private body, that was subject to the law, and his public body that was not.[52]

---

47 See, however, *Taylor v. New Zealand Poultry Board* [1984] 1 N.Z.L.R. 394, 398 per Cooke P.

48 Sir Owen Dixon, 'The Law and the Constitution', *Law Quarterly Review*, 51 (1935): 590, 590–92.

49 See, for example, H.T. Dickinson, 'The Eighteenth-Century Debate on the "Glorious Revolution"', *History*, 61 (1976): 28–45; H.T. Dickinson, 'The Eighteenth-Century Debate on the Sovereignty of Parliament', *Transactions of the Royal Historical Society* (5th Series), 26 (1976): 189–210.

50 I.R. Christie, *Wars and Revolutions: Britain, 1760–1815* (Cambridge, 1982), p. 21.

51 Kenneth Pennington, 'Law, Legislative authority and theories of government, 1150–1300', in Burns, *The Cambridge History of Mediæval Political Thought c.350–c.1450*, pp. 426–7.

52 Part of this problem is discussed in Ernst Kantorowicz, *The King's Two Bodies: A Study in Mediæval Political Theology* (Princeton, 1957), pp. 42–61.

As a consequence, the canonists became the first lawyers in the western tradition to establish law as an essential element of political theory.[53]

The early twelfth-century Norman cleric known as Anonymous of Rouen re-affirmed the dual personality of the King.[54] Inspired by the liturgy, a King was 'by nature an individual man, by grace [through his consecration] a *Christus*, that is, a God-man'.[55] This idea appears exceptionally modern, but was in fact in line with already ancient Carolingian tradition.[56]

In the mid-twelfth century Gratian completed his *Concordia Discordantium Canonum*.[57] This was a direct consequence of the revival of formal legal studies in the late eleventh century.[58] Gratian's understanding of law and its sources was shaped by the *Digest*, which described the emperor's supreme legislative authority.[59]

The majesty of the Holy Roman Emperor had spread all over Europe in the thirteenth century. To this doctrine of the divine right of kings concepts of the greatest consequences have been traced. These include a deep sense of the majesty of the law, and the duty of obedience.[60] When the competing focal points of sovereignty were reconciled in the course of the seventeenth and eighteenth centuries, the splendour of the Crown remained as the legal expression of the sovereignty of the nation. Nevertheless, the supremacy of the Crown necessarily had to give way under the inexorable advance of the supremacy of Parliament. The shadow remained, however, and for long retained real power and significance.

A main theme of English constitutional history was the question of whether the *communitas regni* had a right to force an unwilling King to take cognizance[61]

53 Pennington, 'Law, Legislative authority and theories of government, 1150–1300', p. 427.

54 Anonymous of Rouen, *Die Texte des Normannischen Anonymous*, ed. K. Pellens (Stuttgart, 1966) p. 130.

55 *Itaque in unoquoque gemina intelligitur fuisse persona: una ex natura, altera ex gratia ... In una quippe erat naturaliter individuus homo, in altera per gratiam christus, id est, deus-home.* – Anonymous of Rouen, p. 130.

56 See Kantorowicz, *The King's Two Bodies*, pp. 42–61.

57 Gratian of Bologna, *Concordia discordantium canonum* (or *Decretum magistri Gratiani*), in A. Friedberg (ed.), *Corpus Iuris Canonici* (2 vols, Tauchnitz, 1879), vol. 1. Better known simply as the *Descretum*.

58 Bologna began as a law school but widened its scope to become a true *universitas litterarum*. The University of Bologna remains probably the oldest university still extant; Rashdall Hastings, *The Universities of Europe in the Middle Ages* new ed. Frederick M. Powicke and Alfred B. Emden (Oxford: 1936).

59 Pennington, 'Law, Legislative authority and theories of government, 1150–1300', pp. 424–5.

60 Figgis, p. 266.

61 To recognize the truth of something without the need for that thing being proven.

of the legitimate interest in the Crown of the *communitas regni*.[62] The contention, most clearly expressed by Aquinas, that the King was not restrained by law because he controlled coercion, was widely rejected in thirteenth-century England – by both Crown and people. Royal jurisdiction depended on co-operation.[63] In both England and France (the latter, at this time at least) Giles of Rome's view that 'laws are laid down by the prince and established by princely authority'[64] was disputed.[65] Bracton regarded the magnates as having an essential role in the making of legislation.[66]

John Locke and later commentators rationalized the notion that the Sovereign stood above the law and acted in trust for his subject, whose rights he should be as sedulous to guard as his own.[67] Few in the seventeenth century ever doubted that government was a trust.[68] Where they differed was whether it was a trust created by God or by man, and its details.[69] That the trust might be from the people, rather than from God, was a novel idea,[70] but one which rapidly attracted the attention of more radical thinkers. It is now, of course, accepted wisdom in most, if not all, countries,[71] though natural law would suggest that it may not necessarily be correct.

A strong rearguard action was fought in the seventeenth century. Although he was primarily a writer of the interregnum and died in 1653, Sir Robert Filmer provided the most spectacular defence of royal powers in the 1680s. His best work was probably *Patriarcha*, written before the civil war, but first published

---

62 In 1311 the ordainers thought that they were acting only to subordinate an erring King to the obligations imposed by the Crown, but in doing so they risked the accusation that they had separated the King from the Crown. This fault was in fact committed in 1308, with the opposition to Gaveston; Stanley Chrimes and A.L. Brown, *Select Documents of English Constitutional History 1307–1485* (London, 1961), p. 30.

63 Dunbabin, pp. 505–6.

64 Giles of Rome, *De regimine principum* (2 vols, Rome, 1556), vol. 1, ch. 2, p. 10, 1556 fol. 44v.

65 Aquinas in particular was not convinced by the Latin tag; St Thomas Aquinas, vol. 1, book IIae, qu. 90, art. 3.

66 Henry de Bracton, *On the Laws and Customs of England* ('*Henri de Bracton de Legibus et Consuetudis Angliæ*'), ed. G.E. Woodbine, trans. S.E. Thorne (2 vols, Cambridge, 1968), vol. 2, p. 21.

67 See John Dunn, 'The concept of trust in the politics of John Locke', in R. Rorty (ed.), *Philosophy in History* (Cambridge, 1984), pp. 279–302.

68 In the fifteenth-century words of Sir John Fortescue, 'the king is given for the kingdome, and not the kingdome for the king': Fortescue, *In Praise of the laws of England*, p. 87.

69 In the Remonstrance of 1648 the army called for 'no king be hereafter admitted, but upon the election of, and as upon trust for the people'; William Cobbett (ed.), *The Parliamentary History of England* (12 vols, London, 1806–20), vol. 3, p. 1125.

70 Robert Bennet, *King Charle's Trial Iustified* (London, 1649), p. 4.

71 Iran being a modern example of a theocracy, in which, by definition, this rule cannot hold true.

only in 1680.[72] Despite the fact that Filmer's ideas are now thoroughly outmoded, his views were a product of his time. He argued that God had given sovereignty over the earth to Adam, which was then passed by hereditary descent through the sons of Noah and the heads of the nations into which mankind was divided at the Confusion of Tongues, to all the modern rulers of the world.

Filmer's great contribution was in seeing government as conforming to the generally accepted pattern of social organization in his time. This saw the King as the father of his people, and thus entitled to the obedience of his family. The idea that there was a sovereign authority did not however supersede the older idea of 'natural law' which reason would lead men to acknowledge.[73] The evolutionary view of society was also reflected in the nature of the law.

The common law, by which we mean that body of laws common to all and which are to be distinguished from local custom, statute, royal prerogative and all other exceptional or special laws,[74] is remarkable historically for its formulary nature. The history of the common law is the history of the writ. Yet in its origins English law drew from two distinct traditions, neither of which was overly concerned with niceties of form. The Anglo-Saxon law, from the *Lex Salica*,[75] the laws of Ine[76] and the dooms of Æthbert,[77] to the code of Canute and the ordinances of Ælfred, constitute one of these. The other is the French or Frankish tradition, the capitularies of the Carolingian emperors and the Merovingian kings to Chloding, who led the Franks to Gaul.

The King of the English was expected to publish laws at a time when hardly anyone else in Europe was attempting any such feat – the dooms of Canute are probably the most comprehensive of any code in eleventh century Europe.[78] The Normans, by contrast, had little if any written law to bring with them to England, and had perforce to rely on the relatively well-developed Saxon legal and administrative structure. Yet in the first half of the twelfth century one could still speak of Wessex law, Danish law, Mercian law, and the law of the King's own

---

72 Filmer.

73 J.R. Western, *Monarchy and Revolution – the English State in the 1680's* (London, 1972), pp. 7–14. For Locke's concept of the state of nature see Robert A. Goldwin, 'Locke's state of nature in political society', *Western Political Quarterly*, 31 (1976): 126–35.

74 Including the statute law because that was formerly rare.

75 c.500.

76 c.690.

77 c.600.

78 In western Europe law codes were rare until the twelfth century, when a whole new jurisprudence appeared, as the Roman law of Justinian became better understood and diffused: F.L. Attenborough (ed.), *Laws of the earliest English kings* (Cambridge, 1922); A.J. Robertson, *Laws of the Kings of England* (Cambridge, 1925). The real distinction between law and custom only arose from the twelfth century, as a clear distinction must depend on the monopoly of law enforcement and on a procedure of legislation, and of recording legislation: M. Gluckman, *Politics law and ritual in tribal society* (Oxford, 1977), pp. 196–202.

court, which was apart from and above all these partial systems, though in a way more significant than ever in the Saxon kingdom. The local customs were those of the shires and hundreds, and the King's law came to be ever more pre-eminent, especially as the royal judicial system developed (particularly under Henry II[79]). Royal authority was founded on the constitutional history and structure of society, including the role of the king as the official representative of the community.

Yet even the Saxon kings were more than mere officials, as popular reverence for their real or imagined pedigree shows. Feudalism added to their power by formalizing in a legal structure the already significant ties of fealty. As the tendency of feudalism was to connect jurisdiction with land, so the right to hold the Crown, and to its perquisites, came to be regarded as a proprietary right. The king was also not just the chosen of the people, but also the chosen of God. He was able to command greater resources than any potential rival, unlike the King of France, who was dominated by over-powerful vassals.[80] Yet he remained in essence no different from any of his subjects, who might exercise juridical functions of their own, though on a much smaller scale than those of the King. It might be said that to this origin of the king's powers can be traced the concept of the 'third power' of the Crown.[81]

Thus the scope of public law in the English model is not truly distinct from the private law because the Sovereign as the representative of the state possessed few if any powers which were inherently unavailable to the subject. Ironically however, the Queen's Courts have now generally placed greater restrictions upon the working of the executive, by classifying as prerogative powers those powers of action which the Crown shares with the public. These are now therefore generally amenable to judicial review by the courts.[82]

The example of Carolingian kingship brought a tradition of royal war-leadership and an idea of empire.[83] English developments were influenced by Carolingian models, in political ideas as in institutions and royal ritual. Yet it retained its own traits, and was especially king-centred. The king was in the place of a father, as Christ's representative.[84] Royal peacekeeping was a distinctive feature, as was the drafting of comprehensive codes of laws. The old insular ideas of imperial kingship gained new impetus, not only from the extension of the West Saxon power, but also from English acquaintance with Ottonian and Salian courts.[85]

---

79 Cannon and Griffiths, pp. 111–12.

80 Sir William Anson, *The Law and Custom of the Constitution*, ed. A.B. Keith (5th edn, 1922, Oxford; 3rd edn, 1907), vol. 2, Part 1, pp. 16–17.

81 Bruce Harris, 'The "Third Source" of Authority for Government Action', *Law Quarterly Review.* 109 (1992): 626.

82 *Council of Civil Service Unions v. Minister for the Civil Service* [1985] A.C. 374.

83 Janet L. Nelson, 'Kingship and empire', in Burns, *The Cambridge History of Mediæval Political Thought c.350–c.1450*, pp. 213–29.

84 Wulfstan of York, *An Werk Erzbischof Wulfstans von York – Die 'Institutes of Polity, Civil and Ecclesiastical'*, ed. K. Jost (Tübingen, 1959), pp. 40–42.

85 Nelson, pp. 239–40.

King Ælfred promoted education so that his laws could be understood more widely, but also so that religious works reached a wider readership. The function of the king as law-giver and judge was gradually emphasized at the expense of self-regulation by leading figures in the community. This was partially a consequence of the Christianizing of kingship, with the *Bible*'s stories about great judges and Christian law having long-term effects. From Ine to Æthelred II, the tradition of assembling the pronouncements, administrative regulations and laws of their predecessors, led to the development of a recognizable body of Anglo-Saxon law. To make and proclaim the law became a mark of kingship;[86] the greater the king the more elaborate the codes.

The Norman Conquest brought few changes in the ideal or practice of English rulership; these could be seen to strengthen the Conqueror's authority in the face of an alternative Norman tradition of aristocratic freedom.[87]

The law served to develop the powers of kings, and to direct and limit their action.[88] The balance between the king and the community as the fount of law and the dispenser of justice was perceptibly altered in favour of the king by Ælfred's time.[89] Kings and their subjects were increasingly made aware of the kings' religious and moral duties and responsibilities.[90] The Europe-wide Papal investiture contest led to King John being excommunicated in 1209. Although the king and pope were reconciled in 1213, a Christian king had been declared unworthy of kingship.[91] The Church modified and restrained the scope of the king's authority.[92] The king's duty to maintain the peace in his kingdom and provide justice for his subjects underwent a major transformation in the twelfth century. This emphasized the king's authority throughout England and made more explicit his obligations and the parameters within which he ruled. His role as judge and law-maker was revolutionized.[93]

The change during the twelfth century was more one of availability and effectiveness rather than new laws as such. Under King Henry I especially, new royal officials, including roving or itinerant justices, were introduced. The law itself developed significantly under Henry II, with new formulas making new remedies available.[94] The Statute of Marlborough 1267[95] was a review of the relations between the king and his subjects and of the working of the common law. So comprehensive was the statute that contemporaries wrote of the constitutions

86 Cannon and Griffiths, p. 32.
87 Nelson, p. 241.
88 Cannon and Griffiths, p. 34.
89 Ibid., p. 66.
90 Ibid., p. 104.
91 Ibid., p. 106.
92 Ibid., p. 108.
93 Ibid., p. 110.
94 Ibid., pp. 111–12.
95 52 Hen. III.

or the statutes of Marlborough, rather than of the statute, implying a degree of codification of the common law, rather than a mere change in detail. At this time legislation meant an explicit statement of what the force of existing custom or the ruling of divine law provided for in particular instances. Mostly statutes were non-controversial, for they did not constitute 'new' laws.

As the monarchy grew more authoritarian in the eleventh and twelfth centuries, flaws and weaknesses were exposed that ultimately produced major changes in the course of the thirteenth century. Under the influence of the Crown's continental dominions the monarchy changed from a West Saxon kingdom writ large to a transmarine monarchy those main arteries of royal communications and travel were the Thames Estuary and the south-eastern ports.[96]

King Henry II established permanent government.[97] Legal memory extends only as far back as the coronation of his successor Richard I,[98] by a technical doctrine whose scope was concerned merely with prescriptive rights. It does however illustrate the longevity of the common law, whose roots indeed go back centuries earlier than that date. The English was by the end of the twelfth century the most sophisticated and effective monarchy in Europe.[99] Law and government were inherently linked.

Because of the uncomfortable paradox of monarchy and the unsuitability of some kings, it came to be believed over the course of the thirteenth and fourteenth centuries that one could separate the Crown from the wearer, so that it became possible to correct or even remove the king. Discussion along these lines tended to decline in the fifteenth century because of the weak title of the usurpers in that century. There was no real alternative to hereditary rule, and force of arms was not conducive to stability and order.[100] However, the law provided the cement necessary to keep the edifice together.

In the time from King Henry VIII to the accession of William and Mary the court (royal, not juridicial) was at the very centre of political power. The power of the king was limited by an ancient and strong tradition of consultation, though this may not have been much more a feature of the English monarchy than the French, despite the belief to the contrary held by Fortescue and Smith.[101] It was formalized however, and widely seen as being a major point of distinction. This perception (and perhaps its formalization) was to have real long-term consequences, as a normative influence.

96 Cannon and Griffiths, pp. 148–9.

97 Ibid., p. 156.

98 3 September 1189.

99 Cannon and Griffiths, p. 158.

100 Ibid., p. 217.

101 Ibid., p. 299.

The repudiation of papal authority and the insistence upon the Crown's imperial status, though of great symbolic importance, did not in themselves materially alter the Crown's position.[102] But they helped encourage moves already underway.

Royal authority was founded on the constitutional history and structure of society, including the role of the king as the official representative of the community. From the seventeenth to the nineteenth centuries there was little in the way of formal changes, but with real power now in the hands of politicians, who owed their offices at least in part to the electorate, it was inevitable that the real focus of government would change.

After the long years of the Whig ascendancy, by early in the nineteenth century analytical jurists had made parliamentary sovereignty the pivot of the British legal system.[103] The constitution depended upon the common law, whose creature it largely was. The legal expression of the executive power of the state was always through the Crown. Yet there was nothing which transcended the legislative power of an Act of Parliament.[104] The Sovereign could suspend the law – to some extent at least – and Parliament's power to so was absolute. But this position was reached comparatively recently, and is not necessarily immutable. The modern view of parliamentary sovereignty is largely a twentieth-century re-statement of a seventeenth-century assertion[105] – it does not even apply in any other modern state except New Zealand, now the sole remaining unitary state with an unwritten constitution.

We can see that, not only was there an ongoing political and legal debate about the nature of authority in the early modern state, but in practice the tendency was for centralization, however justified, as the most efficient. It was no coincidence that much of the importance of the British revolutions of 1642–60 and 1688–89, the French revolution of 1789–99, the American revolution of 1776–89 (and the Civil War of 1861–65),[106] and other significant events has been in their determination of the locus of authority. This tendency to centralize was as much for pragmatic functional reasons as for theoretical ones. The king was long seen as the keeper of the peace – and this role required an iron fist. Government was regulatory.

An understanding of the regulatory role of the state must be built upon a conceptual and functional analysis of sovereignty, the organizing and political principle upon which national economic policy-making and regulation, as well as

102 Ibid., p. 322.

103 See William Hearn, *The Government of England: Its Structure and its Development* (London, 1867), which was a major influence on Dicey.

104 Sir Owen Dixon, 593–5. Nor will the courts be eager to question the authority of an Act of Parliament, a principle cited as early as 1455; P 33 Hen. VI 17, 8 at 18 per Fortescue, C.J.

105 For more on this see Chapter 8.

106 These dates are approximate, since the events contained within these revolutionary periods were often loosely conjoined.

international economic co-ordination and regulation are based.[107] Further, proper appreciation of the internal dimension of sovereignty requires an understanding of the relationship between the state and the society it governs.[108] As Tshuma has emphasized, the relationship between the state and civil society over which it exercises sovereignty is historically specific, and the manner in which sovereign power is exercised is shaped by the configuration of social forces.[109] These forces include legal and constitutional rights and limitations. The external dimension of sovereignty is equally circumscribed by an international system where sovereign states are *de jure* equal. The reality is of course that states are not equal politically, economically, militarily or even socially. This means that the legal systems of countries are not all equal in economic, legal, or political importance.

The relationship between law and government may also be seen from an economic perspective – indeed it may be that this is its primary nature. It is especially important at a time when technology has caused a reappraisal of the role of law and state. The liberal interventionist approach to economic policy and regulation in the context of globalization would hold that global problems require international collective action. But, as Matthews has asserted, a shift in power from hierarchical state organizations to multi-layered networks of supra-states, sub-state, and non-state entities, has broken the dominance of hierarchy, and enjoined a revival of the network-based society.[110] This argument has been said to resemble technological determinism which overlooks or downplays the role of politics in the development and diffusion of technology.[111] That is not a charge which could be laid at Castells's door.

Manuel Castells attempted an analysis of contemporary society which extended beyond the concept of the information society.[112] He postulated that society is not purely defined by our technology. Cultural, economical, and political factors contribute to what he styled the Network Society.[113] He stressed the importance of networks rather than hierarchy-ranked global cities. Networks are the basis of one of the most important new technologies – information technology. Those who classify themselves as Internet realists would minimize the extent and breadth of the societal and constitutional influences of the information technology revolution,

---

107 Lawrence Tshuma, 'Hierarchies and Government versus Networks and Governance: Competing Regulatory Paradigms in Global Economic Regulation', *Law, Social Justice and Global Development* (1999) <http://elj.warwick.ac.uk/global/issue/2000-1/tshuma.html>.

108 W.H. Reinicke, 'Global Public Policy', *Foreign Affairs* (1997): 127–38, 129.

109 Tshuma, 'Hierarchies and Government versus Networks and Governance: Competing Regulatory Paradigms in Global Economic Regulation'.

110 J. Matthews, 'Power Shift', *Foreign Affairs*, 76(1) (1997): 50–71.

111 Tshuma, 'Hierarchies and Government versus Networks and Governance: Competing Regulatory Paradigms in Global Economic Regulation'.

112 Susan Hornby and Zoë Clarke (eds), *Challenge and change in the information society* (London, 2003).

113 Manuel Castells, *The Rise of the Network Society* (2nd edn, Oxford, 2000).

but it is clear that technology has a major influence, if not a determinate one, upon the shape of future society. It remains to be seen whether the financial instability of 2008 has long-term implications for states and their regulatory role.

3.3 Flexibility and responsiveness – The rule of law

Constitutional law – however the constitution of a particular state is structured – is the set of rules that describe the powers, authority and functions of the organs of the state. One of the features that may, at first glance, appear common to the states of the West is that they broadly adhere to the constitutional principles that we now know as the rule of law. This adherence may not have contributed to the economic development of the West since the Middle Ages, but there may well be a link. This can be traced to the origins of the Industrial Revolution in the British Isles, at a time when the United Kingdom was particularly advanced constitutionally, but not necessarily at the centre of European political or social life.

The peculiarity in regards to the concept of the rule of law is that it is less a set of rigid principles than a broad understanding of how a constitution ought to operate. This in itself is derived from a particular understanding of the constitution. It is not one based simply on arbitrary authority. It is marked by a singular lack of dogmatism, and an emphasis on freedom, and pragmatism. In British constitutional history this can be traced to Magna Carta, if not earlier, though in these earlier years the freedom was of the nobility rather than of the people.[114] Freedom where social mobility and fluidity is unusually pronounced (as it was in England), tends to spread to wider sections of society than may originally have been intended or anticipated. A non-intrusive state was combined with an unusual degree of legalism, and a comparatively efficient central administration. The weakness of the later mediæval kings, and the Wars of the Roses, which decimated the early mediæval nobility, ensured the growth of the political power of the middle classes. Still, the ancient institutions of government remained; it was the way in which they operated that reflected these changing dynamics.

As the apparatus of government operated according to strict rules, so expectations grew that these would be adhered to in all cases. Much of the legitimacy of a political system derives from the impartiality and objectivity with which it is administered.[115] Thus the very exercise of authority legitimates that authority. To this may be traced the modern concept of the rule of law.

If the rule of law means an absence of arbitrary power, then, as was inherent in the mediæval concept of government, the law, whether human or divine, was

114 Noel Cox, 'Stephen Langton, Magna Carta and Church Law' ('Magna Carta and the Antipodes', English-Speaking Union, Wellington, 29 June 2008).

115 Royal Commission on the Electoral System, *Report of the Royal Commission on the Electoral System 'Towards a better democracy'* (Wellington, 1986), p. 27.

pre-eminent. King James I, in *The Trew Law of Free Monarchies* (1598)[116] and the *Basilikon Doron* (1599),[117] outlined a fairly simple assertion of divine right kingship. Legal authority, though vested in the king as it always had been, was founded on long-established religious principles.

Theories of divine right were outlined by writers such as Sir Robert Filmer.[118] Hobbes and Filmer argued that the will is the source of all law and the form of all authority. They believed in the necessity of a perpetual and absolute submission to the arbitrary dictates of an indivisible sovereign, and in the impossibility of mixed government (or pluralism). They were criticized – perhaps unsurprisingly – by Whig theorists of contract, such as Sidneyand Locke. It would seem that Locke wrote his *Two Treatises of Government* to refute Filmer instead of Hobbes. Hobbes was politically the least important of the principal absolutist writers, although his impact as an analytical thinker was more profound over time. Locke, however, succeeded in seriously undermining Filmer's arguments,[119] which largely reflected an earlier political era.

The doctrine of the divine right of kings was not an academic but rather a popular doctrine. It satisfied deep instincts and fulfilled a distinct function. In its classic definition, it was said that the monarchy is a divinely ordained institution; that hereditary right is indefeasible, that kings are accountable to God alone and that non-resistance and passive obedience are enjoined by God. The doctrine was supported by the authority of the *Bible*.[120] Examples of this support are Samuel's description of a king,[121] on the Jewish nation demanding one,[122] and David's refusal to touch 'the Lord's anointed'.[123] The passage describing the vision of Nebuchadnezzar;[124] 'render unto Cæsar';[125] Christ's words to Pilate;[126] and the behaviour of the primitive Christians; are further examples. Above all we have the direct enjoining by both St Peter and St Paul to obedience to constituted

116 Written 1598, collection published 1616.

117 HM King HM KIngKing James I, *Basilikon Doron* (Menston, 1969, first published 1599).

118 Sir Robert Filmer, *Patriarcha and other writings*, ed. J.P. Sommerville (London, 1991).

119 See, for example, John Dunn, *The Political Thought of John Locke*: *An historical account of the Two Treatises of Government* (London, 1969), ch. VII.

120 This idea, not unknown in earlier times, was most explicitly and universally expressed after the Restoration. The divine right, the impiety of resistance, and of the subjects' duty to render at least passive obedience to royal commands. If the king recovered only an attenuated authority, he possessed it by the most august and sacred of titles.

121 1 Sam. 8–12.

122 Sam vii 10–18.

123 Prov viii 15.

124 David iv.

125 Luke xx 25.

126 John xix 11.

authority.[127] The theory belongs to an age when politics and theology were closely connected.[128]

Critics of the doctrine generally were content to argue on the same lines as its supporters.[129] They maintained that scripture was misunderstood, especially those texts which inculcate the right and duty of resistance; that early Christians exhibited the virtue of passive obedience because they could not do otherwise;[130] that the *Bible* provided an alternative theory in the original compact – the 'law of the Kingdom' of Samuel.[131] Political theory in the twentieth and twenty-first centuries tends to be utilitarian, and we must not judge the seventeenth century by our standards. Sovereignty in the Austinian sense was unknown in any single nation in the middle ages. Bracton knew of no sovereign which was above the laws, because it made them. It is also certain that the notion of a single ultimate authority is a modern one[132] – provided we discount a divine authority (as most will today, and many even in Locke's time).

The origin of the theory of the divine right of kings is to be found in the conflict between the Papacy and the Empire. Even in England, which was only on the periphery of this dispute, where the king, who had a strong sacred character and became, with the advent of Christianity, God's vicar on earth, obedience to the

---

127 Rom xiii 1–7; 1 Pet ii 13–17. The Roman Pontiff, in holy orders a bishop, is in jurisdiction held (by the Roman Catholic Church and by Churches in communion with the Holy See) to be by divine right the centre of all Catholic unity, and consequently Pastor and Teacher of all Christians. There is no recourse against the judgement or decree of the Pontiff, who is regarded in canon law as being the supreme judge for the whole world: *The Code of Canon Law: in English Translation* prepared by the Canon Law Society of Great Britain and Ireland (London, 1983), canons 333 §3, 1442. Note however, that any appeal heard by a subordinate could be appealed to the pope himself, and even appealed from the pope to the pope 'better informed'; Felix Makower, *Constitutional History and Constitution of the Church of England* (London, 1895), pp. 225–7. See also Brian Tierney, *Origins of Papal Infallibility, 1150-1350: a study on the concepts of infallibility, sovereignty and tradition in the Middle Ages* (Leiden, 1972).

128 Figgis, pp. 3–11.

129 Although John Hall did reject biblical arguments – John Hall, *The Grounds and Reasons of Monarchy* prefixed to *The Political Works of James Harrington*, ed. J.G.A. Pocock (Cambridge, 1977).

130 This however is weak, for early Christians positively welcomed persecution, as a means to achieve martyrdom. This was seen as a particularly serious problem; see Joseph Modica, 'The function and purpose of suffering, persecution, and martyrdom in Luke–Acts: An exegetical and theological inquiry' (1995) Drew University PhD thesis.

131 The initial function of Locke's *First Treatise of Government* was to show that Scripture did not show that God had given any man, or order of men, superiority over other men: John Locke, *Two Treatises of Government*, ed. Peter Laslett (Cambridge, 1988), treatise I.

132 *Revocatio Novarum Ordinationum* 1322 Statutes of the Realm (London, 1810–22), vol. 1, p. 189.

king was a religious duty. The effect of the Norman Conquest was to some extent muted because there was no pre-existing theory of sovereignty.

With the accession of King Edward II the election of the king fell into disuse, while the royal prerogative grew. The whole constitutional struggle of the fourteenth century raged around the prerogative, as the king developed his sovereignty. In 1322 the right of Parliament to petition for new laws was made exclusive.[133] The distinction between the personal and political capacity of the king was also caused by the growth of Parliament. Even in the time of Edward II it was a matter of controversy, and was apparently one of the arguments for the banishment of Gaveston. An ordinance of 1311 accused him of 'encroaching to himself royal power and royal dignity and lording it over the state of the king and the people'. Later on, in the trial of the De Spensers, the doctrine that there is any distinction between the king and the Crown was condemned.[134]

Not surprisingly this view, very similar to that held by the Long Parliament, was criticized by Coke in *Calvin's Case*,[135] as a 'damnable and damned opinion'. The formation of a theory of sovereignty in England in the Middle Ages was effectively prevented by feudalism, and the unwritten and pragmatic common law did not encourage it either. Bracton did not ascribe sovereignty to the king, nor make him absolute, as was believed by royalist writers of the seventeenth century.[136] The theory was advanced that resistance to the Crown was only lawful if enjoined by the inferior magistrates. Thus Parliament could pretend that they

---

133 Ibid.

134 Ibid., vol. I, p. 182. The trial criticized the passage which said that:

> Homage and the Oath of Allegiance is more by reason of the Crown than by reason of the person of the king, and it bideth itself more unto the Crown than unto the person; and this appears in that before the Estate of the Crown hath descended, no allegiance is belonging to the person; wherefore if the king by chance be not guided Reason, in right of the Crown, his Liege Subjects are bound by the Oath made to the Crown to guide the king and the Estate of the Crown back again by reason, or otherwise the oath would not be kept. Nor were it to be asked, how they ought to guide the king? Whether by course of law, or by violence? By course of law a man will not be able to get redress, for he will have no judges but such as are the king's, in which case, if the will of the king be not according to reason he certainly will have only Error maintained and confirmed; wherefore it behoveth, in order to save the Oath, that when the king will not redress the matter and remove that which is hurtful to the people at large, and prejudicial to the Crown, it is to be determined, that the king be removed by violence, for he is bound by his oath to govern the people and his liege subjects, and his liege subjects are bound to govern in aid of him and in his default.

135 (1608) 7 Co Rep 1a; 77 ER 377.

136 Figgis, pp. 11–32.

only took up arms against Charles I the person, but were in support of his authority as king.[137]

The divine right of kings is the form taken in the seventeenth century by the theory of sovereignty.[138] Jean Bodin's *Les Six Livres de la République* (1576),[139] stressed the indivisibility of sovereignty and the consequent impossibility of limited or mixed monarchies. The primary attribute of sovereignty was the power to give laws to subjects without their consent. Consultation was a matter of prudence rather than a legal requirement. This theory was simple but its application to all monarchies on principle was peremptory and indiscriminate. In practice the English monarchy relied more on financial reality than on political theory – upon practice as opposed to theory, about which there was generally comparatively little debate.

The difficulty in assessing the nature of constitutional developments when the principle is developed to suit the apparent situation is seen in the divergent views of the early modern monarchy. Stubbs thought that promising constitutional progress was arrested by the vigour of Tudor rule, while Pollard (as well as Elton and Neale) thought that the foundation of later parliamentary rule was laid under that dynasty.[140] There has been a swing back towards Stubbs's view more recently, such as with Roskell.[141]

Locke attacked the idea of sovereignty, rather than the idea of absolute monarchy; although the legislature is supreme, it has limitations.[142] Sidney's *Discourses concerning Government*,[143] and even Milton's *Tenure of Kings and Magistrates*,[144] exhibit similar limitations. The definite ground assumed is that of Rousseau; that the people are sovereign, that this sovereignty comes from God, and that it is inalienable. All governments are in their view merely officials carrying out the will of the sovereign people, and they may therefore be removed at any time. This view is apparently also that of Mariana and Suarez, and is more consistent and logically defensible than the common Whig theory. In comparatively few states even today is the sovereignty legally and formally vested undiluted in the people[145] — perhaps to avoid heightening the risk of demagoguery.

137 Ibid., p. 223. The king was also above the law in the sense that the courts, being his courts, could not try him. A special High Court of Judicature was set up to try Charles I. Henry VI's judges also refused to advise him regarding the claim of the Duke of York, on the grounds that it was not justiciable – Rot Parl V 375–9 in *English Historical Documents* vol. 4, 1327–1485, ed. A.R. Myers (London, 1969), pp. 416–17.

138 Figgis, p. 237.

139 Jean Bodin, *Les Six Livres de la République* ('*The Six bookes of a Commonwealth*'), trans. M.J. Tooley (Oxford, 1955).

140 John Cannon and Ralph Griffiths, *The Oxford Illustrated History of the British Monarchy* (Oxford, 1988), p. 301.

141 Cannon and Griffiths, p. 302.

142 Figgis, p. 242.

143 London, 1698.

144 London, 1649.

145 Ibid., p. 243.

Hobbes was vehemently opposed by the believers in divine right. His system of politics is pure utilitarian, and was largely devoid of religious content. He also, almost alone for his time, realized that politics is not and cannot be a branch of theology. His theory of government was based upon the original compact, which lay at the root of such consistency as the opponents of the theory of divine right had. To those believing in the compact, the state was an artificial creation. To Filmer, Hickes or Leslie it was a natural growth.

For Locke, Sidney or Milton the original compact limits all forms of government and reduces the state to a mechanical instrument that may with ease be destroyed and manufactured afresh. In the view of Hobbes the machine of state, when created, is to last for all time, but it has no quality of life, no principle of internal development. The popular theories of the seventeenth century were a survival of the notion proclaimed by Hildebrand, but hinted at by Aquinas.[146] It was more or less dominant in all the 'Papist' writers. It was simply that the state is a consequence of the fall, existing because in our imperfection we have need of it.[147]

To the believers in the divine right, political society is natural to man. Government and therefore obedience are necessities of human nature. It could be argued that no theory of government was ever more untrue to the reality of political life than is that of Locke, and the difference between him and Filmer is in this respect all in favour of the latter. Even Filmer's theory is based upon the notion that what has always existed must be natural to man and of divine authority, and therefore immutable.[148] The theory forms the necessary transition between mediæval religious and modern secular politics.[149]

Theories of divine right outlined by such as Filmer in *Patriarcha* (1680) were criticized. A doctrine which relied heavily upon biblical authority was bound to suffer damage in the Age of Reason.[150]

Sir Julius Cæsar had doubts about the abortive Great Contract between the king and Parliament, which would have seen the king give up purveyances and modify wardship, in return for an annual parliamentary grant. To abandon prerogative rights in exchange for parliamentary revenue, would lead to democracy. Perhaps then, it is not a coincidence that hereditary revenues were largely surrendered in 1760; little more than generation later the role of the King was to be clearly subordinated to that of his Ministers, and the Reform Act 1832 was to largely complete the process.

Yet the old concept of the Crown living off its own resources made sense no longer. The old constitution was close to stalemate, and the Crown eventually

146 St. Thomas Aquinas, *Summa theologiæ* (London, 1963).

147 Figgis, pp. 249–51.

148 Ibid., p. 252.

149 Ibid., p. 258.

150 Cannon and Griffiths, p. 415.

collapsed due to the exigencies of the Bishops' War in Scotland in 1641–42.[151] With the last of the Stuarts disappeared strict indefeasible hereditary right and much of the mystical power of kingship in the British Isles.[152] The theory lost its popularity because its work was done – the independence of the state had been attained.[153] But where did this leave the Crown, and the rule of law?

The divine right of kings, a doctrine which relied heavily upon biblical authority was bound to suffer damage in the Age of Reason.[154] Rarely were theory and practice so far apart as in the Stuart monarchy, yet it was the practice which had changed, not the theory,[155] which was neglected. In the seventeenth century theorizing about the constitution evolved between models of law which were not always empirically-based.

Ironically, in the absence of a developed constitutional theory, great reliance is placed on legal form as a substitute. Such is the present situation in New Zealand (as an example of the handful of countries without a written constitution). Certainly, recognizing that the acquisition of sovereignty was based on a compact in 1840 would bring this country to a more principled constitutional position, one much discussed in the seventeenth century, that of the compact.[156]

That such a recognition has not yet been fully made is indicative of what Kelsey calls the integration ethic and the self-determination ethic,[157] a desire to accommodate the separateness of Maori culture but also a desire to integrate that culture into mainstream Pakeha society. The future direction of the constitution is not clear, but concepts of Western liberalism require the resolution of grievances resulting from breaches of the Treaty of Waitangi.[158]

---

151 Ibid., pp. 370–76.

152 Ibid., p. 459.

153 Figgis, p. 263.

154 Filmer, following Grotius, had interpreted the evidence to show that procreation gave a right of superiority. This was not only bad observation, but contrary to his own first premise, that man is God's workmanship. Locke, the first systematic ethnologist, made short work of such reasoning; Locke, *Two Treatises of Government*.

155 Cannon and Griffiths, p. 357.

156 The original compact – the 'law of the Kingdom' of Samuel. All political theory in the twentieth century was arguably utilitarian. We must not judge the seventeenth century by our values and standards, any more that we should that of the nineteenth century. See Locke, *Two Treatises of Government*; Jonathan Scott, *Algernon Sidneyand the Restoration Crisis, 1677–1683* (Cambridge, 1991).

157 Jane Kelsey, 'Restructuring the Nation', in Peter Fitzpatrick (ed.), *Nationalism, Racism and the Rule of Law* (Aldershot, 1995), p. 185; See also Bruce Clark, *Native liberty, Crown Supremacy — the Existing Aboriginal Right of Self-Government in Canada* (Montreal, 1990), pp. 191–219. That traditional structures and modern institutions each owe their validity and authority to distinct criteria is obvious. Where a constitution is based on such a pluralistic basis tension is inevitable; Bekithemba Ralph Khumalo, 'Legal Pluralism and constitutional tensions' (1993) York University LLM thesis.

158 Interview with Sir Douglas Graham, 24 November 1999.

Brookfield has looked at what he calls the Crown's seizure of power over New Zealand from 1840, the challenges of Maori, and the establishment of the separate New Zealand Crown. Developing from his earlier writings on law and revolution and on Waitangi matters and indigenous rights, he has examined how a revolutionary taking of power by one people from another may be at least partly legitimated.[159] This process relies heavily upon redressing grievances and upon the development of new concepts of authority. There is no doubt that, as part of this process, during the 1980s in particular, the Treaty of Waitangi was constitutionalized, and, in some views, the basis of government is now founded upon it.[160] The form remained, though the substance may have changed radically.

By using the example of one country, New Zealand, it may be seen that government is both the product of history, and a significant ongoing influence upon the development of both constitutional law, and substantive and procedural laws. Even where the form of constitution is unique or unusual – as in a colonial or post-colonial state – this is apparent. In the context of a country without the restrictions (or safeguards) of an entrenched constitution this justification for government action is particularly clear.

In British jurisprudence generally, after the evolution of parliamentary government the rule of law simply reflected a belief in due process, and certain minimum standards to which government agencies were expected to adhere. The doctrinal basis of this was unlikely to be seen as the social compact as Hobbes argued for, or a modernized divine right. Ultimately individual and community rights prevailed, with the growth of democracy, and this became the basis for the rule of law. Whatever its theoretical basis, from as early as the twelfth century in England, it could be argued that governmental action required the authority of law.[161] Unlike parts of the Continent, where the exaltation of royal authority gained much impetus from the revival of Roman law, local circumstances in England, although not uninfluenced by these developments, remained more insular, and more inclined to view government as consensual and therefore responsive to changing times and circumstances.

In his book *Constitutional Justice*, Allan argues for a normative theory of law. The central thread of his work, which is also reflected in his earlier *Law, Liberty, and justice*, is a conception of the rule of law that is a 'necessary component of any genuine liberal or constitutional democratic polity'.[162] Here 'genuine' is to

---

159 Brookfield, *Waitangi and Indigenous Rights*.

160 P.G. McHugh, 'Constitutional Myths and the Treaty of Waitangi', *New Zealand Law Journal* (1991): 316; David Williams, 'The Constitutional Status of the Treaty of Waitangi: an historical perspective', *New Zealand Universities Law Review*, 14 (1990): 9–36.

161 *Campbell v. Hall* (1774 1 Cowp. 204; 20 State Tr. 239; 98 E.R. 1045 (K.B.).

162 Trevor R.S. Allan, *Constitutional Justice: a liberal theory of the rule of law* (Oxford, 2001), p. 1.

be understood as one that promotes 'the equal dignity of all citizens'.[163] Thus, according to Allan's hypothesis, regimes are only just if they place primary on the dignity of the individual, thereby fostering an environment in which people are able to associate freely, and speak freely and without fear of reprisals. They will also, in certain situations, even have the right to refuse to abide by state-sponsored laws, when those laws offend one's 'personal moral judgement'.[164] A state recognizes 'the citizen's moral authority or independence of mind as an internal characteristic of law',[165] as being a fundamental or vital component of the law is a state that has achieved the standard recognized by Allan. At a very minimum, first principles in such a state include the rule of law, and the separation of powers.

The constitutional principle of the rule of law is based upon the practice of liberal democracies of the Western world. At its simplest, it means that what is done officially must be done in accordance with law. In Europe, where an entrenched Constitution is the touchstone for legitimacy of government, there might be a general grant of power to the executive, and a bill of rights to protect the individual. In the British tradition public authorities must point to a specific authority to act as they do. Much of the legitimacy of a political system derives from the impartiality and objectivity with which it is administered.

As Allan freely acknowledges in his introduction, the concept of rule of law may appear to lack a denominate meaning. That however, is no reason to dispense with the notion, which has a value as a governing principle for constitutional theory and analysis. He seeks to give a coherent, unified, and (in his own words) attractive account of some of the principal questions of legal authority and personal freedom. The emphasis is upon procedural fairness, but Allan rejects any rigid distinction between procedure and substance as artificial and unworkable. The rule of law is explained as a set of closely interrelated principles that together make up the core of the doctrine or theory of constitutionalism. This is explained within a framework of liberalism, which is here utilized to comprise any modern democratic regime that protects a range of familiar civil and political liberties and in which governmental action is constrained by law, interpreted and applied by independent judges.

If a criticism might be made of Allan's thesis, it is that his thesis is infused with the spirit of the common law. Yet, in the face of increasing pressure to allow the reception of Roman law-based laws, which the common lawyers successfully resisted in the sixteenth century, it is good to be reminded of our own legal heritage and the part it has played in preserving our freedoms. This is illustrated in Allan's assertion that a general commitment to certain foundational values that underlie and inform the purpose and character of constitutional government, imposes a natural unity on the relevant jurisdictions that is ultimately more important than the presence or absence of a 'written' constitution, with formally entrenched

163 Ibid, p. 2.
164 Ibid, p. 89.
165 Ibid, p. 89.

provisions. It is the spirit of the law, rather than its form, which is the embodiment of the concept of the rule of law.

These principles – the rule of law and separation of powers, to dissent and disobedience, and equal justice and due process of law – are comparatively rarely litigated. Yet several have come to the fore in recent times. One relates to the executive power and in particular the royal prerogative. Justiciability and the reviewability of political decisions were examined in *Black* v *Chrétien*, a judgment of the Court of Appeal for Ontario.[166]

Conrad Black, a prominent publisher and businessman in both Canada and United Kingdom, submitted his name for one of the peerages to be created for the new-model House of Lords following the House of Lords Act 1999. His ennoblement was approved by the relevant British authorities, and Tony Blair, the Prime Minister, advised The Queen to confer the title upon Mr Black. However, Jean Chrétien, Prime Minister of Canada, intervened, and advised The Queen to not confer the peerage on Mr Black.

Ultimately the action was bound to fail, as the honours prerogative, and by extension the other 'political' prerogatives of the Crown, is non-justiciable. It is now rare for any governmental action to be beyond the review of the courts, and it could be argued that just as the tendency has been to expand the scope of justiciability across the prerogative, so the honours prerogative itself should be included.

The rule of law, as a constitutional principle, has an important influence upon the constitution. The extent of that influence depends upon the degree to which the concept of the rule of law in incorporated into the broader constitutional discourse of the state. Where the rule of law is taken as the accepted standard – even where there may be disagreement as to the precise consequences of the application of the principle – the constitution may reflect this principle both in its formal structure and contents, and (perhaps more importantly), in its application.

In those states where the concept of the rule of law is less well-accepted, disregarded, or treated as an alien implant, it may well still be reflected in the formal constitution due to a widespread desire to legitimate power through the assertion of authority through legal processes, but it may be ill-applied in operation.

Whether the rule of law is based on historical legacies (as in most Commonwealth and non-Commonwealth common law countries), civil law-based legal systems, or some other basis – such as natural law – it is common to see it applied to both the formal constitution and the operation of the constitution. The latter is particularly so where courts have an active role in judicial review, or validating or questioning the constitutional validity of statutes.

166 *Black v Chretien* (2001) 199 DLR (4th) 228, Laskin, Goudge and Feldman JJA.

3.4 Inflexibility and constitutional arteriosclerosis

While the rule of law presupposes the maintenance of certain principles, adherence to the notion of the rule of law is not inherent in any political system. It evolved due to the particular circumstances of states, and especially in the West, notably in the United Kingdom. This led in part to the development of a highly systematized legal apparatus; one which was operating to a large degree independently of political oversight and reliant upon a sophisticated system of courts. The Middle Ages were a time of growing legalism. It was especially significant during the establishment of model of mediæval papacy in the twelfth century, when modern states were also emerging.[167] Despite St Paul's warning against legalism,[168] the mediæval church was to become rigidly legal, perhaps an inevitable result given the wide reach of the universal church and its centralization. Law provided the framework, the skeleton upon which faith was supported and the holy catholic church administered. Even though the laws which regulated this bureaucracy were canon laws – later subject to consolidation and reform in the Roman Catholic Church in 1917[169] and 1983[170] – they were influenced by a desire to achieve a considerable degree of precision of definition, and to clarify authority for action.[171]

The circumstances of the break with Rome in the sixteenth century need not be considered here. It is sufficient to observe that the contest with Rome began as one primarily of jurisdiction[172] – King Henry VIII died avowing himself a good Catholic. The Great Schism had also originally been concerned primarily with authority, and

---

167 Brian Tierney, *Church law and constitutional thought in the Middle Ages* (London, 1979).

168 See Colossians 2.20–23:

> 20 Wherefore if ye be dead with Christ from the rudiments of the world, why, as though living in the world, are ye subject to ordinances,
> 21 (Touch not; taste not; handle not;
> 22 Which all are to perish with the using;) after the commandments and doctrines of men?
> 23 Which things have indeed a shew of wisdom in will worship, and humility, and neglecting of the body: not in any honour to the satisfying of the flesh.

169 *The 1917 or Pio-Benedictine Code of Canon Law: in English Translation*, Edward Peters, Curator (San Francisco, 2001).

170 *The Code of Canon Law* prepared by the Canon Law Society of Great Britain and Ireland (London, 1983).

171 The former of course was the cause of many rifts at the early church councils, and of schisms, including the Nestorian Schism between the Byzantine church of the West and the Assyrian Church of the East in the fifth century; W.A. Wigram, *An introduction to the history of the Assyrian Church or the church of the Sassanid Persian Empire, 100-640 A.D.* (Piscataway, 2004).

172 James Spalding, *The Reformation of the Ecclesiastical Laws of England, 1552* (Kirksville, 1992), pp. 1–57.

the validity of the Holy Orders of the Eastern and Western churches was rarely questioned in either camp. Nonetheless, in England the break with Rome was merely one step in an evolving revolutionary era known as the Reformation.[173] The Church of England, while asserting its catholicity, was to become at least partially doctrinally Protestant, in the sense that the *Thirty-Nine Articles* expressly reject certain key elements of then contemporary Roman Catholic dogma, and include some Zwinglian expressions and manner of thought. This was less the result of government policy than a consequence of the decapitation of the Anglican Church (the loss of papal control),[174] and contemporary religious and political feelings. With the loss of what was portrayed as the 'heavy hand' of Rome[175] English prelates – and lesser clerics and laymen alike – felt able (and even impelled) to offer their own contributions to the reform of the catholic church in England.[176]

The removal of the papal authority necessitated a replacement, since the church was the Church of England – religion remained state sponsored – and organized religion was not a matter which could be left entirely a matter for individual choice.[177] The obvious choice, from a pragmatic perspective, was to simply replace the Pope with the King. Some contemporary prelates and most political leaders were generally able to persuade themselves that this was not necessarily such a radical change as it might at first appear. That the majority of the episcopate did not necessarily agree may be seen in the numbers of vacant sees at time during the sixteenth century – though there were many reasons why a see might remain vacant.[178]

Through the Middles Ages the Church (the *magisterium*) and the state (the emperor or *imperium*, and kings) operated in co-equal spheres, though there were times when 'demarcation disputes' arose. In theory, both the Courts-Christian and the king's (secular) courts were supreme within their own fields. This was in an era which saw an ongoing contest throughout Christendom between the church and secular princes.[179] Most – if not all – modern and post-modern states are predominantly if not exclusively secular, insofar as religious laws are not imposed

173 Owen Chadwick, *The Reformation* (Harmondsworth, 1968).

174 The Sovereign can only be seen as head of the Church of England (in England) in a narrow jurisdictional sense.

175 The reformers in England and elsewhere ignored from the outset the New Testament doctrine of the 'universal' church as an inherent part of the Gospel, but its replacement was a pragmatic necessity; *Catholicity: A Study in the Conflict of Christian Traditions in the West, being a Report presented to His Grace the Archbishop of Canterbury* (Westminster, 1947), p. 36.

176 See Owen Chadwick, *The Reformation* (Harmondsworth 1968); Sir Geoffrey Elton (ed.), *The Reformation, 1520–1599* (2nd ed., Cambridge, 1990).

177 Arthur W. Haddan, *Apostolic Succession in the Church of England* (rev. ed., London, 1883), pp. 9–12.

178 William Haugaard, *Elizabeth and the English reformation* (1968).

179 See, for instance, the conflict between the papacy and the empire over the right of investiture; Uta-Renate Blumenthal, *The investiture controversy: church and monarchy from the ninth to the twelfth century* (Philadelphia, 1988).

upon an unwilling population. Partly this is a consequence of the Reformation, but it probably owes as much to the Enlightenment. Yet this rejection of religious uniformity in favour of plurality is one example where states have undergone profound constitutional change, often without the principal actors (the politicians and bureaucrats) being aware of the degree of change. This is only possible where there is a degree of inherent flexibility. The comparative rigidity of the late mediæval church left it ill-suited to react swiftly to the changes wrought by the Reformation. The Counter-Reformation and the Council of Trent were comparatively speedy responses, and did much to ensure the survival of the Roman Catholic Church.

States – as well as churches – today face similar difficulties to those that led to the Reformation. Examples will be discussed in more detail in later chapters, but for the moment we will consider an early example. The Roman Empire lasted some five hundred years, if its establishment can be dated to Augustus in 27 BC, and its end to the fall of the west to Germanic invaders in 476 AD. However, the eastern empire was to last another thousand years until the fall of Constantinople in 1453. The two were politically and culturally linked, but the flexibility that the imperial constitution offered (to divide and unite the empire as circumstances demanded) compensated for the disadvantage of an uncertain process for determining imperial succession. Indeed, it can be argued that the very uncertainty of succession encouraged the assumption of the imperial mantle by men of inherent personal strength – political, military or familial – who were able to hold the disparate empire together.

By contrast, the government of Poland, during the Middle Ages, included a legislative assembly that represented an exceptionally powerful and privileged nobility. This included the famous (or infamous) provision known as the 'Golden Liberty'. The 'Golden Liberty' distinguished Poland and was a unique exception in an age when absolutism was developing in the principal countries of Europe to the east and west. Freedom and liberty, even if enjoyed only by a single social class – the *szlachta* (nobility) – were rights almost unheard-of elsewhere in Europe, where monarchs tended to have more authority. The excesses of the Golden Liberty resulted in weakness in the central government. The most critical of these excesses was the requirement for unanimity of voting in the *Sejms*, or parliament, after the end of the sixteenth century. This prevented, or at the very least severely inhibited, constitutional reforms after this time. The result was that Poland remained largely unchanged constitutionally from this time, until later external events necessitated radical action. This weakness eventually allowed the Commonwealth's neighbours to paralyse the polity, bring it to the brink of anarchy, and annex the weakened country in the late-eighteenth-century partitions of Poland.

The point to be emphasized is this: the flexibility of a given state's constitution may have a significant effect on that state's stability and ultimately its viability. If the constitution is a largely unreformed entrenched eighteenth-century written constitution, then the ability of that state to respond to changing political, economic and social changes may be restricted. If, however, the constitution is actually supported and surrounded by a corpus of glosses – judicial decisions, administrative edicts and other forms of accretions – then the state is much more likely to be able to respond.

An alternative might be where the constitution is either not entrenched or is largely ignored by the regime. While this would allow a great degree of flexibility, permitting reforms of various sorts to be readily made, the absence of an underlying principle could lead to instability. It would seem that a constitutional structure must be sufficiently robust to provide a viable skeleton upon which the organs of state are hung, but not be too prescriptive or restrictive.

3.5 Conclusion

In this chapter we have considered some of the effects of legal principles upon constitutions, leading to a proposal that the flexibility of a constitution has a direct effect upon the stability of a regime or the viability of a state. The rationale for this argument was that the nature of the relationship between law and government is primarily a binary and dependent one. The principles that underpin the constitution will reflect the ethos of the legal system, and *vice versa*. If the legal system is dominated by a belief in the flexibility of law – whether immanent or otherwise – then the constitution itself is more likely to be flexible. However, there are many instances – indeed the majority of states today – where there a degree of constitutional entrenchment.

This idea will be developed further in the next chapter.

PART II
The Viability of States

In Part I we examined some of the theories that have been proposed to explain the rise and fall of civilizations. Secondly, this was extended and focused on the question of the viability of individual states. Thirdly, we introduced the hypothesis that this book proposes, the concept of the hard and the soft constitution, and the effect that this appears to have upon the success or failure of the state.

This second part of the book builds upon the theoretical underpinnings of the first part, by assessing the hypothesis that the book advances. It does so in relation to a number of state models or case studies. There is much to be said for the argument that attempting to explain why an individual state was successful, or was not successful, is an impossible task. The potential variables are enormous and uncertain – possibly unknowable. However, while recognizing that a genuinely accurate model or theory may be impossible to achieve, this does not mean that the attempt must perforce be abandoned. Sisyphus kept rolling his stone up a hill, knowing that it would roll down again. He kept going – though, unfortunately for him, not because of any desire on his part, but as the result of a curse. We also persist because we must; driven by a desire to understand something of the forces that have shaped our world and which continue to shape it. Unlike Sisyphus, we are not necessarily condemned to futile struggle; some light may be revealed as a result of our research.

As outlined in the previous Part, although environmental factors have a crucial influence upon the development of states, nevertheless, where environmental factors are apparently common to a region but only one country or part of the region prospers or stagnates there must be some other factors at play. As postulated in the last chapter of Part I, it seems that the constitutional paradigm of the state may be one such variable. It may be more than simply one variable of many, it may be crucial. In an age of complex and multivariate societies, developing technology and communications – even in the most deprived parts of the world – the environmental differences between states may indeed be less significant that hitherto. Success and failure may today be due more to the way in which a state is organized, and the way in which it operates, than the existence or absence of resources, or other environmental factors.

In order to explore and test this theory further, in Part II, 'The Viability of States', we will apply the theory to different types of state models. The choice of models made here is not intended to be comprehensive, it is to reflect some models that exist in the world today – and in most cases, have existed, in one form or another, throughout the known history of mankind. These are not intended to be a complete list, but rather to demonstrate a range of possible systems. Each has its own characteristics. Few states actually meet all the criteria for any particular category, and are therefore, to some degree, mixed models. This departure from the models is scarcely surprising; after all are merely academic attempts at categorizing what we see around us and are consequently inherently flawed to some extent. It may, however, be seen as an indication of the hard or softness of the particular constitution. The pragmatic polity is perhaps more likely to succeed that the dogmatic doctrinaire regime.

The models that have been selected for closer scrutiny are the authoritarian and doctrinaire liberal states, empires and supra-national entities, and so-called mixed models. Authoritarian regimes, generally speaking, concentrate power and authority, though there may be an element of diffusion, depending upon circumstances. In concentrating power they may have either a hard or a soft constitution (more likely hard than soft), but real power, as often as not, particularly in the modern era, is not vested in the legal system, but in the political leadership. Centralization of authority also tends to lead to a degree of homogeneity, even in a disparate state, that can stifle or encourage creativity, according to the whim of the leadership. The short and medium term success or failure of such a state is also dependent upon the whim of the leadership. The long-term success is a matter which is less certain, as shall be explored in Chapter 5.

The doctrinaire liberal regimes are those that promote the freedom of the individual, the benefits of hard work and industry, and the evils of interventionist government. North American, Australasian and Western European countries generally may be broadly categorized as belonging to this model, although the development of the welfare state (particularly in the latter two regions) has affected the application of the model to some degree. From the growth of democracy, first in the United Kingdom (we are here excluding the ancient Greek democracies, and the various localized and short-lived experiments in democracy elsewhere), and then, through the nineteenth century, on the continent of Europe, liberalism became the established model. Sometimes this is simply referred to as democracy, but it is more than this. Democracy reflects a particular sociological and political approach. Belief in democracy is enjoined upon us because we are in liberal regimes; whether this promotes or hinders state success is a question that will be considered in Chapter 6.

The empires and supra-national entities (the sole example of the latter today being the European Union, though depending upon definition, there may be several examples of the former), by their very nature, must have a stronger binding force than the national or racial identity of a state, in order to not disintegrate. This may be pure brute force – as occasionally in the past – or it may be a bureaucratic machine of great tenacity and reach – as in ancient China and the modern European Union. If the latter is the case, then this can be seen as a form of hard constitution. Relative inflexibility, coupled with an emphasis upon the precision of detail, regulate aspects of life throughout the empire, to a greater or lesser extent, depending upon the resources of the empire. Whether the hard constitutions of the empires render them more or less likely to be successful is an important question. The consideration of this question is the aim of this chapter.

In the so-called mixed models, there is neither doctrinaire liberalism, nor authoritarianism. There is unity rather than diversity (an empire). Sometimes this is because soft constitutions have allowed or encouraged this; occasionally because hard constitutions have required it. The application of the hard/soft distinction to these hybrid states – to which the majority of modern states can probably be deemed to belong – can be equally useful however. The choice of paradigm can be seen to be a product of the particular history of the state and an important influence upon the success or failure of the state.

This part of the book seeks to ascertain whether in fact the flexibility of constitutions has had an effect upon state viability. A variety of models of state are considered, so as to avoid a comparison of one or two examples that may or may not be comparable. In each model examples are used to tease out the influence that may be ascribed to constitutional flexibility, and this compared and contrasted with the success or failure of the particular states.

Chapter 4
Underlying Theory

4.1 Introduction

In the previous chapter we considered the notion of the hard and the soft constitution. Fluidity, as a whole, would appear to lead to a more realistic assessment of a constitution than the simple question of whether a constitution is formally legally entrenched or not, or is confined to a single document or is spread across a range of disparate sources. Law, in one form or another, is inherent to any constitutional system, it could scarcely be otherwise, but constitutional law is merely a specialized sub-set of law. For this reason an appreciation of how law is understood, rather than an analysis of the provisions of a formal constitution, provides a worthwhile means of understanding the operation of the constitutional structure of any given state. The constitution is thus set within a broader socio-legal context, which must also be understood.

We now move on to ask how the nature of a constitution can contribute to the stability of the regime. The approach that will be taken to this question is as follows: flexibility leads to stability, because the constitution is able to freely adapt itself to changing circumstances. However, too much flexibility can be dangerous. The key is to determine how much flexibility is required for any given state to give it the necessary stability and freedom. As we shall discuss in this and later chapters, the key element is the underlying ethos or *Grundnorm* of the constitution and of the state. The absence of a clear underlying principle is likely to increase the prospect of instability, through excessive or insufficient constitutional rigidity. It is also true that stability may lead to flexibility, though this may not occur if the constitution is rigid but other countervailing influences contribute to stability. A case in point is the United States of America.

In this chapter we will consider the hypothesis that the flexibility of constitutions influences the stability of states. We will commence with a consideration of the influence of legitimacy on constitutional action and thought. This will be followed by discussion of various schools of political thought – such as liberal, conservative, socialist, anarchist, and environmentalist – some of which will be examined in more depth in subsequent chapters when we consider case studies of actual states.

4.2 Legitimacy as a normative influence

Structural flexibility influences action and thought in the operation and perception of the constitution. The degree to which a constitution can change, and the processes involved in this development, are important. The normative influence of these factors includes the ways that structural factors affect the operation of the constitution. The factors are of course both formal and informal in nature.

One of these structural factors is legitimacy. Legitimacy is a more supple and inclusive idea than sovereignty or continuity.[1] Legitimacy offers reasons why a given state deserves the allegiance of its members. Max Weber identifies three bases for this authority – traditions and customs; legal-rational procedures (such as voting); and individual charisma.[2] Some combination of these can be found in most political systems.

With the dominance of democratic concepts of government, it might be thought that if the people believe that an institution is appropriate, then it is legitimate.[3] But this scheme leaves out substantive questions about the justice of the state and the protection it offers the individuals who belong to it.[4] It is more usual to maintain that a state's legitimacy depends upon its upholding certain human rights.[5]

There are three current alternative definitions of legitimacy. The first definition involves the capacity of the system to engender and maintain the belief that the existing political institutions are the most appropriate ones for the society.[6] Second, in the tradition of Weber, legitimacy has been defined as 'the degree to which institutions are valued for themselves and considered right and proper'.[7] Third, political legitimacy may be defined as the degree of public perception that a regime is morally proper for a society.[8]

---

1 Rodney Barker, *Political Legitimacy and the State* (Oxford, 1990), p. 4. For a general discussion of aspects of legitimacy in relation to the Crown, see F.M. Brookfield, *Some aspects of the Necessity Principle in Constitutional Law* (DPhil thesis, University of Oxford, 1972); and F.M. Brookfield, *Waitangi and Indigenous Rights: Revolution, Law and Legitimation* (Auckland, 1999).

2 See Randall Collins, *Weberian Sociological Theory* (Cambridge, 1986).

3 Penelope Brook Cowen, 'Neo Liberalism' in Raymond Miller (ed.), *New Zealand Politics in Transition* (Auckland, 1997), pp. 341–9.

4 Which is illustrated by the study of the application of the model to Mummar Qadhafi's Libya; Saleh Al Namlah, *Political legitimacy in Libya since 1969* (PhD thesis, Syracuse University, 1992).

5 John Rawls, *Political Liberalism* (New York, 1993); Ted Honderich (ed.), *The Oxford Companion to Philosophy* (Oxford, 1995), p. 477; Matthew Lane Swanson, *The social extract tradition and the question of political legitimacy* (PhD thesis, University of Missouri-Columbia, 1995).

6 Seymour Martin Lipset, *Political Man: The Social Bases of Politics* (New York, 1960), p. 77.

7 Robert Bierstedt, 'Legitimacy' in Julian Gould and William Kolb (eds), *A Dictionary of the Social Sciences* (London, 1964), p. 386.

8 Richard Merelmen, 'Learning and Legitimacy', *American Political Science Review*, 60 (1966): 548–61.

Whichever definition is preferred, all are based on belief or opinion, unlike the older traditional definitions, which revolved around the element of law or right.[9] These traditional concepts of legitimacy were built upon foundations external to, and independent of, the assertion or opinion of the claimant.[10] These normative or legal definitions included laws of inheritance and laws of logic. Sources for these included immemorial custom, divine law, the law of nature, or a constitution.[11]

Legitimacy is sought through the advancing and acceptance of a political formula; a metaphysical or ideological formula that justifies the existing exercise or proposed possession of power by rulers, as the logical and necessary consequence of the beliefs of the people over whom the power is exercised.[12] Just what this formula is depends largely upon the history and composition of a country. In modern democratic societies, popular election confers legitimacy upon governments, and is usually perceived as the pre-eminent, if not exclusive, source of such legitimacy. However, legitimacy can also be independent of the assertion or opinion of the claimant. This has been particularly important in late twentieth-century discussion of indigenous rights.[13]

Overall, the desire or need to preserve legitimacy constrains the flexibility of a constitution. Formal, as well as informal, structural influences may be seen in the evaluation of the development of legislative independence in the British Commonwealth. This went through a number of stages, but always was heavily affected by a liberal ethos and a pragmatism largely devoid of doctrinaire assertions or beliefs.

The legislative independence of colonial assemblies, and the later dominions, was limited by technical rules of repugnancy and capacity. Laws which were repugnant to the fundamental principles of the common law of England were held to be invalid, or *ultra vires*.[14] No assembly could pass legislation beyond its limited legal capacity, a capacity defined by the legislation establishing the assembly.[15] Technical rules of repugnancy were the first legislative restrictions

---

9 In an extreme form, the divine right of kings; J.N. Figgis, *The theory of the Divine Right of Kings* (Cambridge, 1914).

10 John Schaar, 'Legitimacy in the Modern State', in William Connolly (ed.), *Legitimacy and the State* (Oxford, 1984), p. 108; Jonathan Waskan, 'De facto legitimacy and popular will', *Social Theory and Practice*, 24 (1998): 25–56.

11 Hannah Arendt, 'What was authority', in Karl Friedrich (ed.), *Authority* (Harvard, 1958), p. 83.

12 Fatos Tarifa, 'Quest for legitimacy and the withering away of utopia', *Social Forces*, 76 (1997): 437–74.

13 See, for example, Sir Elihu Lauterpacht, 'Sovereignty – Myth or Reality?', *International Affairs*, 73 (1997): 137–50.

14 Sir William Blackstone, *Commentaries on the Laws of England*, ed. E. Christian (New York, 1978), book 1 chapter 1, p. 105.

15 Limited, in most instances, to measures for the 'peace order and good government' of the territory. The New Zealand Constitution Act 1852 (15 and 16 Vict c 72) (UK)

on the dominions to be weakened.[16] This relaxation came about, not because of political pressure, but in response to judicial activity, in Australia in particular.

In the late 1860s, Boothby J in South Australia applied very broadly the principle of the invalidity of colonial legislation repugnant to fundamental principles of English law, to the extent of finding the Constitution Act 1855–56 no 2 (South Australia) itself invalid. This decision was in part responsible for the passage, by the imperial Parliament, of the Colonial Laws Validity Act 1865.[17]

This Act ended the old theory and practice that colonial legislatures must respect the fundamental principles of English law applicable to that colony.[18] It made it clear that legislation would only be invalid if repugnant to an imperial Act extending to the colony – or any order or regulation under such Acts.[19] For the first time, the rule of repugnancy was clearly restricted to statute law only.

Perhaps most importantly, the Colonial Laws Validity Act 1865 conferred upon all self-governing colonies a clear power to alter their own constitutions.[20] However, by a proviso, the Act required that any laws designed to exercise these powers were to be passed in such manner and form as required by the law for the time being in force, whether that be imperial Act, letters patent, Order in Council, or colonial law. Thus a limitation of capacity remained.[21]

The advent of the Statute of Westminster 1931 removed, for dominions generally – though not for Canada – the colonial limitations of legislative repugnancy and constitutional incapacity. This did not itself amount to political independence. This had been established at the 1926 and 1930 Imperial Conferences, with the adoption of the principle that 'the Crown is the symbol of the free association of the members of the British Commonwealth of Nations', and that 'they are united by a common allegiance to the Crown'.[22]

The Balfour formula, given statutory form in the Statute of Westminster 1931, prescribed allegiance to the Crown as one of the conditions then obtaining for membership in the British Commonwealth. As the dominions individually entered the international arena,[23] the common allegiance implied less the unity of the

---

conferred upon the General Assembly of New Zealand the authority to make laws for the 'peace order and good government' (s 53) of the country.

16 Though they were to survive for the Australian states until the Australia Act 1986.

17 28 and 29 Vict c 63 (UK).

18 s 3.

19 s 2, although this was an established rule anyway.

20 s 5. A right conferred on all those settled colonies not yet enjoying representative legislative assemblies (such as the Falkland Islands), by the British Settlements Act 1887 (UK).

21 This effect was confirmed in *McCawley's Case* [1920] AC 692 (PC).

22 *Imperial Conference* (1926) Parliamentary Papers, vol 11 1926 cmd 2768; *Imperial Conference* (1930) Parliamentary Papers, vol 14 1930–31 cmd 3717.

23 Originally the doctrine was confined to internal affairs, rather than foreign relations, but the second followed almost as a matter of course.

Crown than its opposite, divisibility.[24] This was driven largely by external factors such as the need to preserve and enhance domestic democratic legitimacy. This included, with the growth of the independence of the dominions, the development of the concept of an indigenous or autochthonous constitution. In such a situation the constitution depended on local legitimacy, and retained only peripheral and derivative legitimacy founded on United Kingdom constitutional sources. This is seen clearly in the development of Canadian constitutional independence.

The granting of legislative independence to Canada was impeded in part by the difficulties of resolving some of these disputes internally. Canada adopted the provisions of the 1931 Act only so far as its federal nature then allowed.[25] This meant that until 1982 the United Kingdom Parliament had to legislate for Canada, with respect to any constitutional provisions.

On the abdication of King Edward VIII in 1936, the distinction between the legal arrangements of the dominions was highlighted. Canada expressed its consent to imperial legislation giving effect to the King's determination to abdicate,[26] by an executive request and consent under s 4 of the Statute of Westminster 1931. Like South Africa,[27] it also subsequently passed an Act to homologate its actions, although the abdication probably would have taken effect automatically upon the passage of the imperial Act, under s 2 of the British North America Act 1867.[28]

In the *Patriation Reference*,[29] the Supreme Court of Canada took the viewpoint of a British court in the face of legislation emanating from the superior and sovereign Parliament at Westminster. At least until 1982 the imperial Parliament retained undiminished powers over the Canadian legislature.[30] However, the formal rules must be seen in the context of the informal reality.

The powers of the Canadian Parliament are limited. This is due to the federal nature of the Constitution, in which certain powers are conferred upon the

24 The question whether the Crown was divisible elicited much legal debate in its day. See A.B. Keith, *The King and the Imperial Crown* (London, 1936); Richard Latham, *The Law and the Commonwealth* (London, 1949) reprinted from W.K. Hancock (ed.), *Survey of British Commonwealth Affairs* (London, 1937).

25 Limitations are inherent where authority is shared, as in a federal system. But in Canada's case further restrictions were necessitated by the absence of the provision for local constitutional amendments.

26 HM Declaration of Abdication Act 1936 (10 Edw VIII and 1 Geo VI c 3) (UK).

27 His Majesty King Edward VIII's Declaration of Abdication Act 1937 (South Africa).

28 Noel Cox, *A Constitutional History of the New Zealand Monarchy: The evolution of the New Zealand monarchy and the recognition of an autochthonous polity* (Saarbrücken, 2008), p. 141.

29 *Reference re Amendment of the Constitution of Canada* [1981] 1 SCR 753 (SCC).

30 A view which coincided with that of the British House of Commons Foreign Affairs Committee; First Report, Session 1980–81 (HC 42), *British North America Acts*, vols 1 and 2 (1981); Foreign Affairs Committee, Second Report, Session 1980–81 (HC 295), *Supplementary Report on the British North America Acts* (1981).

provinces and others upon the federal Parliament and government. The legislative independence of Parliament in such a system must always be subject to some limitations. For Canada, these limitations were contained in the British North America Act 1867.[31]

The Statute of Westminster 1931 ended most of the limitations upon the Canadian Parliament. However, because Canadian political leaders, and particularly the leaders of Ontario and French-speaking Quebec, could not agree upon procedures for future amendments to the Constitution,[32] no general power of constitutional amendment was conferred upon Canada, as it was upon the other dominions, by the Statute of Westminster 1931.[33]

The Colonial Laws Validity Act 1865 ceased to have effect in Canada on 11 December 1931, except for amendments to the British North America Act 1867.[34] This meant that there were limitations of repugnancy as well as capacity. The British North America Act 1867[35] could not be amended by the Canadian legislature *per se*, due to the limitations imposed by the federal structure of the Canadian Constitution, so the imperial Parliament was required to act. Thus, although a Canadian court would not recognize a 'normal' post-1931 Act of the imperial Parliament as part of the laws of Canada, since such an Act would be contrary to the Statute of Westminster, it would recognize an Act purporting to amend the British North America Act 1867,[36] because of the inherent paramountcy of the latter statute, and the absence of any internal amendment procedure,[37] and thus the necessity for imperial Acts to change it.

Until 1982 the Canadian Parliament was incapable, in terms of the statute conferring and defining its powers, of amending the Canadian Constitution. In the absence of this power constitutional amendments were enacted by the British Parliament, although otherwise after 1931 no British legislation applied to Canada. Thus, in 1949 an Act integrated Newfoundland into Canada,[38] and in that same

---

31 30 and 31 Vict c 33 (UK).

32 Timothy Cochran, 'Competing visions of the Canadian Constitution' (University of New Brunswick M.A. thesis, 1995).

33 s 7(1). The statute also excluded 'any power to repeal or alter the Constitution or the Constitution Act of the Commonwealth of Australia or the Constitution Act of the Dominion of New Zealand otherwise than in accordance with the law existing before the commencement of this Act' (ss 8, 9). However, these constitutions already had provision for local amendments.

34 Under ss 2 and 7 of the Statute of Westminster 1931. Newfoundland remained a dominion, latterly under suspension of self-government due to financial collapse, until union with Canada in 1947.

35 30 and 31 Vict c 33 (UK).

36 Ibid.

37 *Reference re Amendment of the Constitution of Canada* [1981] 1 SCR 753.

38 British North America Act 1949 (12 and 13 Geo VI c 22) (UK), now restyled the Newfoundland Act 1949.

year the right to amend the Act in respect of certain internal matters was granted by the British North America Act (No 2) 1949.[39]

Though it had acquired political independence at some point after 1919, and by 1931 at the latest, Canada only achieved full formal legislative independence in 1982,[40] when the Canada Act 1982 removed the residual repugnancy, allowing Canada to amend the British North America Act 1867.[41] In 1982 provision was made for the first time for Canada to amend its own Constitution in its entirety.[42] In terms of the 1982 amendments to the British North America Act 1867, now renamed the Constitution Act 1982, the Canadian Parliament alone is competent to alter the Constitution.

There was no doubting the reality of independence before 1982, but short of relying on a deliberate legal break, there was no pragmatic alternative to using the British Parliament. It was not that attachment to legal form alone required the Canadians to follow the requirements of the British North Act 1867. Any amendment enacted by a contrary method would be held by the Canadian courts to be *ultra vires*. This is grounded on the autochthony of the Canadian constitution, which is the basis, or one of the principal bases, of the legitimacy of the constitution. But its exact nature is unclear, due to the difficulty of reconciling an apparently indigenous nature with legal continuity from an historically prior constitutional parent. Various attempts have been made, largely unsuccessfully, to explain this paradox.

Following the 1982 legislation, the Canadian courts will probably recognize only a Canadian statute as able to amend the Constitution, although its Parliament is still not sovereign, as the Constitution remains in this essential respect paramount, since a special amendment procedure, laid down by the Constitution, must of necessity be followed. This is of course a matter of a limitation on capacity rather than repugnancy.

However, questions remain as to whether the United Kingdom retained, after 1982, the power to legislate for Canada. Political independence was apparently followed by legal independence in 1982. This latter is only real if the United Kingdom Parliament is now incapable of legislating for Canada – either because of s 52(3) or otherwise.

If the Constitution Act 1982, enacted as Schedule B of the Canada Act 1982, can bind Canada, cannot subsequent British Acts also bind Canada? Could not the United Kingdom Parliament repeal the Constitution Act 1982, thereby returning

39 13 Geo VI c 81 (UK).

40 *Madzimbamuto v Lardner-Burke* [1969] 1 AC 645 (PC); *Reference re Offshore Mineral Rights of British Columbia* [1967] SCR 792, 816; *R v Secretary of State for the Foreign and Commonwealth Office* (1982) 2 All ER 118, [1982] QB 892 (CA). Lord Denning's judgment in this respect has been called by Slattery a throwback to the 1930s.

41 30 and 31 Vict c 33 (UK).

42 This is not quite as restrictive as it may appear, since the constitution is actually fairly brief and skeletal, with most constitutional legislation not similarly entrenched.

Canada to the pre-1982 position? The orthodox answer is politically no, and legally perhaps no. While preserving legal continuity the Canadian Constitution has developed local roots.[43] This is despite the fact that the authority of the Canadian Constitution derives, not from an act of the people of Canada, but ultimately from a British statute. This is largely because of the established independence of Canada and the autonomy of its legal system, the basic rules underpinning Canadian law, and the extent of the British Parliament's power to legislate for Canada.[44]

That the answer to the question is qualified, is a reflection of the absence of juridical acceptance of a single new theory or model of the Constitution which would reconcile the political reality with orthodox legal theories of the supremacy of Parliament. Politics and law have coalesced in an uneasy amalgam, with orthodox law sometimes at odds with political reality.

The denial of the legal right of the United Kingdom Parliament to legislate for Canada depends upon acceptance of a change in the constitutional *Grundnorm*. The traditional *Grundnorm* is that of continuing parliamentary sovereignty. But, if 'freedom, once conferred, cannot be revoked',[45] then it would seem that whatever a strict view of the law may suggest, if the political ground rules change, so will the legal.

By establishing an independent legislature, the United Kingdom was creating a new polity in Canada, capable of outgrowing its original powers, and developing distinct attributes and features of its own.[46]

The newly renamed Constitution Act 1982 attributed to itself a position of legal paramountcy.[47] On the model of the American Constitution there was to be no higher legal authority. This assertion however was not especially significant, as the Constitution Act 1982 clearly held a position of paramountcy as a necessary prerequisite to a federal Constitution. Because authority was shared between the federal and provincial parliaments, there must be some higher authority which determines who shall have what power or responsibility.

This did not necessarily mean, however, that the Canadian Constitution could never be regarded as a truly Canadian document, in the sense of the American Constitution, which is devoid of any formal legal antecedents. The process leading to the amendment of the British North America Act in 1981–82 was generally

43 Brian Slattery, 'The Independence of Canada' (1983) 5 Supreme Court Law Review 390.

44 Ibid, pp. 369–71.

45 *Ndlwana v Hofmeyer* [1937] AD 229, 237 (South African CA).

46 See Noel Cox, *A Constitutional History of the New Zealand Monarchy: The evolution of the New Zealand monarchy and the recognition of an autochthonous polity* (Saarbrücken, 2008).

47 s 52. There is no single document which constitutes 'the Constitution', though the Constitution Act 1982 (as the British North America Act 1867 was renamed) provides a framework. Most importantly, because of the federal nature of Canada the legal capacity of the parliaments are limited by an enabling Act which is itself entrenched.

spoken of as patriation,[48] suggesting that the constitution was somehow being bodily moved to Canada. It remains uncertain whether a constitution, whose legal origins may be traced directly to an imperial statute, can ever be fully autochthonous.

There are alternative approaches however. One is simply to ignore the question of legal authority, and introduce a new constitution which was not based on any prior legal authority. Such a deliberate break in continuity was considered by the Canadian Government in 1980,[49] but the tradition of legal justification for government action was to prove too strongly entrenched. With the rule of law one of the benchmarks of the constitution and an essential element in maintaining legitimacy, the Government could scarcely have decided otherwise.

The other alternative is to attempt to rationalize and explain the current position, where the Canadian Constitution is politically, and also legally, supreme. In one model Slattery has argued that Canada's legal independence is based neither on events of 1931 nor of 1982, nor on any decisive legal event, but is 'at root a matter of fact'.[50] In effect he is arguing that legal concepts of authority are essentially meaningless; what counted was the political reality. The acquisition of political independence, sometime between 1919 and 1931, had the legal effect of ending the colonial rule of subordination and replacing it with one of equality. It was therefore independence and not s 2 of the Statute of Westminster 1931 which ended the relationship of subordination between the Canadian and United Kingdom parliaments, and ended the latter parliament's ability to legislate for Canada.[51]

Hogg holds a similar view. However, he concludes that the concept of autochthony is neither very clear nor very useful.[52] In preference he borrows and slightly modifies Marshall's test for patriation.[53] Hogg asks whether a legally effective termination of British legislative authority has occurred.[54]

Although s 2 of the 1982 Act appears to be an obvious candidate for having accomplished this termination of authority, it cannot have done so on its own, at least in orthodox constitutional theory, because of the doctrine of parliamentary supremacy.

---

48 Or as 're-patriation', a somewhat mystifying term.

49 David E. Smith, *The Invisible Crown: The First Principle of Canadian Government* (Toronto, 1995), p. 158.

50 Brian Slattery, 'The Independence of Canada' (1983) 5 Supreme Court Law Review 369, 391.

51 Peter Oliver, 'Cutting the Imperial link – Canada and New Zealand', in Philip Joseph (ed.), *Essays on the Constitution* (Wellington, 1995), pp. 368, 378–9.

52 P.W. Hogg, *Constitutional Law of Canada* (3rd edn, Scarborough, Ontario, 1992), p. 54n.

53 Geoffrey Marshall, *Constitutional Theory* (Oxford, 1971), p. 63.

54 Ibid, p. 55.

Hogg argues that the Supreme Court of Canada would not allow an Act of the United Kingdom Parliament passed after 1982 to extend to Canada as part of its laws,[55] and that 'freedom, once conferred, cannot be revoked'.[56] Still, he acknowledges that it is difficult to reconcile this view with parts of the *Patriation Reference*,[57] which suggested that there had been, at least prior to 1982, no diminution of the legal authority over Canada of the United Kingdom Parliament since colonial times.[58]

Clearly any attempt by the United Kingdom Parliament to legislate for Canada would be doomed to failure, but no satisfactory theoretical explanation for this has yet been accepted. One possibility is that the view put forward in 1886 by James Bryce, drawing a distinction between legal and political sovereignty,[59] is a more accurate way of describing the constitution than the traditional, legalist approach. The practical difficulty is that the law is what the courts say it is, and thus, to a lawyer, political sovereignty can be seen as meaningless.[60] If the legal theorists cannot agree that a fundamental shift in political power can alter their long held constitutional concepts, then the Canadian constitution can never be seen as autochthonous.

Section 52 has an important symbolic role, like the Crown itself. It is almost certain in that the Canadian Constitution is autochthonous, rather than derived from the laws of the United Kingdom – though, without a deliberate legal break, it is hard to see this as technically true.[61] Constitutional law has always followed constitutional practice,[62] and the evolution of the Canadian polity will likely gradually assume a truly autochthonous nature, if it has not yet reached this point.

Elsewhere in the (former) British empire, similar issues of legitimacy have had to be addressed. The autochthony of the 1922 constitution of the Irish Free State

55 P.W. Hogg, *Constitutional Law of Canada* (3rd edn, Scarborough, Ontario, 1992), p. 56.

56 *Ndlwana v Hofmeyer* [1937] AD 229, 237 (South African CA).

57 *Reference re Amendment of the Constitution of Canada* [1981] 1 SCR 753.

58 Peter Oliver, 'Cutting the Imperial link – Canada and New Zealand', in Philip Joseph (ed.), *Essays on the Constitution* (Wellington, 1995), pp. 368, 379–80.

59 To a lawyer, political sovereignty is a meaningless concept – in law sovereignty means authority, not might; See also H.R. Gray, 'The Sovereignty of Parliament Today' (1953–54) 10 University of Toronto Law Journal 54; For an attempt to bridge this gap see Ian Loveland, 'Parliamentary Sovereignty and the European Community: the Unfinished Revolution?' (1996) 49(4) Parliamentary News 517.

60 Sir Ivor Jennings, *Law and the Constitution* (3rd edn, Bickley, 1943).

61 See however, Noel Cox, *A Constitutional History of the New Zealand Monarchy: The evolution of the New Zealand monarchy and the recognition of an autochthonous polity* (Saarbrücken, 2008); Noel Cox, 'Republican Sentiment in the Realms of the Queen: The New Zealand Perspective' (2001–2002) 29(1) Manitoba Law Journal 1–28.

62 See Daniel O'Connell and Ann Riordan, *Opinions on Imperial Constitutional Law* (Sydney, 1971).

was recognized by the Supreme Court of Eire in *The State (Ryan) v Lennon*.[63] The legitimacy of the state, which had emerged through a deliberate rejection of United Kingdom hegemony, required the rejection of a prior British legal authority, whatever the constitutional and legal reality might have been. Perhaps unsurprisingly, at about the same time, the Judicial Committee of the Privy Council, in *Moore v Attorney-General (Irish Free State)*,[64] was of the contrary opinion to the Irish Supreme Court. They emphasized the inheritance of legal form and authority from the Parliament of the United Kingdom. In the absence of a genuine legal break – not a mere assertion of an indigenous and autochthonous nature – the constitutional legitimacy remained primarily derived from legal continuity, and thus from United Kingdom laws. Marshall has observed that even a break in legal continuity cannot necessarily imply legal independence.[65] Necessity, and similar principles, may fill the gap.

The need for legitimacy – and especially one influenced by a strongly legalistic and jurisprudential perspective – has militated against radical constitutional reforms, such as deliberate breaks in legal continuity. A constitution tries to be all things to all people, and thus draws legitimacy from a number of sources, including technical rules of capacity and repugnancy. This then has an influence on the flexibility of the constitution, and the way in which it operates.

4.3 The necessity for inherent strength

It might be argued that it is a truism that a constitution needs to be inherently strong enough to hold a state together. This strength may derive from legitimacy, adherence to the rule of law, or convention, or other informal influences, or it may derive from the formal structures of the law and the constitution itself. Examples of the latter might include rigid entrenchment, especially manner and form entrenchment to escape from the Diceyan formula of parliamentary supremacy.[66]

The necessity for strength may be seen in the influence of flexibility on constitutional action and thought. It is dangerous to allow too much flexibility, whether formally or informally; the Soviet constitution was ostensibly democratic and fairly well-balanced, but the reality, derived from the informal manner in which it was administered and the socio-political reality, was that it masked the tyranny of a communist dictatorship. Authoritarian government, or the tyranny of the masses, are both possible where the constitutional checks and balances

63 [1935] IR 170.

64 [1935] AC 484.

65 Geoffrey Marshall, *Constitutional Theory* (Oxford, 1971).

66 See *The Prince's Case* (1606) 8 Co Rep 1a; 77 ER 481, *Stockdale v Hansard* (1839) 9 Ad and E 1; 112 ER 1112 (QB), cf. *R (Jackson) v Attorney-General (UK)* [2006] 1 AC 262 (HL) (The Fox Hunting case).

are inadequate, or inadequately adhered to. This is also affected by formal and informal adherence to the rule of law.

The risks inherent in excessive flexibility may appear obvious, on one level: if a constitution is too vague, uncertain or fluid there may be insufficient rigidity to support the maintenance of the rule of law and of democracy. This may lead to greater uncertainty. However, constitutions are rarely as precise as this, and even the most vague or skeletal may actually be reinforced by a range of muscles, tendons, sinews and similar supports, to continue an anatomical metaphor. These can be in the form of extra-legal glosses, regulations, convention, statutes and common law principles. In part these supports bolster the constitution through the details they provide, but also because they help establish and maintain a culture of constitutionalism.

4.4 Political ideology underlying the *Grundnorm*

Dyzenhaus has argued that there is an unwritten constitution of law, exemplified by the common law constitutions of Commonwealth countries. This is based on cases decided in the United Kingdom, Canada and Australia, to show that even in the absence of an entrenched Bill of Rights the law provides a moral resource.[67] This may be seen, at least partially, as the principle underlying the *Grundnorm* of the constitution.

The role of law can be seen as a tool in pursuit of equality. Tensions exist between the law as a protector of individual liberty and as a tool of democratic self-rule.[68] This approach focuses on Schmitt's critique of liberal politics and his politicization of constitutional law. Schmitt prefers to find an underlying tendency for laws to well up from a fount of authority based on self-interest and an authoritarian centralizing tendency.[69]

Dyzenhaus is in favour of the unity of public law based in fundamental constitutional values such as human rights, expressed in administrative law, constitutional law, and public international law.[70] This approach suggests that the public international lawyer, the constitutional lawyer and the administrative lawyer might have more in common than hitherto thought – though it might be noted that the Advocates of Doctors' Commons, which itself was abolished in 1857, trained in the civil law tradition, served the ecclesiastical courts, the Court of Admiralty,

67 David Dyzenhaus, *Constitution of Law: Legality in a time of emergency* (Cambridge, 2006).

68 David Dyzenhaus and Arthur Ripstein (eds), *Law and Morality: readings in legal philosophy* (Toronto, 1996).

69 David Dyzenhaus (ed.), *Law as politics: Carl Schmitt's critique of liberalism* (Durham, 1998).

70 David Dyzenhaus (ed.), *The Unity of Public Law* (Oxford, 2004), p. v.

and for arbitrations involving questions of international law.[71] It has been argued that this unity of public law comes from natural law. This is on the grounds that neither legal positivism nor interpretavism provide an ultimate source. However, the mere fact that the basis of this unity – if unity there is – remains uncertain and unsettled suggests that it does little to identify the principles underlying the constitutional *Grundnorm*. Perhaps little can be added to the basic principle of the rule of law, uncertain and often unhelpful though that is. Another possibility is that the rule of law has been extended in the western liberal democracy, so that liberalism, rather than the rule of law *per se*, is the ruling belief. Yet this cannot, of itself, be sufficient, due to difficulties with the idea of liberalism.

The term 'liberalism' conveys two distinct positions in political philosophy. One is a pro-individualist theory of people and government. The second is a pro-statist or what is perhaps better termed a 'social democratic', conception. In the nineteenth century occurred a shift towards more liberal and socialist perspectives. Liberalism therefore doesn't necessarily mean today which it did to a prior generation. There is no generally accepted meaning for the term 'liberal', but it might be said to include acceptance of rights against persons and the existence of certain basic rights, such as those to health care and education.

However there is an inherent difficulty in this definition, for it includes freedom to succeed as well as freedom to be nurtured even in the absence of attempting to succeed. J.S. Mill, John Rawls, Will Kymlicka, Ronald Dworkin and others have tried to create order out of chaos, though that very act is arguably illiberal in nature. However, they emphasize toleration, plurality and justice, though they differ on their interpretation of toleration, public and private roles, and the perceived need for opportunities to be created. The survival of the welfare state in the twenty-first century economy is a problem not just for pragmatists.

Liberalism in the twentieth century imposed positive obligations upon the state. The state's duty to ensure a just and fair opportunity for all to compete and flourish in a civil society is, according to Dworkin, fundamental to the role of the state. This activist approach would be anathema to the classical liberal, those non-interventionist, *laissez-faire* approach, which strongly opposes imposing taxes, for instance, on one sector of society in order to benefit another.

Conservatives are not opposed, *per se*, to change, but they are distrustful of the ability of a current generation to have sufficient wisdom and discernment to be able to make radical changes to what has evolved over time. They favour gradual change, rather than no change at all, for, as Tennyson wrote, 'The old order changeth, yielding place to new, and God fulfils himself in many ways, lest one good custom should corrupt the world' (from 'The Passing of King Arthur'). They also tend to support some redistribution, in order to maintain stability, and will also approve some revolutionary actions where the alternatives are even less palatable.

---

71 See George Squibb, *Doctors' Commons: a history of the College of Advocates and Doctors of Law* (Oxford, 1977).

Socialists are more liberal than the liberals, but not in the sense of moderation; they support more radical change, sometimes amounting to revolutionary distribution of property and power. The more moderate are all-but-indistinguishable from the liberals, the more extreme can become anarchists, where property rights, *inter alia*, are irrelevant, and the state of society is akin to the state of nature, with life being 'nasty, brutish and short' (Hobbes's *Leviathan*).

Most constitutions are not dominated exclusively by one or other of the above political or philosophical ideologies, theories or principles. Most are either a hybrid, or are what may be described as pragmatic rather than dogmatic. This may reflect elements of the conservative, the liberal, and the authoritarian. They respond to events, rather than flow from fundamental principles of government. This may be seen in one case study, that of New Zealand in the context of recent discourse around the notion of constitutional reform.

It is a common misconception that New Zealand does not have a written constitution. It is true that there is no one document called 'the constitution'. But the principal Acts which establish, empower and regulate the organs of government are readily identifiable.[72] The meaning behind the assertion that New Zealand does not have a written constitution is simply that New Zealand's constitution is not entrenched. Thus Parliament can, and does, amend the constitution through a simple majority vote.[73]

In the modern world New Zealand, together with the United Kingdom, is virtually alone in not having an entrenched constitution. Unlike the United States, Canada and Australia – not coincidentally all federal systems, New Zealand cannot look to one single document embodying its constitution. But, although the provisions of the Constitution Act 1986 are not entrenched,[74] and major constitutional changes could legally be effected virtually overnight by a bare majority of the House of Representatives,[75] the issue is not purely or even mainly the legal one of entrenchment.

The approach of the New Zealand constitution is one of flexibility. The written rules are underpinned by what are called conventions. They are rules of political practice which are regarded as binding by those to whom they apply. Laws are

72 One of the purposes of the Constitution Act 1986 (NZ) was to bring together in one place important constitutional provisions.

73 Though there is a procedural entrenchment of parts of the Electoral Act 1993 (NZ), it is doubtful whether this is effective.

74 Whether Parliament can in fact entrench an enactment remains controversial. The Union with Scotland Act 1706 (6 Ann c 11) (Eng.) was declared to be entrenched, but has been subject to repeated amendments. Most recently, article 22 was repealed by the Statute Law (Repeals) Act 1993 (U.K.), s 1(1) and schedule 1.

75 Although it may be questioned whether the Governor-General could, or indeed should, decline to give the royal assent to such a measure. See Sir Owen Dixon, 'The Law and the Constitution' (1935) 51 L.Q.R. 590.

enforceable by the courts, conventions are not.[76] The major convention upon which the constitution is built is the constitutional principle known as the rule of law. This is based upon the practice of liberal democracies of the western world.[77] It means that what is done officially must be done in accordance with law.[78]

In Europe, where an entrenched constitution is the touchstone for legitimacy of government,[79] there might be a general grant of power to the executive, and a bill of rights to protect the individual. In the British tradition, which New Zealand is alone in following in this respect, public bodies must point to a specific authority to act as they do.[80] Thus we rely upon numerous specific grants of authority to the various organs of government, a much more flexible approach.

New Zealand might choose to adopt an entrenched constitution, but this would mean adopting a new approach to public law. In Canada, the newly renamed Constitution Act 1982 attributed to itself a position of legal paramountcy.[81] On the model of the American Constitution there was to be no higher legal authority. This has meant that the Supreme Court of Canada has had to become increasingly involved in the political arena.

Indeed, it is a debatable point whether New Zealand has lost anything by not having an entrenched constitution. Not only would an entrenched constitution require the courts to assume a greater, more controversial role, thereby increasing the possibility of political selection of judges, but entrenched constitutions also tend to become out of date. This is due to the difficulty of amending them to take into account changes in circumstances. In Australia it was this latter aspect which was the underlying cause of the sacking of the Whitlam government in 1975.

An entrenched constitution is in no way a guarantee of better government, nor necessarily a limitation upon excessive legislative independence. Those countries which suffer most from military coups, revolutions, putsches and similar upheavals normally have entrenched constitutions. The way in which society functions, the emotional attachment to democratic processes, are a better safeguard than a so-called written constitution.

Because in Canada and Australia authority is shared between the federal and provincial or state parliaments, there must be some higher authority which determines who shall have what power or responsibility. As a unitary state, there is

---

76 *Madzimbamuto v. Lardner-Burke* [1969] 1 A.C. 645 (P.C.); N.O. 1968 (2) S.A. 284.

77 Robert Heuston, *Essays in Constitutional Law* (2nd edn, London: Stevens and Son, 1964), 40–41.

78 *Arthur Yates and Co Pty Ltd v The Vegetable Seeds Committee* (1945) 72 C.L.R. 37, 66 per Latham C.J.

79 Hardin, I. and N. Lewis, *The Noble Lie*: *The British Constitution and the Role of Law* (London: Hutchinson, 1987), 7.

80 *Entick v Carrington* (1765) 19 State Tr. 1030 per Lord Camden.

81 s 52.

no need for the New Zealand constitution to be entrenched, apportioning authority and placing limits on the powers of Parliaments.

It is generally agreed that Parliament is a sovereign body, able to enact, repeal or amend any law, including any self-imposed limitations. Such limitations are only effective in a federal state, where limitations on capacity are, by definition, part of the constitutional structure. Short of adopting a federal system of government precisely to entrench a constitution, it is doubtful whether any constitution would be held by the courts to be truly entrenched.

In August 1998 the Supreme Court of Canada considered the question of the Canadian constitution being circumvented by a referendum, thereby affirming the sovereignty of the people. But it felt that political institutions draw their legitimacy from the rule of law, which precluded such action.[82] In the New Zealand context, this would mean that any attempt to introduce a truly entrenched constitution would threaten the legitimacy of the established legal order, because of its reliance upon inherited authority.

Revision of constitutional arrangements to reflect national identity requires agreement as to what precisely is New Zealand's national identity. The Maori and Pakeha cultural heritage, the special position of the Maori and their relationship with the Crown, are all aspects which are currently reflected in the New Zealand constitution. An entrenched constitution would be alien to New Zealand's constitutional traditions, but would make formal entrenchment of the Treaty of Waitangi into the constitution easier (assuming for the moment that this was necessary or desirable). However, whether this would be acceptable to the Pakeha majority is unclear.

Although some may argue that New Zealand's present system is *ad hoc* and lacking in conceptual uniformity, this is itself a reflection of national identity. There has traditionally been a reluctance to address strongly theoretical issues. Nor, in fact, is the constitution lacking in a theoretical basis. The present system reflects both a degree of inclusiveness and a flexibility that would be hard to emulate in a deliberately constructed constitution. This does not preclude the adoption of such a constitution. But the rationale for such an innovation would have to be developed, and would be at least as important a question as the composition of any such constitution.

Such pragmatism leads to considerable constitutional flexibility, but one which is bounded, not by strict rules of jurisdiction, but rather more by expectations and accepted ways of acting – the principles of the rule of law, for instance, and quasi-binding or binding convention. In the 1980, centre-left neo-liberalism drove radical economic reforms which amounted, in their eventual development, to significant political, structural and economic change. They were not inhibited by the pragmatic and flexible constitution, and the national tendency to pragmatism and the expense of principle allowed – if not encouraged – piecemeal reform, which led a decade later to formal constitutional reform.

82 'Breaking New Ground' (1998) 111(135) Maclean's 18.

4.5 Conclusion

Constitutional flexibility, in the sense of the hard or the soft constitution, is distinct from the narrower question of democracy. However, the political ethos which underpins the formal constitution also affects the operation of the constitution. Whether the former is liberalism or authoritarianism, it influences the ways in which the constitution is seen by the people, and thus functions on a daily basis. In part this is related to the question of the proper scope and reach of government, but it also involves questions of how the nature of a constitution can contribute to the stability of the regime. Flexibility leads to stability, because the constitution is able to freely adapt itself to changing circumstances. However, too much flexibility can also be dangerous, and the determining question is how the constitution is perceived, whether this be liberally, narrowly or widely.

Chapter 5
Authoritarianism

5.1 Introduction

In the previous chapter we began to consider how the nature of a constitution can contribute to the stability of the regime, in particular through the underlying ethos or *Grundnorm* of the constitution. The absence of a clear underlying principle is likely to increase the prospect of instability, through excessive or insufficient constitutional rigidity. It is also true that stability may lead to flexibility, though this may not occur if the constitution is rigid but other countervailing influences contribute to stability, for instance through consistent economic growth.

Authoritarian regimes, generally speaking, tend to concentrate power and authority. There may be an element of diffusion, depending upon circumstances, such as through the creation of competing elements, designed to act as a check upon each other. In concentrating power they may have either a hard or a soft constitution (perhaps more commonly hard than soft), but real power is often as not, particularly in the modern era, not vested in the legal system, but rather in the political leadership. Centralization of authority also tends to lead to a degree of homogeneity; even in a disparate state centralization can stifle or encourage creativity according to the whim of the leadership. The short- and medium-term success or failure of such a state is also dependent upon the whim of the leadership. The long-term success is a matter which is less certain, as shall be explored in Chapter 5.

5.2 Egypt

It has commonly been argued that the inundation of the Nile Valley of northern Africa through the annual flooding of the river Nile was eventually to lead to the development of cultivation and ultimately to a settled civilization. This was because it encouraged intensive agriculture,[1] and all which developed from that. The precarious nature of the flood – too much and the soil would be washed away, too little and there would be insufficient to ensure a harvest – required strong centralized government, including the use of levies for public works, writing and

1 See Robert C. Allen, 'Agriculture and the origins of the state in ancient Egypt', *Explorations in Economic History*, 34 (1997): 135–54; Arthur Mirsky, 'Influence of geologic factors on ancient Egyptian civilization', *Journal of Geoscience Education*, 45 (1997): 415.

record-keeping, and of taxation.[2] The waters had to be harnessed and this had to be done in a timely fashion, or there would be famine and disease in the following season. This harnessing of the productive or potentially destructive energy of the river might be undertaken by a single family or a small community, but only a stable political environment afforded the peace and stability requisite for even that small-scale enterprise to be safely and regularly undertaken. It was more efficient to band together in increasingly large and complex communities, for the good of all, and hence the good of the individual.

In comparatively early times the Nile valley developed what is now classed as the pre-dynastic state (or states) of Egypt. They were states because they were political entities which brought together for a common purpose people of many different families, tribes, villages, and towns. Unity of purpose – in this case the cultivation of the land while the annual inundation provided sufficient water for a crop – required unity of government. The relative simplicity of the requirement produced a relatively simple solution – a single leader. This individual was at once the organizational focus for those public works and private enterprise which were required, as well as the intermediary through which the people might seek the intercession of the many gods with which the creative imagination of the Egyptians peopled the skies. The control of the rains was beyond the direct powers even of the divine Pharaoh (as the leader was styled from early times in Egypt), but he might seek the blessings of the gods through the observance of the proper religious ceremonies.

The Pharaoh also owed his[3] political pre-eminence to his control of the army,[4] which in itself may be seen as mastery of technology having constitutional consequences. Loss of crops due to a failure in the flood (or excessive flooding)[5] could, and sometimes did, lead to political change,[6] despite the Pharaoh's control

2 See, generally, David A. Warburton, *State and economy in ancient Egypt: fiscal vocabulary of the New Kingdom* (Göttingen, 1997).

3 Hatchepsut, in the eighteenth dynasty, ruled as a female Pharaoh, not as a queen regnant. Cleopatra, and others of her Macedonian Lagidæ line, were of the post-dynastic Ptolemaic era; See Joyce Tyldesley, *Hatchepsut: the female pharaoh* (London, 1996); Michel Chauveau, *Cleopatra: beyond the myth* (Ithaca, 2002).

4 See Nigel Strudwick, *The administration of Egypt in the Old Kingdom* (London, 1985).

5 The Egyptians realized quite well that their prosperity and welfare depended on the health of the river Nile. This river provided its people with most of what they needed to survive: fish and wildlife, mud for building materials, a 'highway' for easy transportation, and papyrus for writing. Most importantly, the Nile floods annually from June to October, watering the ground and replenishing the soil with a rich fertile layer of silt; The Egyptians called their land kmt ('the Black land') after this layer of silt. The real heartland of Egypt consisted of a long thin strip of land along the Nile that was never more than a few kilometres wide. Outside of this strip was the 'Red land', the desert.

6 The Biblical ten plagues of Egypt could be seen as an example of technology having constitutional effects – Moses and the elders of Israel contended with the priests of Egypt

of the army. Often it was the general of a victorious army who took the throne of a Pharaoh who showed himself incapable of rule through his inability to intercede successfully with the gods. Between the Middle and the New Kingdoms, beginning about 1700 BC (the Second Intermediate Period), a series of unpredictable floods struck the Nile and Egypt, and at least partly as a result of this failure of technology,[7] fragmented Egypt into two kingdoms.[8] The sphere of influence of each Pharaoh was circumscribed by the physical limitations of the ruler's ability to exercise control, the poverty of his treasury, and the parochial nature of the worship of his attendant gods and goddesses. North and south (Lower and Upper Egypt respectively) looked to the Near East and Mediterranean, and to Africa, and developed similar though distinct identities.

Egypt's geopolitics were similar to and yet also very different from those of Mesopotamia.[9] Both cultures had evolved in hot dry river valleys that required irrigation, which in turn required a comparatively advanced and robust form of organization, and a strong government that led in turn to the development of civilization.[10] The Egyptians depended so much on irrigation and the high level of organization and authority needed to maintain it, that they considered their rulers, the Pharaohs, gods[11] – though it is true that the rulers of the city states of early Mesopotamia were also ascribed divine status due to their role as intermediaries of the gods (if not indeed actually descended from the gods).

In Egypt there was a direct correspondence between the power and effectiveness of these god-kings and the country's prosperity, which itself depended on the floods' regularity and the effectiveness of the irrigation system that was required to take full and efficient advantage of it.[12] The greater the success the organized irrigation was, the greater the need for a central organization to maintain the

---

for mastery (Exodus, 7–10); See Richard D. Patterson, 'Wonders in the heavens and on the earth: Apocalyptic imagery in the Old Testament', *Journal of the Evangelical Theological Society*, 43 (2000): 385–403.

7 This was not merely a failure of nature, for the annual inundation was merely the first part of a technological process largely controlled by the state.

8 See K.S.B. Ryholt, *The Political Situation in Egypt during the Second Intermediate Period, c.1800–1550 BC* (Copenhagen, 1997).

9 See Gwendolyn Leick, *Mesopotamia: the invention of the city* (London, 2001).

10 See David Warburton, *Egypt and the Near East: politics in the Bronze Age* (Neuchâtel, 2001); Bruce G. Trigger, *Early civilizations: ancient Egypt in context* (Cairo, 1993).

11 See Regine Schulz and Matthias Seidel (eds), *Egypt: the world of the Pharaohs* (Köln, 1998). Whilst the Mesopotamian rulers were also seen as gods, this might be seen as due to the need for the people to have an intermediary with the gods not dwelling on earth. More importantly, each city boasted its own god-king, and there was no comparable unity as found in Egypt; HIH Prince Takahito Mikasa of Japan (ed.), 'Monarchies and socio-religious traditions in the ancient Near East' (International Congress of Human Sciences in Asia and North Africa, Cairo, 1984).

12 See Allen.

systems necessary to ensure its success. The control of agricultural technology led to a strongly centralized government – and in turn the centralized government fostered intensive agriculture which depended upon the careful use of the available technology, limited though it was.[13] The maintenance of a standing army for the protection of the country from aggressors, and for the occasional conquest of neighbouring countries, also gave the Pharaoh political power. It further assisted in the centralizing of authority in the state, as well as the development of the notion of the state (as distinct from a loose collection of city states into which Egypt sometimes briefly fell in times of crisis).

It would be unduly simplistic to assist that the irrigation of the Nile river led to the development of the Egyptian monarchy. But it would nevertheless appear true that the technological and logistical implications of the systematic use of irrigation, the maintenance of a permanent civil bureaucracy for the service of the Pharaoh and the gods of Egypt, and of the standing army which was necessary for the defence of the Pharaoh, gods and land, were instrumental in the development of the pharaonic kingdom.

The centralization of power in the hands of an authoritarian ruler was effective in ensuring a relatively stable and efficient government in an era where weakness meant division and subjugation by outside forces. A clear process for selecting the ruler (in contrast to the Roman model in later centuries) helped maintain stability, as did a strong religious element to the constitution; the king was not merely the temporal ruler, but also a god. However, concentrating power in the hands of an individual, untrammelled by institutional or constitutional limitations excepting religious norms and expectations, rendered the state liable to decay or weakness under a less than capable pharaoh.

5.3 Political collapse and *laissez-faire* economies

The collapse of communism in eastern Europe was primarily a politically-driven change to the legal system, spurred by external developments, primarily the weakened state of the Soviet Union and the ideological poverty of the system which it purported to represent.[14] However, it constituted a paradigm shift for the legal systems concerned.

---

13 Here, technology is largely agricultural, in particular the use of irrigation. Other major civilizations have also depended upon irrigation – or been created by them – as, for example, the Khmer kingdom; See Charles Higham, *The civilization of Angkor* (London, 2001).

14 Cynthia B. Schultz and Tamara Raye Crockett, 'Economic development, democratization, and environmental protection in Eastern Europe', *Boston College Environmental Affairs Law Review*, 18 (1990): 53.

The Communist era was marked by a history of inefficient industrialization in Eastern Europe,[15] guided by the region's centralized political leadership. It was chiefly responsible for a long inventory of ecological disasters, and has left a legacy of pernicious, long-term environmental contamination.[16] Economies however can evolve more quickly, giving opportunities for business entrepreneurs, including privatization.[17]

The fall of communism and the rise of nationalism in central and eastern Europe created a large number of new states that qualify as developing countries economically while they undergo this political transition. They have begun interacting with the industrialized countries accordingly.[18] For many observers, the recent transition phenomenon represents one of the two most important economic developments of the twentieth century, the other being the Great Depression of the 1930s.[19] According to Stern, transition involves 'the establishment of a competitive market economy where central planning once prevailed, including the full range of institutions that are required to support a decentralised economy'.[20] But it has not been wholly successful.[21]

Business takes advantage of privatization, but most of all of opportunities to embark on new ventures hitherto prohibited. The more marginal the opportunity the greater the return. However, this is rarely productive investment. The encouragement of longer-term investment might require deregulation to be gradually implemented. Yet, this has seldom been the case in eastern Europe since the late 1980s.

---

15 See Vlad Sobell, 'The CMEA's Future: The Demise of the Soviet-Centered Model', RAD Background Report/17, Radio Fred Europe Research Reports, 17 January 1989, at 2.

16 See Cornelius van der Veen, 'Facts and figures on Rhine pollution', *International Business Lawyer*, 9(2) (1981): 41–52; D.J. Peterson, *Troubled lands: the legacy of Soviet environmental destruction* (Boulder, 1993).

17 Bruno Dallago, Gianmaria Ajani and Bruno Grancelli (eds), *Privatisation and entrepreneurship in post-socialist countries: economy, law, and society* (New York, 1992). Privatization is a set of policies designed to curtail the size and influence of the public sector through the sale of public assets; Mariusz Mark Dobek, *The Political logic of privatisation* (Westport, 1993) 1.

18 Vinod Rege, 'Economies in transition and developing countries: prospects for greater co-operation in trade and economic fields', *Journal of World Trade (Law-Economics-Public Policy)* 27(1) (1993): 83–115.

19 Nauro Campos and Fabrizzio Coricelli, 'Growth in Transition: What We Know, What We Don't, and What We Should', *Journal of Economic Literature*, 40 (2002): 793–836.

20 Nicholas Stern, *Transition: Private Sector Development and the Role of Financial Institutions* (London, 1994) Working paper no 13. XY/N-1.

21 Martin Krygier and Adam Czarnota (eds), *The Rule of Law After Communism* (Brookfield 1998); P. Sarcević, *Privatisation in Central and Eastern Europe* (London, 1992).

One example of an eastern European country undergoing the process of marketization is Bulgaria. Since the fall of Communism in 1989 Bulgaria embraced economic reform and is gradually becoming a viable investment market. The goal was to achieve 'complete intellectual and moral reconstruction' for total economic restructuring to occur and for the establishment of a new institutional system.[22] Bulgaria's strategic geographic location provides easy access to the European, Asian and North African markets. The lack of ethnical tensions makes the country a centre of economic and political stability on the Balkans. The costs of Bulgarian labour are significantly lower than the European average and various trade agreements with neighbouring countries ensure a duty-free movement of goods and services within a market of 550 million consumers.[23]

Yet, Bulgaria's favourable geographic location and low labour cost failed to attract foreign investors. Despite the great advantages Bulgaria offers, there were concerns based on recent political and economic history. Internally, fears of inflation, an inefficient judiciary, an uncertain legislative framework, inefficient government bureaucracy, a protracted privatization process, and corruption continued to deter foreign investment.[24] Internally, however, the picture was slightly different. As in most of post-Communist eastern Europe, domestic businesses flourished, often sporadically,[25] but in a relatively unregulated manner similar to the growth of the US economy during the nineteenth century.

Even in areas not normally thought of as 'commercial' there were opportunities for business and business models in post-Communist Eastern Europe. With the old hierarchical structures disintegrating and cultural policy largely dismantled throughout Central and Eastern Europe, the issue of privatization and the concomitant threat of a commercialization or 'marketization'[26] of the arts and culture began to dominate the policy debates.[27] As Schuster has argued,

---

22 See Csaba Varga, 'Transformation to Rule of Law From No-Law: Societal Contexture of the Democratic Transition in Central and Eastern Europe', *Connecticut Journal of International Law*, 8 (1993): 487, 488.

23 Bulgarian Foreign Investment Agency, 'Bulgarian Business Guide: Legal, Tax, and Accounting Aspects' 6 (2002), available at <http://www.bfia.org> (as at 19 December 2003).

24 Dora Djilianova, 'To be or not to be: What went right in the Bulgarian foreign Investment climate after 1997', *Thomas Jefferson Law Review*, 25 (2002): 223.

25 As in the growth of the opportunist 'black market'.

26 That is, a movement away from a centrally planned economy and toward a market system integrated with the world economy; Emily Stoper and Emilia Ianeva, 'Democratisation and women's employment policy in post-Communist Bulgaria', *Connecticut Journal of International Law*, 12 (1996): 9.

27 A. van Hemel and N. van der Welen (eds), *Privatisation/desetatisation and culture. Conference reader for the Circle Round Table 1997* (Amsterdam, 1997).

privatization became a 'buzzword' indiscriminately used for a whole range of processes and rationales for policy action.[28]

Although the arts and culture were subject to governmental control and censorship in the party-states of the Warsaw Pact, the supply of artistic and cultural goods and services was plentiful, and widely accessible. It was also heavily subsidized, which in turn led to what would be seen, to a free marketer, as a distortion of the economy. With the demise of socialism as an economic and political system, and the fall of the Berlin Wall, which was widely – though perhaps inaccurately perceived as the victory of the capitalist west – concerns arose as to what the change of systems might mean for the future of the arts in Central and Eastern Europe. This uncertainty was felt equally strongly in the Newly Independent States (NIS) of the former Soviet Union,[29] including the Russian Federation itself.

Because of the tremendous political, economic and social challenges of the transition from controlled socialist-style economy to broadly capitalist economy, it was inevitable that this period be marked by uncertainty and disruption. A widespread privatization of cultural assets, if not a complete abandonment of the support of culture by the state, was the logical if undesired outcome of the revolution after the immediate post-1989 euphoria had subsided; though a similar withdrawal of support was also discernible in the free market west during the 1980s and the heyday of liberalization policies. Many countries in the region (central and eastern Europe) saw reforms as 'the march through the "valley of death" [take] its toll',[30] with the initial dismantling of certain cultural institutions such as cultural centres, movie houses, theatres, and youth and music clubs.[31] Industrial enterprises and scientific institutions, especially those with military links also suffered significantly during this period.

Although the cultural industries[32] have mostly been transferred to the private or market sector, the state has not relinquished its primary responsibility for the institutions of high culture in the region. Moreover, a third, or non-profit, sector has also developed between the state and the market as a result of the loss of certain forms of state patronage and of pre-existing, less institutionalized venues

---

28 J.M. Schuster, 'Deconstructing a Tower of Babel: Privatisation, decentralisation and devolution as ideas in good currency in cultural policy', *Voluntas*, 8(3) (1997): 261–82.

29 Stefan Toepler, 'From Communism to civil society? the arts and the nonprofit sector in Central And Eastern Europe', *Journal of Arts Management, Law and Society*, 30(1) (2000): 7.

30 O. Novotny, 'Key issues in the transformation of culture in the post-socialist countries: With particular reference to the Slovak Republic', *European Journal of Cultural Policy*, 1(2) (1995): 217–23, 218.

31 G. Muschter, 'Kunstlerforderung in der Bundesrepublik Deutschland', in R. Strachwitz and S. Toepler (eds), *Kulturforderung: Mehr als Sponsoring* (Wiesbaden, 1993), pp. 35–40.

32 Including publishing, cinema, recording, and the media.

of cultural activity and production in the socialist era.[33] These cultural industries have been relatively successful because of such enterprises. Generally speaking, the degree of economic success seems to depend upon the infrastructure – political, social, economic, and legal.

A decade of experience with the transition from centrally planned to market economies has shown that the strength of a country's market-supporting 'institutions' has a powerful effect on the transition success.[34] The decisions made by former countries of the Soviet Union – newly independent states ('NIS') – to build free market economies require appropriate legal structures. New civil codes have been successfully adopted in many of the NIS. Work on the new Civil Code in Ukraine based on free-market principles is still in progress.[35] The form of the legal system may not be influenced by the business community, but business is still able to take advantage of the reforms which have occurred, particularly privatization.

The legal codes entrench 'western'-style free market models, including private ownership of business enterprises. Over the past decade, privatization has been advanced as these countries have moved to dismantle their previous, dominantly state-owned economies.[36]

The massive redistribution of property that occurred reshaped not only their economic systems but their political and social systems as well. However, in the absence of significant restructuring, privatization alone could not solve the underlying problems facing the previously state-owned enterprises.[37] A hurdle that had to be overcome in privatization was the fact that Communist rule was long intertwined within the countries of Eastern Europe, and that the judicial system was directly affected by it. Consequently, it has become very hard to find judges who are qualified to rule on the actions and policies of their former Communist rulers.[38] Nor was the rule of law in its broader aspects necessarily fully embedded.[39]

More significantly, mass privatization left new owners and managers with the responsibility of implementing the investments and reforms necessary to make

33 See Toepler, 'From Communism to civil society?'.

34 Bernard S. Black and Anna S. Tarassova, 'Institutional reform in transition: A case study of Russia', *Supreme Court Economic Review*, 10 (1993): 211.

35 Alexander Biryukov, 'The Doctrine of Dualism of Private Law in the Context of Recent Codifications of Civil Law: Ukrainian Perspectives', *Annual Survey of International and Comparative Law*, 8 (2002): 53–4.

36 See Varga, 'Transformation to Rule of Law From No-Law: Societal Contexture of the Democratic Transition in Central and Eastern Europe'.

37 See International Labour Organisation, *World Labour Report* (London, 1995), p. 64. See Mariusz Dobek, *The political logic of privatisation* (Westport, 1993), p. 68 (discussing the steps that Poland made in privatization).

38 See Mark Gibney, 'Decommunization: Human Rights Lessons from the Past and Present, and Prospects for the Future', *Denver International Law and Policy*, 23 (1994): 7, 88.

39 See Varga, 'Transformation to Rule of Law From No-Law: Societal Contexture of the Democratic Transition in Central and Eastern Europe'.

their enterprises viable.[40] These investments and reforms were created through free trade in the newly capitalized markets.[41] Some of the new enterprises were run by the 'old guard' – bureaucrats from the Communist era, but most passed to the new business elite.

Post-Communist eastern Europe saw business reacting enthusiastically to the relaxation of previously strict and prohibitive legal regulation. The immediately consequence, especially where political uncertainly remained, was frequently unregulated growth. It was often not in productive sectors – such an industry and agriculture – but rather where large short-term profits could be most readily made.[42]

The potential for profits was greatest where embarking on new enterprises, rather than reviving inefficient Communist-era enterprises. Unfortunately, this meant decay in what were often the more productive sectors of the economy (such as heavy industry), while the ephemeral grew. But business reacted to deregulation by seizing any opportunity now allowed to make money, in preference to maintaining the old economies. This encouraged an opportunistic spirit of *laissez faire*, the almost inevitable result of the ending of centralized planning.

The collapse of the political elite led to the rapid decline of centralization and the advent of unregulated economic, social and political change. This was perhaps the inevitable result of the loss of central leadership. But perhaps more fundamentally, even where the leadership remains intact, it represents a prescriptive leadership, rather than the management, of the state. This in turn leads to a dependence culture, and a loss of internal self-regulation, self-reliance and innovation. Such a constitutional model is almost inevitably doomed to failure when external factors, such as the loss of a patron state, impose new or unexpected tensions and challenges. Communist regimes collapsed in eastern Europe because they lack real local support. Their authoritarian nature inhibited real commitment from the people, and precluded the development of legitimacy through acquiescence or longevity of rule.

5.4 Conclusion

Over-centralization, and the concentration of power in the hands of an individual, or an elite group, renders a state liable to collapse due to the weakness of the

40 See International Labour Organisation, *World Labour Report* (London, 1995), p. 64.

41 See Varga, 'Transformation to Rule of Law from No-Law: Societal Contexture of the Democratic Transition in Central and Eastern Europe', 492 (discussing how the transition period enabled former Communist countries to set historic new directions for their future).

42 This was often in marginally legal or illegal activities, such as gambling, drugs, and prostitution.

leadership. This can occur due to the advent of a less capable individual leader, or it may be due to the collapse of a sponsor state or the intellectual or economic poverty of the system. Constitutional continuity is inhibited by a lack of institutional strength independent of the personality of the ruler or the political elite – the collapse of the empire of Alexander the Great after his death is a classic case in point. There was great strength through the military and political strength of the leader, but the unifying element was not a bureaucracy, or a permanent principle or national identity, but the leader himself. Upon his death state failure, to use the term around which this book is based, was inevitable. It was not inherent – or constitutional – strength.

Whatever the cause, an overly rigid, authoritarian state is unlikely to engender long-term commitment from the population unless it is underpinned by an ideology which genuinely grips the population. It succeeded in Egypt because of the strength of the religious heritage of the state; it failed in eastern Europe because communist regimes were widely and increasingly seen as impositions from the Soviet Union and were insufficiently flexible socially, politically, or economically, to meet the demands of the population in a more complex political and economic environment.

Chapter 6
Doctrinaire Liberalism

6.1 Introduction

The United States of America and the United Kingdom may both be seen as classic examples of doctrinaire liberal states. There are certain constitutional implications of that status, not least of which may be categorized by asking the question of whether democracy itself hinders or promotes state success.

The doctrinaire liberal regimes are those that promote the freedom of the individual, the benefits of hard work and industry, and the perceived evils of interventionist government. North American, Australasian and Western European countries generally may be classified as belonging broadly to this model, although the development of the welfare state (particularly in the latter two regions) has affected the application of the model to some degree. But from the growth of democracy, first in the United Kingdom (we are here excluding the ancient Greek democracies, and the various localized and short-lived experiments in democracy elsewhere, due to their relative impermanence), and then, through the nineteenth century, on the continent of Europe, liberalism became the established model. Sometimes this is simply referred to as democracy, but it is more than this. Democracy reflects a particular sociological and political approach. Belief in democracy is enjoined upon us because we are in liberal regimes. This, and a strong belief in the rule of law, and a preference for *laissez-faire* principles, underpin such states.

6.2 Liberalism as a legal/political influence

When we think about liberalism today we seem to be confronted with at least these two competing images.[1] First, there is a 'classical' liberalism emphasizing the virtues of tolerance, diversity and openness together with ambivalence about moral truth. This classical version is epitomized by Nagel's indecisive liberal and Flanders' and Swann's ironic injunction against cannibalism. John Stuart Mill's work is imbued with some of this ethos of tolerance and, more recently, John Gray, the English political philosopher, has referred to it as the 'modus vivendi',

---

1 There are many ways to distinguish liberalisms from ranging from Isaiah Berlin's Two Views of Liberty to the disputes between egalitarian liberals (represented by John Rawls (A Theory of Justice (Cambridge, 1971))) and libertarians represented by the likes of Robert Nozick or Frederick Hayek.

that is, the idea of liberalism as a procedure for organizing relations among diverse communities.[2] It is also reflected in a disinclination within at least one liberal strand of international law to make judgements about the politics of the state. The United Nation's approach to membership after about 1950, as anticipated in the Admissions Case, is an example of this form of liberalism.[3]

However, there is a second image of what it means to be a liberal. This is liberalism (sometimes characterized as neo-liberalism) endowed with a sort of moralistic fervour, a conviction and, at times, an intolerance of the illiberal. Louis Hartz, in his study of American liberalism, described it as 'this fixed, dogmatic liberalism of a liberal way of life' and traced its roots in American liberalism's lack of internal enemies and resultant lack of plausible alternatives.[4] This liberalism produces a profoundly illiberal 'conformitarianism' according to Hartz. In various writings about international affairs, Francis Fukayama's liberal triumphalism is the starkest example of this liberalism but it is there, also, in Fernando Tesón's strident Kantian theory of international law, Michael Reisman's peremptory dismissal of the illiberal in his pro-democratic intervention work and in Anne-Marie Slaughter's distinctions between liberal and non-liberal states.[5] It is the liberalism of certainty, or what we may call 'liberal anti-pluralism'; a liberalism that can be exclusive and illiberal in its effects. In international law, it differs from the Charter liberalism identified above most obviously in its lack of tolerance for non-liberal regimes.[6]

---

2 John Gray, *The Two Faces of Liberalism* (Cambridge, 2000). Louis Hartz located this liberalism in a European tradition in which there was a 'sense of relativity … acquired through an internal experience of social diversity and social conflict'. *The Liberal Tradition in America* (New York, 1955), p. 14. This view of liberalism emphasizes the idea of open political process and pragmatic compromise over the competing idea of absolute rights and legal standards. It is liberalism as a mechanism for making political choices in a world of disagreement as opposed to liberalism as a system designed to erase those disagreements altogether.

3 *Membership Case*, ICJ Reports (1948).

4 Louis Hartz, *The Liberal Tradition in America* (New York, 1955), pp. 8–9. Curiously enough Hartz associates this with the constitutional fetishism which sees the Supreme Court 'resolve' moral dilemmas for the nation. It may be that this escape from politics and ethics is peculiarly American. It is no surprise given this tradition that the end of history and the triumph of liberal democracy have been proclaimed by American scholars nor that these American scholars have embraced a sort of legalism to pursue liberal ends at the international level.

5 Thomas M. Franck, 'The Emerging Right to Democratic Governance', 86 *American Journal of International Law* (1992): 46–91; Fernando Tesón, 'The Kantian Theory of International Law', 92 *Columbia Law Review* (1992): 53–102, at 54; Anne-Marie Slaughter, 'International Law in a World of Liberal States', *European Journal of International Law*, 6 (1994): 503–38.

6 Gerry Simpson, 'Two Liberalisms', 12 *European Journal of International Law* (2001): 537–72.

Slaughter's version of liberal theory builds upon Andrew Moravcsik's challenge to prevailing state-centric theories of international relations, including most prominently, realism. Like Moravcsik, Slaughter contests all the fundamental assumptions that realists make, namely (a) that states, the primary international actors, are rational, functionally identical, and unitary actors; (b) that states' preferences are exogenous and fixed; and (c) that the anarchic structure of the international systems create such uncertainty and mistrust that power, exercised in typically zero-sum games, is the only constant.[7]

Following Moravcsik, Slaughter argues that state preferences are not fixed or autonomous but are the aggregation of individual and group preferences and that these preferences are the primary determinant of what states do.[8] But while Moravcsik seeks to up-end traditional verities within political science, Slaughter's target is international law. Slaughter contends that international lawyers, through recourse to nebulous concepts such as 'sovereignty' and 'sovereign equality' and reliance on state-centric sources of legal obligation, have been, no less than the realists of political science, equally willing to treat states as so many indistinguishable 'black boxes' despite differences in political ideology and domestic institutions and equally oblivious to the impact of non-state entities, including subgovernmental units. Classical international law, with its fixation on liberal internationalist institutions on the model of the United Nations premised on hierarchical authority and universal membership, is increasingly irrelevant because it has failed to include the new, more effective modes of international governance emerging in the wake of the 'disaggregating' state.[9]

According to this latest version of liberal theory,[10] 'how States behave depends on how they are internally constituted'.[11] Liberal theory is not, however, a pale

7 See, for example, Anne-Marie Slaughter, 'International Law in a World of Liberal States', *European Journal of International Law*, 6 (1995): 503–38, at 507. See also Andrew Moravcsik, 'Taking Preferences Seriously: A Liberal heory of International Politics', *International Organisation*, 51 (1997): 513, at 516–24.

8 See, e.g., Anne-Marie Slaughter, 'International Law in a World of Liberal States', *European Journal of International Law*, 6 (1995): 503–538; Andrew Moravcsik, 'Taking Preferences Seriously: A Liberal Theory of International Politics', *International Organisation*, 51 (1997): 513; Anne-Marie Slaughter, 'A Liberal Theory of International Law', *Proceedings of the American Society of International Law* (2000): 1.

9 See, e.g., Anne-Marie Slaughter, 'The Real New World Order', *Foreign Affairs*, 76 (1997): 183. See also Anne-Marie Slaughter, 'Government Networks: The Heart of the Liberal Democratic Order', in Gregory H. Fox and Brad R. Roth (eds), *Democratic Governance and International Law* (Cambridge, 2000), p. 199; and Anne-Marie Burley, 'Toward an Age of Liberal Nations', *Harvard International Law Journal*, 33 (1992): 393–405.

10 See Gerry Simpson, 'Two Liberalisms', *European Journal of International Law*,12 (2001): 537–72.

11 Anne-Marie Slaughter, 'International Law in a World of Liberal States', *European Journal of International Law*, 6 (1995): 503–38, at 537.

application of the familiar interest-group or rent-seeking models applied by public choice theorists. It 'transforms states into governments':[12] unlike traditional international law, liberal theorists distinguish between types of regimes, including between liberal and non-liberal regimes. While Slaughter has wavered over time on how sharply distinctions between 'liberal' and 'non-liberal' need to be drawn,[13] she has consistently argued that liberal theory 'permits, indeed mandates, a distinction among different types of States based on their domestic political structure and ideology'.[14]

At the same time, however, Slaughter, again following Moravcsik, has suggested that liberal theory applies to all states, even totalitarian, authoritarian or theocratic regimes, since all 'can all be depicted as representative of some subset of actors in domestic and transnational society, even if it is a very small or particularistic slice'.[15] While its potential for universal applicability has consequences for liberal

12 See, e.g., Anne-Marie Slaughter, 'International Law in a World of Liberal States', *European Journal of International Law*, 6 (1995): 503–38, at 2.

13 The sharpest dichotomy between liberal and non-liberal appears in Anne-Marie Burley, 'Law Among Liberal States: Liberal Internationalism and the Act of State Doctrine', *Columbia Law Review*, 92 (1992): 1907. In this 1992 piece, Slaughter (then Burley) argued that liberal insights required rejecting the cornerstone of the international lawyers' pluralist project: the concept of universally applicable sources of law. Slaughter argued that, since only liberal states operate in a 'zone of law', courts in those states ought to use the act of state doctrine to repudiate the laws and legal system of non-liberal states; Slaughter argued that liberal courts ought to impose a badge of 'alienage' on non-liberal states. Ibid, at 1990. The act of state doctrine, she argued, ought to be used as a democratizing tool: to help 'nudge nonliberal states toward the liberal side of the divide'. Ibid, at 1912. Despite Slaughter's claims that the act of state doctrine has been applied in this fashion by US courts, there appears to be not a single judicial citation to Slaughter's controversial article since its publication and it is not clear whether even its author would today defend its central thesis. Slaughter's most recent work, on the relevance of transnational networks, avoids drawing such clear fault lines between liberal/non-liberal, but still maintains that 'the emerging transgovernmental order is concentrated among liberal democracies' of the West. Anne-Marie Slaughter, 'Government Networks: The Heart of the Liberal Democratic Order', in Gregory H. Fox and Brad R. Roth (eds), *Democratic Governance and International Law* (Cambridge, 2000), p. 199, at 201. See also Anne-Marie Slaughter, 'International Law in a World of Liberal States', *European Journal of International Law*, 6 (1995): 503–38, at 507. See also Andrew Moravcsik, 'Taking Preferences Seriously: A Liberal Theory of International Politics', *International Organisation*, 51 (1997): 513, at 12 ('I do subscribe to a distinction between liberal and non-liberal states as a positive predictor of how they are likely to behave in a wide variety of circumstances, including within or toward international organizations').

14 Anne-Marie Slaughter, 'International Law in a World of Liberal States', *European Journal of International Law*, 6 (1995): 503–38, at 504 (noting the growing body of evidence highlighting the 'distinctive quality of relations among liberal democracies').

15 Ibid., at 509. See also Andrew Moravcsik, 'Taking Preferences Seriously: A Liberal Theory of International Politics', *International Organisation*, 51 (1997): 513, at

theory's claims to analytical priority over rival accounts within political science,[16] Slaughter's liberal theory has not gone in this direction. Instead, liberal theory is promoted as a corrective to the inclinations of universalist international lawyers precisely because it 'permits more general distinctions among different categories of States based on domestic regime-type'.[17] The liberal view of international law builds upon the purportedly distinctive quality of legal relations among liberal democracies, and especially the members of the European Union and the system of human rights centred at Strasbourg.[18]

Slaughter's liberal theory has both a philosophical and an empirical basis and attempts to build a bridge between political science and law. It traces its origins to Immanuel Kant's prediction, in 1795, that liberal states would some day form a 'free federation' blessed by perpetual peace,[19] but it is most directly grounded in the work of Michael Doyle and other neo-Kantians who have attempted to provide empirical evidence of the 'liberal' or 'democratic' peace.[20] Slaughter builds on

518 (arguing that all states are 'representative institutions subject to capture and recapture, construction and reconstruction by coalitions of social actors').

16 See, e.g., Andrew Moravcsik, 'Taking Preferences Seriously: A Liberal Theory of International Politics', *International Organisation*, 51 (1997) 513, at 538–49.

17 Anne-Marie Slaughter, 'International Law in a World of Liberal States', *European Journal of International Law*, 6 (1995): 503–38, at 509. As Slaughter has suggested in presentations on liberal theory, this is because, even though non-liberal nations may 'represent' some particularistic segment of society, the small size and unity of that segment means that for all practical purposes the non-liberal state behaves much like the unitary actor of realist theory. Anne-Marie Slaughter, 'A Liberal Theory of International Law', presentation at Columbia Law School, 2 December 1999.

18 See, e.g., Anne-Marie Burley, 'Toward an Age of Liberal Nations', *Harvard International Law Journal*, 33 (1992): 393–405, at 402–3. See also Anne-Marie Burley and Walter Mattli, 'Europe Before the Court: A Political Theory of Legal Integration', *International Organisation*, 47(1) (1993): 41–76; Anne-Marie Burley, 'Democracy and Judicial Review in the European Community', *University of Chicago Legal Forum* (1992): 81; Anne-Marie Slaughter and Laurence R. Helfer, 'Toward a Theory of Effective Supranational Adjudication', *Yale Law Journal*, 107 (1997): 273–391; Walter Mattli and Anne-Marie Slaughter, 'Revisiting the European Court of Justice', *International Organisation*, 52 (1998): 177. See also Daniel S. Sullivan, 'Effective International Dispute Settlement Mechanisms and the Necessary Condition of Liberal Democracy', *Georgetown Law Journal* 81 (1993): 2369, at 2374–87.

19 See Anne-Marie Burley, 'Toward an Age of Liberal Nations', *Harvard International Law Journal*, 33 (1992): 393–405, at 394 (citing Kant's prerequisites for such a free federation, namely (1) co-operation among republics with market economies that respected equality before the law and private property rights; (2) an agreement between these republics to refrain from the use of force against one another; and (3) extensive international commerce). See Emmanuel Kant, *Perpetual Peace*, reprinted in Carl Joachim Friedrich (ed.), *The Philosophy of Kant* (New York, 1949), pp. 430–76.

20 Michael Doyle, 'Kant, Liberal Legacies and Foreign Affairs' in Michael E. Brown, Sean M. Lynn-Jones, and Steven E. Miller (eds), *Debating the Democratic Peace*

Kant's perceptiveness as well as the neo-Kantians' premise that liberal states do not go to war with one another.[21] At the same time, her version of liberal theory denies that it is either a normative or an abstract interdisciplinary exercise. Its 'unsentimental analysis of the domestic origins of international behaviour'[22] is purportedly grounded in positive fact.

Slaughter's liberal theory professes to be, first, an accurate description of that growing part of the world that is composed of liberal states. Liberal theory explains 'legal relations among States such as the United States, Canada, the Member States of the European Union, Japan, Australia, and New Zealand' and provides at least a 'point of departure' for 'conceptualizing the legal relations' of others (presumably those that are almost as democratic?), namely, 'among Argentina, Chile, Brazil, Ecuador, Mexico; Poland, Hungary, and the Czech Republic; Taiwan, South Korea, and the Philippines; India, Israel, and, with luck, South Africa'.[23] Much of liberal scholarship is accordingly devoted to showing how the growing number of states that are 'functioning democracies' – loosely defined as those with a freely elected government, a flourishing civil society according respect for human rights, and a free market that respects private property – 'strengthen and expand' international norms and institutions while enjoying the fruits of a 'separate' peace.[24]

Liberal theory assumes that liberal states will comply more readily with the treaties that they sign and that these treaties are more likely to be subject to effective judicial enforcement at either the international or domestic level (or both).[25] Liberal states are also more likely to turn to alternative mechanisms not captured by the traditional sources of international law (and that obviate the need for some

(Cambridge, 1996).

21 See, e.g., Anne-Marie Burley, 'Law Among Liberal States: Liberal Internationalism and the Act of State Doctrine', *Columbia Law Review*, 92 (1992): 1907, at 1914–16. See, generally, the contributions by Michael W. Doyle, Bruce Russett, and John M. Owen in Michael E. Brown et al. (eds), *Debating the Democratic Peace* (Cambridge, 1996).

22 See, e.g., Anne-Marie Burley, 'Toward an Age of Liberal Nations', *Harvard International Law Journal*, 33 (1992): 393–405, at 395; Anne-Marie Slaughter, 'International Law in a World of Liberal States', *European Journal of International Law*, 6 (1995): 503–38, at 509. See, generally, Jack S. Levy, 'Domestic Politics and War', in Robert I. Rotberg and Theodore K. Rabb (eds), *The Origin and Prevention of Major Wars* (Cambridge, 1988), p. 88 (discussing the 'liberal peace', the 'closest thing we have to an empirical law in the study of international relations').

23 Anne-Marie Burley, 'Toward an Age of Liberal Nations', *Harvard International Law Journal*, 33 (1992): 393–405, at 393.

24 Anne-Marie Slaughter, 'International Law in a World of Liberal States', *European Journal of International Law*, 6 (1995): 503–38, at 514–15.

25 Anne-Marie Burley, 'Toward an Age of Liberal Nations', *Harvard International Law Journal*, 33 (1992): 393–405, at 395. Slaughter's definition of a 'liberal state' faithfully adheres to Doyle's. See Doyle, 'Kant, Liberal Legacies, and Foreign Affairs', in Michael W. Doyle, Bruce Russett and John M. Owen in Michael E. Brown et al. (eds), *Debating the Democratic Peace* (Cambridge, 1996), pp. 5–6.

treaties altogether), including efforts by liberal judges to build a 'transnational community of law' through a readiness to cite one another's opinions, as well as through international obligations, co-operative ventures by liberal regulators on a range of issues from antitrust to criminal law enforcement, and transnational regulatory networks engaged in everything from securities regulation to the setting of interest rates by central banks.[26] Liberal theory also professes to explain the legal relations (or lack thereof) between liberal and non-liberal states, including the relative ineffectiveness of legal institutions attempted by 'mixed' groups of states.[27] Liberal theory speculates about but does not draw definitive conclusions about what causes the democratic peace or general law-abiding behaviour among liberal nations.

While Slaughter argues that the precise mapping of cause and effect for the democratic peace 'does not matter', she outlines the correlative attributes that characterize the world of liberal states as follows: (1) mutual assurances that inter-state disputes will not be resolved by military means; (2) representative governments secured by the separation of powers, constitutional guarantees of civil and political rights, juridical equality, and a functional judicial system dedicated to the rule of law; (3) market economies based on private property rights ensuring an economic sphere distinct from the state; (4) a dense network of transnational social and economic relations among individuals and groups; (5) informal ties between governmental elites, including direct meetings and communications among bureaucrats from different countries; and (6) the relative parity of security with economic and environmental issues, along with the breakdown of a firm distinction between 'foreign' and 'domestic' politics.[28]

---

26 Anne-Marie Slaughter, 'International Law in a World of Liberal States', *European Journal of International Law*, 6 (1995): 503–38, at 530 and 533–4; Anne-Marie Slaughter and Alec Stone Sweet, 'Assessing the Effectiveness of International Adjudication', in *Structures of World Order: Proceedings of the 89th Annual Meeting*. Washington D.C.: *American Society of International Law*: 91–3. See, generally, Anne-Marie Burley and Walter Mattli, 'Europe Before the Court: A Political Theory of Legal Integration', *International Organisation*, 47(1) (1993): 41–76.

27 See, e.g., Anne-Marie Slaughter, 'Government Networks: The Heart of the Liberal Democratic Order', in Gregory H. Fox and Brad R. Roth (eds), *Democratic Governance and International Law* (Cambridge, 2000), p. 199; Anne-Marie Slaughter, 'A Typology of Transjudicial Communication', *University of Richmond Law Review*, 29 (1995): 99; Anne-Marie Slaughter, 'The Real New World Order', *Foreign Affairs*, 76 (1997): 183.

28 See, e.g., Anne-Marie Slaughter, 'International Law in a World of Liberal States', *European Journal of International Law*, 6 (1995): 503–38, at 515. See also Anne-Marie Slaughter and Laurence R. Helfer, 'Toward a Theory of Effective Supranational Adjudication', *Yale Law Journal*, 107 (1997): 273–391 (contrasting the relative ineffectiveness of the International Court of Justice and the Human Rights Committee with the integrating successes achieved by the European Court of Justice and the European Court of Human Rights); Anne-Marie Burley, 'Toward an Age of Liberal Nations', *Harvard International Law Journal*, 33 (1992): 393–405, at 393 ('nonliberal states … are freer now

In more recent work on transnational contacts among subcomponents of liberal governments – that is, among liberal courts, regulatory agencies, executives and legislatures – Slaughter speculates that the emerging transgovernmental order is concentrated among Western industrialized states for a number of reasons: liberal nations' (slavish) devotion to the norms of separation of powers (and the quasi-autonomous governmental institutions that result), the 'unified foreign policy stance' that comes with the 'certainty' that conflicts will not become military confrontations, the macroeconomic interdependence that accompanies economic development among mature democracies, and shared political values of pluralism and tolerance.[29] Slaughter's liberal theory is, secondly, prescriptive. It is not content with merely trying to explain matters that classical international law and its state-centric sources of legal obligation leave out. It seeks to provide prescriptions to policy-makers intent on creating effective legal institutions and instruments that are useful because they are more firmly rooted in the way state preferences arise and take shape. The liberal theory of international relations, or 'transgovernmentalism', is accordingly presented as a 'blueprint for the international architecture of the 21st century', offering nothing less than 'answers to the most important challenges facing advanced industrial countries'.[30]

Notwithstanding normative disclaimers, Slaughter's sympathies for the law-making regimes and the political institutions of the West are never in doubt. The political message liberal theory conveys to international policy-makers is not subtle: 'hopes for international order should be pinned on our hopes for democracy'.[31] While Slaughter avoids the most provocative normative claims

---

than at any time since 1945 to pursue their ambitions, however defined, and when frustrated, to settle their grievances by force').

29 Anne-Marie Slaughter, 'International Law in a World of Liberal States', *European Journal of International Law*, 6 (1995): 503–38, at 510 and 511–14. Slaughter does not try to explain just how each of these six correlatives, intended to be congruent with those suggested by Kant, work in tandem to produce the liberal peace, but speculates that factor (1) 'establishes a different psychological and political context' for the resolution of disputes; that (2) assures the operation of civil society and makes available a neutral arbiter for private disputes; that (3) is an engine for social interaction that is a source of demand for legal rules and institutions and the stability these bring; that (4), (5) and (6) all inhibit governments from acting violently toward one another, and that the degree of transnational free market contacts between liberal states result in foreign and domestic policies that are increasingly 'subject to the same constraints'. Ibid, at 511–14.

30 Anne-Marie Slaughter, 'Government Networks: The Heart of the Liberal Democratic Order', in Gregory H. Fox and Brad R. Roth (eds), *Democratic Governance and International Law* (Cambridge, 2000), p. 199, at 201 and 221–6.

31 See, for example, Anne-Marie Burley, 'Toward an Age of Liberal Nations', *Harvard International Law Journal*, 33 (1992): 393–405, at 399–405; Anne-Marie Slaughter, 'Government Networks: The Heart of the Liberal Democratic Order', in Gregory H. Fox and Brad R. Roth (eds), *Democratic Governance and International Law* (Cambridge, 2000), p. 199, at 226; and Anne-Marie Slaughter, 'International Law in a World of Liberal

made by some of her fellow neo-Kantians, such as Fernando Tesón, she endorses the more restrained reformist agenda of scholars like Thomas Franck.[32] Unlike Tesón, who prescribes war against illiberal nations for the sake of bringing about Kant's perpetual peace,[33] Slaughter is the more tempered liberal, urging patient transmittal of liberal values over time (through the expansion of a 'liberal zone of law') as the more effective way to liberal peace.[34]

6.3 Constitutions in liberal states – informal limitations in New Zealand

Liberal states – those countries which have a prevailing liberal political ethos – exhibit a variety of constitutional structures. Curiously perhaps, but largely the result of the historical circumstances which formed them, the two oldest liberal democracies, the United States of America, and the United Kingdom, have constitutions which exhibit certain profound similarities and differences. The United States of America has an eighteenth-century 'rigid' constitution, entrenched, written and codified. In contrast to the United States, the United Kingdom has a flexible unwritten constitution, almost a non-constitution in a formal sense. New Zealand is in a similar situation, perhaps even more clearly so, for the United Kingdom is neither strictly a unitary state, nor has it a truly flexible constitution; the Act of Union 1706 (Eng),[35] and the various treaties under which it is a member of the European Union, limit its true sovereignty and uniformity.

But even in the case of New Zealand, rigidity is not absent. There is a type of manner and form entrenchment to escape from the Diceyan formula of parliamentary supremacy. Parliament is only sovereign when acting in a regulated manner.[36] The Electoral Act 1956 (NZ) attempted to introduce a form of statutory entrenchment (s 189), though it is doubtful whether this was legally effective, at least in a formal sense.

Perhaps our view of parliamentary sovereignty – which effectively requires that we acknowledge that there is a high degree constitutional flexibility (Parliament can change any law it wishes) – has changed since the mid-twentieth century. Newer concepts of self-embracing sovereignty (see Latham, Jennings and

States', *European Journal of International Law*, 6 (1995): 503–38, at 538. See also Brian Fitzgerald, 'An Emerging Liberal Theory of International Law and the Non-Enforcement of Foreign Public Laws', *Australian Yearbook of International Law*, 16 (1995): 311, at 315 (describing liberal theory's reliance on the liberal peace).

32 Anne-Marie Burley, 'Toward an Age of Liberal Nations', *Harvard International Law Journal*, 33 (1992): 393–405, at 403.

33 Ibid, at 404.

34 See, e.g., Fernando R. Tesón, *A Philosophy of International Law* (Boulder, 1998), pp. 62–3. For Tesón's answer to the 'neoliberals', see ibid, at 65–6.

35 Union with Scotland Act 1706 (6 Anne c 11) (Eng.).

36 Richard Latham, 'What is an Act of Parliament?', *King's Council,* (March 1939): 152–62.

Heuston), rather than asking 'Can Parliament bind itself?' say that the question should be 'What comprises Parliament?' or 'How must Parliament combine formally to express itself?' In such an approach constitutional flexibility – or rather specifically, the ability of Parliament to bind its successors – is more limited.

This requires consideration of the rules defining Parliament. Parliament of the United Kingdom comprises the Queen, the House of Lords and the House of Commons; thus requiring (formally at least) three separate assents[37] – except for legislation under the provisions of the Parliament Acts 1911–49 (UK). The Parliament of New Zealand – which was the 'General Assembly of New Zealand' to 1986,[38] lost the upper house, the Legislative Council, in 1950. The Queen replaced the Governor-General in 1986 (though the latter remains, as representative of The Queen). This means that Parliament post-1986 is not the same as before, despite s 14(2) of the Constitution Act 1986 (NZ), perhaps requiring a deeming provision.[39] But in political reality – and probably legally also – there is no doubting that Parliament remains the sovereign entity, and is the lineal descendant of the legislature established at the advent of British rule over New Zealand in 1840. Hence there is some flexibility in the formal provisions, and the constitutional is interpreted, and operates, in a pragmatic, not a technical, manner.

Having observed that, parliamentary assent must be real, as seen in a 1976 case in Australia.[40] Formal words of enactment are required. An enacting clause is also needed – Heuston thought there must be formal words of enactment,[41] but despite *The Prince's Case*[42] (1606) it may not be a formal requirement, and has not been included in reprinted statutes since 1979. Rules for identifying Parliament's statutes are prescribed however in s 4 of the Acts and Regulations Publication Act 1989 (NZ): the Chief Parliamentary Counsel prints and publishes statutes.

In *Attorney-General (NSW) v Trethowan*,[43] (1931) the Privy Council looked at New South Wales statutes, and concluded that it did not follow that sovereign legislatures couldn't be bound by manner and form restrictions. In *Harris v Minister of the Interior*[44] (1952) the South Africa Parliament was found to be sovereign, and the court endorsed the manner and form school, where a requirement for a special vote was binding – until it was followed Parliament had not acted. In *Bribery Commissioner v Ranasinghe*[45] (1965) the Privy Council held that manner and form entrenchment provisions did not limit the sovereign powers of Parliament.

37 *The Prince's Case* (1606), *Stockdale v Hansard* (1839).
38 New Zealand Constitution Act 1852 s 32, cf Constitution Act 1986 s 14.
39 *R v Norfolk CC* (1891).
40 E. Campbell, 'Royal Assent to Bills' (2003) P.L.R. 9, 11.
41 *Essays in Constitutional Law* (2nd edn, London, 1964).
42 (1606) 8 Co Rep 1a; 77 ER 481.
43 (1931) 44 CLR 394.
44 1952 (2) S A 429.
45 [1965] AC 172 (PC).

In New Zealand, entrenchment provisions remain under the Electoral Act. The entrenching mechanism requires a 75 per cent vote, or a referendum (s 189 of the 1956 Act is now represented by s 268 of the Electoral Act 1993 (NZ)) for six sections. These are s 28 (Representation Commission), s 35 (method of drawing boundaries), s 36 (margin of tolerance), s 74 (qualification of electors), s 168 (method of voting), and s 17(1) of the Constitution Act 1986 (NZ) (a three years term for Parliament). The conventional understanding remains that s 268 is not itself entrenched, a deliberately choice, on the understanding that double entrenchment would not work.[46]

However, in *R (Jackson) v A-G (UK)*[47] (The *Fox Hunting* case), the House of Lords finally endorsed the efficacy of manner and form requirements and rejected the hitherto conventional understanding of single entrenchment. The majority of the bench believed that the special enacting procedures under the Parliament Acts 1911–49 (UK) were legally as efficacious as double entrenchment.

The changing understanding of the limitations upon Parliament in the United Kingdom and New Zealand are examples where informal limitations exist, but are flexible enough to change over time. Democracy is a major element driving this, though it is a belief in representative democracy, rather than direct democracy.

6.4 Constitutions in liberal states – a change of *Grundnorm*: Ireland

Whenever there is a fundamental change of political ideology or structure, a constitution may undergo changes which are sometimes ill-understood. One such example is Ireland, where the advent of independence from the United Kingdom, and the subsequent adoption of a republican form of government, left a legacy of uncertainty with respect to the royal prerogative, and particularly as it applied to the executive function granting armorial bearings.

In 2006 a Private Member's Bill to establish clear legal authority for the Genealogical Office and the granting of armorial bearings by the Chief Herald of Ireland was withdrawn from the Seanad Éireann, after the Minister responsible for the National Library of Ireland, in which the Genealogical Office is located, indicated that he would not support it. The rationale for the Genealogy and Heraldry Bill 2006 was the continued uncertainty, at least in some quarters, over the legal authority for grants of arms. This derived from the means by which the Genealogical Office inherited the role and responsibilities of Ulster King of Arms in 1943. This had ostensibly been based in the royal prerogative, which was not inherited by the Irish State in 1922, nor when it became a *de facto* republic in 1937, or a *de jure* republic in 1949. This uncertainty was resolved, or so it was believed, by s 13 of the National Cultural Institutions Act 1997 (Ireland), which came into force in 2005. However, as shall be seen, although this provision has

46 (1956) 310 NZPD 2839).

47 [2006] 1 AC 262 (HL).

gone some way to resolving this long-standing and unsatisfactory situation, it has not brought an end to the doubt and uncertainty that surrounds the Genealogical Office, and by association, Irish genealogy and heraldry in general.

On several recent occasions it has been suggested that the Kings of Arms and Heralds of the College of Arms had declined to record or otherwise recognize grants of armorial bearings[48] made by the Chief Herald of Ireland. This had allegedly been because the College was unsure of the legal basis upon which Irish grants were made, and because of a changed policy with respect to the registration of overseas grants. It may indeed matter little whether the heraldic authority of another country approves or disapproves of the status of one's own heraldic authority, except for two considerations. The first is that the College of Arms is the foremost surviving heraldic authority, whose views must be given due weight. Secondly, the College was not alone in expressing concerns about the status of Irish grants; indeed, there had been many voices heard, in the Irish Republic and elsewhere, much louder than the College of Arms.

There are two important questions raised by this reported action of the College of Arms, and by the broader issues that it highlighted. One is the question of the authority for the granting of arms by the Chief Herald of Ireland.[49] The second distinct, though related question, is that of the recognition of Irish grants by the College of Arms.

The Genealogy and Heraldry Bill 2006, published 11 May 2006[50] and sponsored by the Genealogical Society of Ireland, was intended to rectify the situation, at least with respect to the first question. It was hoped that it would place the Office of the Chief Herald of Ireland on a sound legal footing and lay to rest any concerns that might exist – at least with respect to the question of the validity of the granting authority. Whether this would lead to the College of Arms registering Irish grants – as distinct from recognizing them – would remain a secondary issue, and not one necessarily resolved or resolvable by legislation in the Irish republic. The Bill was

48 These are variously styled coat armour, armorial bearings, arms, or coats of arms, and in some countries, though not all, are a legally enforceable right. Although their original function was to enable knights to identify each other on the battlefield, they soon acquired wider, more decorative uses. They are still widely used today by countries, public and private institutions and by individuals. The law which governed their use was called the Law of Arms, or the laws of heraldry. The officials who administer these arcane matters are styled pursuivants, heralds, or kings of arms, depending upon their seniority, or the tradition of the country concerned. Generally, see Noel Cox, 'The Law of Arms in New Zealand', *New Zealand Universities Law Review*, 18(2) (1998): 225–56.

49 Or, indeed, the Genealogical Office, as the distinction between the Office and the Herald is unclear. The National Cultural Institutions Act 1997 appears to indicate that grants are actually made by the Board of the National Library of Ireland, through its department known as the Genealogical Office, rather than by the Chief Herald of Ireland, as a corporation sole.

50 Second Reading in the Seanad Éireann 12 December 2006.

not, in the event, passed, but was withdrawn by leave after its Second Reading in the Seanad Éireann, on 12 December 2006.

The argument, which was accepted by the Seanad Éireann, was that there was sufficient legal authority for the Genealogical Office in the National Cultural Institutions Act 1997 (Ireland), and that therefore additional legislation was not required – though the issues that the Bill raised would, it was said, be considered. The justification for this confidence remains uncertain, however, as shall be discussed.

The Chief Herald of Ireland was said to be 'unaware of any notion that the College of Arms does not recognize the validity of Irish grants'.[51] However, Michael Merrigan, Honorary Secretary of the Genealogical Society of Ireland, and other proponents of the 2006 Bill, believed that the College of Arms was correct in its assessment of the legal position of the Chief Herald of Ireland and therefore in its refusal to accept the validity of Irish grants.[52] This was rooted in the history of the Genealogical Office,[53] which arose during the transitional period when Ireland was a republic in almost all respects except in name (1937–43), and when the existence of Kings of Arms or heraldic and genealogical offices was probably not the most pressing concern of the Irish Government – or indeed of the United Kingdom Government.

To some extent the questions surrounding the authority of the Genealogical Office are a consequence of the process, sometimes radical or even revolutionary, sometimes measured and legalistic, by which the major part of the island of Ireland was converted from being a part of the United Kingdom of Great Britain and Ireland, to being the Republic of Ireland.

It is also possible that there may be a grain of truth in the assertion contained in a 1945 minute of the Dominions Office, that 'excursions of kings of arms into the field of constitutional theory generally produce surprising results'.[54] It is also unfortunate that these developments took place at a time when the modern concept of the division or separation of the Crown was in its early stages,[55] leading to some conceptual uncertainly, and – what now appears as – ambiguous or even inconsistent actions.

The essence of the concerns was that it was not clear that the office was authorized, when it was established in 1943, to grants armorial bearings. It is not possible to simply assume that this right exists. Despite these doubts, it has been

51 Fergus Gillespie, Chief Herald of Ireland to Michael Merrigan, Honorary Secretary of the Genealogical Society of Ireland, 6 September 2006.

52 Michael Merrigan to the Author, 31 July 2006.

53 For a history of the Office see Susan Hood, *Royal Roots Republican Inheritance: The Survival of the Office of Arms* (Dublin, 2002).

54 16 February 1945, Dominions Office, DO35/113.

55 See Noel Cox, 'The control of advice to the Crown and the development of executive independence in New Zealand', *Bond Law Review*, 13(1) (2001): 166–89.

said[56] that common attitudes in Ireland to this concern included the following rejoinders:

1. The office is legal because of the State's inheritance of the royal prerogative;
2. The office is legal because of the Ministers and Secretaries Act 1924;
3. The office is legal due to the transitional provisions of the 1937 Constitution;
4. The office is legal because of the National Cultural Institutions Act 1997, s 13
5. The office is legal because it has existed for 63 years (as of 2006).

Although it was the fourth argument that prevailed in the Seanad Éireann, all of these are possible explanations. It will be seen, however, whether they, or any of them, can withstand close scrutiny. It is important to understand the nature of grants from 1943, because without doing so we fail to appreciate a large element of the nature of the Law of Arms of Ireland, and even of the nature of the establishment of the Irish Republic. Continued uncertainty can do little to raise the reputation of heraldry and genealogy in Ireland, suffering as it is in the aftermath of a serious scandal, and subject to continued legal doubts – notwithstanding the views of the members of the Seanad Éireann.

In the meantime, it is unfortunate that such uncertainty should have surrounded the status of Irish grants, particularly at a time when the prestige of the Genealogical Office has suffered from the repercussions of the MacCarthy Mór chiefly titles scandal. This arose when the Chief Herald recognized Terence MacCarthy as The MacCarthy Mór, although his pedigree was later shown to be unreliable.[57] The legal authority for the Genealogical Office to recognize Gaelic chiefly titles was also challenged,[58] and the practice of doing so has now ended, hopefully only temporarily.

This section will address the question of the legal basis for Irish grants of armorial bearings. It may be, as has been suggested by Merrigan, that there are now several categories of arms in the Republic of Ireland. His suggested categories were as follows:

- Grants made by the Ulster King of Arms between 1552 and 31 March 1943;
- Grants made by the Chief Heralds of Ireland between 1 April 1943 and 19 March 1997;
- Grants made between the date of enactment and the date of implementation of s 13 of the National Cultural Institutions Act 1997 in 2005;
- Grants made since the implementation of s 13.[59]

56 Michael Merrigan to the Author, 31 July 2006.

57 Sean J. Murphy, *Twilight of the Chiefs: The Mac Carthy Mór Hoax* (Bethesda, 2004).

58 Attorney-General's advice to the Minister of Arts, Sport and Tourism in June 2002.

59 Michael Merrigan to the Author, 31 July 2006.

It is the purpose of this section to attempt to unravel the situation as of 2006, and identify the legal basis – if any – for the granting of arms in the Republic of Ireland. These categories, or rather the events which punctuate the periods that mark the categories, are the structure upon which the section is constructed.

The related question of the recognition of Irish Arms by the College of Arms (and by other non-Irish bodies) will then be addressed.

In most respects the legal system of the Republic of Ireland is derived from that of that part of Ireland that formerly constituted a part of the United Kingdom. Put simply, most Irish laws were similar to, or indeed identical with, the laws of England[60] – for most civil and criminal matters – and of the United Kingdom for constitutional matters, subject to the usual changes to suit local circumstances. The Law of Arms in Ireland was in the same position. In the absence of an imperial Law of Arms (that is, one common to all the realms of the King, irrespective of otherwise differing legal systems) England and Wales, Scotland and Ireland (and now also Northern Ireland)[61] enjoyed their own Law of Arms. Those of Ireland were, however, essentially the same in most respects to those in England.

According to the usual description of the Law of Arms, coats of arms, armorial badges, flags and standards and other similar emblems of honour may only be borne by virtue of ancestral right, or of a grant made to the user under the authority of the Crown.[62] Ireland shared with the rest of the United Kingdom the principle that armorial bearings are within the exclusive control of the Crown. The power to grant and confirm coats of arms is part of the royal prerogative.

The power to grant armorial bearings was and is currently delegated by the Crown to the kings of arms.[63] In a republican regime the *fons honorum* (or font of honour) would become the President, state or some other organ of government, according to the terms of their respective constitutions, but the principle of state control would remain the same, unless armorial bearings were entirely deregulated, or the Law of Arms were specifically and explicitly altered by competent legal process.

The applicable Law of Arms in Ireland prior to the early to mid-twentieth century was in most particulars identical with that in England, just as the common law in Ireland was very close to that in England. But they were separate and distinct laws, although in both countries grants depended on the royal prerogative for their legal authority. From 1382, and the appointment of a dedicated King of Arms for the Kingdom of Ireland – Ireland King of Arms – the laws of heraldry

60 *Harris v Saunders* (1825) 4 Bl. & C. 411; 3 L.J. (o.s.) K.B. 239.

61 Prior to 1922, arms granted by Ulster King of Arms were undoubtedly governed by the Irish law; Sir Crispin Agnew of Lochnaw, Bt, 'The Conflict of heraldic laws', *Juridical Review* (1988): 61, 62.

62 As in *Halsbury's Laws of England* (3rd edn, 1960) vol.. 29, pp. 239–70.

63 The Crown's prerogative as fount of honour remains exercisable personally by the Sovereign.

in Ireland were administered in a manner similar to that in England (where the College of Arms had not yet been created[64]).

The office of Ireland King of Arms lapsed with the fall of King Richard III in 1485, and indeed the extent to which Ireland King of Arms was ever an effective heraldic authority is uncertain. But in 1552 Ulster King of Arms was appointed. This post remained in use throughout the whole of the period with which we are concerned, and undoubtedly operated in much the same manner as the Kings of Arms in England and Wales, and Scotland, in granting and confirming armorial bearings.

From the extension of the Crown's authority to Ireland until the relinquishing of that authority in the course of the twentieth century the legal authority of the Crown to confer armorial bearings on its Irish subjects was legally-speaking, unimpeachable.[65]

Ignoring, for the purposes of this exercise, grants made prior to 1552, it can scarcely be doubted that within the Kingdom of Ireland,[66] the authority to grant armorial bearings lay with Ulster King of Arms, as the King's authorized deputy. The applicability of the royal prerogative everywhere in the empire, whether settled, ceded or conquered, was never doubted.[67] This is regardless of the fact that the Law of Arms is not part of the common law[68] and the common law Courts have no jurisdiction over matters of dignities and honours,[69] such as armorial bearings.[70]

64 The kings of arms and heralds were incorporated by letters patent in 1484, as the Corporation of the Kings, Heralds and Pursuivants of Arms. On the death of King Richard III his acts were declared void, and the College of Arms received a new charter in 1556. However, the existence or absence of legal authority for the collegiate government of the College did not affect the heraldic jurisdiction of the individual Kings of Arms and heralds, which was and remains based upon their own individual letters patent of appointment, and subject to the authority of the Earl Marshal, who authorizes each individual grant, by warrant.

65 Heraldry in Ireland before the Anglo-Norman kingdom is another matter, but, suffice to say, the long era of Anglo-Irish law either extinguished or more likely subsumed any surviving earlier heraldry.

66 The Kingdom of Ireland was constituted 1541, and the revival of an Irish King of Arms can be seen as consistent with the policy of Henry VIII's government of regularizing the position of Ireland within the King's domains.

67 The Crown could rely on the royal prerogative to govern colonies: *Kielley v Carson* (1824) 4 Moo PCC 63; 13 ER 225; *Phillips v Eyre* (1870) LR 6 QB 1; *Sabally and N'Jie v Attorney-General* [1965] 1 QB 273; [1964] 3 All ER 377 (CA); *Gilbertson v State of South Australia* [1978] AC 772, 782 (PC). Once a representative assembly was created, as in Ireland in 1541, then Acts of Parliament were the primary means of legislation.

68 *R v Parker* (1668) 1 Sid 352; 82 ER 1151 per Keeling CJ.

69 *Manchester Corp v Manchester Palace of Varieties Ltd* [1955] 2 WLR 440; [1955] 1 All ER 387; [1955] P 133 per Lord Goddard.

70 *Duke of Buckingham's Case* (1514) Keil 170; 72 ER 346.

The Law of Arms is regarded as a part of the laws of Ireland (or of England, as the case may be), and the common law Courts will take judicial notice of it as such.[71]

The Crown in right of the United Kingdom had executive authority over British subjects wherever domiciled.[72] The imperial jurisdiction of the King – primarily through the Earl Marshal – was held to extend to the arms of at least some of the former Indian princes.[73] Subjects of the King of Ireland were unquestionably entitled to seek grants of arms from the King's authorized minister – Ulster King of Arms – and the authority for any subsequent grant lay in the royal prerogative.

Prior to 1922, arms granted by Ulster King of Arms, who since 1943 has been an officer of the College of Arms and an 'English' herald (though his responsibilities extend to Northern Ireland), were undoubtedly governed by the Irish Law of Arms,[74] which conferred the same type of territorial monopoly upon Ulster King of Arms as was conferred upon Garter, Clarenceaux and Norroy Kings of Arms in England and Wales, and Lord Lyon King of Arms in Scotland.[75]

From 1922 the situation became more complicated, with the constitution of the Irish Free State remaining silent on the question of the royal prerogative – which was clearly not then transferred to the government of the state, but which probably preserved the royal prerogative in the hands of the King. It seems that the royal prerogative of arms, and the authority of the Ulster King of Arms to confer arms, was unaffected by the advent of the Irish Free State – at least until 1937 (or rather 1936, as shall be seen), and the effective creation of an Irish republic. The 1943 merger of the offices of Ulster King of Arms and Norroy King of Arms, and establishment of an Irish Genealogical Office, were possibly a different matter. But we may fairly conclude that grants of arms by Ulster King of Arms prior to 1936 were as valid as any.

One might speculate as to the status of grants made by Ulster King of Arms between 1936 and 1943, given the creation of a *de facto*, if not *de jure*, republic. But most likely however these grants were entirely lawful, since the citizens of Ireland remained as if they were subjects of the Crown,[76] at least until 1949.[77] Ulster King of Arms – and later Deputy Ulster – was therefore quite within his authority to confer arms upon Irish citizens at this time. The royal prerogative was

71 *Paston v Ledham* (1459) YB 37 Hen VI, Pasch 18 per Nedham J.

72 Sir Francis Grant, *A Manual of Heraldry* (Edinburgh, 1924), p. 9.

73 In the opinion of the law officers of the Crown, quoted by L.G. Pine, *International Heraldry* (Rutland, 1970), p. 214.

74 Sir Crispin Agnew of Lochnaw, Bt, 'The conflict of heraldic laws', *Juridical Review* (1988): 61, 62.

75 The position of Ulster grants is considered in Sir Christopher Lynch-Robinson, Bt and Adrian Lynch-Robinson, *Intelligible Heraldry. The application of a Mediæval System of Record and Identification to Modern Needs* (London, 1948), pp. 112–13. They also concur that Ulster King of Arms enjoyed a monopoly of authority – subject of course to certain peculiarities of the Irish Law of Arms.

76 *Murray v Parkes* [1942] All ER 123.

77 British Nationality Act 1948 (11 and 12 Geo VI c 56) (UK).

not transferred or assigned to the Irish government in 1936 or 1937, but continued to be lawfully exercised by the King of Arms.

This was so despite the fact that from 12 December 1936 the King ceased to be such for all purposes except signing treaties and accrediting envoys, since Irish citizens remained subjects of the Crown. It meant, however, that the legal status of grants from 1936 to 1943 is subtly different to earlier grants, since Ulster King of Arms was acting as delegate of the King of the United Kingdom, rather than as King of Ireland. This doesn't invalidate them, however (and we must remember that the notion of the separation of the Crowns was not fully developed at this time[78]), but it does show that the transitional period was one in which clear and simple solutions were not always to be obtained.

With the steady progress of the Irish Government's policy of cutting links with the Crown, the Genealogical Office, later to be also known as the Office of Chief Herald of Ireland, was established 1 April 1943. The last Ulster King of Arms, Major Sir Nevile Wilkinson, had actually died in 1940, but had not been replaced, and his responsibilities being undertaken by his deputy, Thomas Sadlier. The office of Ulster King of Arms was merged with that of Norroy King of Arms in 1943, as a member of the College of Arms with ongoing responsibility for that part of the island of Ireland which still remained part of the United Kingdom. Ironically, for the first time since the office was created the title of 'Ulster' King of Arms now reflected to a much greater degree the actual extent of his territorial jurisdiction. The subsequent history of Ulster King of Arms need not concern us here, and our focus now turns to the new Office of Chief Herald of Ireland.

The establishment of the Genealogical Office in 1943 was without legislative authority – and it seems without regulations either. Legislative authority would not however have been necessary if the powers of the office were purely within the scope of the royal prerogative, or entirely ministerial or executive rather than judicial. We will consider each of these possibilities in turn.

The granting of coats of arms is usually regarded as being part of the royal prerogative. These dignities, as they are called, have legal standing[79] Arms are a form of property, as incorporeal and impartible hereditaments,[80] inalienable,

78 Generally, see Noel Cox, 'The control of advice to the Crown and the development of executive independence in New Zealand', *Bond Law Review*, 13(1) (2001): 166–89.

79 *Manchester Corp v Manchester Palace of Varieties Ltd* [1955] 2 WLR 440; [1955] 1 All ER 387; [1955] P 133 per Lord Goddard. As early as *Scroop v Grosvenor* (1389) Calendar of Close Rolls, Ric II, vol. 3, 586, it was established that a man could have obtained at that time a definite right to his arms, and that this right could be enforced against another.

80 For a discussion of corporeal and incorporeal property, see Noel Cox, 'The British Peerage: The Legal Standing of the Peerage and Baronetage in the Overseas Realms of the Crown with Particular Reference to New Zealand', *New Zealand Universities Law Review*, 17 (1997): 379.

and descendable according to the Law of Arms.[81] The ownership of arms may survive the cessation of new grants, for example due to government policy, or legal impasse. While armorial bearings are a form of property, the power of conferring of them is generally regarded as an exercise of the royal prerogative – something made explicit in the delegation of the royal prerogative to the Canadian Heraldic Authority in 1988.[82] It is the exercise of a royal prerogative, not a merely administrative act.

The question now becomes, what happened to the royal prerogative in Ireland after 1943 (or rather, 1937, which was the year the Constitution of Ireland came into force,[83] or 1936, when the Executive Authority (External Relations) Act 1936 (Ireland) replaced the King as Sovereign, and retaining the King – as an organ – only for certain limited external purposes)?

It has been claimed that the authority to grant arms survived the effective declaration of a republic in 1937, because of the state's inheritance of the royal prerogative. Unfortunately this does not seem to be correct. In the case of *Byrne v Ireland*[84] the Supreme Court of Ireland categorically established that the Irish Republic did not inherit the royal prerogative.[85] It was apparently excluded – indeed this occurred in 1922,[86] rather than in 1937, or in 1949, when Ireland became officially, as well as effectively, a republic.

Had the royal prerogative been included in the 1922 constitution, or subsequently assigned to the Irish State, it would have transferred to the new one in 1937; however it is not clear that it was included. No express provision was made for royal prerogatives in the 1922 Constitution.[87] Certain royal prerogatives continued to be exercised by the King until 1936 – and Ulster King of Arms continued to confer armorial bearings on the direct delegation he had from the Crown. The royal prerogatives were left with the King after 1922, and not incorporated into the Constitution.

---

81 Arms descend, with due and proper differencing, in the first instance to male descendants of the grantee, and then through females as heraldic heiresses in the event of the failure of the male line, as quarterings: *Wiltes Peerage Case* (1869) LR 4 HL, 126, 153 per Lord Chelmsford.

82 Letters Patent authorizing the granting of armorial bearings in Canada, dated 4 June 1988. This was sealed with the Great Seal of Canada, on the advice of the Privy Council of Canada.

83 Constitution (Amendment No 27) Act 1936.

84 [1972] I.R. 241 (Sup Ct (Irl)).

85 Supported by *Webb v Ireland* [1988] I.R. 353 and *Geoghegan v Institute of Chartered Accountants* [1995] 3 I.R. 86. See also Garter King of Arms to Secretary-General of the Most Venerable Order of St John of Jerusalem (Rear-Admiral Andrew Gough, CB), 19 October 2006.

86 The Constitution of Saorstát Éireann 1922.

87 Kevin Costello, 'The Expulsion of Prerogative Doctrine from Irish Law: Quantifying and Remedying the Loss of the Royal Prerogatives', *Irish Jurist*, 32 (1997): 145–94, 164.

The Executive Authority (External Relations) Act 1936 (Ireland) restricted the powers of the Crown to signature of treaties and accreditation of envoys; no express provision was made for the powers of Ulster King of Arms to be transferred to the Irish State at this or any subsequent time. The Act itself did more than restrict the powers of the Crown. In an adroitly worded section,[88] it was provided that, from the passage of the Act (12 December 1936), the King 'cease[d] to be King' for 'all other (if any) purposes', except for those of s 3(1). The King for the purposes of s 3(1) would be the person who would be his successor under the law of the Irish State – the Act provided for the abdication of King Edward VIII. Section 3(1) does not make the 'King' King of Ireland, but rather provides that the King of Australia, Canada, Great Britain, New Zealand, and South Africa, had certain limited and defined responsibilities with respect to Irish foreign relations.

This affected the status of Ulster King of Arms as outlined above, since he could no longer be seen as exercising his responsibilities as a delegate of the King of Ireland – even if that legal entity had survived the 1922 Constitution. The royal prerogative however enjoys an imperial unity all of its own. It is clear that the major royal prerogatives apply throughout the Commonwealth (and for this purpose including Ireland). They are applied as a pure question of law,[89] even in a country, such as Malta, where the common law is not otherwise in force.[90] Minor royal prerogatives apply in all common law countries, except that they may be excluded or modified by local circumstances. Given the general circumstances of Ireland, it might be supposed that the whole of the royal prerogative – except for the ecclesiastical prerogatives – extended to the country. From 1936 however, there was no longer a King, except for certain limited external purposes, and therefore Ulster King of Arms must be seen to have been acting as a British King of Arms, rather than an Irish one.

These grants would have been valid, despite the absence of a King from the Irish Constitution. In 1935 the Irish Free State was the first dominion to introduce its own citizenship status. But Irish citizens were still treated as subjects of the Crown.[91] The Kings of Arms may, and do, grant armorial bearings to subjects of the Queen in Australia, New Zealand, Canada, and her other realms and territories.[92]

88 Executive Authority (External Relations) Act 1936, s 3(2).

89 Noel Cox, 'The Dichotomy of Legal Theory and Political Reality: The Honours Prerogative and Imperial Unity', *Australian Journal of Law and Society*, 14 (1998–99): 15, 19; *Black v Chretien* (2001) 199 DLR (4th) 228, paras 26 per Laskin J.A. (Court of Appeal of Ontario).

90 *Sammut v Strickland* [1938] AC 678 (PC). See also *Sabally and N'Jie v Attorney-General* [1965] 1 QB 273, 293; [1964] 3 All ER 377, 380, 381 (CA). The prerogative cannot however operate against an alien in an alien land; *Attorney-General v Nissan* [1970] AC 179, 229; [1969] 1 All ER 629, 654 per Lord Pearson.

91 *Murray v Parkes* [1942] All ER 123.

92 See Sir Crispin Agnew of Lochnaw, Bt, 'The conflict of heraldic laws', *Juridical Review* (1988): 61; George Squibb, 'Heraldic Authority in the British Commonwealth', *Coat of Arms*, 10 (no 76) (1968): 125.

Foreign citizens and foreign-domiciled corporations may only receive honorary grants, which have limited legal effect as they are issued by the kings of arms in their private capacities. From 1949 citizens of Ireland have been deemed not to be aliens.[93] But they do not owe allegiance to the Crown, and are therefore disbarred from receiving a grant of arms. From 1922 to 1949 (rather than 1937) they remained subjects of the Crown, and were thus entitled to apply for grants of arms. Ulster King of Arms' own letters patent of appointment dated from 1908, and thus predated the 1922, 1936 and 1937 constitutional changes.

But from 12 December 1936 grants of arms were arguable completely divorced from the Irish state, and the question as to whether they were and remain governed by the Law of Arms of Ireland, or of England, is an interesting one. Sensibly, the Law of Arms of Ireland should be the applicable law, however, since Ulster King of Arms was appointed to grant arms in accordance with that law.

On 29 December 1937 a new Constitution was adopted which was republican in form, if not in name. It made no mention of the Sovereign, who had effectively been removed as of the precious December by the Executive Authority (External Relations) Act 1936 (Ireland). This Act continued in force. The Sovereign was no longer the head of the Irish executive, but merely an organ or instrument, authorized by the Government of Ireland, to play a specific role in external affairs.

If the transitional provisions of the 1937 Constitution preserved the royal prerogative,[94] then the Genealogical Office may have inherited the requisite authority through the transitional provisions of the Irish Constitution 1937. Article 49 of the new Constitution provided for the transmission of the powers, functions, rights and prerogatives held by the Irish State before 11 December 1936,[95] to the Oireachtas. The crucial elements are that the powers that were transferred under Article 49 were those held by the State at that time, and that these powers were transferred to the legislature, not the executive.

Although the Executive Authority (External Relations) Act 1936 (Ireland) had effectively excised the King as of the 12 December 1936, the new Constitution preserved all 'prerogatives' held by the Irish state as of the previous day. The question then becomes this: were the royal prerogatives of the King held by the Irish state on 10 December 1936? If they were, then they were inherited, under the

93 A principle established in 1948 (British Nationality Act 1948 (11 and 12 Geo VI) c 56 (UK)), However, Irish citizens were still treated as subjects of the Crown, and they are still not regarded as foreign, even though Ireland is not a member of the Commonwealth. See now the British Nationality Act 1981 (UK), ss 37 (1) (a), (b) and 50 (1).

94 Generally, see Kevin Costello, 'The Expulsion of Prerogative Doctrine from Irish Law: Quantifying and Remedying the Loss of the Royal Prerogatives', *Irish Jurist*, 32 (1997): 145–94 (for the argument that no elements of the royal prerogative were transferred to the Irish State in 1922).

95 The Executive Authority (External Relations) Act 1936 provided that Edward VIII remained king in the Irish Free State till 12 December 1936. The effect of Article 49(1) was that none of the royal prerogatives held by King George VI were transferred.

1937 Constitution, by the Oireachtas. If they were held by the King, as distinct from the state – if that distinction could be made – then they were not inherited.

It would be usual to assume that the powers of the King would be counted among the powers of the state. In the 1922 Constitution the King was envisaged as being part of the state.[96] Article 2 stated that 'All powers of government and all authority, legislative, executive, and judicial, in Ireland are derived from the people of Ireland, and the same shall be exercised in the Irish Free State (Saorstát Eireann) through the organisations established by or under, and in accord with, this Constitution.' Article 51 provided that 'The Executive Authority of the Irish Free State (Saorstát Eireann) is hereby declared to be vested in the King, and shall be exercisable, in accordance with the law, practice and constitutional usage governing the exercise of the Executive Authority in the case of the Dominion of Canada, by the Representative of the Crown.' Together these would appear to suggest that the royal prerogative – which is probably not mentioned in the Constitution because it is regarded as being a distinct type of law – would be a 'prerogative of the state'.

The 1937 Constitution stated that 'the powers, functions, rights and prerogatives held by the Irish State' before 11 December 1936 were inherited by the new Constitution. Articles 12 and 51 of the 1922 Constitution could be interpreted as embracing the royal prerogative as part of the powers, not of the Constitution *per se*, but of the King as the person in whom was vested the Executive Authority of the Irish Free State. However, in 1922 the concept of the division of the Crown was not well developed, and it is likely that the royal prerogative was not intended to be patriated in this manner. Indeed, it would seem that the British Government was opposed to a transfer of the office to the control of the Irish Free State because of the concern that this would harm the unity of the Crown and the royal prerogative. This attitude could only be maintained if the royal prerogative is seen as being distinct from the 'executive authority' of the 1922 Constitution.

Thus it is not clear whether the royal prerogative was a 'prerogative held by the Irish State', and therefore inherited by that State in 1937. Although it might be a conceptually stronger argument to assert that the royal prerogative was included in the 1922 Constitution, we are bound by the decisions in *Byrne v Ireland*,[97] and subsequent cases, that the royal prerogative was not transferred to the Irish State. It would be unwise to assert that an office (namely the Genealogical Office) had authority to act simply on the basis of a legal argument that directly contradicted a series of Supreme Court decisions, however appealing the above argument may

96 Though he was, in the 1922 Constitution, part of Parliament: 'All powers of government and all authority, legislative, executive, and judicial, in Ireland are derived from the people of Ireland, and the same shall be exercised in the Irish Free State (Saorstát Eireann) through the organisations established by or under, and in accord with, this Constitution' (Article 12).

97 [1972] I.R. 241 (Sup Ct (Irl)).

appear. Unfortunately, the Genealogical Office has suffered more than enough from assumptions, and complacency with respect to its legal powers.

The safest conclusion is that the royal prerogative was not transferred to the Irish Government in 1922, or subsequently prior to 11 December 1936, and that Ulster King of Arms continued to exercise the non-delegated royal prerogative until 1943. Practice in Canada and elsewhere in the realms of the Queen has shown that the royal prerogative to grant arms can only be delegated by express grant of the Crown, and this was not done at any stage before or after 1922.

If all the royal prerogatives were inherited by the Irish Government after 1922 the Genealogical Office might have authority to grant arms. But the decision of the Irish Government to allow Ulster to remain in office until his death, and the reluctance of the British Government to transfer the office, suggests that the Irish Government had no reason to believe that they now possessed control of the royal prerogative of arms, or indeed had any wish to acquire it. It remained an imperial prerogative, and was expected to die with the last exerciser of that royal prerogative. Surprisingly perhaps, it lingered from Sir Nevile Wilkinson's death in 1940, until 1943, when the Genealogical Office was established, and, perhaps surprisingly, the granting of arms was deemed to be one of its functions.

It remains unclear why the Genealogical Office did not receive an express grant of authority in 1943, unless it was due to mistaken understanding of the nature of the office of Ulster King of Arms, and of the source of his authority. The interval between 1936 and 1943, and the death of the last Ulster, might have contributed to the situation developing as it did.

Ironically, if Ulster King of Arms – or Deputy Ulster – had continued to reside in Dublin Castle after 1943, it would seem that he would have retained the right to confer arms, according to the Irish Law of Arms, for so long as Irish citizens remained subjects of the Crown, which they did until 1949.[98]

The authority for deputy Ulster to confer arms from 1922 to 1943 derived exclusively from the royal prerogative, and was independent of the Irish government or state – it was not extinguished, merely not delegated. The Irish Free State might have sought to obtain control over the office between 1922 and 1937, but this was not done. From 1936 the royal prerogative was apparently that of the United Kingdom, but at the time the distinction between the prerogative of one realm and other was not firmly established, and probably had little practical effect.

From 1943 the Genealogical Office assumed that it succeeded to the powers and functions of Ulster King of Arms, but it would seem that it cannot have done so since the royal prerogative was not preserved in Ireland. So much then for the possibility of the royal prerogative as the basis for the authority for the Chief Herald of Ireland to grant arms after 1943.

So far we have considered the possibility that the Genealogical Office could exercise the royal prerogative after 1943 – and rejected this option, as contrary to Supreme Court precedents that confirm that the royal prerogative was extinguished.

98 British Nationality Act 1948 (11 and 12 Geo VI c 56) (UK).

What about ministerial or executive authority? If the granting of arms were a purely administrative function it would require neither the exercise of the royal prerogative nor legislation. While there is a common perception that executive governmental powers must be derived from either the royal prerogative or statute, there is in fact a third source.[99] The Crown – or in this case, the Chief Herald of Ireland, acting as an organ of the government of Ireland (after 1949 of the Irish Republic) – has the same powers of a natural person to assign property, or create legal rights.

Unfortunately, although this would mean that the Chief Herald might have the right to seek copyright protection for coats of arms,[100] or otherwise exercise the rights and privileges of any natural or artificial person, the Law of Arms is different. If we are concerned here with the granting of armorial bearings of the same essential nature as those granted before 1943, then they must be seen as being granted in accordance with the Law of Arms. This is *sui generis*, and is a right confined – in the Irish Law of Arms as in that of England – in the Sovereign, or *fons honorum* – after 1937, or at least 1949, presumably the President or his lawfully deputised representative. The Office might grant arms that did not have a basis in the royal prerogative, if there was specific legislative authority for this, but none existed, doubtless because it was thought – mistakenly it would appear – that the Office could simply 'inherit' the royal prerogative hitherto exercised by Ulster King of Arms.

The Chief Herald of Ireland also believed that from 1943 until 2005 the Genealogical Office operated under an Order made under the Ministers and Secretaries Act 1924 (Ireland) (and the later Ministers and Secretaries (Amendment) Act 1939 (Ireland)), and that no specific legislation was required.[101] The use of regulations under an Act is of course an option. However, since the Act would appear to be intended solely to assign governmental functions between departments, it would appear *prima facie* to be ineffective as the legal basis for conferring arms.[102]

The Adoption of Charters Act 1926 (Ireland) deemed bodies established by royal charter or letters patent to be statutory bodies for the purposes of the Ministers and

99 Bruce Harris, 'The "Third Source" of Authority for Government Action', *Law Quarterly Review*, 109 (1992): 626–51.

100 In the National Cultural Institutions Act 1997 it is indeed provided that any copyright subsisting in armorial bearings would be vested in the Board of the National Library of Ireland; s 13(3). The wording suggests that there may have been some doubt as to whether copyright did subsist in armorial bearings, for which question see Noel Cox, 'The intellectual property laws and the protection of armorial bearings', *Australian Intellectual Property Journal*, 12(1) (2001): 143–52.

101 Fergus Gillespie, Chief Herald of Ireland to Michael Merrigan, Honorary Secretary of the Genealogical Society of Ireland, 6 September 2006.

102 This was certainly the view of the College of Arms; Garter King of Arms to Secretary-General of the Most Venerable Order of St John of Jerusalem (Rear-Admiral Andrew Gough, CB), 19 October 2006.

Secretaries Act 1924 (Ireland), and it may also be questioned whether Ulster King of Arms was such a body, although he did have seal and was a corporation sole.

Even if the Office of Ulster King of Arms were a body corporate established by letters patent, and therefore a 'statutory body' for the purposes of the 1924 Act, it is necessary to examine the relevant Order, the Allocation of Administration (Genealogical Office) Order 1943 (Ireland), to see whether it was, in fact, ineffective, for the reason cited above, namely that the Act was designed to facilitate the assignment of departments, and did not authorize the granting of legal rights.

The Order is very brief. The single substantive clause states simply 'The administration and business of the Genealogical Office are hereby allocated to the Department of Education.' This would not have the effect of creating any additional powers or authority; it does not even formally establish the Genealogical Office, an action which, of itself, may be achieved by administrative act alone. The Attorney-General gave advice to the Minister in June 2002 to this effect. Nor is there a clear statement (or even an unclear one) that the Genealogical Office is the successor to the Office of Ulster King of Arms.

From 1943 the Genealogical Office seems to have operated under the dubious authority of the Allocation of Administration (Genealogical Office) Order 1943 – which was scarcely authority for anything – and a belief that the office had 'succeeded to the powers and functions' of Ulster King of Arms (as stated on the Genealogical Office's website). There was an interval of more than fifty years before the next legislative or regulatory measure affecting the Office was enacted, though doubts had arisen from time-to-time before then.

On 27 November 1996 the National Cultural Institutions Act 1997 (Ireland) was passed by the Seanad Éireann. On 19 March 1997 the Dáil Éireann passed the Act. The Act endeavoured to regularize matters by declaring that the non-statutory Genealogical Office was a branch of the National Library of Ireland – but it did not establish the office nor specify its functions or powers. In part the former may have been due to a desire to emphasize the continuity of the office, not merely with the Genealogical Office of 1943, but also the Ulster King of Arms of 1552.[103] Despite the sections – the key ones being 12 and 13 – it is not clear that the situation has been clarified or improved.

The Chief Herald of Ireland believed that the Act did quite clearly provide specific legislative authority.[104] The key provision is s 13,[105] which only came into

103 Consistent with this is the preservation of a continuous series of Arms Registers, pre-dating the establishment of the Genealogical Office, until today.

104 Fergus Gillespie, Chief Herald of Ireland to Michael Merrigan, Honorary Secretary of the Genealogical Society of Ireland, 6 September 2006.

105 The complete section is as follows:

13.— (1) For the avoidance of doubt, it is hereby declared that the Genealogical Office is a branch of the Library.

effect in 2005. Thus from 1997 to 2005 the legal position of the Genealogical Office was unchanged from what it was in 1943.

The Attorney-General's advice to the Minister in June 2002 that there was no legislative basis for the granting of arms by the Chief Herald on behalf of the State was provided before s 13 was brought into effect, but took that section into account. However, as shall be seen, s 13 did little to help matters.

Section 13 was brought into force in 2005.[106] Section 13(1) does not create the Genealogical Office, but rather states that:

> **13.**—(1) For the avoidance of doubt, it is hereby declared that the Genealogical Office is a branch of the Library.
>
> This does not assign any specific powers, and achieves no more than the 1943 Order did. Subsection 2, however, is crucial. It states that:
>
> —(2) The Board shall, from time to time as occasion requires, designate a member of its staff to perform the duty of researching, granting and confirming coats of arms and such member shall use the appellation Chief Herald of Ireland or, in the Irish language, Príomh-Aralt na hÉireann while performing such duties.

This appears to finally confer an express authority – statutory rather than prerogative – to grant arms. The words 'to perform the duty of researching, granting and

(2) The Board shall, from time to time as occasion requires, designate a member of its staff to perform the duty of researching, granting and confirming coats of arms and such member shall use the appellation Chief Herald of Ireland or, in the Irish language, PríorahAralt na hÉireann while performing such duties.

(3) The Board shall be entitled to any copyright subsisting in coats of arms granted or confirmed under this section.

(4) (*a*) The Board of the Library shall as soon as may be after the Library establishment day appoint a committee to be known as the Committee on Genealogy and Heraldry (referred to subsequently in this subsection as 'the Committee') to perform such of the functions of the Board, as in the opinion of the Board, may be better or more conveniently performed by it and are assigned to it by the Board.

(*b*) There may be included in the membership of the Committee such number (not being more than half of the membership of the Committee who are entitled to vote) of persons who are not members of the Board.

(*c*) The appointment of a person to act as a member of the Committee shall be subject to such conditions as the Board may think fit to impose when making the appointment.

(*d*) A member of the Committee may be removed from office at any time by the Board.

(*e*) The acts of the Committee shall be subject to the approval of the Board.

(*f*) The Director of the National Library and the Chief Herald of Ireland shall be included in the membership of the Committee but shall not be entitled to vote.

(*g*) The Board may regulate the procedures of the Committee but, subject to any such regulation, the Committee may regulate its own procedure.

106 National Cultural Institutions Act, 1997 (Commencement) Order 2005.

confirming coats of arms' are important. Does this amount to the delegation of authority – presumably inherent in the powers of the Irish legislature – to grant arms? By way of comparison let us look at the wording used in the 1988 letters patent establishing the Canadian Heraldic Authority. This states that it authorizes:

> the Governor General of Canada to exercise or provide for the exercise of all powers and authorities lawfully belonging to Us as Queen of Canada in respect of the granting of armorial bearings in Canada.[107]

This is much more explicit than the formula in s 13 of the National Cultural Institutions Act 1997 (Ireland). The usual wording of letters patent appointing a King of Arms states that 'We do give and by virtue of these Presents grant into the said […] Authority Power and Licence with the consent of the Earl Marshal of England or his Deputy for the time being in writing under their hands and seals from time to time first given or signified of granting and appointing to eminent men Letters Patent of Arms and Crests … .'[108] This is quite explicit, and in marked contrast to the wording of ss 12 and 13.

The greatest difficulty with the wording of s 13 is that it is effectively repeating the error of the 1943 Order, it is stating that the function of granting arms is to be carried out by a certain officer, but does not actually confer the authority to make grants. This may seem a very nice distinction to make, but legally it is significant. Section 13 provides a clearer view of what was intended (than does the Order), and comes closer to achieving that, but alas it also falls short of resolving all uncertainty.

The limitation in the wording in s 13 is echoed in s 12, which describes the functions of the Board of the National Library of Ireland. This provides, inter alia, that

> (2) The Board shall have all such powers as it considers necessary or expedient for the performance of its functions under this Act including, but without prejudice to the generality of the foregoing, the following powers:
>
> (*c*) to facilitate, encourage, assist and promote the granting and confirming of coats of arms,

This clearly does not expressly authorize the granting of arms, indeed is seems to presuppose that the ultimate authority for grants lies elsewhere – perhaps in the inherited royal prerogative, which, as we have seen, is an inadequate basis for authority.

---

107 4 June 1988.

108 From the Letters Patent appointing John Philip Brooke Brooke-Little Norroy and Ulster King of Arms and Principal Herald of the North Part of England and of Northern Ireland, 7 July 1980.

Section 13(1) continues the practice of emphasizing the continuity of the Genealogical Office. This would not necessarily present a difficulty, even though the office was apparently never formally established. The key point is that the office exists now as a department of the National Library, and that one of the officers of the library is authorized to perform the duties of 'granting and confirming coats of arms', subject of course to the authority of the Board, which is empowered to 'to facilitate, encourage, assist and promote the granting and confirming of coats of arms'. This is a wholly inadequate basis for the granting of armorial bearings, and reliance upon ss 12 and 13 will do little to raise the reputation of the Genealogical Office.

Perhaps equally seriously, s 13 fails to address the status of pre-2005 grants of arms, the legal status of which is subject to serious question.

The primary concern remains whether the imprecise wording that was used in ss 12 and 13 of the National Cultural Institutions Act 1997 (Ireland) can confer the right to grant arms. This is a particular problem because we are not here concerned with the known and familiar royal prerogative grants, where, as above, the Queen of Canada can easily provide for the Governor-General of Canada to 'exercise or provide for the exercise of all powers and authorities lawfully belonging to Us'. In Ireland we see a non-prerogative authorization, apparently (but not unambiguously) legislative. Are these 'coats of arms' legally the same as pre-1943 coats of arms; does the Irish Law of Arms apply to them, or are they a new form of grant? [109] These are unanswered, and as the legislation currently stands, unanswerable questions.

On the question of the lack of express creation of the Genealogical Office, that may not necessarily matter. The power to grant arms – note, not to recognize chiefly titles – is conferred upon the Chief Herald, not the Genealogical Office, but only as an officer of the National Library of Ireland. Continuity is primarily a concern because there was arguably no legal authority for the granting of arms from 1943 to 2005 (and possibly even after that).

Additional difficulties and uncertainties may have been created. The National Cultural Institutions Act 1997 (Ireland) appears to indicate that grants are actually made by the Board of the National Library of Ireland, through its department known as the Genealogical Office, rather than by the Chief Herald of Ireland, as a corporation sole. Irish grants of arms themselves do not accurately reflect this legal arrangement. They are in the name of the Chief Herald of Ireland, and include the key phase that 'by virtue of the authority vested in me in that behalf do by these Presents grant and assign unto the said … the Arms following … to have and to hold the said Arms … according to the Laws of Arms and the practice

109 The grants themselves specifically refer to the Law of Arms, see, for instance the Grant of Arms to Stephen Patrick Cracroft-Brennan, 11 February 1986 (Vol. W, fol.43, per Donal Begley, Chief Herald of Ireland).

of this Office'.[110] Unfortunately it is not clear that the Chief Herald of Ireland is authorized to grant arms, though it could be argued that s 13 can be read to mean that the Chief Herald for the time being has this authority vested in him. It would perhaps be more accurate to say that the authority is vested in the Board of the National Library of Ireland, and is being exercised on its behalf by the Chief Herald of Ireland.[111]

The 2006 Bill would have repealed what has been described as the fundamentally flawed s 13 of the National Cultural Institutions Act 1997 (Ireland). Section 13 does apparently give some form of authority to the Chief Herald of Ireland to grant arms. But it is not explicit, especially when read in conjunction with s 12. Given that doubts have lingered for sixty years it is unfortunate that a more precise provision were not provided – especially as the draftsmen were alerted by many interested parties, to the deficiencies of the proposed section.

As a final point on the legal authority for the granting of arms in the Irish Republic, there has been an argument that the Genealogical Office is legal because it has existed for over sixty years. Unfortunately prescription – which may operate in some areas of private law – does not provide authority for the granting of armorial bearings. The Genealogical Office exists as an institution of government by administrative action. But it needs clear authority to grant arms, or the arms it purports to grant have no legal standing in the Irish Law of Arms. This is a matter of embarrassment to the state, and of real concern to grantees, who have paid for

110 Wording from May 2005. Letters Patent of Grant of Arms to the Association of Professional Genealogists of Ireland, 7 July 2006 (Vol. Z, fol.75, per Fergus Gillespie, Chief Herald of Ireland).

It may also be noted that this grant was to a corporate body that was registered as a company on 17 August 2006 in the Companies Registration Office, Dublin (number 425002). The letters patent purport to make the grant to the Association, although at the date of the grant the Association, which was founded in 1986, may have been unincorporated. The letters patent also make the grant to the Association of Professional Genealogists *of* Ireland, although the correct title of the organization is now (from incorporation as a company) the Association of Professional Genealogists *in* Ireland Limited. There would not appear to be any legal authority for the grant of arms to an unincorporated body, and it must be doubted whether a retrospective grant would be effective; the Association may, however, have been incorporated in some other manner prior to 2006, but this is not evident from the letters patent themselves.

111 Until 2003 the wording was 'by these Presents, acting on behalf of and by the authority of the Government of Ireland, [do] grant and assign unto the said … the arms following … according to the Laws of Arms'. Letters Patent of Grant of Arms to Stephen Patrick Cracroft-Brennan, 11 February 1986 (Vol. W, fol. 43, per Donal Begley, Chief Herald of Ireland). This wording is also unsatisfactory, for the same reasons, though it could be argued that the Chief Herald was acting by the authority of the Government of Ireland in a loose sense, assuming of course that the Government itself had the authority to grant arms.

the privilege of having Irish armorial bearings, and might reasonably expect to get a valid grant.[112]

This situation would be amusing if it were not deplorable. The difficulty could have been avoided by a relatively simple amendment to the 1997 Act. The 2006 Bill met some opposition due to its comprehensiveness, particularly in light of the short passage of time since the implementation of s 13. The easiest solution, in terms of short-term correction of the uncertainty, is an amendment to ss 12 and 13 of the National Cultural Institutions Act 1997 (Ireland). The Genealogy and Heraldry Bill 2006 should however form the basis for a more comprehensive reform of Irish genealogy and heraldry. Few would deny that events surrounding the Genealogical Office in recent years do suggest that there is a need for some fairly radical (but carefully reasoned) reforms.

By way of suggestion, s 12(2) could be amended as follows (new text in italics):

> (2) The Board shall have all such powers as it considers necessary or expedient for the performance of its functions under this Act including, but without prejudice to the generality of the foregoing, the following powers:
>
> *(c) to grant and confirm coats of arms in accordance with the Law of Arms of Ireland,*

Section 13 could become

> **13.**—(1) For the avoidance of doubt, it is hereby declared that the Genealogical Office is a branch of the Library, *and is the successor in law to all the rights, privileges, powers and immunities of the Office of Ulster King of Arms as existed prior to 1st April 1943, and for the further avoidance of doubt the Genealogical Office shall be deemed to have existed since 1st April 1943 and to have enjoyed the said rights, privileges, powers and immunities without interruption since that date.*

Doubtless more detailed drafting could create a more robust provision, but it is essential that the continued doubts be speedily put to rest. Ideally the Genealogical Office should be a stand-alone entity (though this would require a more complex amendment to the Act, or a new Act such as the proposed Genealogy and Heraldry Bill), and the Chief Herald – perhaps even renamed Ireland King of Arms – made

112 According to the Genealogical Office website, 'The fee for a personal grant of arms is €3,300. The sum of €300 is payable when lodging the application, a further €1,500 is payable when work on the design begins and the balance of €1,500 must be paid before work on the actual grant of arms is put in hand by the herald painter. For a grant of arms to a local authority, or a school, club etc, the fee is €5,000. For a grant of arms to other corporate bodies and organisations, the fee is €10,000' (http://www.nli.ie/fr_offi.htm) as at 14 December 2006.

its executive head, with specific authority to confer arms, and to recognize chiefly titles.

The doubts surrounding the legal status of Irish grants of arms must be said to remain, despite (or perhaps even because of) the enactment of s 13 of the National Cultural Institutions Act 1997 (Ireland). This can do little to persuade heraldic authorities abroad, and least of all the College of Arms, which had already expressed its disquiet, that all was not well in Irish heraldry and genealogy.

One illustration of the consequences of this unsatisfactory situation is in the refusal of the College of Arms to register Irish grants of arms. The following is the account of one instance. In 1974, John E. Flynn, then of Ireland, later Scotland, and now living in England, obtained a Confirmation of Arms from the Chief Herald of Ireland.[113] In 1975 he was advised by Lancaster Herald that these arms could be registered in the College of Arms, provided they were first registered in Scotland (since he was then domiciled in Scotland).[114] The arms were matriculated at the Court of the Lord Lyon of Scotland in the same year. Mr Flynn however took no action at that time to register his Irish arms in the College of Arms.

Some years later, in 2002, he sought to have his arms registered in London. This time he was advised, by Clarenceaux King of Arms, that the College of Arms was not now registering arms originating from the Chief Herald of Ireland.[115] Further advice, in 2004, from Norroy and Ulster King of Arms, was that arms granted by the Chief Herald of Ireland were treated in the same way as all foreign grants of arms. Since 1999 the entering of any foreign arms in the Foreign Arms Register at the College of Arms had been discontinued, with the sole exception of grantees who were British subjects who had previously borne the same arms under another jurisdiction. Only grants and matriculations of the Lord Lyon King of Arms were now entered in the records of the College of Arms.[116] Canadian grants since 1988 could however also be recorded, an example being the grant to Graeme John Leonard Hall, of arms, crest and motto, 10 January 1995, recorded in August 2004.[117]

This refusal to register Irish grants was not grounded on any concern as to the legal standing of the Genealogical Office, or doubts as to the legal basis for the Chief Herald of Ireland's powers to grant arms – at least none that were expressed. It was based instead on a policy decision, justified by doubts as to the College of Arms own legal powers in this respect, to only register grants of arms made by Officers of Arms of the Crown.

113 Volume U, folio 19.

114 Sedley Andrus, Lancaster Herald, to J.E. Flynn, 1 October 1975.

115 Hubert Chesshyre, Clarenceaux King of Arms, to J.E. Flynn, 16 July 2002.

116 Thomas Woodcock, Norroy and Ulster King of Arms, to Vernon Coaker, MP, 1 October 2004.

117 With the reference Canada 1/12; The College of Arms Newsletter, November 2004, no 3, p 3.

This was made clear in a letter from Garter King of Arms in 2004, that grants by Lord Lyon or by the Chief Herald of Canada may sometimes be noted in the appropriate book of records at the College of Arms: 'This does not apply to others who are not subjects of the Crown.' 'In the past there were occasional efforts to note certain Arms granted by other authorities. Unfortunately, this caused a number of problems concerning such matters as the eligibility of grantees and the eligibility of the granting authority. Our own authority to embark on this remained doubtful; and the correct procedure was deemed to be to restrict our activities to the terms of our respective appointments, and what was known to be correct.'[118]

In 2006 Garter King of Arms clarified that the College of Arms were not prepared to accept the 1975 Scottish matriculation for registration, as it was not a grant as such: 'Essentially it is the recognition of an Irish grant and not an original grant made in Scotland.'[119] In other words, in accordance with the policy stated in 2004, only grants made to 'subjects of the Crown'[120] would be recorded. It would seem that the grants also had to be made by the Crown to qualify for inclusion, since only grants by Lord Lyon and the Chief Herald of Ireland were being registered. Though it is possible that the College had not been asked to register arms conferred on a subject by a foreign authority, this is unlikely.

In the light of recent publicity regarding the disputed status of Irish grants, the College now also expressed its own concerns,[121] but this would not have had any effect upon the decision not to register Irish grants. This was based on the status of the recipient as much as the authority of the granting authority.

The College of Arms, or rather the Kings of Arms who work there, are authorized to grant coats of arms to subjects of the Crown – and may make honorary grants to foreigners and others who are not subjects of the Crown. As noted earlier, honorary grants are issued by the kings of arms in their private capacities, and it may indeed be questioned whether these have legal standing.

The existence of mechanisms in the United Kingdom and the Irish Republic for the mutual recognition of the institutions of each state in relation to Northern Ireland has little bearing upon the question of the registration of Irish grants. The Chief Herald of Ireland believed that the Belfast Agreement[122] was not relevant as the College of Arms is 'not a department of Government but a private corporation'.[123]

---

118 Peter Gwynn-Jones, Garter Principal King of Arms, to Vernon Coaker, MP, 8 December 2004.

119 Peter Gwynn-Jones, Garter Principal King of Arms, to John E. Flynn, 7 July 2006.

120 Peter Gwynn-Jones, Garter Principal King of Arms, to Vernon Coaker, MP, 8 December 2004.

121 Peter Gwynn-Jones, Garter King of Arms to Secretary-General of the Most Venerable Order of St John of Jerusalem (Rear-Admiral Andrew Gough, CB), 19 October 2006.

122 10 April 1998.

123 Fergus Gillespie, Chief Herald of Ireland to Michael Merrigan, Honorary Secretary of the Genealogical Society of Ireland, 6 September 2006.

This is incorrect. The corporation may be private – though that is doubtful since all members are appointed by the Crown, and the Earl Marshal is Visitor of the College, but it also indicates that there may have been a misconception as to the nature of grants in England and Wales. Grants of arms are not made by the College of Arms, even though that is a corporate body, but rather by the Kings of Arms, pursuant in each instance to a warrant from the Earl Marshal.

The Belfast Agreement, and other treaties and conventions between the United Kingdom and the Republic of Ireland, allow for the reciprocal recognition of certain processes, and for co-operation and consultation. But although the Belfast Agreement in particular enjoins the state parties to work together, it does not mean that Irish grants would necessarily be treated in a manner different to those of other states. The key issue here is that only grants to subjects of the Crown are recognized (and apparently only when receiving grants from the Crown, though this is less clear).

It has long been the position that those domiciled in the realms of the Crown should only use arms granted by the Crown.[124] It would follow that those domiciled within the realms of the Crown should not obtain grants from foreign heraldic authorities, but that if they do they should seek registration in the College of Arms, Lord Lyon, or the Chief Herald of Canada, as applicable. Whatever the law and practice may be in Scotland and Canada, in England and Wales – and indeed Northern Ireland – the College of Arms appears to hold the view that only Scottish and Canadian grants (not confirmations) can be recognized.

It may well be that this is the correct position to maintain, and it is certainly within the discretion of the College of Arms to register whatever arms it sees fit to register, because of the overarching principle that those domiciled in the realms of the Crown should only use arms granted by the Crown.

It might be observed that the question of whether a recipient of arms is a subject or not is less important than their domicile. An Irishman, or person of Irish descent, who has obtained a grant of arms from the Chief Herald of Ireland, and who is domiciled in England, Wales, or Northern Ireland, would not have a right to have his arms registered in the College of Arms. Firstly, they should only use arms granted by the Crown, and the registration of foreign arms has always been discretionary.

124 In much the same way foreign honours and titles held by subjects of the Crown are not officially recognized, though their social use is common. As Queen Elizabeth I said, 'there was a close tie of affection between the Prince and subject, and that as chaste wives should have no glances but for their own spouses, so should faithful subjects keep their eyes at home and not gaze upon foreign crowns; that we for our part do not care that our sheep should wear a stranger's marks, nor dance after the whistle of every foreigner'. Foreign knighthoods have not been recognized since the early nineteenth century, and in 1932 King George V revoked all remaining royal warrants authorizing the use of foreign titles of nobility by British subjects, saving the current holders and their immediate heirs where named in the warrants.

Secondly, and perhaps most importantly from the perspective of the special position of Irish grants, especially since the Belfast Agreement, the College of Arms is probably correct in only registering arms granted by other heraldic authorities of the Crown (setting aside the vexed question of whether the Canadian Crown is the same as the United Kingdom Crown[125]). Its function is to grant armorial bearings, and confirm others borne by virtue of ancestral right.[126] Just as there is no right to a grant – one must convince an Officer of Arms, then the Chapter of the College of Arms, and finally the Earl Marshal, that one is worthy of a grant of arms – so there is no right to have foreign arms registered.

This general principle of state exclusivity can be applied elsewhere also. Each state may decide for itself whether heraldry will be regulated, and if it is, what form that regulation will take. They may choose to allow the use only of duly registered arms – and may or may not recognize and register foreign arms.[127] As with any aspect of dignitary law, the state is the final arbiter. However close the social, political and historical links between countries, it is not generally the case that one can insist upon the mutual recognition of one's title in another country, and this applies to armorial bearings also.[128]

There is of course nothing preventing an agreement being entered into that would allow the College of Arms to routinely register grants made by the Chief Herald of Ireland to men and women domiciled in England, Wales or Northern Ireland (or possibly just those domiciled in Northern Ireland, which would make more sense in principle). Because this would amount to a departure from the standard policy, because these grants are not made on behalf of the Sovereign, and in light of doubts as to its legality, specific authority would have to be sought from the Queen.

There is no reason to believe that such authority would not eventually be forthcoming. However, it would be a matter for Her Majesty, doubtless as advised by her British Ministers and taking into account the political circumstances of the situation, to decide. Hopefully Her Majesty would be allowed to express her own view, and not be treated as simply a pawn in a larger political game. Undoubtedly the present unsatisfactory state of the heraldic laws in Ireland would rightly prove a barrier to any such arrangement being entered into in the short or medium term.[129]

---

125 For a case that suggests it is, see *R v Secretary of State Foreign and Commonwealth Office, Ex parte Indian Association of Alberta* [1982] QB 892 (CA; cf. *Attorney-General for the United Kingdom v Wellington Newspapers Ltd* [1988] 1 NZLR 129 (HC and CA).

126 As in *Halsbury's Laws of England* (3rd edn, 1960) vol. 29, 239–70.

127 Internationally, providing full legal protection for even domestic coats of arms is the exception rather than the rule.

128 An analogous situation is seen with honours. Honours and awards conferred by the Queen in one or other of her capacities are generally recognized in other realms. But awards conferred by foreign heads of state, or even by the heads of state of republics within the Commonwealth (or even indigenous monarchies), are not.

129 It is the writer's personal view, for what it is worth, that such an arrangement would not be appropriate. Only grants made by the Crown should be registered by the

Irish grants of arms by the Chief Herald of Ireland are now made under the less than satisfactory authority of ss 12 and 13 of the National Cultural Institutions Act 1997 (Ireland). It is fairly clear that this authority is not derived from the royal prerogative, and it must therefore be of legislative or administrative origins. The latter is improbable, the former possible, but unlikely, due to the wording of the sections.

Unfortunately the uncertainty which has lingered since 1943 has not been removed by the enactment of these sections, nor was the position of pre-2005 grants clarified when the sections came into force in 2005.

The Genealogy and Heraldry Bill 2006 did offer an opportunity to correct these uncertainties. Unfortunately this opportunity was not taken, and the status of Irish grants of arms remains uncertain. It might be that steps will be taken to correct this anomalous situation. However, what it clearly shows is that the change of *Grundnorm* which occurred when Ireland moved from being a part of the United Kingdom, to being an independent republic, was both ill-understood, and had unexpected flow-on effects. This was not dealt with directly even when it was recognized, perhaps for fear that this would be an acknowledgement that the republican (doctrinaire liberal) principles of the state may have not been as clear as was expected. However the flexibility of the constitution meant that these were manageable and correctable – though the steps to correct the situation have been slow in coming.

6.5 Conclusion

Doctrinaire liberal states are founded upon, and promote, concepts such as the rule of law, and democracy. They are therefore driven by imperatives which are derived from these, including the maintenance of legal continuity, and a tradition of legalism.

The particularly strong influence of legalism in England was partly due to the contemporary strength of the common law, and the antithetical attitude of the latter for the former.[130] Despite St Paul's warning against legalism,[131] the mediæval

College of Arms. To include any others would conflict with the principle of exclusivity. It could also, potentially, open the prospect for other claims of special circumstances, for instance, to also register South African or Zimbabwean grants.

130 Noel Cox, 'The Influence of the Common Law and the Decline of the Ecclesiastical Courts of the Church of England', *Rutgers Journal of Law and Religion*, 3(1) (2001–2002): 1–45.

131 See Colossians 2.20–23:

> 20 Wherefore if ye be dead with Christ from the rudiments of the world, why, as though living in the world, are ye subject to ordinances,
> 21 (Touch not; taste not; handle not;

church was to become comparatively legalistic, a perhaps inevitable condition given the wide reach of the (western) universal church and its centralization. The state, influenced by the church, and drawing upon its jurisprudence, and developing its own common law traditions, in its turn became legalistic. In part it was possibly due to the importance of *stare decisis*[132] and precedent in the common law, the nature of the legal profession, and the way in which common law judges were appointed in England.

Even in terms of concepts of European legalism, the evolution of the constitution in New Zealand since 1840 has presented problems for its legitimacy. The Crown of the United Kingdom, having assumed sovereignty over New Zealand by an act of State or cession, the United Kingdom Parliament never formally renounced power to legislate for New Zealand.[133] Nor did New Zealand legislate to end this power until 1986. This was due rather to inertia than to any lingering sentiment of imperial unity.[134] The effect was that the nature of legitimacy was primarily evolutionary. The limitations of the constitutional approach and a narrow legalism, both in discussion of the scope of government,[135] and in understanding the nature of the constitution, are apparent in considering the development of post-colonial regimes, especially, as in Ireland, legal continuity is maintained.

Democracy, *per se*, does not appear to hinder state success, but nor does it necessarily promote it. What appears more directly relevant is the existence of a working system of the rule of law, coupled with democracy and legitimacy.

---

22 Which all are to perish with the using;) after the commandments and doctrines of men?

23 Which things have indeed a shew of wisdom in will worship, and humility, and neglecting of the body: not in any honour to the satisfying of the flesh.

132 The rule that precedents set by earlier court decisions must be followed where applicable.

133 F.M. Brookfield, 'Parliamentary Supremacy and Constitutional Entrenchment', *Otago Law Review* 5 (1984): 603; Bruce Harris, 'Law-making powers of the New Zealand General Assembly', *Otago Law Review*, 5 (1984): 565.

134 F.M. Brookfield, *The Constitution in 1985* (1985), 9.

135 J. Dearlove, 'Bringing the State Back In', *Political Studies* (1989): 521.

Chapter 7
Empires and Supra-national Entities

7.1 Introduction

Political entities which transcend the nation-state, empires and supra-national entities, exhibit features which render them uniquely incapable of precise categorization. In order to preserve an element of political unity, the constitutional binding force in these forms of state, must exhibit an unusual degree of flexibility and strength – flexibility to respond to the various demands of the constituent peoples, and strength to ensure that diversity does not become disunity.

The empires and supra-national entities (the sole example of the latter today being the European Union, though, depending upon definition, there may be several examples of the former), by their very nature, must have a stronger binding force than the national or racial identity of a state, in order not to disintegrate. This may be pure brute force – as occasionally in the past – or it may be a bureaucratic machine of great tenacity and reach – as in ancient China (and arguably in the modern European Union). If the latter is the case, then this can be seen as a comparatively hard constitution. Relative inflexibility, coupled with an emphasis upon the precision of detail, regulates aspects of life throughout the empire, to a greater or lesser extent, depending upon the resources of the empire. Whether the hard or soft constitutions of the empires render them more or less likely to be successful is an important question. The consideration of this question is the aim of this chapter.

7.2 Rome

While Egypt was an early, at in some respects a rather primitive form of state – primitive in that the dynamics between Pharaoh and people was fairly simple, almost that of overseer and peasant – that of the empire which was Rome was, by comparison, highly complex. It also was the product of physical environment, but whereas the environment which formed Egypt's civilization was a comparatively benign but narrowly-confined fertile valley, Rome's empire (like the earlier, but short-lived, empire of Alexander the Great before it) was spread across much of the known world. Thus, at once it offered greater opportunities to the ruler for the enlargement and the exercise of power, but at the same time it required (and inaugurated) a wholly distinct form of government. The development of this government was to tax the mental and physical resources of the empire, and eventually resolve itself (from the time of Diocletian onwards) into a form of decentralized autocracy – prior to the eventual collapse of the empire in the face of mounting internal and external challenges.

The Roman Empire was also dependent upon technology for its political survival, and this also influenced the nature and form of the constitution.[1] For an empire which lacked a clearly defined border, such as Egypt had,[2] communications was essential to government. Initially this was heavily dependent upon the sea – it is not coincidental that the empire developed around the margins of the Mediterranean Sea, nor that the Romans called it the Mare Nostrum, or 'our (Roman) sea'. As McGinnis has noted, one of the most important ways in which technology transforms the environment is by reducing transportation and communication costs.[3] Such reductions made possible new forms of constitutional structures[4] – in the case of Rome – an empire.[5] The advent of roads led to unity, just as unity led to the construction of roads to exploit the new markets and preserve the unity. The saying that 'all roads led to Rome' had a profound meaning in the empire.

Rome depended upon these communications systems for its survival, as the size of the empire meant that military forces had to be moved swiftly wherever necessary to meet a new threat.[6] As the empire expanded into the hinterland of Europe, Asia and North Africa so it became necessary to develop landward communications arteries, both through military necessity, and as the provinces became more settled, administration convenience.

In the Roman world these communications arteries included roads,[7] military networks,[8] and system of civil and military administration – including the legal

---

1 The law in general was also influenced by economic and social factors; See Jean-Jacques Aubert and Boudewijn Sirks (eds), *Speculum iuris: Roman law as a reflection of social and economic life in antiquity* (Ann Arbor, 2002).

2 Most other civilizations such as the Tigris-Euphrates, and Indus valleys in the Old World and the Valley of Mexico and the mountain and coastal valleys of Peru in the New World also enjoyed defined borders – even if, like Mesopotamia, and the Indus valley, it was a water catchment area. See also Robert L. Carneiro, 'A Theory of the Origin of the State', *Science*, 169 (1970): 733–8, 734.

3 John O. McGinnis, 'The Symbiosis of Constitutionalism and Technology', *Harvard Journal of Law and Public Policy*, 25 (2001): 3–14, 6.

4 Ibid., 6.

5 While not the first empire in Europe – that distinction might go to Alexandra, or to the Minoans (or any of a number of earlier peoples), it was the first viable multinational empire. See Clifford Ando, *Imperial ideology and provincial loyalty in the Roman Empire* (Berkeley, 2000); S.E. Finer, *The history of government from the earliest times* (Oxford, 1997).

6 See Thomas S. Burns, *Barbarians within the gates of Rome: a study of Roman military policy and the barbarians, ca. 375–425 A.D* (Bloomington, 1994).

7 See Raymond Chevallier, *Roman roads*, trans. N.H. Field (Berkeley, 1976).

8 See, for instance, D.J. Woolliscroft, *Roman military signalling* (Stroud, 2001).

system.[9] This involved a degree of constitutional centralization,[10] but occasionally this failed.[11] These occasional failures were less serious that might perhaps otherwise have been the case because the next constitutional tier below the imperial government were the provinces, which were run as part of a relatively homogenous imperial system (though the provinces were initially under senatorial governors, this also reflected a significant degree of centralization).[12]

In the later centuries of the empire fiscal, military and population collapse[13] – brought about in part by the increasingly serious invasions from the east – led to the empire being divided, first temporarily and eventually permanently, into east and west.[14] Yet, while the communications systems were operating properly, Rome was able to oversee – if not always aid – provinces many hundreds and even thousands of kilometres from the imperial city.[15] Unfortunately, because the mechanisms through which the empire operated depended greatly upon the army, and particularly because the formal constitutional powers of the emperors' were long disguised (and therefore the management of the imperial succession was often difficult), the army was often to assume a decisive political role.[16] While

9 See Jean-Jacques Aubert and Boudewijn Sirks (eds), *Speculum iuris: Roman law as a reflection of social and economic life in antiquity* (Ann Arbor, 2002). Roman law forms the basis of the civil law system, which is one of the principle legal systems in use today.

10 This was especially so after the evolution of the imperial constitution – such as it was – through the adoption of the eastern model of divine ruler. See J. Rufus Fears, *Princeps a diis electus: the divine election of the emperor as a political concept at Rome* (Rome, 1977).

11 There was, for instance, no satisfactory imperial succession law; See Fears. When the succession was disputed provincial governors, or generals, might contend for the imperial purple. See, for example, in the year of the three emperors; John Grainger, *Nerva and the Roman succession crisis of AD 96–99* (London, 2003).

12 See Andrew Lintott, *Imperium Romanum: politics and administration* (London, 1993). Governors might vie for the purple, but a province would rarely secede for very long.

13 See F.W. Walbank, *The awful revolution: the decline of the Roman Empire in the West* (Liverpool, 1969).

14 See Timothy D. Barnes, *The new empire of Diocletian and Constantine* (Cambridge, 1982).

15 This was at least until the conditions facing the imperial heartlands rendered all contact – and aid – uncertain. See, for instance, Venerable Bede, *Bede's Ecclesiastical history of the English people: a historical commentary*, ed. J.M. Wallace-Hadrill (Oxford, 1988), ch. 13:

> To Agitius (Aetius), thrice consul, the Groans of the Britons ... the barbarians drive us to the sea, the sea drives us to the barbarians; between these two means of death we are either killed or drowned. There is no reply.
>
> – from *The Groans of the Britons* (446 AD). By Agitius Gildas presumably meant Aetius. Aetius held his third consulship from 446 to 454.

16 See J.B. Campbell, *The Emperor and the Roman Army, 31 BC–AD 235* (Oxford, 1984); Lukas de Blois, *The Roman army and politics in the first century before Christ* (Amsterdam, 1987).

this led, at times, to instability, it also could cause the rise to the purple of capable military and political leaders. Politico-strategic changes – including an increased emphasis upon the provinces along the eastern borders, meant that a single imperial government was incapable of effectively administering the whole empire.

Communications and transportation technology allowed the Roman empire to be run in a centralized fashion.[17] As utilization of technology declined in effectiveness – partly through over-commitment – decentralization increased.[18] Communications technology of this type made a significant contribution to the form of the imperial Roman imperial constitution and was fostered by a regime built on public works and military technology.

Political unity depended, in common with that in ancient Egypt, on the unity of the position of head of state. The succession to the imperial purple, and the choice of emperor, were always central to Roman unity, and became increasingly important as the exigencies of imperial government, especially from the third century, became increasingly military and defensive in nature. Roman strength lay in its military and engineering genius, and later its jurisprudence; its weakness lay in its inability to development a consistent law and policy of imperial succession. Under a strong emperor some measure of success could be anticipated, but failure to ensure a smooth succession often acted as a harbinger of civil war, rebellion, invasion or political and economic chaos.

If Egypt may be categorized as showing the development of a simple centralized monarchical government around a single pre-eminent technological requirement, Rome may be seen as the evolution of an artificial state through the requirements of a more complex physical and human environment. Rome became a multi-headed empire because of the failure of communications, but its existence at all was a tribute to the comparatively advanced nature of communications in the ancient world, and to its successful utilization. Unfortunately, eventual failure could be ascribed to the privations of invaders and political disunity, due to a lack of a common law or succession, or a coherent national ethos. Whilst it would be an exaggeration to ascribe this to the advent of Christianity, the loss of the cohesion of the imperial religious cult, and the decline in adherence to the ancient religions, would have accelerated the decline.[19]

---

17 Aqueducts, public granaries, etc allowed the city of Rome to become a metropolis of at least half a million people; See Gerda de Kleijn, *The Water Supply of Ancient Rome: City Area, Water, and Population* (Amsterdam, 2001); Glenn R. Storey, 'The population of ancient Rome', *Antiquity*, 71 (1997): 966–78.

18 Aqueducts failed, secure food supplies dwindled, people left the cities, causing a decline of the city-state government; See Robert Coates-Stephens, 'The walls and aqueducts of Rome in the early Middle Ages, A.D. 500–1000', *The Journal of Roman Studies*, 88 (1998): 166–78.

19 Ferdinand Lot, *The end of the ancient world and the beginnings of the Middle Ages* (London: 1953).

7.3 European Union

Two thousand years later another empire lies at the cross-roads of success or failure. This also may be categorized as dependent upon the absence of a coherent cultural or political ethos, and a lack of political unity and continuity at the highest levels.

The European Union is, in essence, a refutation of the classical model of sovereignty. European Union members have delegated or 'pooled' their sovereignty in the interest of an unprecedented degree of unification. Developments in the European Union and elsewhere have caused some theorists to posit that a 'new sovereignty' has been forged, one that is based far less on the dictation of outcomes or classical exclusivity and more on bargaining, negotiation, cooperation, and earned recognition as a member of the international community.

The European Union is one of the largest organizations in the world, today comprising of 27 member states, and millions of people. There are however deep divisions and conflicts in how the European Union should be managed, and how the current expansion and integration process should be handled. There are many views, ranging from the complete dismantlement of the European Union, back to independent nation-states with no integration, to those seeking complete integration and the forming of a unitary state.

Many critics of the European Union see the process of integration to be elitist, undemocratic and insufficiently transparent.[20] The European Union also seems to be suffering from having too many labels; there is no consensus over what the European Union should be called. Some of these labels are: quasi-state; intergovernmental organization; supranational polity; federation; confederation, and multilevel system of government. Whatever the label given, the European Union is causing considerable debate, especially over the direction its future should take. The European Constitution attempted to define Europe's future, by giving it a new structure in which to work.

This section will look at some of the issues surrounding the future of the European Union, looking specifically at the views of Eurosceptics and Federalists. These two groups form the two extremes of the debate over integration, the Eurosceptics favouring the maintenance or the re-establishment of the nation-state, the federalists favouring complete integration into a unitary state. This section will begin with a brief history of the European Union, and what the founding fathers originally envisioned. It will attempt to conclude with how the process of integration may be managed in the future.

The European Union is an organization that began life in the late 1940's, born in the aftermath of the Second World War. At this time, there was a consensus between Western European nations, that some kind of European integration or network was needed to help rebuild Europe, and to prevent another war occurring.

---

20 G. Morgan, *The Idea of a European Superstate: Public Justification and European Integration* (Princeton, 2005).

It was facilitated partly by the United States of America and the Marshall Plan. This plan was designed to stimulate economic growth, and politically to combat the threat of communism from the Soviet Union. In 1948, the Organization for European Economic Cooperation (OEEC) was established, created to administer and organize the economic help from the USA, as laid out in the Marshall Plan. By 1949, the Council of Europe was established to create political cooperation among European nations; its aim was to strengthen democratic systems, and human rights within member states.

France and Germany were two countries hit hardest by the destruction of the Second World War. They were also two countries that were deeply opposed to each other politically. The Schuman Declaration attempted to confront both these issues:

> Europe will not be made all at once, or according to a single plan. It will be built through concrete achievements which first create a de facto solidarity. The coming together of the nations of Europe requires the elimination of the age-old opposition of France and Germany. Any action taken must in the first place concern these two countries. With this aim in view, the French Government proposes that action be taken immediately on one limited but decisive point.
>
> It proposes that Franco-German production of coal and steel as a whole be placed under a common High Authority, within the framework of an organisation open to the participation of the other countries of Europe. The pooling of coal and steel production should immediately provide for the setting up of common foundations for economic development as a first step in the federation of Europe (...).[21]

This declaration forged the way for the European Coal and Steel Community, created in 1951 through the Treaty of Paris. Four other members, Italy, Belgium, the Low Countries and the Netherlands, joined France and Germany, thus creating the first European Community.

The foreign ministers of this community lead by the Belgium Foreign Minister, met in 1955 at a conference in Messina, Italy. As a result of these meetings, in March 1957 the Treaties of Rome were signed, creating the European Economic Community (EEC). After a ratification process undertaken by all six countries home parliaments, the Treaty of Rome came into effect on 1 January 1958. The treaty's aim was to 'channel political and economic reconstruction, and particularly that of Germany'.[22] The hope was that closer European integration would make another war unthinkable.

Other members have slowly been added to this community, in 1973 three new members joined: Ireland, Denmark and the United Kingdom. Greece joined in

---

21 Quote taken from <http://www.historiasiglo20.org/europe/anteceden2.htm> (18 April 2007).

22 A.S. Sweet, *The Judicial Construction of Europe* (Oxford, 2004).

1981; Spain and Portugal in 1986; and Austria, Sweden and Finland in 1995. In 1993 however, certain qualifying conditions were approved, by the EU, for the admittance of central and eastern European states. In 2004 ten new members were admitted,[23] but Bulgaria, Rumania and Turkey's applications were delayed, as criteria were not meet. Bulgaria and Rumania however became full members on 1 January this year, although they face penalties if improvements are not seen in certain areas.[24] Turkey's admission was delayed in December 2006 after European Union foreign ministers suspended talks, this was due in part to Turkey's refusal to open sea and air ports to European Union member Cyprus,[25] which Turkey doesn't recognize, having their own regime in north Cyprus. It would be interesting if Turkey joined the European Union, then went to war with Greece – as it nearly did several times in the 1970s and 80s.

In 1991 the Maastricht Treaty turned the European Community into the European Union, creating an even closer political and economic union between countries. It was ratified by home parliaments, coming into force in May 1993.[26] As well as the name change, the Maastricht Treaty paved the way for monetary union, and greater social policy coherence. It also introduced European Union citizenship, allowing citizens of any European Union country to live, work and vote in any other European Union country. Currently the European Union has a tripartite division of power: the European Council, the European Commission, and the European Parliament.

As well as creating the European Economic Community, the Treaty of Rome also created what became known as the Common Market. This was designed to reduce and eliminate tariffs on trade between member countries, and create a common tariff for goods coming in from third countries. It also formed the Common Agricultural Policy (CAP), creating a free market for agricultural products within the EEC, by guaranteeing prices for farmers, protectionist policies were promoted.

In the first few decades of the European Community (EC), establishing and maintaining free movement of trade was the primary concern. However, other issues gradually came to the forefront such as: fiscal and monetary policy; social policy and health care; environmental protection and human rights. These issues have been addressed in subsequent Acts and treaties,[27] which have been formally incorporated into the Treaty of Rome by member states, thus expanding the scope and competences of the EC outside of the original agenda.

---

23 These countries were: the Baltic states; Cyprus; the Czech Republic; Hungary; Malta; Poland; Slovakia and Slovenia.

24 Some of these areas are: curbing organized crime and corruption, ensuring food safety standards are met, and the proper use of European Union funds is managed.

25 BBC Website.

26 Ibid.

27 Some of these are: The Single European Act (1986), the Treaty on the European Union (1993), and the Treaty of Amsterdam (1999).

The recent effort to adopt a European Union constitution was another attempt to expand the scope of the European Union. Although the United Kingdom claimed it was 'merely a tiding-up exercise',[28] the fact that the treaty was signed in the same place as The Treaty of Rome, 'the symbolism thus declared that this was a treaty to re-found the European Union'.[29] This move was outside the original scope of The Treaty of Rome, which, after all, was primarily economic, and was ultimately unsuccessful.

Lord Carrington, who helped the United Kingdom become a member in 1973, believed that the European Union has gone too far, which is why the Constitution failed. 'I thought we were joining a common market. It did not occur to me that the Europeans would interfere in our affairs.'[30] Lord Carrington however argues that the average person is not anti-European, but that the British public were sold the idea of a Common Market, not an integrated European State; 'What worries me about the Union is that so many rules and regulations come out of Brussels that are not, broadly speaking, anything to do with the Common Market.' It is the increasing bureaucracy of Brussels that many people are against, and the over-regulations that accompanies it. Quite apart from any political or economic arguments, there is danger inherent in a bureaucracy becoming too powerful. The feeling that 'you should be left to run your own affairs unless it affects the Common Market' is the reason, according to Lord Carrington, that the Constitution failed.

The European Community however has never fitted into a conventional typology, it is seen by some as an intergovernmental organization with a voluntary 'pooling of sovereignty'[31] by member states. Others see it a 'quasi-federal state system', however when The Council of Europe was established back in the 1940's, it did not ask for the surrender of sovereignty from member states, neither calling itself a union nor a federation of states.[32] With the evolving of the European Union (EU) however, many now see it as a 'complex blend of supranational and intergovernmental modes of governance'.[33] There are elements of governance found in international law, but also elements that are parallel to national constitutional law and federalism.[34] The lack of definition over the status of the European Union is one area that causes tension among member states. And if we don't know exactly what it is, how can we sell if to anyone? The European Community has evolved from a Free Trade Area (FTA), taking on more areas of

---

28 R. Whitman, 'No and After: Options for Europe', *International Affairs*, 81(4) (2005): 673–87.

29 Ibid.

30 Daily Telegraph Website: Con Coughlin, 'EU has gone too far, says man who helped Britain join'.

31 A.S. Sweet, *The Judicial Construction of Europe* (Oxford, 2004).

32 <http://www.historiasiglo20.org/europe/anteceden2.htm> (18 April 2007).

33 Ibid.

34 J.A. Caporaso, 'The European Union and Forms of State: Westphalian, Regulatory or Post Modern?', *Journal of Common Market Studies*, 34(1) (1996): 19–52.

responsibility, but has not yet fully evolved into a single federal state. Member states still technically hold full sovereign rights, but more decisions concerning the governing of territory is given up to the European Council. How to move the European Union forward is a major area of contention, an example of which was the rejection of the European Constitution.

In 1958, the Treaty of Rome harmonized nearly 200 laws,[35] and the process has continued. Today 60 per cent of national legislation of European Union member states originates in Brussels. According to Schmitter 'there is no issue area that was the exclusive domain of national policy in 1950 and that has not somehow and in some degree been incorporated within the authoritative purview of the EC/EU'.[36] If this is the case, then it follows that there must be some impact on the sovereignty of individual member states (see European Union directives on changing light bulbs). Indeed many believe that only a residual sovereignty now remains. Wiener however argues that sovereignty is reinforced by the 'pooling effect', reasserting state sovereignty. A view supported by Harrison and Mungall,[37] who state that through harmonization and agreement of policy changes among national states, there is an explicit avoidance of interfering with national sovereignty.

In 2001 a grocer in England was convicted of selling one pound of bananas, the defence argued that the British Weights and Measures Act 1985 allowed goods to be sold in both imperial and metric measures, however this is not the case in European Law. As a member of the European Union, the United Kingdom is required to 'recognize both the "direct effect" and "supremacy" of European Law over competing national laws'.[38] This case sparked a debate over who was actually governing the nation, Westminster or Brussels.[39] Legally speaking, subject to a right – which presumably still exists – to leave the European Union, there is not much doubt that it is ultimately Brussels, and has been for some time. It is an ongoing debate that is being carried out across Europe, together with whether or how far European integration and expansion should continue.

Treaties can in some cases lead to federal states being formed, such as Germany in 1870. Usually however, treaties produce alliances, leagues, confederations or goals that are confined to specific areas.[40] The Treaty of Rome began as a way to unite Europe and focus on rebuilding and creating economic growth, and essentially constitutes the European Community.[41] Thus, the governing authority

---

35 J. Wiener, *Globalisation and the Harmonisation of Law* (London, 1999).

36 Cited in G.F. Mancini, 'Europe: The Case for Statehood', *European Law Journal*, 4(1) (1998): 29–42.

37 Cited in J. Wiener, *Globalisation and the Harmonisation of Law* (London, 1999).

38 G. Morgan, *The Idea of a European Superstate: Public Justification and European Integration* (Princeton, 2005).

39 Westminster being the home of the British Parliament, and Brussels being the home of the European Parliament.

40 G.F. Mancini, 'Europe: The Case for Statehood'.

41 A.S. Sweet, *The Judicial Construction of Europe*.

has been distributed among different institutions, with the establishment of legal rules and procedures. The European Community therefore, differs from the conventional view of treaties, as polity was established, member states and citizens have become subject to a European rule of law, over and above their own domestic law.

Within Europe it would appear that individual domestic institutions (or member states) have yielded to bureaucratic directives from Brussels, with 'national sovereignty seem[ing] to have been merged into a supranational framework'. There is an increasing system of standards and controls that reach far inside every state. In the 1970's the Constitutional Court of Germany ruled that certain EC regulations could not be enforced as they conflicted with rights guaranteed in the German constitution. The *Internationale Handelsgesellschaft* ruling by the European Court of Justice (ECJ) maintained that European Union law must take precedence over national constitutions. By signing the Treaty of Rome, Germany had bound itself to a higher authority than its own constitution. Thus, it can be claimed that in some part, member states' sovereignty has been handed to the European Union. The question follows as to why a country would bind itself to a supranational authority that can override its own constitution. One theory is to view the European Union as an embryo state; indeed as an increasing number of laws are made at European Union level it is a convincing argument. This thought was present before the European Union was realized. Some people consider that Winston Churchill took the first step towards European integration in 1946 when seeking a remedy to the 'tragedy of Europe', stating:

> What is this sovereign remedy? It is to recreate the European Family, or as much of it as we can, and to provide it with a structure under which it can dwell in peace, in safety and in freedom. We must build a kind of United States of Europe.[42]

Thus the idea of a federal Europe is not a new one – and Hitler had similar ideas. Although is has been noted that the closer the union moves towards statehood, the greater the resistance becomes.

Mancini argues that the European Union does already possess a federal character. Power is severely detracted from the sovereignty of national parliaments, through an incremental process that national parliaments have no control over and have not consented to.[43] This has however been denied, which critics of the European Union suggest is due to its undemocratic structure.

The European Union as an organization is still growing and changing; new members are still being admitted and discussions for new treaties are being held for further integration. This is known as the 'deepening and widening process'. It is not however a process that is without its difficulties, and there are many

---

42 <http://www.historiasiglo20.org/europe/anteceden2.htm> (18 April 2007).

43 G.F. Mancini, 'Europe: The Case for Statehood'.

opponents and supporters, both of the European Union as a whole, but also the way in which further integration is being handled. According to Morgan, the arguments surrounding the 'problem of the EU' are three sided, there are: the Eurosceptics; the Postsovereignists; and the federalists, which all have differing opinions on how the process should be managed and to what extent integration should occur. Loosely defined, the Eurosceptics want to maintain independent nation-states, whereas the postsovereignists want a radically new multilevel, decentralized polity. The federalists on the other hand favour a more 'United States of Europe', based on the model seen in the United States of America.

Morgan states that there are four main areas of contention, two institutional disagreements, and two big policy disagreements.[44] The institutional disagreements are the division of competences and the distribution of power.

The division of competences concerns the level in which decisions are made, at a European level, national or local level. For postsovereignists, the decision on any issue should be taken at the level closest to those being affected.[45] This issue links closely to that of the distribution of power. Eurosceptics advocate that power should be concentrated in institutions that member states control, with national vetoes for any decisions taken. Federalists on the other hand, promote distributing power to institutions that member states do not control, and also want majority voting. Thus ensuring that powerful states cannot veto decisions that may not necessarily benefit them but would be of benefit to the majority of other states. These divisions are fundamental to the running of the European Union, and causing major disagreements over the best way to progress the 'deepening and widening process'.

In addition to these institutional disagreements, are those surrounding policies. Market-constraining regulatory policies are one area causing contention, and also drive much of the disagreements on the division of competences. Each member country wants to be able to implement policies that will benefit their economy; however these economies do not have the same cycles and thus benefit from differing levels of intervention. For example, the United Kingdom favours minimal governmental intervention, however there is a fear that federalism will generate a series of market constraining polices that will impede economic performance. Conversely, France and Germany have the opposite view. The concern being that further European Union expansion will limit the capacity for national governments to impose market constraining polices, such as anti-takeover legislation.

The second major policy disagreement concerns foreign and security policies, and to a lesser extent the European Union's relationship with the United States of America. This is considered to be the biggest unresolved issue for the European Union, and the recent war in Iraq has exposed deep divisions. The United Kingdom has always maintained close relations with the United States of America, and has

44 There are other areas of contention, but too many to go into detail here.

45 Thus if the decision affected Europe at a whole if would be taken at that level, if it only affected Scotland, the decision would be taken in Edinburgh at the Scottish parliament.

supported the Iraq war. Many mainland European nations however are sceptical of American policies, and are outspoken in their opposition to current events. Currently the European Union has no official foreign policy, and there is not a 'European Army', although the European Parliament does make statements concerning world security issues. Currently though, member states determine their own foreign and security polices.

Eurosceptics are those that are opposed to further European expansion. Many in this group believe that the European Union is wasteful, unnecessary, unaccountable, corrupt, protectionist, anti-democratic, and 'foreign'.[46] These are views that are said to have originated in Britain, but have spread throughout mainland Europe. The overriding fear is that Europe will turn into a federal entity, as the current process of integration has far reaching and irreversible changes. They argue that the process of expansion and integration is secretive, bureaucratic and deceptive, with many decisions being taken that greatly affect individual nations, but are not voted upon. They oppose the idea of a European super state, or United States of Europe, and want to maintain independent nation-states. Critics of the Eurosceptic movement argue that due to the current level of integration, returning to un-integrated nation-states would require as much departure from the *status quo* as moving towards a federal state. Therefore implying that Eurosceptics seek a level of independence that can no longer be sustained.

Mancini states that the history and practices of European member states, 'promises the implicit vision of a supranational, rather than a statal Europe'.[47] However, the Maastricht Treaty took the symbols of statehood, with the ideas of citizenship, foreign policy and defence. Ideas that are traditionally associated with the nation-state. Thus the Eurosceptic may be justified in fearing that Europe will turn into a federal entity.

The real issue according to Mancini is the inability to 'conceive of statehood in any other terms than the nation-statehood, or, in a nutshell, to divorce the state from the nation'. The German Constitutional Court looked at the Maastricht Treaty in comparison to German Basic Law, and found in Article 20 that:

> The 'principle of democracy requires that each and every execution of sovereign rights derives directly from the "people of the State"' (Staatsvolk).[48]

For the European Union, the issue is that there is no 'European People'. In democratic countries, national parliaments are subject to public opinions, the opinions of their citizens. The German Courts argue that public opinion is formed through the free exchange of ideas, and that a certain degree of homogeneity is needed for this to occur. Thus, it naturally occurs within the nation-state. Justice

46 G. Morgan, *The Idea of a European Superstate: Public Justification and European Integration* (Princeton, 2005).

47 G.F. Mancini, 'Europe: The Case for Statehood'.

48 Ibid.

Grimm[49] points out that the chief obstacle to development, which 'dooms to failure' any attempt to create a functioning political system is the absence of a common language,[50] and a common language is required for the exchange of ideas to occur. Justice Grimm goes onto say that because there is not a 'European People'; the European Union assembly is not a popular representative body. Member states consist of an ethnically homogenous and socially coherent group of people that renders democracy possible. Europe on the other hand lacks this ethnic uniformity to allow the same level of democracy to occur, thus Justice Grimm suggests that a single European state is not possible, if it is to remain democratic.

It is a view upheld by other Eurosceptics, in that European political integration will lead to the demise of the European Sozialstaat.[51] The fear is that there will be a return to a 'classical liberal Rechstaat',[52] a Europe capable of protecting basic liberties and the rule of law, but will be unable to maintain a socialized market, a welfare state, and progressive taxation policies, which have been the accomplishment of the Sozialstaat. Eurosceptics believe that further European integration will result in a Europe without social justice.

Mancini however, refutes the idea that a lack of ethnic uniformity means democracy cannot be fully realized in a European state. Mancini cites two examples, that of South Africa and India. South Africa consists of eight black ethnic groups; a large number of 'coloureds'; two Asian communities; two white 'tribes', and has eleven official languages. India has countless ethnic groups; six religions (all with over three million followers); 15 regional languages; the official language, Hindi, is spoken only by 38 per cent of the population, and only four in every hundred can speak English, which is the language of influential newspapers. Both of these countries have huge problems; such as hostility between ethnic groups and high illiteracy rates, democracy however is flourishing. Mancini argues that as Europe has better material and social conditions than either of these countries, a European state should work. Marxist-Leninist theory also maintained that Communism would have worked in Russia had it been more developed in 1917. However, South Africa and India are already a nation-state, and thus have the incentive to ensure democracy works. Europe on the other hand, is a collection of several countries, with large groups of people not wanting to create one state, thus the comparison with India and South Africa may be unfair.

In regard to Turkey's admittance to the European Union, cultural issues appear to be an important aspect, Jose Manuel Barroso, President of the European Commission stated: 'First of all (it will be) very demanding for them but also demanding for us here to be ready to accommodate such an important big country that is seen by so many of us as culturally different from, let's say, mainstream

---

49 Justice Grimm is a senior German Judge.

50 G.F. Mancini, 'Europe: The Case for Statehood'.

51 G. Morgan, *The Idea of a European Superstate: Public Justification and European Integration* (Princeton, 2005).

52 Ibid.

Europe.' Therefore, on a political level, Mancini is mistaken in suggesting that ethnic uniformity is not an important factor.

Part of the reasons against a federal Europe are however ideological, rather than if it is technically possible. The political ramifications of uniting the nation-states into a single nation are likely to be far reaching. A major concern for everyday people is the loss of their national identity. The Treaty of Amsterdam took these concerns seriously when discussing the possibility of national identity cards, stating that union membership was to complement, but not replace member state nationality.

The failure of the European Constitution reinforces the Eurosceptics' views. The constitution needs to be fully ratified by all member states, which in some countries was done through a referendum. Both France and the Netherlands voted against the constitution, in France one of the reasons given was that concern that France was ceding too much sovereignty to the European Union.[53] As yet, Europe does not hold sovereignty, this remains with individual states, thus under international law, unless member states voluntarily surrender their sovereign rights to the EU, a 'United States of Europe' is not legally possible.

Morgan identifies that there are two types of federalists within Europe, what has been termed *genuine* federalists and European federalists. Although essentially wanting the same for Europe, that of moving away from independent nation-states, there are subtle differences between the two.

It is argued that European federalists are seeking a 'unitary federal superstate'. They favour locating the centre of power at Brussels, with all-important political functions taking place at the European level. They argue that the European people form the constituting power and the state represents the people. Thus, European federalists seek the transfer of sovereign power from the nation-states to the European Union.

What has been classified as *genuine* federalists however, seek a different vision for the European Union. These federalists can also be termed post-sovereignists. They aspire to a decentralized, multi-level federal polity, replacing sovereignty and the nation-state. The aim is a disposal of power, rather than concentrating power in a centralized political authority.

Federalism in its *genuine* meaning in defined as:

> the linking of individuals, groups, and polities in lasting but limited union in such a way as to provide for the energetic pursuit of common ends while maintaining the respective integrities of all parties … Federalism has to do with the constitutional diffusion of power, so that the constituting elements in a federal arrangement share in the processes of common policy-making and administration by right, while the activities of the common government are conducted in such a way as to maintain their respective integrities.[54]

---

53 Cited on BBC website <http://news.bbc.co.uk/1/hi/world/europe/4596005.stm>.

54 Defined by Daniel Elazar as cited in G. Morgan, *The Idea of a European Superstate.*

Thus, the federal polity represents the 'constitutive "'member states"',[55] which in turn represent the people of that state, hence forming a type of double representation. The ideal form for a federal polity is a 'constitutionally entrenched formal equality' rather than a hierarchical one between the two levels of authority. This view contrasts with European federalists seeking a unitary state, which creates a central authority and all other jurisdictions are subordinate to it. However, it is conceded that this form of double representation federal polity is rarely, if ever, achieved.

As already stated, one of the major fears for Eurosceptics is the idea of Europe becoming the United States of Europe. Looking at the concept of federalism, the comparison of Europe to the United States of America is natural. There are however some distinct differences between Europe and the USA. At present the member states of the European Union have sovereign rights; they are independent nation-states, recognized as such on the world stage. The states of America though, while maintaining some distinction and separation of federal and state levels of powers, do not have sovereign status. The United States of America is therefore closer to that of a unitary state, than that of a true federal polity. The federal level is considered a higher form of authority than individual states, and does not include the states in federal decision-making. It is this that Eurosceptics fear, that political power will be taken away, with decisions taken at a higher level. Unlike the European Union, the United States of America does not have a European Council in which all member states participate, deciding on the political directions and policies.

There is an argument that suggests that the European Union is already an international state, but lacks an international government, in the 'sense of a highly centralised, hierarchical political structure, independent of the Governments of Member states, and capable of acting (authoritatively) on a broad range of issues'.[56] However, the European Union does have a recognized international structure of governance. The European Parliament sets rules or laws governing inter-state relations, and has a 'soft-law'[57] for the acceptance of national methods to achieve the Commission's objectives. It sets defence budgets, mobilizes troops and sends diplomats abroad, among other things. With the exclusion of certain political decisions, Caporaso states that the 'ongoing economic and political relations between Member states mediated by the institutions of the European Union, [the European Union] is already an international state'. The exclusion of some political decisions does not seem to affect the status of the European Union, as this can be explained through devolution. Even though Scotland has its own

55 Ibid.

56 J.A. Caporaso, 'The European Union and Forms of State: Westphalian, Regulatory or Post Modern?', *Journal of Common Market Studies*, 34(1) (1996): 19–52.

57 Wellens and Borchardt (1989), 'Soft Law in European Community Law' *European Law Review* cited in J.A. Caporaso, 'The European Union and Forms of State: Westphalian, Regulatory or Post Modern?', *Journal of Common Market Studies*, 34(1) (1996): 19–52.

parliament and makes decisions, it is still nonetheless part of the sovereign state of the United Kingdom. Thus, member states such as the United Kingdom, France or Germany can still make political decisions and also be part of the European Union state.

In 1576 Bodin wrote the 'Six Livres de la Republique' in which he set out the Marks of Sovereignty:[58]

> The power of law-making
> The power to declare war and make peace
> The power to establish offices of State
> The ultimate right of judgement
> The power of pardon
> The right of coining money
> The right of taxation

By looking at these Marks of Sovereignty, is almost like a checklist for the European Union. The European Union is able to make laws and enforcement them, albeit through member state parliaments; it has established offices of state; the European Courts pass judgments and pardons; and the European Union also coins its own money. As yet the European Union does not tax individuals, but a tax or 'contribution' is given by member states that has been taken from individuals. Declaring war or peace is the one area where member states have a unilateral decision. Therefore, Caporaso may be right in thinking that a European state does already exist.

The European Union's future is currently being debated in many political circles, especially since the failure of the constitution through the French and Dutch 'No' votes in their referendums. Germany has attempted to revive the constitution, by proposing a new treaty that does not contain the controversial elements of the old Constitution. This would still create closer integration, but sovereignty would not be such a direct issue. However, the United Kingdom, the Netherlands and the Czech Republic have asked for further 'constitutional trappings' to be dropped to ensure that ratification by referendums would not be necessary. Former British Prime Minister Tony Blair however created controversy by announcing that a referendum would not be held to ratify the new treaty. This led to accusations of 'introducing a scaled down constitution through the back door'. French President, Nicholas Sarkozy also favours 'ratifying an EU mini-treaty created from the ashes of the 'constitution' without a referendum'.[59] Therefore two of the main countries whose citizens were against a European Union constitution are planning

---

58 Cited in M. Loughan (ed.), *The Ten Tenets of Sovereignty* (Oxford, 2003).

59 Harry de Quetteville: 'Full in-tray challenges a man in a hurry' The Daily Telegraph 7 May 2007 http://www.telegraph.co.uk/news/main.jhtml?xml=/news/2007/05/07/wfra207.xml.

ways of ensuring that it does still happen. Therefore, the suggestion is that further integration may happen regardless of what the citizens of Europe want.

There is an increasing argument that the European Union needs to become a full unitary state to effectively deal with the issues in security that have arisen since the attacks in America in 2001. Morgan argues that if terrorists attacked Europe, such as Westminster in London, the Louvre in Paris, the Vatican and the Reichstag, killing thousands, Europe would not be able to defend itself in a coherent manner.[60] The USA is tied up with the war in Iraq, and may be unwilling to provide Europe with military support, especially with public support waning. As the European Union currently does not have a unilateral security stance or a unified military, it is in a vulnerable position to outside threats. Becoming a single state, would allow the European Union to deal with security issues quicker and more efficiently. The Irish Republican Army – partly funded by tax-deductable donations in the United States of America – carried out many attacks in London and elsewhere without the European Union or the United States of America getting involved.

At the end of April 2007, the European Union and United States of America signed up to a new transatlantic economic partnership, focusing primarily on economic, rather than political or environmental issues. The pact has been designed to 'boost trade and investment by harmonising regulatory standards, laying the basis for a United States-European Union single market'.[61] An economic council will be set up to advance regulatory convergence in forty different areas, including intellectual property rights, financial services, business takeovers, and the motor industry, as well as many others. The aim is to increase trade and lower costs.

An Open Skies Deal has also been reached, designed to reduce fares and increase traffic on transatlantic routes. Taking effect at the end of March 2008, European Union carriers were allowed to fly anywhere in the United States of America, and *vice versa*. It is also hoped that an Open Aviation Area will be created in the future, 'in which investment can flow freely and in which European and United States airlines can provide air services without any restriction'.[62] The European Union is also petitioning the United States of America to withdraw visa requirements for citizens from certain European Union countries, making travel even easier.

Agreeing to a single market with the United States of America could have major implications for the European Union. Trade should increase and become easier between these two regions. However, it may make the campaign for returning to fully independent nation-states become less relevant. If trade with the United States of America is easier being inside the European Union, there will be strong reluctance for politicians to pull their countries out of the European Union.

60 G. Morgan, *The Idea of a European Superstate: Public Justification and European Integration*.

61 'US and EU agree "Single Market"', BBC Website <http://news.bbc.co.uk/2/hi/europe/6607757.stm>.

62 Ibid.

Therefore, this may in turn lead to increased pressure to integrate the European Union further, making trade between European Union countries and those outside the European Union even easier. If Turkey joined the United States of America might get upset, security-wise, and impose more restrictions on all European Union members.

The European Union has gone through many changes since in inception sixty years ago. It started out as a collection of six countries, uniting under a Coal and Steel Treaty to rebuild after the ravages of the Second World War. Since then it has grown to include 27 countries, with increasing levels of integration, harmonizing laws, practices and recently a common currency. For many these are all steps towards a fully integrated, unitary state. There has however been opposition at every stage, with claims that state sovereignty is being eroded, and accusations that Europe interferes with ordinary people's lives. Despite these conflicting views however, Europe has continued to evolve, accepting new members and integrating to ever-deeper levels. Due to recent developments, such as the agreement with the USA over a 'single market' and both Britain and France pushing for a 'mini-constitution' that does not need a referendum, it would appear that the European Union will continue along the path of further integration. The conflict surrounding this process will probably always be present, but the commitment of Europe's politicians suggests that the development will continue.

There are however, issues and concerns that have not been dealt with by European politicians. For instance, would France and the United Kingdom be willing to surrender their seats at the United Nations Security Council, in favour of one European seat. At present 'current plans for reforming the [European] Council [do not] envisage a single European seat on the Security Council'.[63] However, for full integration to occur, this is one issue that will need to be addressed and one that is likely to cause disagreements. Thus, further integration of the European Union will continue to be surrounded by disagreements and conflicts, as new issues continue to arise.

7.4 Conclusion

Supra-national entities and empires are not inherently constitutionally dissimilar to nation-states. But they may, almost by definition, manifest the advantage and disadvantage of their federal nature (whether formally a federation or not). Thus there is unlikely to be a strong unifying cultural or political ethos – beyond adherence to a common leadership, or belief in the rule of law, or democracy. Christians in the early Roman empire suffered persecution, not because they worshipped the new Christ god (for the Roman state, whatever its people may have thought individually, was relatively tolerant), but they refused to sacrifice to

63 E. Bloom, F. Bgnami, P.-J. Kuijper and P. Lachmann, 'The European Union's New Ambitions', *Proceedings of the American Society of International Law* (2005).

the Caesar god – and hence were seen as subversive, as potential enemies of the state. The decline of the old paganism in the fourth century was accompanied by a state-encouraged Christianization, but the challenges to the empire from within and without had already irretrievably weakened the empire, at least in the west.

The European Union, lacking the unifying symbol – and strong leader – of a Caesar or Augustus, and devoid of a common ideology or religion, is potentially in a much weaker position than the Roman empire. It may be that the legalistic and bureaucratic apparatus of the European Union acts as a substitute, at least to some extent, for the centralizing influence of the emperors. But this is dependent upon the adherence of both populations and member governments. Whilst the latter retain the independence of action and policy formation to which they cling it may be impossible to develop a truly lasting 'imperial' entity. Whether this is a good thing or not is another question, but its implications are that the unity of the European Union depends upon the support of member governments.

Chapter 8
Mixed Models

8.1 Introduction

In the so-called mixed models, there is neither doctrinaire liberalism, nor authoritarianism. There is unity rather than diversity (the latter being perhaps more typical of an empire). Sometimes this is because soft constitutions have allowed or encouraged this; occasionally it is because hard constitutions have required it. The application of the hard/soft distinction to these hybrid states – to which the majority of modern states can probably be deemed to belong – can be equally useful however. The choice of paradigm can be seen to be a product of the particular history of the state, and still has an important influence upon the success or failure of the state.

8.2 Modern doctrinaire liberalism and authoritarianism

In the Westminster parliamentary system of government, whether located in the United Kingdom or elsewhere, there are a number of common elements. These reflect aspects of doctrinaire liberalism and authoritarianism. In the former may be seen the rule of law; the latter is reflected in the doctrine of parliamentary sovereignty or supremacy.

The sovereignty of Parliament is perhaps the most fundamental principle of the British constitution.[1] The traditional, Diceyan, theory of parliamentary sovereignty or supremacy was one of continuing sovereignty. Thus the Westminster Parliament, in English law, could continue to legislate for ex-colonies, whatever the Statute of Westminster or any other Act might say.

But the independence of the Dominions was protected by well-established conventions, which held that Westminster would not act without the Dominion following the procedure specified in the Statute of Westminster 1931, that of request and consent.[2] This allowed for post-independence legislation for these countries, legislation which would be equally valid in both United Kingdom and local law.

---

1 Sir Henry Wade, 'The Basis of Legal Sovereignty', *Cambridge Law Journal* (1955): 172–97.

2 See Richard Latham, *The Law and the Commonwealth* (London, 1949) reprinted from W.K. Hancock (ed.), *Survey of British Commonwealth Affairs* (London, 1937).

But since the United Kingdom Parliament is, in English law, supreme, it always has the authority to enact any legislation it wishes, including legislation which ended the independence of the former Dominions.

But the political reality is very different. It is highly unlikely that courts would now accept this traditional view of sovereignty, despite its inherent logic, if an alternative were available.[3] For to do so would be to admit that the legal authority of the country was still subordinate to that of the United Kingdom, and would for ever remain so.

A revolutionary break would be one way for a constitution to become autochthonous, for if there has been a break in authority there can be no dependence upon prior legal authority. But revolutionary actions are contrary to the rule of law, and political tradition in the Commonwealth.[4] There remains the possibility of an alternative.

The view that Parliament cannot bind its successor, well established as it is,[5] is not of great antiquity.[6] The formalization of the doctrine of the sovereignty of Parliament was largely the work of Oxford theorists, especially Hobbes, Blackstone, and Dicey.[7] Blackstone, while he had some qualms relating to the lack of limitations on the legislature that that logically imposed,[8] observed that 'what the Parliament doth, no power on earth can undo'.[9]

By 1930 it was generally agreed that the imperial Parliament was a sovereign body, able to enact, repeal or amend any law, including any self-imposed

---

3 Peter Oliver, 'Cutting the Imperial link – Canada and New Zealand', in Philip Joseph (ed.), *Essays on the Constitution* (Wellington, 1995) 368–404, 393–4.

4 In August 1998 the Supreme Court of Canada considered the question of the Canadian Constitution being circumvented by a referendum, thereby affirming the sovereignty of the people. But it felt that political institutions draw their legitimacy from the rule of law, which precluded such action; 'Breaking New Ground', *Maclean's* 111(135) (1998): 18.

5 Sir William Anson, 'Government of Ireland Bill and the Sovereignty of Parliament', *Law Quarterly Review* (1886): 427, 434–41; Albert Dicey, *Introduction to the Study of the Law of the Constitution* introduction and appendix by E.C.S. Wade (10th edn, London, 1959), pp. 64–6; *Ellen Street Estate Ltd v Minister of Health* [1934] 1 KB 590 (CA) per Maugham L.J.; *British Coal Corporation v R* [1935] AC 500 (PC) at 520 per Lord Sankey, LC.

6 It was certainly not the common view in the fourteenth century. The Observance of Due Process of Law Act 1368 ((42 Edw. III c 3) (Eng.)), for instance, enacted that any legislation created contrary to Magna Carta was void.

7 Robert Heuston, *Essays in Constitutional Law* (2nd edn, London, 1964), p. 1.

8 Thus statutes contrary to the law of God, impossible to be performed or with 'absurd consequences manifestly contradictory to common reason' were invalid: Sir William Blackstone, *Commentaries on the Laws of England*, ed. E. Christian (New York, 1978), book I, p. 91.

9 Sir William Blackstone, *Commentaries on the Laws of England*, ed. E. Christian (New York, 1978), book 1, p. 161.

limitations.[10] One consequence of this view was that the Westminster Parliament could, in English law, continue to legislate for ex-colonies, whatever the Statute of Westminster or any other Act might say. Yet at the same time, the development of dominion-status was lessening the scope of imperial control.

After the adoption by the Dominions of the Statute of Westminster, domestic law apparently ceased to recognize the validity of British Acts in the Dominions, except any passed in accordance with the provisions of that Act. But if the imperial Parliament is alone sovereign, then it would have authority to repeal the Statute of Westminster, and enact legislation for the Dominions. Yet the local courts would not necessarily recognize such laws. This would suggest that the focus of the constitution had passed from the United Kingdom to the Dominion; had become, at least in some sense, autochthonous.

According to traditional nineteenth-century legal theory, Parliament could only abdicate its sovereignty entirely, as by dissolving itself, or by transferring its authority to a new legislative body.[11] Following Dicey, a new view of sovereignty was developed. This held that Parliament could bind itself as to manner and form of legislation, if not permanently shed a part of that sovereignty.[12]

A more popular line of reasoning stated that Westminster had abdicated part of its sovereignty, as, for example, in its power to legislate for New Zealand or Canada.[13] Thus, sovereignty, once conferred, could not be revoked. But the courts remained unconvinced,[14] though in *Blackburn v Attorney-General*[15] the English Court of Appeal did ponder the question of whether an Act of the United Kingdom Parliament implementing the Treaty of Rome would be irrevocable.[16]

It has often been said that whatever view a British court might take of any post-1986 legislation passed by the United Kingdom Parliament for New Zealand, local courts would ignore it.[17] But the United Kingdom Parliament itself never purported to abdicate its power to legislate for New Zealand.

---

10 Though this has only been established by a series of *obiter dicta* judicial statements, which may have authority, but are not binding in any other court.

11 Such as the Parliament of the United Kingdom replacing that of England in 1707; *MacCormick v Lord Advocate* 1953 SC 396; 1953 SLT 255 (Sess Ct); Geoffrey Marshall, *Constitutional Conventions – The Rules and Forms of Political Accountability* (Oxford, 1986), p. 209.

12 See Sir Ivor Jennings, *The Law and the Constitution* (5th edn, London, 1959), ch. 4; Geoffrey Marshall, *Parliamentary Sovereignty and the Commonwealth* (Oxford, 1957), chs 2–4.

13 See Geoffrey Marshall, *Constitutional Conventions – The Rules and Forms of Political Accountability* (Oxford, 1986), p. 209.

14 *Reference re Amendment of the Constitution of Canada* [1981] 1 SCR 753 (SCC).

15 [1971] 2 All ER 1380 (CA).

16 [1971] 2 All ER 1380 (CA) at 1383 per Salmon LJ.

17 Geoffrey Marshall, *Constitutional Conventions – The Rules and Forms of Political Accountability* (Oxford, 1986), p. 63.

In the *Patriation Reference*,[18] the Supreme Court of Canada took the viewpoint of a British court in the face of legislation emanating from the superior and sovereign Parliament at Westminster. At least until 1982 the Imperial Parliament retained undiminished powers over the Canadian legislature.[19]

The undiluted sovereignty or supremacy of Parliament may be seen as authoritarian. But that does not mean that these systems do not also reflect aspects of liberalism. This may be seen in the operation of a western liberal state of the Westminster model; New Zealand.

New Zealand has a constitution which contains what might appear at first glance to be a dichotomy. It is a democratic monarchy, with executive power (and elements of legislative and judicial authority) vested in the Sovereign – or Crown, as the entity which the Sovereign represents is styled. Yet it has a government responsible to Parliament and thence to the electorate. This arrangement, typical of the nineteenth century British genius for improvisation and compromise (or what has also been described as muddle and hypocrisy), seems to work despite – or perhaps because of – its apparent weakness in principle.

New Zealand statutes have tended to use the terms 'Her Majesty the Queen' and 'the Crown' interchangeably and apparently arbitrarily.[20] There appears to have been no intention to draw any theoretical or conceptual distinctions. This may simply be a reflection of a certain looseness of drafting, but it may have its foundation in a certain lack of certainty felt by legal draftsmen as much as by the general public.[21] 'The Crown' itself is a comparatively modern concept in Commonwealth jurisprudence. As Maitland said, the king was merely a man, though one who does many things.[22] For historical reasons the king or queen came to be recognized in law as not merely the chief source of the executive power, but also as the sole legal representative of the state or organized community.

According to Maitland, the crumbling of the feudal state threatened to break down the identification of the king and state, and as a consequence Coke recast the king as the legal representative of the state. It was Coke who first attributed legal

18 *Reference re Amendment of the Constitution of Canada* [1981] 1 SCR 753 (SCC).

19 A view which coincided with that of the British House of Commons Foreign Affairs Committee; First Report, Session 1980–81 (HC 42), *British North America Acts*, vols 1 and 2 (1981); Foreign Affairs Committee, Second Report, Session 1980–81 (HC 295), *Supplementary Report on the British North America Acts* (1981).

20 The word 'Sovereign' appears in New Zealand statutes only in the Sovereign's Birthday Observance Act 1952. Otherwise the usage is generally such as is found in s 2 of the Public Finance Act, where 'Crown' is defined as 'Her Majesty the Queen in right of New Zealand; and includes all Ministers of the Crown and all departments'.

21 For this conceptual uncertainty, see Janine Hayward, 'In search of a treaty partner' (1995) Victoria University of Wellington PhD thesis; Interview with Sir Douglas Graham, 24 November 1999.

22 'The Crown as a Corporation', *Law Quarterly Review*, 17 (1901): 131–46.

personality to the Crown.[23] He recast the king as a corporation sole, permanent and metaphysical.[24]

The king's corporate identity[25] drew support from the doctrine of succession that held that the king never dies[26] – so that there might be no interregnum or lacuna of authority. It was also supported by the common law doctrine of seisin of land, where the heir was possessed at all times of a right to an estate even before succession.[27] Blackstone explained that the king:

> is made a corporation to prevent in general the possibility of an interregnum or vacancy of the throne, and to preserve the possessions of the Crown entire.[28]

Thus the role of the Crown was eminently practical. In the tradition of the common law constitutional theory was subsequently developed which rationalized and explained the existing practice – as, for example, in the development of the law of succession to the Crown.[29]

Generally, and in order to better conduct the business of government, the Crown was accorded certain privileges and immunities not available to any other legal entity.[30] Blackstone observed that '[t]he King is not only incapable of doing

---

23 Maitland, 'The Crown as a Corporation'.

24 It was as late as 1861 that the House of Lords accepted that the Crown was a corporation sole, having 'perpetual continuance'; *Attorney-General v Kohler* (1861 9 HL Cas 654, 671.

25 A corporation is a number of persons united and consolidated together so as to be considered as one person in law, possessing the character of perpetuity, its existence being constantly maintained by the succession of new individuals in the place of those who die, or are removed. Corporations are either aggregate or sole. A corporation aggregate consists of many persons, several of whom are contemporaneously members of it. Corporations sole are such as consist, at any given time, of one person only; *Mozley and Whiteley's Law Dictionary*, ed. E.R. Hardy Ivamy (10th edn, London, 1988), p. 109.

26 It was at the time of Edward IV that the theory was accepted that the king never dies, that the demise of the Crown at once transfers it from the last wearer to the heir, and that no vacancy, no interregnum, occurs at all; William Stubbs, *The Constitutional History of England* (4th edn, Oxford, 1906), vol. 2, p. 107.

27 Howard Nenner, *The Right to be King – The Succession to the Crown of England, 1603–1714* (London, 1995), p. 32.

28 Sir William Blackstone, *Commentaries on the Laws of England*, ed. E. Christian (New York, 1978), book 1, p. 470. That Blackstone was at least partly incorrect can be seen in the development of a concept of succession to the Crown without interregnum of the heir apparent. Since this concept had fully developed by the time of Edward IV, this cannot have been the principal reason for the development of the concept of the Crown as a corporation sole.

29 Noel Cox, 'The Law of Succession to the Crown in New Zealand', *Waikato Law Review*, 7 (1999): 49–72.

30 Bruce Harris, 'The "Third Source" of Authority for Government Action', *Law Quarterly Review*, 109 (1992): 626–51.

wrong, but even of thinking wrong; he can never mean to do an improper thing, in him is no folly or weakness'.[31] Mathieson has proffered the notion that the Crown may do whatever statute or the royal prerogative expressly or by implication authorizes, but that it lacks any natural capacities such as an individual or juridical entity may possess.[32]

In the course of the twentieth century the concept of the Crown has succeeded the king as the essential core of the corporation, which is now regarded as a corporation aggregate rather than a corporation sole.[33] In a series of cases in both the United Kingdom and New Zealand, we can see the courts struggling to categorize the nature of the Crown.[34]

In *Re Mason*[35] Romer J stated that it was established law that the Crown was a corporation, but did not indicate whether it was a corporation sole (as generally accepted) or a corporation aggregate (as Maitland argued). Maitland believed that the Crown, as distinct from the king, was anciently not known to the law but in modern usage had become the head of a 'complex and highly organized 'corporation aggregate of many' – of very many'.[36] In *Adams v Naylor*,[37] the House of Lords adopted Maitland's legal conception of the Crown.[38]

Although the House of Lords in 1977, in *Town Investments v Department of the Environment*,[39] accepted that the Crown did have legal personality, it also adopted the potentially confusing practice of speaking of actions of the executive as being performed by 'the government' rather than 'the Crown'.[40] The practical need for

31 Blackstone, book 1, p. 254.

32 'Does the Crown have Human Powers?', *New Zealand Universities Law Review*, 15 (1992): 118–42. Contrary case law includes *Sutton's Hospital Case* (1613) 10 Co Rep 23a; *Clough v Leahy* (1905) 2 CLR 139, 156–7; *New South Wales v Bardolph* (1934) 52 CLR 455, 474–5; *R v Criminal Injuries Compensation Board* [1967] 2 QB 864, 886; *Malone v Metropolitan Police Commissioner* [1979] Ch. 344, 366; *Attorney-General of Quebec v Labrecque* [1980] 2 SCR 1057, 1082; *Davis v Commonwealth* (1988) 166 CLR 79 (HCA).

33 Philip Joseph, 'Suspending Statutes Without Parliament's Consent', *New Zealand Universities Law Review*, 14 (1991): 282, 287.

34 To the question, 'What is the Crown', there have been what Wade calls 'some extraordinary answers'; Sir William Wade, 'The Crown, Ministers and Officials: Legal Status and Liability', in Maurice Sunkin and Sebastian Payne (eds), *The Nature of the Crown: A Legal and Political Analysis* (Oxford, 1999), p. 23, referring to *Town Investments Ltd v Department of the Environment* [1978] AC 359; *M v Home Office* [1992] 1 QB 270 (CA); [1993] 3 All ER 537 (HL).

35 [1928] 1 Ch 385, 401.

36 Maitland, 'The Crown as a Corporation'.

37 [1946] AC 543, 555 (HL).

38 It has also been accepted by the Supreme Court of Canada: *Verreault v Attorney-General of Quebec* [1977] 1 SCR 41, 47; *Attorney-General of Quebec v Labrecque* [1980] 2 SCR 1057, 1082.

39 [1978] AC 359, 400 per Lord Simon of Glaisdale (HL).

40 *Town Investments Ltd v Department of the Environment* [1978] AC 359, 380–81 per Lord Diplock.

this distinction is avoided if one recognizes the aggregate nature of the Crown.[41] 'The government' is something which, unlike the Crown, has no corporate or juridical existence known to the constitution. Further, its legal definition is both legally and practically unnecessary.

In *Town Investments*[42] Lord Simon, with little argument, accepted that the Crown was a corporation aggregate, as Maitland had believed. This appears to be in accordance with the realities of the modern state, although it was contrary to the traditional view of the Crown. Thus, the Crown is now seen, legally, as a nexus of rights and privileges, exercised by a number of individuals, officials and departments, all called 'the Crown'.

More recently, in *M v Home Office*,[43] the English Court of Appeal held that the Crown lacked legal personality and was therefore not amenable to contempt of court proceedings.[44] But it is precisely because in the Westminster-style political system we do not have the Continental notion of a state, nor an entrenched constitution,[45] that the concept of the Crown as a legal entity with full powers in its own right arose. *Town Investments* must in any event be regarded as the definitive statement of current English law.

The development of the concept of the aggregate Crown from the corporate Crown provides sufficient flexibility to accommodate the reality of government, without the need for abandoning an essential legal *Grundnorm*[46] in favour of a very undeveloped and inherently vague concept of 'the government'.[47] Thus, for

41 Some writers, following *Town Investments*, have preferred the expression 'government' rather than 'Crown' or 'State', for example Harris, 'The "Third Source" of Authority for Government Action', 634–5. The government has never been a juristic entity, so in trying to abandon one legal fiction in *Town Investments*, their Lordships adopted a new one; Philip Joseph, 'Crown as a legal concept (I)', *New Zealand Law Journal* (1993): 126, 129.

42 *Town Investments v Department of the Environment* [1978] AC 359, 400 (HL).

43 [1992] 1 QB 270.

44 However, in the House of Lords, Lord Templeman spoke of the Crown as consisting of the monarch and the executive, and Lord Woolf observed that the Crown had a legal personality at least for some purposes; [1993] 3 All ER 537.

45 That is, one which claims for itself legal paramountcy, and which limits executive and legislative powers in such a way that the constitution itself, rather than any institution of government, becomes the focus of critical attention.

46 In Kelsen's philosophy of law, a *Grundnorm* is the basic, fundamental postulate, which justifies all principles and rules of the legal system and which all inferior rules of the system may be deduced; Michael Hayback, 'Carl Schmitt and Hans Kelsen in the crisis of Democracy between World Wars I and II' (1990) Universitaet Salzburg DrIur thesis.

47 For a critique of these propositions generally see Joseph, 'The Crown as a legal concept (I)'; and Philip Joseph, 'The Crown as a legal concept (II)', *New Zealand Law Journal* (1993): 179; F.M. Brookfield, 'The Monarchy and the Constitution today', *New Zealand Law Journal* (1992): 438.

reasons principally of convenience, the Crown became an umbrella beneath which the business of government was conducted.

The Crown has always operated through a series of servants and agents, some more permanent than others. The law recognizes the Crown as the body in whom the executive authority of the country is vested, and by which the business of executive government is exercised.

Whether New Zealand has a Crown aggregate or corporate, the government is formally that of the Sovereign,[48] and the Crown has the place in administration held by the state in other – principally civil law – legal traditions. The Crown, whether or not there is a resident Sovereign, acts as the legal umbrella under which the various activities of government are conducted, and with whom, in the specifically New Zealand context, the indigenous Maori people may negotiate as treaty partner with the Crown.[49] Indeed, the very absence of the Sovereign has encouraged this modern tendency for the Crown to be regarded as a concept of government quite distinct from the person of the Sovereign.[50]

The monarchy does, however, have a role beyond the symbolic. In his analysis of the British Crown in his own day (1865), Bagehot seriously underestimated its surviving influence.[51] His famous aphorism, that a constitutional Sovereign has the right to be consulted, to encourage, and to warn,[52] can hardly express the residual royal powers of even the late nineteenth century.[53] It may describe the royal powers today – in the United Kingdom if not the overseas realms of Queen Elizabeth II – but does not explain why the inherited concept of the supremacy of the Crown should leave the constitution apparently centred upon an institution lacking real power.

But Bagehot, like Palmerston and Gladstone wanted the monarchy relegated to the status of a museum piece, despite the Sovereign 's 'right to be consulted, to encourage, and to warn'.[54] This passive role was not that envisaged by George IV, William IV, Victoria or Edward VII (though the latter's sons and granddaughter

48 A concept which is alive today, in part as a substitute for a more advanced concept of the constitution; Interview with Sir Douglas Graham, 24 November 1999.

49 Generally, see Janine Hayward, 'In search of a treaty partner' (1995), Victoria University of Wellington PhD thesis.

50 See, for instance, Noel Cox, 'The Theory of Sovereignty and the Importance of the Crown in the Realms of The Queen', *Oxford University Commonwealth Law Journal*, 2(2) (2002): 237–55.

51 Following the example set by Bagehot, British historians since 1945 have very largely neglected the continuing political influence of the monarchy under George VI and Elizabeth II; Peter Hennessy, 'The throne behind the monarchy', *Economist*, 24 December 1994, pp. 77–9.

52 'The English Constitution', in the *Collected Works of Walter Bagehot*, ed. Norman St John-Stevas (5 vols, London, 1974), vol. 5.

53 Frank Hardie, *The Political Influence of Queen Victoria, 1861–1901* (London, 1935), pp. 23–7.

54 Bagehot, 'The English Constitution', vol. 5, p. 253.

were each to later study Bagehot in their schooldays), nor that held by the majority of statesmen and text-book writers over this period. They felt that the Sovereign's role as head of state in a popular parliamentary system had still to be satisfactorily defined, and might well be rather wider than that assigned to it by Bagehot.[55]

Dicey and Anson, the leading authorities of their own day, were inclined to advocate a stretching of the royal discretion (or rather to acknowledge a broader discretion than Bagehot had done), and, to some extent at least, the monarchy ostensibly operated at a political level under Edward VII in much the same way as it did under George IV[56] But there had been a clear change in the basis of royal authority. This was now almost totally dependent upon parliamentary support. But there has been no study which offers evidence to show that the exercise by the Crown of the rights to be consulted, to encourage, and to warn, has influenced the course of policy.[57]

The Crown is more than just the mechanism through which government is administered. It is also itself one of the sources of governmental authority, as a traditional source of legal sovereignty. Not only is government conducted through the Crown (as discussed above), but some governmental authority is derived from the Crown as the legal focus of sovereignty.

'Sovereignty' put simply, is the idea that there is a 'final authority within a given territory'.[58] Foucault identified four possible descriptions of the traditional role of sovereignty:

1. to describe a mechanism of power in feudal society;
2. as a justification for the construction of large-scale administrative monarchies;
3. (as an ideology used by one side or the other in the seventeenth century wars of religion; and
4. in the construction of parliamentary alternatives to the absolutist monarchies.[59]

---

55 The limitations of the distinction between dignified and efficient, so central to Bagehot's model, can be seen in Laura Jackson, 'Shadows of the Crown' (1994), University of Chicago PhD thesis.

56 H.J. Hanham, *The Nineteenth Century Constitution, 1815–1914* (Cambridge, 1969), p. 24.

57 David E. Smith, 'Bagehot, the Crown, and the Canadian Constitution', *Canadian Journal of Political Science*, 28 (1995): 622–37. An example of the use of influence through an 'exchange of views' has been given in Kenneth Rose, *Kings, Queens and Courtiers: Intimate Portraits of the Royal House of Windsor from its foundation to the Present Day* (London, 1985), p. 92.

58 F. Hinsley, *Sovereignty* (2nd edn, Cambridge, 1986), p. 1; Stephen Krasner, 'Sovereignty', *Comparative Political Studies*, 21(1) (1988): 66–94, 86.

59 From Michel Foucault, *The Foucault Effects: Studies in Governmentality*, ed. Graham Burchell, Colin Gordon and Peter Miller (London, 1991), pp. 97–8, 101–2. See also David Held, *Political Theory and the Modern State* (Cambridge, 1989), pp. 216–25.

Whatever rationale applied to the embryonic English Crown, the old theory of sovereignty has been democratized since the nineteenth century into a notion of collective sovereignty, exercised through parliamentary institutions. The fundamental responsibility for the maintenance of society itself is much more widely dispersed throughout its varied institutions and the whole population. To some degree this equates to the concept of the aggregate Crown favoured by the more recent jurists.[60]

But the concept of sovereignty, however understood, is especially important because it has become part of the language of claims by indigenous people, as in New Zealand, where Maori claims are based on the conflicting concept of tino rangatiratanga, or chiefly authority.[61] The particular problems this causes in New Zealand are that it represents the claims of an antecedent regime to juridical survival despite apparently ceding sovereignty to the Crown in the Treaty of Waitangi in 1840. Indeed, it is significant that most talk of 'sovereignty' in the second half of the twentieth century concentrated upon the sovereignty of racial groups, and particularly, the so-called indigenous peoples.[62]

Sovereignty has assumed different meanings and attributes according to the conditions of time and place, but at a basic level it requires obedience from its subjects and denies a concurrent authority to any other body.[63] In New Zealand, the Sovereign is responsible for the executive government, and indeed is specifically so appointed by the Constitutions of most Commonwealth countries of which Her Majesty is head of state.[64]

It will be immediately apparent that there is a divergence between abstract law and political reality, for substantial political power lies in politicians rather than the Sovereign. Political orthodoxy also appears to hold that for a constitution to be legitimate it must derive from the people. Yet, our constitution is not apparently based legally on the sovereignty of the people, but rather on that of the Queen–in–Parliament.

---

60 Sovereignty is always limited in some way. Genesis 1: 26–30 makes it clear that God created mankind to subdue the earth and to exercise dominion over it under God; Rousas John Rushdoony, *The Institutes of Biblical Law* (Philadelphia, 1973), pp. 448–51.

61 P.G. McHugh, 'Constitutional Theory and Maori Claims', in Sir Hugh Kawharu (ed.), *Waitangi: Maori and Pakeha Perspectives of the Treaty of Waitangi* (Auckland, 1989), p. 25.

62 Sir Elihu Lauterpacht, 'Sovereignty – Myth or Reality?', *International Affairs*, 73(1) (1997): 137–50.

63 Daniel Philpott, 'Sovereignty', *Journal of International Affairs*, 48(2) (1995): 353–68.

64 See, for example, the Barbados Independence Order 1966, the Schedule of which is the Constitution of Barbados. Section 63(1): 'The executive authority of Barbados is vested in Her Majesty.'

In the Westminster tradition, it is Parliament, in contrast to the Crown, which is widely regarded as being the focus of political power.[65] Joseph assumes therefore that it is the people rather than Parliament who is sovereign.[66] But it would seem that sovereign authority is legally vested in the Crown–in–Parliament, politically in the people.[67] Legally, this can be seen as less than ideal, or even confused. However, a constitution is more than merely a legal structure.[68]

The authority of government is based upon several sources. Even were authority legally derived from the people, as it appears to now be in Australia,[69] it is not clear how the position of the Maori can be reconciled,[70] in particular, the preservation of their *tino rangatiratanga*, or chiefly authority. For the Maori retained for themselves at least some degree of political power under the Treaty of Waitangi, power which has its origins in traditional sources rather than the popular will. The Crown also claims some degree of authority based upon traditional sources, including mystique and continuity.[71]

The origins and nature of constitutional authority, whether in a monarchy or a republic, are important. But although a formal constitution can say, as does that of Papua New Guinea, that it is derived from the popular sovereignty of the people,[72]

---

65 See Allan Kornberg and Harold Clarke, *Citizens and Community – Political Support in a Representative Democracy* (Cambridge, 1992); Carol Harlow, 'Power from the People?', in Patrick McAuslan and John McEldowney (eds), *Law, Legitimacy and the Constitution*: *Essays marking the Centenary of Dicey's Law of the Constitution* (London, 1985); J.R. Mallory, 'The Appointment of the Governor General', *Canadian Journal of Economics and Political Science*, 26 (1960): 96.

66 Philip Joseph, *Constitutional and Administrative Law in New Zealand* (Sydney, 1993), pp. 284–5.

67 In early America, there was no question, whatever the form of government, that all legitimate authority was derived from God. The influence of the classical tradition revived the authority of the people, which historically is equally compatible with monarchy, oligarchy, dictatorship, or democracy, but is not compatible with the doctrine of God's authority; Rushdoony, p. 214.

68 Particularly in respect of what might be called policy legacies; Theda Skocpol, *States and Social Revolution* (Cambridge, 1979), p. 27. Indeed, a Constitution exists in the imagination of those who create it, use it, and thus know it; Joseph Jacobs, *The Republican Crown*: *Lawyers and the Making of the State in Twentieth Century Britain* (Aldershot, 1996), p. 6.

69 The Australian Constitution has been held to be based on popular sovereignty, as it was adopted by popular vote; *Australian Capital Television Pty Ltd v Commonwealth* (1992) 177 CLR 106, 138 per Mason CJ; *Theophanous v Herald & Weekly Times Ltd* (1994) 182 CLR 104, 171 per Deane J; *McGinty v Western Australia* (1996) 186 CLR 140, 230, 237 per McHugh, J.

70 Canada has the same type of conceptual difficulty; Peter Russell, *Constitutional Odyssey*: *Can Canadians become a Sovereign People*? (Toronto, 1992).

71 The Australian Labour Party wanted a republic partly for symbolic nationalist reasons, but partly also to deprive the Governors-General of their association with royal legitimacy; R. Lucy, *The Australian Form of Government* (Melbourne, 1985), p. 17.

72 Constitution of the Independent State of Papua New Guinea 1975.

this may be confusing legal authority with political authority.[73] Where the Crown exists, and no formal entrenched Constitution has been adopted, difficult questions of the basis of governmental authority can be avoided.

There has been to date comparatively little theoretical analysis of the conceptual basis of governmental authority in countries with informal constitutions such as New Zealand.[74] There has been much discussion focused on the legitimacy of government derived from written constitutions, and in New Zealand, from the Treaty of Waitangi[75] – since it is a written document of apparent if not formal legal authority. But there has been little work done towards an understanding of the nature of governmental authority in New Zealand, except by those who argue that there is too much (or too little) involvement of government in individual lives.[76] This dearth of work may be due to apathy,[77] but it could also be influenced by an underlying suspicion of abstract theory which can be traced in British tradition of political thought from the seventeenth century, if not earlier.[78]

In Canada, in contrast, there have been several major studies of the conceptual basis of government. In particular, in 1985 the Law Reform Commission of Canada released a working paper which called for a re-examination of the concept of the Federal Crown in Canadian law.[79] The working paper called for the recognition of a unitary federal administration in place of the legal concept of the Crown.[80] The paper specifically asked:

73 See Harold Laski, 'The Theory of Popular Sovereignty', *Michigan Law Review*, 17 (1919): 201–15.

74 Indeed, it has been said that few care for such esoteric matters; Interview with Sir Douglas Graham, 24 November 1999.

75 For example, F.M. Brookfield, *Waitangi and Indigenous Rights: Revolution, Law and Legitimation* (Auckland, 1999); Andrew Sharp (ed.), *Leap into the dark: the changing role of the state in New Zealand since 1984* (Auckland, 1994); Andrew Sharp, *Justice and the Maori: the philosophy and practice of Maori claims in New Zealand since the 1970s* (2nd edn, Auckland, 1997); Richard Mulgan, 'Can the Treaty of Waitangi provide a constitutional basis for New Zealand's political future?', *Political Science*, 41(2) (1989): 51–68.

76 See, for example, the recent writings on the State; Jane Kelsey, *Rolling Back the State: Privatisation of Power in Aotearoa/New Zealand* (Wellington, 1993); Richard Mulgan, *Democracy and Power in New Zealand: A study of New Zealand politics* (2nd edn, Auckland, 1989).

77 As former Prime Minister David Lange believed; Interview with David Lange, 20 May 1998.

78 See Michael Foley, *The Silence of Constitutions: Gaps, 'Abeyances' and Political Temperament in the Maintenance of Government* (London, 1989). The wars of the seventeenth century were, to no small degree, between competing conceptions of the State, and engendered a suspicion for such speculation. It is probable that the long dominance of Whig ideology also contributed to this attitude.

79 Law Reform Commission of Canada, *The Legal Status of the Federal Administration* (Ottawa, 1985).

80 *Bank voor Handel v Slatford* [1952] 1 All ER 314, 319 per Devlin J:

> to what extent should Canada retain the concept of the Crown in federal law? Should we replace the concept of Crown with the concept of State or federal administration?

The Commission briefly described what it termed the chaotic and confusing historical treatment of 'the Crown' in English and Canadian law. Historical inconsistencies and contradictions in the treatment of the concept of the Crown cannot and need not be rationalized. Judges, legislators, and writers are not always taking about the same thing. They may mean the Sovereign herself, the institution of royal power, the concept of sovereignty, the constitutional head of state, judicial instructions, or actors.[81]

To recognize the political reality the authors of the working paper suggested that the concept of the Crown should be abolished, and the Sovereign relegated to the status of constitutional head of state.[82] Discarding monarchical terminology and limiting the Crown to its purely formal role would, in the opinion of the Commission 'reduce terminological confusion, historical biases, and anti-democratic and non-egalitarian concepts so far as they affect individuals in the relationships between bureaucrats and the majority'.[83] The Crown would be replaced by the 'administration'. The authors of the working paper wanted to recognize the executive branch of the state.[84] The legal nature of the Crown or state in Canada has also been considered by others,[85] but the issue is not yet settled.[86]

> The Crown is a convenient term, but one which is often used to save the asking of difficult questions. It is a description of the powers that formerly at common law were exercised by the king in person, and that latterly have been bestowed by statute on the king in council or on various Ministers.

81 In this, parallels may be seen with the position of the Crown in New Zealand, in the Maori–Crown context. In Australia debate on whether The Queen is head of state continues.

82 The King of Sweden, for instance, has been so relegated; Constitution of Sweden (1975). Note the Canadian paper spoke of the Crown as an institution, rather than of the person of the Sovereign, or of their representatives.

83 David Cohen, 'Thinking about the State', *Osgoode Hall Law Journal*, 24 (1986): 379–409.

84 In effect a republican form of government.

85 Neil Komesar, 'Taking Institutions seriously', *University of Chicago Law Review*, 51 (1984): 366; P.W. Hogg, *Liability of the Crown in Australia, New Zealand and the United Kingdom* (Sydney, 1971); Law Reform Commission of British Columbia, *Legal Position of the Crown* (Vancouver, 1972).

86 Because Canadians never severed their ties with Britain, they never found it crucial to define themselves in a way which rendered them distinct from the 'mother country'; Smith, 'Empire, Crown and Canadian Federalism', 471.

Cohen believed that the methodology of the working paper itself was flawed because it focused on theoretical and abstract analyses of the state.[87] Essentially, the difficulty is that there is no developed concept of the state or nation in Commonwealth constitutional theory.[88] Moore attributes this to parliamentarian mistrust inspired by the association between civil law and Baconian theory.[89] But it is equally true that modern theoretical studies of the state have been limited even in Continental Europe.[90]

In New Zealand executive authority is also, like that of Canada, formally vested in the Crown.[91] The government does not require parliamentary approval for most administrative actions; nor need it show popular approval or consent for these actions – though the rule of law, a long tradition of political restraint, political expediency, and the strictly limited range of powers held by the Crown, prevent authoritarian Crown government.[92]

The executive authority of a country could be vested in a president, the Governor-General, or the Queen irrespective of the basis of sovereignty. But in the constitutional arrangements of New Zealand the principal if not indeed the sole focus of legal authority is the Crown-in-Parliament (there remains some debate over the role of the indigenous Maori people. This institution enjoys full legal sovereignty or supremacy. The Crown itself is allocated executive functions, and, within a limited field, requires no other legal authority than its own prerogative.[93]

This approach has the advantage of simplicity, leaving broader questions of sovereignty unanswered.[94] As such it owes much to the British tradition of a constitution as something which evolves, and for which theory is sometimes

87 Cohen, 'Thinking about the State'.

88 Sir William Moore, 'Liability for the Acts of Public Servants', *Law Quarterly Review*, 23 (1907): 112; Sir William Corbett, '"The Crown" as representing the State', *Commonwealth Law Review*, 1 (1903): 23, 145; H.T. Postle, 'Commonwealth and Crown', *Australian Law Journal*, 3 (1929): 109; Harold Laski, 'The Responsibility of the State in England', *Harvard Law Review*, 32 (1919): 447–72, 472; Maitland, 'The Crown as a Corporation', 136.

89 Sir William Moore, 'Law and Government', *Commonwealth Law Review*, 3 (1905): 205.

90 J. Dearlove, 'Bringing the State Back In', *Political Studies* (1989): 521–39.

91 Harris, 'The "Third Source" of Authority for Government Action'.

92 For an example of the application of such limits on government see *Fitzgerald v Muldoon* [1976] 2 NZLR 615.

93 Harris, 'The "Third Source" of Authority for Government Action'.

94 Which suits most political leaders and the general public alike; Interview with Sir Douglas Graham, 24 November 1999.

developed subsequent to the practice.[95] One aspect of this paucity of theory, if it may be so called, is the weakness – or absence, of a general theory of the state.[96]

In Canada, problems with the place of the French-speaking minority, and the federal nature of the country, meant that difficult questions of the location and nature of governmental authority had to be addressed. Thus, claims by Quebec for special status within the federation required an analysis of the nature of power exercised by federal and provincial governments. The existence of an entrenched constitution also meant that this could substitute for the Crown, as in the United States of America, as a conceptual focus of government.

Clarke argues that in Canada the marriage of the parliamentary form of government to the federal principle makes the determination of legislative authority problematic, at least in part, because it fails to develop an adequate conceptualization of sovereignty. In the absence of a better understanding authority is described merely in terms of a division of power.[97]

There have been neither technical nor practical reasons for these difficult questions of the sources of governmental authority to be answered in New Zealand. To some extent, the asking of such questions was also avoided.[98] Thus, the existence of the Crown, whilst providing a convenient legal source for executive government, has also acted as an inhibitor of abstract constitutional theorizing. As a consequence, in Laski's view, the Crown covered a 'multitude of sins'.[99] Whilst this might not be desirable, it provides a convenient and pragmatic cover behind which the business of government is conducted, unworried by conceptual difficulties.

The principal reason why the Crown has been regarded in New Zealand as a legal source of executive authority is historical. Not only is the Crown a source of legal authority, it serves to personify the political community. Thus the legal role of the Crown is important at three conceptual levels. First, and most fundamentally, it is a metonym for state. Secondly, it is a source of legal authority. Third, it is the means through which government is conducted. In most political systems the

95 By contrast Australia's Constitution may be described as a social covenant drawn up and ratified by the people; J.A. La Nauze, *The Making of the Australian Constitution* (Melbourne, 1972).

96 The sovereignty of the Crown is not merely a legal fiction, as Bercuson argued, since it has practical consequences, including a measure of public perception as a source of authority; David Bercuson and Barry Cooper, 'From Constitutional Monarchy to Quasi Republic', in Janet Ajzenstat (ed.), *Canadian Constitutionalism, 1791–1991* (Ottawa, 1992); cf David E. Smith, *The Republican Option in Canada, Past and Present* (Toronto, 1999), p. 18; Interview with Sir Douglas Graham, 24 November 1999.

97 Gregory Clarke, 'Popular Sovereignty and Constitutional Reform in Canada' (1997), Acadia University MA thesis.

98 At least, by Pakeha. Maori showed a greater willingness, if only because they saw thereby a means of increasing their share of authority; Interview with Hon Georgina te Heuheu, 7 December 1999.

99 Laski, 'Responsibility of the State in England'.

executive power and the state are synonymous.[100] The state may be classified as that which refers to some or all of the legal administrative or legislative institutions operating in a community.[101] In the British system, and those derived from it,[102] it is questionable whether there is a state, at least as a formal constitutional entity or concept. Most legal commentators had traditionally given it little treatment, or simply answered in the negative. Political scientists considered the question from a different perspective, though not one which is necessarily any more complete.[103] These differing approaches to understanding the constitution are rooted in the different constitutional histories of countries. There was a common element to many, especially in Europe, but experiences were not identical, and affected the relationship of law and government.

The character of communities in the central middle ages was rooted and grounded in older traditions than those created by the study of Roman and canon law, which was the basis for much later conceptualizations of the state in continental Europe.[104] Nor did the rediscovery of Aristotle by western scholars, the development of modern government,[105] or demographic and economic changes significantly affect them. The traditional bonds of community owed much to ties of kinship, much to loyalties of war-bands, very much to Christianity, and perhaps

---

100 Sir Ernest Barker defined a modern State as:

> generally a territorial nation, organized as a legal association by its own action in creating a constitution ... and permanently acting as such an association, under that constitution, for the purpose of maintaining a scheme of legal rules defining and securing the rights and duties of its members.
>
> This is to be distinguished from a nation, which 'is a society or community, whose unity is based primarily on space ... and in that common love of the natal soil (or patria) which is called patriotism'; and 'on time, or the common tradition of centuries, issuing in the sense of a common participation in an inherited way of life, and in that common love for the inheritance which is called nationalism.

– Sir Ernest Barker, Reflections on Government (London, 1942), p. xv.

101 Held; J.R. Strayer, *On the Mediæval Origins of the Modern State* (Princeton, 1970).

102 Excepting those countries, such as the USA, which were compelled to address this often difficult issue, because of the republican and federal nature of their government.

103 Bernard Susser (ed.), *Approaches to the Study of Politics* (New York, 1992), p. 180. In recent decades State-centred theorists have sought to bring the State back, arguing that it is more autonomous than society-centred theorists have claimed. As Bogdanor found, it is necessary to range across law, politics, and history to understand a historic constitution; Vernon Bogdanor, *The Monarchy and the Constitution* (Oxford, 1995).

104 Ernst Kantorowicz, 'Kingship under the impact of scientific jurisprudence', in Marshall Clagett et al (eds), *Twelfth century Europe* (Madison, 1961), p. 89.

105 Strayer.

most strongly, from legal practices and values.[106] In these communities the king was representative of the people, to whom his people owed allegiance, and who, in turn, was held responsible for the government of a nation.[107]

Hobbes, with Bodin, Machiavelli, and Hegel did much to stimulate European state theory, a theory which had not been fully reconsidered in the context of the British constitution since Hobbes and his contemporaries, though recent work has sought to correct this imbalance. Hobbes's *Leviathan* (1651) was perhaps the greatest piece of political philosophy written in the English language. Like Machiavelli's *The Prince* (1532), it offered a dramatic break with the usual apologies for the Christian feudal state of the Middle Ages.

The modern territorial state, the concept of political absolutism, and the principle of *quod principi placuit, legis nabet vigorem*[108] spelled the end of the mediæval nexus of rights and duties, counterbalanced powers, and customs. Hobbes excluded religion as a source of morality, and based ethical values, as well as political theory, on the human impulse toward self-preservation.[109] The reality of early modern government throughout Europe was that it was essentially driven by political realists or pragmatists, who sought the centralization of power for the good of the country.[110]

Since the modern states inherited the papal (and imperial) prerogative, it must, then, govern all within the geographical confines of the country. Speculation in France was centred on a sovereign state with a royal organ to declare its sovereign purposes. This regime collapsed because in eighteenth century France the political and social atmosphere was similar to that which caused such profound changes in England a century earlier, and the unity of the state failed when the strain proved too much for one institution to survive.

Inspired by the political changes in England, and in part directed by the theories of such as Rousseau[111] and Montesquieu,[112] the French people had become the

---

106 Susan Reynolds, 'Law and Community in Western Christendom', *American Journal of Legal History* (1981): 206.

107 Dark Age kings were expected to hold fast the territory of their own communities, to master or conqueror their neighbours, and to protect their own people and enable them to live securely; Kantorowicz, 'Kingship under the impact of scientific jurisprudence', pp. 89–111.

108 'What hath pleased the prince has the force of law.'

109 Thomas Hobbes, *Leviathan* (New York, 1962); Quentin Skinner, 'Conquest and Consent: Thomas Hobbes and the Engagement Controversy', in G.E. Aylmer (ed.), *The Interregnum – The Quest for Settlement, 1640–1660* (Hamden, 1972).

110 Typified by Machiavelli.

111 He argued for a version of sovereignty of the whole citizen body over itself; Jean-Jacques Rousseau, *The Social Contract and other later political writings*, trans. and ed. Victor Goureatres (Cambridge, 1997).

112 He outlined what he believed was the equilibrium of the British political system, which he compared to the French – to the disadvantage of the latter; Charles de Secondat

masters of the state. This example was followed elsewhere in the course of the nineteenth century, though usually with less overt violence.[113]

However, for two interrelated reasons, the state never became a legal concept in English law. Most countries have a date at which they can be said to have begun their constitutional existence, but not the United Kingdom.[114] The need to create (or recreate) a concept of the state has not been generally felt since 1688,[115] and even then the feeling was half-hearted.[116] Nor was there a general reception of the Roman civil law, with its concept of the state. The common law, through common law courts and judges, was always happier developing theories to describe the realities of the law, rather than moulding the law around abstract theories.[117] 'The supreme executive power of this kingdom', as Blackstone knew, was vested in the king;[118] and there the matter was allowed to rest.

As a consequence of this jurisprudential weakness, if it can be so called, there had been in the Commonwealth (excepting perhaps in Canada) comparatively little thought given to theories of the structure of the state. In particular, there had been little consideration of the theory of government in New Zealand beyond questions of 'state responsibility', and the proper role of the state.[119] Yet, the history of this country, and in particular, the existence of the Treaty of Waitangi, makes this a curious deficiency.[120]

Baron de Montesquieu, 'The Spirit of the Laws', in Arend Lijphart (ed.), *Parliamentary versus Presidential Government* (Oxford, 1992), p. 48.

113 Harold Laski, *Authority in the modern State* (New Haven, 1919), pp. 21–4.

114 The United Kingdom can, of course, be dated to the Union with Union with Ireland Act 1800. British constitutional law has been essentially that of England – though not without dispute; Sir Thomas Smith, 'Pretensions of English Law as "Imperial Law"', in *The Laws of Scotland* (Edinburgh, 1987), vol. 5, paras 711–19.

115 Though in recent decades there have been some movements in this direction, for legal rather than political reasons; see Jacobs.

116 Vernon Bogdanor, 'Britain and Europe' in R. Holme and Michael Elliott (eds), *1688–1988 Time for a New Constitution* (London, 1988), p. 81.

117 Indeed, a Continental observer would find two of the distinguishing characteristics of English law (and by extension that of the common law world) to be its antiquity and continuity, and its predominantly judicial character and the absence of codification; Henri Levy-Ullmann, *The English Legal Tradition: Its Sources and History*, trans. M. Mitchell rev. and ed. Frederick Goadly (London, 1935), pp. xlvi–liii.

118 s 8: 'The Queen's excellent Majesty, acting according to the laws of the realm, is the highest power under God in the kingdom, and has supreme authority over all persons in all causes, as well ecclesiastical as civil'; see *The Canons of the Church of England* (London, 1969) Canon A7; *Thirty-Nine Articles of Religion* (1562, confirmed 1571), Art. 37.

119 Kelsey, for example, speaks of the State where constitutional lawyers would traditionally speak of the Crown, or some political scientists the government; Kelsey, *Rolling Back the State*. See also Sharp, *Leap into the dark*.

120 Or, perhaps not so curious, given the uncertainty felt by many Maori about the scope of *kawanatanga* and *tino rangatiratanga*; Interview with Sir Douglas Graham, 24 November 1999.

Since the 1980s, however, there has been more consideration given in New Zealand to the more abstract notions of governmental authority.[121] Inspired by the predominantly neo-liberal market-economy reforms initiated by the 1984 Labour Government,[122] commentators saw a resurgence of the state as a subject worthy of serious study.[123] In the writings of Mulgan[124] and Sharp,[125] for example, are seen the formulation of new conceptions of the state – though not ones which necessarily have much direct influence on politicians or the general public. The disputes between neoliberals,[126] pluralists,[127] feminists,[128] Marxists[129] and others in the 1980s and 1990s[130] have however begun a process towards developing a comprehensive theory of government.

Few of these studies have considered the Crown as an entity of government, let alone a pivotal one. The ideological dominance of neo-liberalism may be in part responsible for this, for whatever its advantages and disadvantages, neo-liberalism is largely ahistorical. Pluralism, at least in its classical form, considers more fully the historical evolution of governmental institutions,[131] and this is critical to an understanding of a political construct like the Crown.

Jacob has postulated that the notion of the state has now begun to evolve in the United Kingdom, as a consequence of the development of public law in place of an emphasis on Crown immunities. His thesis is that since the Franks Report and the consequent Tribunals and Inquiries Act 1958 (United Kingdom), judicial activism has developed an embryonic state.[132] This has been due, so his argument goes, to the increasingly common platform between those politicians who desired to

---

121 See, for example, the 'Building the Constitution' conference held in Wellington in 2000; Colin James (ed.), *Building the Constitution* (Wellington, 2000).

122 Shaun Goldfinch, 'The State', in Raymond Miller (ed.), *New Zealand Government and Politics* (Melbourne, 2001), pp. 511–20, 516–17.

123 For example, in the chapters devoted to the various interpretations of the State in Miller, *New Zealand Government and Politics*.

124 *Democracy and Power in New Zealand.*

125 *Leap into the dark*; *Justice and the Maori.*

126 John Morrow, 'Neo-Liberalism', in Miller (ed.), *New Zealand Government and Politics*, pp. 521–32.

127 Richard Mulgan, 'A pluralist analysis of the New Zealand State', in Brian Roper and Chris Rudd (ed.), *State and Economy in New Zealand* (Auckland, 1993), pp. 128–46.

128 Rosemary Du Plessis, 'Women, Feminism and the State', in Brian Roper and Chris Rudd (eds), *The Political Economy of New Zealand* (Auckland, 1997), pp. 220–36.

129 Chandra Dixon, 'Marxism', in Raymond Miller (ed.), *New Zealand Politics in Transition* (Auckland, 1997), pp. 350–58.

130 Sharp, *Leap into the dark*; Kelsey, *Rolling Back the State*; Pat Moloney, 'Pluralist Theories of the State', in Miller, *New Zealand Politics in Transition*, pp. 317–28.

131 Pat Moloney, 'Neo-Liberalism: A Pluralist Critique', in Miller, *New Zealand Government and Politics*, pp. 533–43, 542.

132 Jacobs.

'roll back the frontiers of the state',[133] or at least placed their emphasis on individual rights, and the attitude of judges asserting the inherent power of the common law. It was not fashioned out of a desire for centralized power. It was, according to Jacob, both judicially and politically created in order to limit it.[134]

Modern Anglo-American constitutional theory is preoccupied with the problem of devising means for the protection and enhancement of individual rights in a manner consistent with the democratic basis of our institutions. In the United Kingdom the focus is on the need for, or the advisability of, imposing restraints on the legislative sovereignty of Parliament – though this latter concept has suffered significantly from the devolution of power in the United Kingdom.[135]

But it would be precipitate to claim the development of a state has been universally accepted in either New Zealand or the United Kingdom. More in keeping with the tradition of historical development found in those two countries[136] would be an acceptance of the evolution of a new form of aggregate Crown, one in which the distinction between person and office is increasingly great.[137]

Allegedly right-wing elements in New Zealand opposed the use of the term 'state', and sought alternatives, such as the pre-existing concept of the Crown, not because of any attachment to monarchy, but because of opposition to anything evocative of interventionist government.[138] In part because of the neo-liberal attempt to 'roll back the state', there was also a corresponding weakening of the legal status of the Crown in late twentieth-century New Zealand.[139] However, there has been some work done on the Crown in its continuing important role as signatory of the Treaty of Waitangi, some of which has led to tentative discussion of concepts of government.[140] It is in this symbolic role that the modern function of the Crown appears to lie.

It may be that the Sovereign lacks personal power, but the organs of royal government, whether they are Ministers or departments, enjoy the benefit of the residual power of the Crown, as an institution in which the *maiestas* of law and

133 See Kelsey, *Rolling Back the State*.

134 Jacobs, p. 24.

135 Gavin Little, 'Scotland and Parliamentary Sovereignty', *Legal Studies*, 24(4) (2004): 540–67.

136 This evolutionary and legalistic approach has been remarked upon regularly by Continental observers; Levy-Ullmann, *The English Legal Tradition*.

137 A conclusion in accordance with the findings of Janine Hayward, 'In search of a treaty partner' (1995), Victoria University of Wellington PhD thesis.

138 Gordon McLauchlan, 'Of President and Country', *New Zealand Herald*, 17 February 1995.

139 Joseph, 'The Crown as a legal concept (I)'; 'The Crown as a legal concept (II)'. See also Kelsey, *Rolling Back the State*.

140 See Janine Hayward, 'In search of a treaty partner' (1995), Victoria University of Wellington PhD thesis; Margaret Wilson, 'The Reconfiguration of New Zealand's Constitutional Institutions: The Transformation of Tino Rangatiratanga into Political Reality', *Waikato Law Review*, 5 (1997): 17.

government is vested. This institution is more important than the person of the Sovereign.[141] The Crown can be seen as a living thing, personified by the Queen and the Governor-General, and distinct from any obscure concept of governmental state. This was the basis of Bagehot 's analysis of the British constitution,[142] and it remains important in New Zealand today. The exact definition of the Crown may at times be uncertain, but it has the advantage over the state of being the structure of government which is actually utilized in New Zealand, and therefore somewhat better known, if not well understood.

In both Canada and Australia the existence of entrenched constitutions have resulted in at least a partial shifting of emphasis from the Crown to the entrenched written constitution. Indeed, revolutionary necessity required this in the United States more than two hundred years ago. But the technical and legal concept of the Crown continues to pervade the apparatus of government and law in New Zealand.

No new generally accepted theory of government has been postulated in New Zealand, nor would such a project be likely to attract the attention which it deserves. In so far as such matters have been considered, the focus has been on the sovereignty, or supremacy of Parliament, and the possibility that there may be limits to such sovereignty.[143] For Dicey, sovereignty of Parliament was matched by the rule of law, or supremacy of law.[144]

Political sovereignty may lie in practice with the people,[145] but legally this is less certain,[146] though legitimacy derives principally from the people. Indeed, as a constitution characterized by its uncodified (or 'unwritten') nature, the New Zealand constitution cannot be anything but a traditional evolutionary Burkean type.[147] Yet, whether this remains the basis of the constitution in New Zealand is uncertain, for two major reasons.

---

141 There was a real interregnum between the death of one king and the election and coronation of another. The hereditary right to be considered eventually became the right to be elected. As the conception of hereditary right strengthened the practical inconvenience of the interregnum was curtailed; Frederic Maitland and Sir Frederick Pollock, *History of English Law before the Times of Edward I* (2nd edn, Cambridge, 1895), vol. 1, p. 507.

142 'The English Constitution'.

143 This question has been called 'the most puzzling constitutional conundrum of all'; Andrew Sharp, 'Constitution', in Miller, *New Zealand Government and Politics*, pp. 37–47, 40. *Taylor v New Zealand Poultry Board* [1984] 1 NZLR 394, 398 per Cooke P.

144 With the courts supervising the exercise of a common law power of government, as in *Wolfe Tone's Case* (1798) 27 State Tr 614.

145 Laski, 'The Theory of Popular Sovereignty'.

146 Though the Australian Constitution has been held to be based on popular sovereignty, as it was adopted by referendum, and may only be changed by referendum: *Australian Capital Television Pty Ltd v Commonwealth* (1992) 177 CLR 106, 138 per Mason CJ; *Theophanous v Herald & Weekly Times Ltd* (1994) 182 CLR 104, 171 per Deane J; *McGinty v Western Australia* (1996) 186 CLR 140, 230, 237 per McHugh J.

147 Edmund Burke saw a constitution as based on a social contract which evolved from generation to generation; Russell, *Constitutional Odyssey*, pp. 10–11.

First, the non-Maori population seems, by and large, influenced by basically Lockean ideas of government as a direct compact.[148] Though they may not directly question the basis of governmental authority, the possibility of such questioning in the future cannot be discounted. This is particularly so given the impetus to reform given by the introduction of a system of proportional voting in 1996.[149]

By contrast, Maori tend to see government, and society, in more evolutionary terms.[150] Most importantly, however, claims to Maori sovereignty do not rest upon claims to popular sovereignty as such, but upon the cession, or non-cession, of *kawanatanga* and *tino rangatiratanga* to the Crown in 1840. The sovereignty of the Crown, in the context of the Treaty of Waitangi, is more than merely a legal doctrine; it has a continuing political relevance. Merely redefining the location of sovereignty as the people, a reconstituted Parliament, or a president, would not necessarily satisfy the other party to the Treaty, for it would constitute the removal of one party to the Treaty.[151] The difficult task of determining what constitutional structures will satisfy both perspectives remains.[152] This task may not be urgent.

8.3 Conclusion

In those mixed models, where there is neither a predominance of doctrinaire liberalism, nor authoritarianism, state flexibility is generally well-developed. The unity of legal continuity, and a sovereign Parliament, or other constitutional focus, ensures that the diversity of a modern society, with its disparate elements, is not too diverse to function. Predominantly this is because soft constitutions have allowed or encouraged this; in the British constitutional tradition only government actions which have authority in law may be undertaken. This limits the actions of government, but only insofar as prior authority must be sought, usually, though not invariably, from Parliament.

However, there are dangers, which stem primarily from the weakness inherent where there is no clear underlying constitutional ethos. The stability of the regime depends neither upon rigid authoritarian rule, nor upon liberal democratic principles, but rather upon a juxtaposition of the two. As discussed in Chapter 2, Foucault's view of government was not so much the political or administrative structures of the modern state as 'the way in which the conduct of individuals or of

148 The Prince of Wales was reported as believing that a referendum on the monarchy in the United Kingdom would provide a new and lasting legitimacy for the Crown; 'Prince wants British to choose', *New Zealand Herald*, 8 November 1999.

149 Alan Simpson (ed.), *Constitutional Implications of MMP* (Wellington, 1998).

150 Dona Awatere, *Maori Sovereignty* (Auckland, 1984).

151 See Janine Hayward, 'In search of a treaty partner' (1995), Victoria University of Wellington PhD thesis.

152 Jock Phillips, 'The Constitution and Independent Nationhood', in James, *Building the Constitution*, pp. 69–76.

groups might be directed: the government of children, of souls, of communities, of families, of the sick … To govern, in this sense, is to structure the possible field of action of others.'[153] This principle of governmentality emphasizes the importance of the active subject as the entity through which, and by means of which, power is actually exercised. The actors, rather than necessarily any underlying principles – such as democracy or the rule of law – determine the nature of the polity. In such a norm-less environment the state is potentially exposed to failure from loss of legitimacy through inconsistency or hesitancy in responding to immediate economic, political or social threats to community cohesion.

153 *The Foucault Effects: Studies in Governmentality*, ed. Graham Burchell, Colin Gordon and Peter Miller (London, 1991).

Chapter 9
Conclusions

9.1 Introduction

In this book we considered the degree to which constitutional flexibility, rather than broader societal and environmental factors, may have led to the rise of 'successful' states, and to the decline of 'unsuccessful' states, by promoting stability. It was the underlying hypothesis of this book that the constitutional paradigm of a country is a prime influence upon that country's success or failure. Thus, although environment, broadly defined, is often a crucial element, the model of constitution, or shape of the body politic, is critical.

The model of the constitution does not necessarily mean any particular type of government, democratic, parliamentary, presidential, monarchical, or any other form that may be imagined, but rather the nature of the constitution. Is it rigid or flexible, can it adapt itself to changing circumsta nces, or is it too flexible that it lacks a necessary degree of coherency? The absence of an inherent ethos, whether social, political, economic, or religious, is important. Equally important is the degree of popular acceptance of this.

Constitutional flexibility, and hence the degree of state 'success', depends upon the existence of a unifying conceptual identity of the state. This may be the product of an imposition – such as where a democratic model of government is imposed by a colonial power (as in the former British colonies, or the post-Saddam Hussein Iraq and post-Taleban Afghanistan), or it may develop through a process of historical evolution, as in the United Kingdom, or the settled colonies of British North America and Australasia. In the former situation it seems to have worked less successfully than in the latter, though it may be as yet difficult to be sure. But the lesson might be that impositions are at least as unlikely to be effective over time as xenotransplantation in biology, and for similar reasons. A natural evolution is more contextualized, if not more conducive to thrive in the native soil. In other words, the ability of the constitution to adapt to the cultural environment affects its survival.

In Part I, 'Legal Paradigms', we considered some of the theories that have been advanced in an attempt to explain the rise and fall of civilizations. Some of these are valuable in general, others contribute to an understanding of the process by which these variables can be isolated and studied. The focus then changed, in the second and third chapters, to look at a small number of individual states, and the factors that appeared to have led to their success and failure. Finally, the concept of the hard and soft constitutions was introduced and explained. This was based on the notion that the formal constitutional flexibility of states is a major factor in determining their success and failure. Flexibility refers to the ability of the state structure to respond to changing circumstances, whether it be a reduction in economic stability, or the advent of new technologies which undermine the authority of the state through increased education and a freer mass media. This is also distinct from the concept that the development and application of the rule of law contributed largely to stability, though the rule of law is indeed one aspect of the flexible and adaptable constitution.

In Part II, 'The Viability of States', we applied this theory to different types of state models. These included authoritarian, doctrinaire liberal, empires and supra-national entities, and mixed models. None were exclusively of the soft or the hard constitution type. But some have been markedly less successful than others, and we examined the performance of these state models, with the purpose of ascertaining, if it is possible to do so, whether it might be the flexibility of the underlying constitutional paradigm, rather than the form of the model itself, that helped determine state stability and viability.

This part comprised a series of case studies, of particular states at particular points in time. The case studies included eastern Europe in the late twentieth century. In these and other examples the focus was upon the responsiveness of the constitution to changing circumstances. Given the limitations of the study in both geography and time it is not possible to derive conclusions with any degree of certainty. But there were some indications of value.

As had been discussed in Chapter 1, in a state like Somalia institutional government was weak, and the 'state' depended upon internal checks and balances to maintain stability – or an element of stability such as was necessary for the preservation of settled government. Post-colonial states generally, including Somalia, sought to emulate the strong government models of the West – whether or not these were suited to their own particular circumstances. In some cases such approaches, rather than instilling a much needed element of unity, built upon tribal and other differences (as in many parts of Africa, in particular, where corruption encouraged this), to destabilize the regime. Excessive constitutional rigidity – including a wilful adherence to state authority – often prevented the fundamental internal realignments which were actually necessary to enable the state to flourish in the post-colonial era, when the externally-imposed order no longer existed.

The world community generally also sought to impose certain standards domestically, such as democracy and the rule of law, again irrespective of the applicability of such concepts, which were assumed (ultimately perhaps correctly, but with a more nuanced approach being necessary) to be ubiquitous.

9.2 Flexibility and stability

The greater the degree of flexibility in a constitution, the greater the prospect for satisfactory response to changing circumstances. But this must be fettered in some degree. In the United Kingdom the juridical test in public law for rationality is 'manifest unreasonableness'; that in the European Union is proportionality ('manifest disproportionality').[1] Both are tests which ensure that judicial response to executive action. Both ensure that there is some constraint on actions. But in addition to formal rules, conventions also ensure that the system operates efficiently. Flexibility is required, and is provided, but it is hedged around with legal rules and principles.

Historically, the stability of the United Kingdom depended upon a number of factors including constitutional continuity, which was of course also itself a product of relative stability. It did however allow the development of certain principles, and was in turn encouraged by them, including the rule of law, and the precedent-based common law. Government early became subordinate to law, whose creature it was, rather than the other way around. In part this came from a legal and constitution tradition which could be traced to Bracton, and Langton, the latter a major influence on Magna Carta. The Great Charter was not merely the product of baronial strength and regal weakness, but was also a reflection of evolving concepts of law. This law included the nascent common law, and the principles of the newly revived *ius commune ecclesiasticum*[2] or canon law. The influence upon Magna Carta of canon law, and the Church, was very great, and few individuals had as much personal influence as Stephen Cardinal Langton, Archbishop of Canterbury.

Langton, who may have written Magna Carta, and at the very least had a significant role in its drafting, was a canon lawyer with a Europe-wide reputation as a scholar (he had studied and taught at the University of Paris for 25 years). It was from his canon and civil law training, rather than from the principles of the common law, or of the practices of English feudalism, that he derived much of his inspiration. From such traditions as these could be traced underlying principles and approaches which continued to influence the development of English law, and thus the constitutional form of the United Kingdom, and later the British Empire and Commonwealth, for the best part of a millennia. Whether we accept the natural law, or the positive law approach, either helped to understand the development of a western legal tradition. This brought with it inherent stability but also the ability to adapt – though it might be said that this was more readily apparent in common law than civil law jurisdictions.

The authoritarian regimes of eastern Europe in the late twentieth century depended for their existence on centralized planning, political control, and adherence to an anti-democratic ideology. Their underlying inspiration, or principles, were less the product of gradual pragmatic evolution built upon a bedrock of Christian monarchical jurisprudence, than the result of socialist ideology based on the writings of one man, Karl Marx. It was almost inevitable that their flexibility was limited. The advent of external and internal economic

1 Paul Craig and Adam Tomkins (eds), *The Executive and Public Law: Power and Accountability in Comparative Law* (Oxford, 2006), p. 9.

2 Evers v. Owen (1627) Godbolt's Report 432 (K.B.) per Whitlock J.

and social pressures – including the absence or weakness of genuine emotional adherence – meant that they were ill-equipped to respond to changing conditions, and *thus* failed. In contrast, the markedly more democratic, and thus adherence-inducing, regimes in the United States and the United Kingdom in the nineteenth and twentieth centuries, were able to respond to the advent of industrialization, and later its decline. This was not without difficulty, but it did not lead to social and political upheavals which threatened to destroy the state itself.

9.3 Hard and soft constitutions, democracy and the rule of law

One of the reasons for the success of the western liberal democracies lay not in their being democracies, *per se*, though that meant that governments were inherently more responsive to social, economic and political changes. Rather, it lay in the flow-on effect of a long-standing tradition of the rule of law. It has been said (perhaps with some degree of accuracy, though it is dangerous to generalize) that some societies – notably those of the West – are profoundly law-abiding. 'In western societies on the whole the laws are felt in fono interno, and not just by reason of their sanctions … the provisions of constitutions do effectively constrain the organs of government and empower large sections of the public.'[3] This adherence stems from the acceptance that the system of government, and its application, is fair and reasonable, efficient and for the good of the people. This, in turn, is only possible because of the tradition under which this has, by and large, been true (even when pre- or un-democratic).

Democracy is a major element in ensuring flexibility – and the rule of law provides the rigidity. But more is needed to provide the constitution with a direction and an underlying ethos. The social compact theories of the seventeenth century might point to one partial solution. But this wouldn't be sufficient of itself, especially since social compacts would be bound to fall victim to democratically-inspired majoritarianism.

9.4 Conclusion

Only the broadest conclusions, if any, can be drawn from the empirical comparisons made in this book, and from the theoretical modelling which accompanies this. In those states where there has been a fundamental change in *Grundnorm*, such as in eastern Europe, the loss of an ideological unity led to institutional paralysis or collapse, followed by the advent of unregulated free markets.

Essentially this book was an exercise in discovering how the one element of the character or ethos of a legal system has influenced economic, social and political

3 S.E. Finer, Vernon Bogdanor and Bernard Rudden, *Comparing Constitutions* (Oxford, 1995), p. 14.

success. In part this was a consideration of the contribution of law, broadly defined, to the success of states.

We considered the degree to which constitutional flexibility, rather than broader societal and environmental factors, appears to have contributed to stability, and thus led to the rise of 'successful' states and to the decline of 'unsuccessful' states. The emphasis was upon identifying the elements of state success and failure – if any – that may be ascribed to the underlying nature of the constitution. The findings, it would appear, are that the formal constitutional rules are less important than the degree of adherence. This in turn depends upon the existence of a unifying ideology or ethos (such as liberal democracy) which is accepted by the majority of the population. The absence of such an ethos renders a state weak, even if its formal constitutional provisions are otherwise satisfactory – such as in the former Soviet Union.

Adherence to principle is fundamentally important. Abandonment of them could seriously undermine the long-term stability of a state. These principles, for more than a century for much of the world, and for rather longer in some states, have included democracy and the rule of law. A state must be flexible enough to adapt its structure and organs to meet new conditions, but it should not be so flexible that it discards the ethos, or underlying nature of the state itself. A state is not merely a country, nor it is a collection of communities let alone individuals. A warning might be given. Recent discussion in Europe about what are core values underlying the nature of the continent concentrated on such comparatively modern ideals as human rights (about which, naturally, there was some disagreement). Christianity was rejected, despite strong attempts from some quarters to include it. Perhaps what has been missed is that it was Christianity which formed the basis of much of the civil law, and provided a guiding hand even in the common law-dominated laws of England. Rejecting Christianity, presumably on the grounds that there is, or should be a separation of church and state (an irrelevancy in the context of a Europe-wide debate), and that religious believe is a personal matter, may have been short-sighted. The deeper issue is the nature of the European-wide constitutional and legal ethos – which is ultimately based on the canon and civil law and thus strongly influenced by Christian principles, just as the common law was, and is still today.

This is not to say that rejection of such an underlying principle threatens to undermine European states. Their survival would scarcely be threatened by such a step. But their flexibility is due, in part, to this ethos. A bureaucratic ethos, based on individual inherent human rights, and democracy, may prove a sufficiently flexible and robust substitute. But unconsciously perhaps, since the Enlightenment this evolution has been gradually occurring (coupled with a shift from a belief in natural law to a largely positive law-based legal system). This has, so far, proven to have provided a sufficient stable yet flexible basis upon which to construct constitutions. States which enjoy such a basis are generally stable. Those states which have a more strongly developed ideology, or where there is no ideology barring survival, are most at risk.

Bibliography

Abbott, Alison, 'Europe's Life Patent Moratorium May Go', *Nature*, 393 (1998): 200

——, 'EuroVote Lifts Block on Biotech Patents .... But Parliament Wants Closer Scrutiny', *Nature*, 388 (1997): 314–15

——, 'Transgenic Patents a Step Closer in Europe', *Nature* 390 (1997): 429

Abbott, Frederick M., 'Distributed governance at the WTO–WIPO: An evolving model for open-architecture integrated governance', *Journal of International Economic Law*, 3 (2000): 63–81

Abbott, K., 'Modern International Relations Theory: A Prospectus for International Lawyers', *Journal of International Law*, 14 (1989): 335–411

Academy of Sciences, *The Patentability of the Genome* (Academy of Sciences, Paris, 1995) Paris Bilingual Report No. 32

Ackerman, Bruce, *We the People* (Cambridge: Harvard University Press, 1991)

Adams, Mark D. et al, 'Complementary DNA Sequencing: Expressed Sequence Tags and Human Genome Project', *Science*, 252 (1991): 1651–6

Adkins, Jocelyn C., 'The Internet: a critical technology for the state of environmental law', *Villanova Environmental Law Journal*, 8 (1997): 341–57

Adler, Reid G., 'Controlling the Applications of Biotechnology: A Critical Analysis of the Proposed Moratorium on Animal Patenting', *Harvard Journal of Law and Technology*, (1988): 1–62

Agamben, Giorgio, *Homo Sacer: Sovereign Power and Bare Life*, trans. D. Heller-Roazen (Stanford: Stanford University Press, 1998)

Agnew of Lochnaw, Bt, Sir Crispin, 'The Conflict of heraldic laws', *Juridical Review* (1988): 61–76

Ahrens, Judith D. and Gerardo A. Esquer, 'Internet's potential as a global information infrastructure: A case study and assessment', *Journal of Global Information Management*, 1 (1993): 18–27

Akdeniz, Y., C. Walker and D. Wall, *The Internet, Law and Society* (Harlow: Longman, 2000)

Akerlof, George A., 'The Market for "Lemons": Quality Uncertainty and the Market Mechanism', *Quarterly Journal of Economics*, 84 (1970): 488–500

Alderson, Stanley, *Yea or nay?: referenda in the United Kingdom* (London: Cassell, 1975)

Alker, Hayward R., 'Dialectical Foundations of Global Disparities', *International Studies Quarterly*, 25 (1981): 69–98

——, Thomas J. Biersteker and Takashi Inoguchi, 'From Imperial Power Balancing to People's Wars: Searching for Order in the Twentieth Century', in James

Der Derian and Michael J. Shapiro (eds), *International/Intertextual Relations: Postmodern Readings of World Politics* (Lexington: D.C. Heath, 1989) 135–62

Allan, Trevor R.S., *Constitutional Justice: a liberal theory of the rule of law* (Oxford: Oxford University Press, 2001)

——, *Law, liberty, and justice: the legal foundations of the British constitution* (Oxford: Oxford University Press, 1993)

Allen Consulting Group, *Economic perspectives on copyright law: research paper* (Strawberry Hills: Centre for Copyright Studies, 2003)

Allen, Robert C., 'Agriculture and the origins of the state in ancient Egypt', *Explorations in Economic History*, 34 (1997): 135–54

Alvarez, José E., 'Do Liberal States Behave Better? A Critique of Slaughter's Liberal Theory', *European Journal of International Law*, 12 (2001): 183–246

Anderson, W. French, 'Human Gene Therapy', *Science*, 256 (1992): 808–13

Anderson, Christopher, 'NIH Drops Bid For Gene Patents', *Science*, 263 (1994): 909–10

——, 'United States Patent Application Stirs Up Gene Hunters', *Nature*, 353 (1991): 485–6

Ando, Clifford, *Imperial ideology and provincial loyalty in the Roman Empire* (Berkeley: University of California Press, 2000)

Andreau, Jean, *Banking and business in the Roman world*, trans. Janet Lloyd (Cambridge: Cambridge University Press, 1999)

Anonymous of Rouen, *Die Texte des Normannischen Anonymous*, ed. K. Pellens (Stuttgart: Franz Steiner Verlag, 1966)

Anson, Sir William, 'Government of Ireland Bill and the Sovereignty of Parliament', *Law Quarterly Review* (1886): 427–41

——, *The Law and Custom of the Constitution*, ed. A.B. Keith (5th edn, Oxford: Clarendon Press, 1922, 3rd edn, 1907)

Aoki, Keith, 'Weeds, seeds and deeds: Recent skirmishes in the seed wars', *Cardozo Journal of International and Comparative Law*, 11 (2003): 247–331

Aquinas, St Thomas, St Thomas Aquinas, *On Kingship to the King of Cyprus*, trans. G.B. Phelan and I.T. Eschmann (Toronto: Pontifical Institute of Mediæval Studies, 1949, first published 1260–65)

——, *Summa theologiæ*, ed. John A. Oesterle (Englewood Cliffs: Prentice-Hall, 1964)

Arendt, Hannah, 'What was authority', in Carl Friedrich (ed.), *Authority* (Cambridge: Harvard University Press, 1958) 81–112

Aristotle, *Ethica Nicomachea*, ed. R.A. Gauthier and E.J. Brill (Rotterdam: Brouwer, 1972–74)

——, *The Politics of Aristotle*, trans. Ernest Barker (London: Oxford University Press, 1958)

Armstrong, Harvey W. and Robert Read, 'Comparing the economic performance of dependent territories and sovereign microstates', *Economic Development and Cultural Change*, 48(2) (2000): 285–306

Arnold, Guy, *World government by stealth: the future of the United Nations* (New York: St Martin's Press, 1997)

von Arx, Kim G., 'ICANN – Now and then: ICANN's Reform and its problems', *Duke Law and Technology Review* (2003) 7

Astraudo, A., 'Saint-marin et l'Ordre de Malta', *La Revue Diplomatique* (1935): 7

Atiya, Aziz Suryal, *Crusade, commerce and culture* (Bloomington: Indiana University Press, 1962)

Attenborough, F.L. (ed.), *Laws of the earliest English kings* (Cambridge: Cambridge University Press, 1922)

Aubert, Jean-Jacques and Boudewijn Sirks (eds), *Speculum iuris: Roman law as a reflection of social and economic life in antiquity* (Ann Arbor: University of Michigan Press, 2002)

Austin, John, *Lectures on Jurisprudence, or The Philosophy of Positive Law*, R. Campbell (ed.) (2 vols, 4th edition, rev., London: John Murray, 1879)

——, *The Province of Jurisprudence Determined*, W. Rumble (ed.) (Cambridge: Cambridge University Press, 1995, first published, 1832)

Austin, John, *Sense and sensibilia* (Oxford: Oxford University Press, 1959)

Avi-Yonah, Reuven S., 'Globalization, Tax Competition, and the Fiscal Crisis of the Welfare State', *Harvard Law Review*, 113 (2000): 1573–676

Awatere, Dona, *Maori Sovereignty* (Auckland: Broadsheet, 1984)

Aylmer, Gerald, *The struggle for the constitution, 1603–1689: England in the seventeenth century* (4th edn, London: Blandford, 1975)

Bacon, Sir Francis, 'Religious Meditations, Of Heresies', in *Bacon's essays* with annotations by Richard Whately (London: J.W. Parker, 1858, first published 1597)

Baechler, Jean, *Les Origines du Capitalisme* (Paris: Gallinard, 1971)

Baer, Klaus, *Rank and title in the Old Kingdom; the structure of the Egyptian administration in the fifth and sixth dynasties* (Chicago: University of Chicago Press, 1960)

Bagner, Jessica, Vanessa Kaye Watson and K. Brooke Welch, 'Internet auction fraud targeted by FTC, state and local law enforcement officials', *Intellectual Property and Technology Law Journal*, 15 (2003): 22

Baker, Sir John, 'English Law and the Renaissance', *Cambridge Law Journal* (1985) 46–61

Bangert William V., *A History of the Society of Jesus* (2nd edn, rev. and updated, St Louis: Institute of Jesuit Sources, 1986)

Banting, Keith G. and Richard Simeon (eds), *Redesigning the state: the politics of constitutional change* (Toronto: University of Toronto Press, 1985)

Barker, Sir Ernest, *Reflections on Government* (London: Oxford University Press, 1942)

Barker, Rodney, *Political Legitimacy and the state* (Oxford: Clarendon Press, 1990)

Barlow, Frank, *The Feudal Kingdom of England, 1042–1216* (2nd edn, London: Longmans, 1961, first published 1955)

——, *William Rufus* (London: Methuen, 1983)

Barnes, Timothy D., *The new empire of Diocletian and Constantine* (Cambridge: Harvard University Press, 1982)

Barrow, G.W.S., *Feudal Britain: The Completion of the Mediæval Kingdoms, 1066–1314* (London: Edward Arnold, 1956)

Barrow, Sir John, *Some Account of the Public Life, and a Selection from the Unpublished Writings, of the Earl of Macartney* (London: T. Cadell and W. Davies, 1807)

Barry, A., T. Osbourne and Nicolas Rose (eds), *Foucault and Political Reason: Liberalism, Neo-Liberalism and Rationalities of Government* (London: UCL Press, 1996)

Bartlett, Joseph W., *Venture capital: law, business strategies, investment planning* (New York: J. Wiley, 1988)

Barton, Simon and Peter Linehan (eds), *Cross, crescent and conversion: studies on medieval Spain and christendom in memory of Richard Fletcher* (Leiden: Brill, 2008)

Battra, Shelly P., Robert E. Lutz, Ved P. Nanda, David A. Wirth, Daniel Magraw and Gunther Handl, 'International transfer of hazardous technology and substances: caveat emptor or state responsibility? The case of Bhopal, India', *Proceedings of the Seventy-Ninth Annual Meeting of the American Society of International Law* (1985): 303–22

Baxi, U., 'Constitutionalism as a Site of State Formative Practices', *Cardozo Law Review*, 21 (2000): 1183–1210

Bean, J.M.W., *The decline of English feudalism, 1215–1540* (Manchester: Manchester University Press, 1968)

Beaumont, P., C. Lyons and Neil Walker (eds), *Convergence and Divergence in European Public Law* (Oxford: Hart, 2002)

Bede, Venerable, *Bede's Ecclesiastical history of the English people: a historical commentary*, ed. J.M. Wallace-Hadrill (Oxford: Clarendon Press, 1988)

Bell, Tom W., 'Free speech, strict scrutiny, and self-help: how technology upgrades constitutional jurisprudence', *Minnesota Law Review*, 87 (2003): 743–78

Bellamy, Richard (ed.), *Constitutionalism and Democracy* (Aldershot: Ashgate, 2006)

Bennet, Robert, *King Charle's Trial Iustified* (London: R.A., 1649)

Benson, Bruce, 'The Spontaneous Evolution of Commercial Law', *Southern Economic Journal*, 55 (1989): 644–61

Bercuson, David and Barry Cooper, 'From Constitutional Monarchy to Quasi Republic', in Janet Ajzenstat (ed.), *Canadian Constitutionalism, 1791–1991* (Ottawa: Canadian Study of Parliament Group, 1992) 17–27

Berger, Carl (ed.), *Imperialism and Nationalism, 1884–1914: A Conflict in Canadian Thought* (Toronto: Copp Clark, 1969)

Berger, Klaus Peter, *The Creeping Codification of Lex Mercatoria* (The Hague: Kluwer Law International, 1999)

Berman, Harold J., *Law and Revolution: The Formation of the Western Legal Tradition* (Cambridge: Harvard University Press, 1983)

Berman, Paul Schiff, 'Cyberspace and the state Action Debate: The Cultural Value of Applying Constitutional Norms to "Private"' Regulation', *University of Colorado Law Review*, 71 (2000): 1265–6

Bernard, Nick, *Multilevel Governance in the European Union* (The Hague: Kluwer Law International 2002)

Bernstein, Jodie, Director, Bureau of Consumer Protection, US Federal Trade Commission, 'Fighting Internet Fraud: A Global Effort', *Economic Perspectives, An Electronic Journal of the United States Department of State*, 5 (May 2000), available at <http://usinfo.state.gov/journals/ites/0500/ijee/-ftc2.htm> (as at 1 December 2003)

Berry, Roberta M., 'The Human Genome Project and the End of Insurance', *Florida Journal of Law and Public Policy*, 7 (1996): 205–56

Best, Geoffrey, Humanity in Warfare: The Modern History of the International Law of Armed Conflict (New York: Columbia University Press, 1980)

Bierstedt, Robert, 'Legitimacy', in Julian Gould and William Kolb (eds), *A Dictionary of the Social Sciences* (London: Tavistock Publications, 1964) 386–7

Bill, Stephen and Arthur Kerrigan, 'Practical application of European Value Added Tax to E-Commerce', *Georgia Law Review*, 38 (2003): 71–83

Birch, Anthony, *The British System of Government* (4th edn, London: George Allen and Unwin, 1980, 9th edn, London: Routledge, 1993)

Birchall, Frederick T., 'Burning of the Books, May 10, 1933', in Louis L. Snyder (ed.), *National Socialist Germany: Twelve Years that Shook the World* (Malabor: Krieger, 1984)

Bird, M., Richard, 'Taxation and e-commerce', *Canadian Business Law Journal*, 38 (2003): 466–71

Biryukov, Alexander, 'The Doctrine of Dualism of Private Law in the Context of Recent Codifications of Civil Law: Ukrainian Perspectives', *Annual Survey of International and Comparative Law*, 8 (2002): 53–4

Black, Bernard S. and Anna S. Tarassova, 'Institutional reform in transition: A case study of Russia', *Supreme Court Economic Review*, 10 (1993): 211–78

Blackburn, Robert G., 'The role of the Canadian government in encouraging innovations', *Canada United States Law Journal*, 15 (1989): 229–36

Blackstone, Sir William, *Commentaries on the Laws of England*, ed. E. Christian (New York: Garland Publishing, 1978)

Blamont, Jacques, *Le Chiffre et Le Songe: Histoire politique de la découverte* (Paris: Odile Jacob, 1993)

Blank, Robert H., *The political implications of human genetic technology* (Boulder: Westview Press, 1981)

Bloch, Marc, *Feudal Society* (Chicago: University of Chicago Press, 1961)

Bloom, E., Bgnami, F. Kuijper P.-J. and Lachmann P., *The European Union's New Ambitions* (2005) Proceedings of the American Society of International Law

Blum, Jerome, *The end of the old order in rural Europe* (Princeton: Princeton University Press, 1978)

Blumenthal, Uta-Renate, *The* investiture *controversy: church and monarchy from the ninth to the twelfth century* (Philadelphia: University of Pennsylvania Press, 1988)

Bodin, Jean, *Les Six Livres de la République ('The Six bookes of a Commonwealth')*, trans. M.J. Tooley (Oxford: Blackwell, 1955)

Boer, Ben, 'The Globalization of Environmental Law: The Role of the United Nations', *Melbourne University Law Review*, 20 (1995): 101–25

Bogdanor, Vernon, 'Britain and Europe', in R. Holme and Michael Elliott (eds), *1688–1988 Time for a New Constitution* (London: Macmillan, 1988) 81–102

——, *The Monarchy and the Constitution* (Oxford: Clarendon Press, 1995)

Boister, Neil, 'The Trend to Universal Extradition over Subsidiary Universal Jurisdiction in the Suppression of Transnational Crime', *Acta Juridica* (1993): 287–313

Bolingbroke, Henry St John Viscount, *The Idea of a Patriot King: With respect to the Constitution of Great Britain* (London: T.C., 1740)

Booth, Rev Ken, 'A Pakeha Perspective on Te Tino Rangatiratanga', in J. Crawford (ed.), *Church and State: Te Tino Rangatiratanga* (Auckland: College of St John the Evangelist, 1998) 1–36

Boston, Jonathan, Stephen Levine, Elizabeth McLeay, Nigel Roberts and Hannah Schmidt, 'Caretaker governments and the evolution of caretaker conventions in New Zealand', *Victoria University of Wellington Law Review*, 28 (1998): 629

Botkin, James, Dan Dimancescu, Ray Stata and John McClellan, *Global stakes: the future of high technology in America* (Cambridge: Ballinger Publishing Co., c.1982)

Boucher, David and Paul Kelly (eds), *The social contract from Hobbes to Rawls* (London: Routledge, 1994)

Bowman, James E., 'Symposium Genetics and the Law: the Ethical, Legal and Social Implications of Genetic Technology and Biomedical Ethics: The Road to Eugenics', *University of Chicago Law School Roundtable*, 3 (1996): 491

Bracton, Henry de, *On the Laws and Customs of England* ('*Henri de Bracton de Legibus et Consuetudis Angliæ*'), ed. G.E. Woodbine; trans. S.E. Thorne (Cambridge: Belknap Harvard: 1968)

Bradley, Ian, *God Save the Queen: The Spiritual Dimension of Monarchy* (London: Darton, Longman and Todd, 2002).

Branscomb, Anne Wells, 'Jurisdictional Quandaries for Global Networks', in Linda M. Harasim (ed.), *Global Networks: Computers and Informational Communication* (Cambridge: MIT Press, 1993)

Brash, Anthony, 'Ecclesiastical Law and the Law of God in Scripture', *Ecclesiastical Law Journal*, 5(22) (1998): 7

Braudel, Fernand, *Civilisation and Capitalism, 15th–18th century* (London: HarperCollins, 1985, first published Paris by Armend Colin, 1979 as *Civilisation matérielle, économie et capitalisme, XVe–XVIIIe siècle*)

Braun, Christopher K., 'Alternative rhythms in law and economics: the Posner–Malloy dialectic', *The Legal Studies Forum*, 15 (1991): 153–65

Brinton, Clarence, *From many one: the process of political integration, the problem of world government* (Cambridge: Harvard University Pres, 1948)

Brookfield, F.M., *The Constitution in 1985: The Search for Legitimacy* (Auckland: University of Auckland Press, 1985)

——, 'The Monarchy and the Constitution today', *New Zealand Law Journal* (1992): 438

——, 'Parliamentary Supremacy and Constitutional Entrenchment', *Otago Law Review*, 5 (1984): 603–34

——, 'Some aspects of the Necessity Principle in Constitutional Law', University of Oxford DPhil thesis (1972)

——, Waitangi and Indigenous Rights: Revolution, Law and Legitimation (Auckland: University of Auckland Press, 1999)

Brown, Andrew and Anthony Grant, *The law of intellectual property in New Zealand: an exposition of the New Zealand law relating to trade marks, passing off, copyright, registered designs, patents, trade secrets and the Fair Trading Act 1986* (Wellington: Butterworths, 1989)

Brownlie, Ian, *Principles of Public International Law* (5th edn, New York: Clarendon Press, 1998)

Bryce, James, *Constitutions* (London: Oxford University Press, 1901)

Buchanan, James, *The Limits of Liberty: Between anarchy and Leviathan* (Chicago: University of Chicago Press, 1975)

Bull, Hedley, *The Anarchical Society: A Study of Order in World Politics* (London: Macmillan, 1977)

Burk, Dan L., 'Federalism in Cyberspace', *Connecticut Law Review*, 28 (1996): 1095–1127

——, 'Muddy Rules for Cyberspace', *Cardozo Law Review*, 21 (1998–99): 121–79

——, 'Patents in Cyberspace: Territoriality and Infringement on Global Computer Networks', *Tulane Law Review*, 68 (1993–94): 1–67

——, 'Trademarks Along the Infobahn: A First Look at the Emerging Law of Cybermarks', *University of Richmond Journal of Law and Technology*, 1 (1995): 1

Burke, Edmund, *Selected Writings and Speeches*, ed. Peter J. Stanlis (Washington: Regnery Publications, 1997)

Burns, Thomas S., *Barbarians within the gates of Rome: a study of Roman military policy and the barbarians, ca. 375–425 A.D.* (Bloomington: Indiana University Press, 1994)

Buscaglia, Edgardo, Maria Dakolias and William Ratliff, *Judicial Reform in Latin America: A Framework for National Development* (Washington: Hoover Institute Press, 1995)

Cain, Bruce E., 'The Internet in the (dis)service of democracy?', *Loyola of Los Angeles Law Review*, 34 (2001): 1005–21

Campbell, J.B., *The Emperor and the Roman Army, 31 BC–AD 235* (Oxford: Clarendon Press, 1984)

Campbell, James, *Essays in Anglo-Saxon History* (London: Hambledon Press, 1986)

Campos, Nauro and Fabrizzio Coricelli, 'Growth in Transition: What We Know, What We Don't, and What We Should', *Journal of Economic Literature*, 40 (2002): 793–836

Cannataci, Joseph A. and Jeanne Pia Mifsud Bonnici, 'Can self-regulation satisfy the transnational requisite of successful Internet regulation?', *International Review of Law, Computers and Technology*, 17 (2003): 51–61

Canning, J.P., 'Law, sovereignty and corporation theory, 1300–1450', in J.H. Burns (ed.), *The Cambridge History of Mediæval Political Thought c.350–c.1450* (Cambridge: Cambridge University Press, 1988) 454–76

Cannon, John and Ralph Griffiths, *The Oxford Illustrated History of the British Monarchy* (Oxford: Oxford University Press, 1988)

Caporaso, J.A., 'The European Union and Forms of State: Westphalian, Regulatory or Post Modern?', *Journal of Common Market Studies*, 34(1) (1996): 19–52

Cardinale, Hyginus Eugene, *The Holy See and the international order* (Toronto: Macmillan of Canada, 1976)

Cardozo, Benjamin N., *The Nature of the Judicial Process* (New Haven: Yale University Press, 1921)

Carey, Gilbert L., 'The resurgence of states' rights creates new risk to intellectual property', *Albany Law Journal of Science and Technology*, 11 (2000): 123–52

Carlyle, Sir Robert and A.J. Carlyle, *A History of Mediæval Political Theory in the West* (Edinburgh: Blackwood, 1928–36)

Carneiro, Robert L., 'A Theory of the Origin of the State', *Science*, 169 (1970): 733–8

Carr, Robert, *Black nationalism in the new world: reading the African American and West Indian experience* (Durham: Duke University Press, 2002)

Carter, F.W. and David Turnock (eds), *Environmental problems in Eastern Europe* (London: Routledge, 1993)

Caskey, C. Thomas, 'Molecular Medicine; A Spin-Off from the Helix', *JAMA*, 269 (1993): 1986–92

Castel, Jean Gabriel, *International Law: Chiefly as Interpreted and Applied in Canada* (3rd edn, Toronto: University of Toronto Press, 1976)

Castells, Manuel, *The Rise of Network Society* (London: Blackwell, 1996, 2nd edn, 2000)

Cates, Christopher, 'Property in Human Tissues: History, Society and Possible Implementations', *Appeal: Review of Current Law and Law Reform*, 4 (1998): 32–43

Catholicity: *A Study in the Conflict of Christian Traditions in the West, being a Report presented to His Grace the Archbishop of Canterbury* (Westminster: Dacre Press, 1947)

Cell, John W., *British colonial administration in the mid-nineteenth century: the policy-making process* (New Haven: Yale University Press, 1970)

Chadwick, Owen, *The Reformation* (Harmondsworth: Penguin, 1968)

Chambers, Jasemine, 'Patent eligibility of biotechnological inventions in the United States, Europe, and Japan: How much patent policy is public policy?', *George Washington International Law Review*, 34 (2002): 223–46

Chander, Anupam, 'Whose Republic?', *University of Chicago Law Review*, 69 (2002): 1479–1500

Charlton, John, *The Chartists: the first national workers' movement* (London: Pluto Press, 1997)

Charnovitz, S., 'Opening the WTO to Non-Governmental Interests', *Fordham International Law Journal*, 24 (2000): 173

Chauveau, Michel, *Cleopatra: beyond the myth*, trans. David Lorton (Ithaca: Cornell University Press, 2002)

Cheshire, G.C., *Modern Law of Real Property*, ed. E.H. Burn (13th edn, London: Butterworths, 1982)

Chester, Sir Norman: *The English administrative system, 1780–1870* (Oxford: Clarendon Press, 1981)

Chevallier, Raymond, *Roman roads*, trans. N.H. Field (Berkeley: University of California Press, 1976)

Chichilnisky, Graciela, 'The Knowledge Revolution', *Journal of International Trade and Economic Development*, 7 (1998): 39–45

Chikuhwa, Jacob, *A crisis of governance: Zimbabwe* (New York: Algora Publishing, 2004)

Chien, Colleen, 'Cheap drugs at what price to innovation: Does the compulsory licensing of pharmaceuticals hurt innovation?', *Berkeley Technology Law Journal*, 18 (2003): 853–908

Chomsky, Noam, *Failed States: The abuse of power and the assault on democracy* (Crows Nest, N.S.W.: Allen & Unwin, 2006)

Chopra, J., 'Achilles' Heel in Somalia: Learning from a Conceptual Failure', *Texas International Law Journal*, 31 (1996): 495–525

Chrimes, Stanley and A.L. Brown, *Select Documents of English Constitutional History 1307–1485* (London: A. and C. Black, 1961)

Chrimes, Stanley, C.D. Ross and R.A. Griffiths (eds), *Fifteenth-century England 1399–1509* (Manchester: Manchester University Press, 1972)

Chrimes, Stanley, *Lancastrians, Yorkists and Henry VII* (2nd edn, London: Macmillan and Co., 1966)

Christie, I.R., *Wars and Revolutions: Britain, 1760–1815* (Cambridge: Edward Arnold, 1982)

Ciggaar, Krijnie N., *Western travellers to Constantinople: the West and Byzantium, 962–1204: cultural and political relations* (Leiden: E.J. Brill, 1996)

Clanchy, M.T., *England and its Rulers, 1066–1272: Foreign Lordship and National Identity* (London: Fontana, 1983)
——, *From memory to written record, England 1066–1307* (Oxford: Blackwell, 1993)
Clark, Bruce, *Native liberty, Crown Supremacy – the Existing Aboriginal Right of Self-Government in Canada* (Montreal: McGill-Queen's University Press, 1990)
Clark, J. Desmond, *The common heritage: the significance of hunter-gatherer societies for human evolution* (Canberra: Australian National University, 1990)
Clarke, Sir Arthur C., *The Wind from the Sun: stories of the space age* (London: Corgi, 1962)
Clift, J., 'The UNCITRAL Model Law and electronic equivalents to traditional bills of lading', *Journal of the Section on Business Law of the International Bar Association*, 27 (1999): 311–17
Coates-Stephens, Robert, 'The walls and aqueducts of Rome in the early Middle Ages, A.D. 500–1000', *The Journal of Roman Studies*, 88 (1998): 166–78
Cobbett, William (ed.), *The Parliamentary History of England* (12 vols., London: Nelson, 1806–20)
Cohen, David, 'Thinking about the State', *Osgoode Hall Law Journal*, 24 (1986): 379–409
Cohen, Linda R. and Roger G. Noll, 'Intellectual Property, Antitrust and the New Economy', *University of Pittsburgh Law Review*, 62 (2001): 453–73
Coleman, S. (ed.), *2001: Cyber Space Odyssey: The Internet in the UK Election* (London: Hansard Society, 2001)
Collins, Lawrence (ed.), *Dicey and Morris on the Conflict of Laws* (13th edn, London: Sweet and Maxwell, 2000)
Collins, Randall, *Weberian Sociological Theory* (Cambridge: Cambridge University Press, 1986)
Colomer, Josep M., 'Disequilibrium Institutions and Pluralist Democracy', *Journal of Theoretical Politics*, 13(3) (2001): 235–48
——, *Political Institutions: Democracy and Social Choice* (Oxford-New York: Oxford University Press, 2001)
Congleton, Roger D. and Birgitta Swedenborg (eds), *Democratic Constitutional Design and Public Policy. Analysis and Evidence* (MIT Press, 2006)
Conley, Richard, 'Sovereignty or the Status Quo? The 1998 pre-referendum debate in Quebec', *Journal of Commonwealth and Comparative Politics*, 35 (1997): 67–92
Cooke, Philip, 'Globalization of economic organization and the emergence of regional interstate partnerships', in Colin H. Williams (ed.), *The Political Geography of the New World Order* (London: Belhaven Press, 1993)
Cooter, Robert D., 'Structural adjudication and the new law merchant: A model of decentralised law', *International Review of Law and Economics*, 12 (1994): 215–31

Corbett, Sir William, '"The Crown" as representing the State', *Commonwealth Law Review*, 1 (1903): 23

Corcoran, Elizabeth, 'A Tiny Mouse Came Forth', *Scientific American* (1989): 73

Cortada, James W., *Making the Information Society: Experience, Consequences and Possibilities* (Paramus: Prentice Hall, 2001)

Cosandey, David, *Le Secret de l'Occident* (Paris: Arléa, 1997)

Costello, Kevin, 'The Expulsion of Prerogative Doctrine from Irish Law: Quantifying and Remedying the Loss of the Royal Prerogatives', *Irish Jurist*, 32 (1997): 145–94

Cowen, Penelope Brook, 'Neo Liberalism', in Raymond Miller (ed.), *New Zealand Politics in Transition* (Auckland: Oxford University Press, 1997) 341–9

Cox, Noel, 'The acquisition of sovereignty by quasi-states: The case of the Order of Malta', *Mountbatten Journal of Legal Studies*, 6(1 and 2) (2002): 26–47

——, 'The British Peerage: The Legal Standing of the Peerage and Baronetage in the Overseas Realms of the Crown with Particular Reference to New Zealand', *New Zealand Universities Law Review*, 17 (1997): 379–401

——, *Church and State in the Post-Colonial Era: The Anglican Church and the Constitution in New Zealand* (Auckland: Polygraphia (NZ) Ltd, 2008)

——, 'The Consequences for the World Legal Order of the War on Iraq', *New Zealand Armed Forces Law Review* (2003): 11–17

——, *A Constitutional History of the New Zealand Monarchy: The evolution of the New Zealand monarchy and the recognition of an autochthonous polity* (Saarbrücken: V.D.M. Verlag Dr. Müller Aktiengesellschaft & Co. K.G., 2008)

——, 'The control of advice to the Crown and the development of executive independence in New Zealand', *Bond Law Review*, 13 (2001): 166–89

——, 'Developments in the Laws of War: NATO attacks on Yugoslavia and the use of force to achieve humanitarian objectives', *New Zealand Armed Forces Law Review* (2002): 13–24

——, 'The Dichotomy of Legal Theory and Political Reality: The Honours Prerogative and Imperial Unity', *Australian Journal of Law and Society*, 14 (1998–99): 15–42

——, 'The extraterritorial enforcement of consumer legislation and the challenge of the internet', *Edinburgh Law Review*, 8 (2004): 60–83

——, 'The intellectual property laws and the protection of armorial bearings', *Australian Intellectual Property Journal*, 12(1) (2001): 143-52

——, 'The Law of Arms in New Zealand', *New Zealand Universities Law Review*, 18(2) (1998): 225–56

——, 'The Law of Succession to the Crown in New Zealand', *Waikato Law Review*, 7 (1999): 49–72

——, 'The regulation of cyberspace and the loss of national sovereignty', *Information and Communications Technology Law*, 11 (2002): 241–53

——, 'Tax and regulatory avoidance through non-traditional alternatives to tax havens', *New Zealand Journal of Taxation Law and Policy*, 9 (2003): 305–27

——, *Technology and Legal Systems* (Aldershot: Ashgate, 2006)

——, 'The Theory of Sovereignty and the Importance of the Crown in the Realms of The Queen', *Oxford University Commonwealth Law Journal*, 2 (2002): 237–55

Cox, Robert W., *Production, Power, and World Order: Social Forces in the Making of History* (New York: Columbia University Press, 1987)

Craig, Paul and Adam Tomkins (eds), *The Executive and Public Law: Power and Accountability in Comparative Law* (Oxford: Oxford University Press, 2006)

Craven, M., 'The EC Arbitration Commission on Yugoslavia', *British Yearbook of International Law*, 66 (1995): 333

Crawford, James, *The Creation of States in international law* (Oxford: Clarendon Press, 1979)

Creveld, Martin van, *The Rise and Decline of the State* (Cambridge: Cambridge University Press, 1999)

Czarnota, Adam, 'A few reflections on Globalization and the constitution of society', *University of New South Wales Law Journal*, 24 (2001): 809–16

Dadge, David, *Casualty of* war*: the Bush administration's assault on a free press* (Amherst: Prometheus Books, 2004)

Dahrendorf, Ralf, 'Transitions: Politics, Economics, and Liberty', *Washington Quarterly*, 13 (1990): 133–42

Dallago, Bruno, Gianmaria Ajani and Bruno Grancelli (eds), *Privatisation and entrepreneurship in post-socialist countries: economy, law, and society* (New York: St Martin's, 1992)

Dancy, R.M., *Plato's introduction of forms* (Cambridge: Cambridge University Press, 2004)

Darwin, Charles, *On the origin of species by means of natural selection*, ed. Joseph Carroll (Peterborough: Broadview Press, 2003, first published 1859)

Dauvergne, Catherine (ed.), *Jurisprudence for an interconnected globe* (Aldershot: Ashgate, c.2003)

Davenport, T.R.H., 'Civil Rights in South Africa, 1910–1960', *Acta Juridica* (1960): 11–28

Davidson, Nicholas S., *The Counter-Reformation* (Oxford: Blackwell, 1987)

de Blois, Lukas, *The Roman army and politics in the first century before Christ* (Amsterdam: J.C. Gieben, 1987)

de Bruin, Ronald, *Consumer trust in electronic commerce: time for best practice* (The Hague: Kluwer Law International, 2002)

De Jager, Charles F., 'The Development of Regulatory Standards for Gene Therapy in the European Union', *Fordham International Law Journal*, 18 (1995): 1303–39

de Malynes, Gerard, *Consuetudo vel Lex Mercatoria, or the Ancient Law Merchant* (London: Adam Islip, 1622, facsimile Amsterdam: Theatrum Orbis, 1979)

de Oliveira Souza, Henrique Freire, 'Genetically Modified Plants: A Need for International Regulation', *Annual Survey of International and Comparative Law*, 6 (2000): 129–74

Dean, M., *Governmentality: Power and Rule in Modern Society* (London: Sage, 1999)
Dearlove, John, 'Bringing the State Back In', *Political Studies* (1989): 521–39
Delibasis, Dimitrios, 'The right to use force in cyberspace: Defining the rules of engagement', *Feature*, 11(3) (2002): 255–68
DeNoce, Kevin G., 'Internet privacy jurisdiction begins to develop; courts and legislators address e-mail confidentiality and other New Age constitutional issues', *The National Law Journal*, 19 (1997): B11
Derrett, J.D.M., 'The Administration of Hindu Law by the British', *Comparative Studies in Society and History*, 4 (1961): 10–52
Dewald, Jonathan, *The European nobility, 1400–1800* (Cambridge: Cambridge University Press, 1996)
Diamond, Jared, *Guns, Germs and Steel: The Fates of Human Societies* (London: Jonathan Cape, 1997)
Diamond, Larry, Yun-han Chu and Hung-mao Tien (eds), *Consolidating the Third Wave Democracies* (Baltimore: Johns Hopkins University Press, 1997)
Dicey, Albert, *Introduction to the Study of the Law of the Constitution* introduction and appendix by E.C.S. Wade (10th edn, London: Macmillan, 1959)
Dickinson, H.T., 'The Eighteenth-Century Debate on the "Glorious Revolution"', *History*, 61 (1976): 28–45
——, 'The Eighteenth-Century Debate on the Sovereignty of Parliament', *Transactions of the Royal Historical Society (5th Series)*, 26 (1976): 189–210
Dixon, Chandra, 'Marxism', in Raymond Miller (ed.), *New Zealand Politics in Transition* (Auckland: Oxford University Press, 1997): 350–58
Dixon, Sir Owen, 'The Law and the Constitution', *Law Quarterly Review*, 51 (1935): 590
Djilianova, Dora, 'To be or not to be: What went right in the Bulgarian foreign Investment climate after 1997', *Thomas Jefferson Law Review*, 25 (2002): 223
Dobek, Mariusz Mark, *The Political logic of privatisation* (Westport: Praeger, 1993)
Dolgin, Janet L., 'Embryonic discourse: Abortion, stem cells, and cloning', *Florida State University Law Review*, 31 (2003): 101–62
Donat, Kim JoDene, 'Engineering Akerlof lemons: Information asymmetry, externalities, and market intervention in the genetically modified food market', *Minnesota Journal of Global Trade*, 12 (2003): 417–59
Donne, John, *Devotions Upon Emergent Occasions*, ed. Anthony Raspa (Montreal: McGill-Queen's University Press, 1975 first published 1624)
Doyle, Michael, 'Kant, Liberal Legacies and Foreign Affairs' in Michael E. Brown, Sean M. Lynn-Jones, and Steven E. Miller (eds), *Debating the Democratic Peace* (Cambridge, MA: MIT Press, 1996)
Drahos, Peter and John Braithwaite, *Global Business Regulation* (Cambridge: Cambridge University Press, 2000)
——, *Information Feudalism – Who owns the Knowledge Economy?* (New York: New Press, 2003)

Driesen, David M., *The economic dynamics of environmental law* (Cambridge: MIT Press, 2003)
Drury, Shadia B., *Alexandre Kojève: The Roots of Postmodern Politics* (Basingstoke: Macmillan, 1994)
Dudley, Leonard, 'Explaining the great divergence: Medium and message on the Eurasian land mass 1700–1850', in Alain Marciano and Jean-Michel Josselin (eds), *Law and the State: A Political Economy approach* (Cheltenham: Edward Elgar, 2005)
Du Plessis, Rosemary, 'Women, Feminism and the State', in Brian Roper and Chris Rudd (eds), *The Political Economy of New Zealand* (Auckland: Oxford University Press, 1997) 220–36
Dunbabin, Jean, 'Government', in J.H. Burns (ed.), *The Cambridge History of Mediæval Political Thought c.350–c.1450* (Cambridge: Cambridge University Press, 1988) 477–519
Dunn, John, 'The concept of trust in the politics of John Locke', in R. Rorty (ed.), *Philosophy in History* (Cambridge: Cambridge University Press, 1984) 279–302
——, *The Political Thought of John Locke: An historical account of the Two Treatises of Government* (London: Cambridge University Press, 1969)
Dunstan, David, *Governing the Metropolis: politics, technology and social change in a Victoria city: Melbourne* (Carlton: Melbourne University Press, 1984)
Duzan, Stephen A., 'The 1992 Biotechnology Agenda: A Message for Candidates Bush and Clinton', *Healthspan*, 9 (1992): 12–15
Dworkin, Ronald, *Law's Empire* (Cambridge: Belknap Press, 1986)
Dyson, Kenneth, *The State Tradition in Western Europe: A Study of an Idea and Institution* (Oxford: Oxford University Press, 1980)
Dyson, Kenneth and Kevin Featherstone, *The road to Maastricht: negotiating Economic and Monetary Union* (Oxford: Oxford University Press, 1999)
Dyzenhaus, David, *Constitution of Law: Legality in a time of emergency* (Cambridge: Cambridge University Press, 2006)
Dyzenhaus, David (ed.), *Law as politics: Carl Schmitt's critique of liberalism* (Durham: Duke University Press, 1998)
——, *The Unity of Public Law* (Oxford: Hart, 2004)
Dyzenhaus, David and Arthur Ripstein (eds), *Law and Morality: readings in legal philosophy* (Toronto: University of Toronto Press, 1996)
Easterly, Ernest, III, 'The rule of law and the new world order', *Southern University Law Review*, 22 (1995): 161–83
Eaton, Howard O., *Federation: the coming structure of world government* (Norman: University of Oklahoma Press, 1944)
Egerton, H.E., *Short History of British Colonial Policy* (London: Methuen, 1897)
Eiselen, S., 'Electronic commerce and the United Nations Convention on Contracts for the International Sale of Goods (CISG) 1980', *EDI Law Review: Legal Aspects of Paperless Communication*, 6 (1999): 21–46

Eisenberg, Rebecca S., 'Genes, Patents, and Product Development', *Science*, 257 (1992): 903–8

Elkind, Jerome (ed.), *The impact of American law on English and Commonwealth law: A book of essays* (St Paul: West Publishing Co., 1978)

Elliott, C., 'The Internet – A New World without frontiers', *New Zealand Law Journal* (1998): 405–7

Elliott, E. Donald, 'The Genome and the law: Should increased genetic knowledge change the law?', *Harvard Journal of Law and Public Policy*, 25 (2001): 61–70

Elster, John, 'Forces and Mechanisms in Constitution-Making,' *Duke Law Review*, 45 (1995): 364–96

Elster, John and Rune Slagstad (eds), *Constitutionalism and Democracy* (Cambridge: University of Cambridge Press, 1988)

Elton, Sir Geoffrey, *Reform and Reformation, 1509–1558* (London: Edward Arnold, 1979)

——, *The Reformation, 1520–1599* (2nd ed., Cambridge: Cambridge University Press, 1990)

Empie, Derek E., 'The dormant Internet: are state regulators of motor vehicle sales by manufacturers on the Information Superhighway obstructing interstate and Internet commerce?', *Georgia State University Law Review*, 18 (2002): 827–57

English Historical Documents 1327–1485, ed. A.R. Myers (London: Eyre and Spottiswoode, 1969), vol. 4

Eppstein, John, *The Catholic Tradition of the Law of Nations* (London: Burns, Oates and Washbourne, 1935)

Epstein, L., J. Knight et al., 'The role of constitutional courts in the establishment and maintenance of democratic systems of government,' *Law and Society Review* (2001): 117

Ertman, Thomas, *Birth of the leviathan: building states and regimes in mediæval and early modern Europe* (Cambridge: Cambridge University Press, 1997)

Esty, Daniel C., J. Goldstone, T.R. Gurr, P.T. Surko and A.N. Unger, 'State Failure Task Force Report', in Robert I. Rotberg (ed.), *State Failure and State Weakness in a Time of Terror* (Washington: Brookings Institute, 2003)

Ewens, Lara E., 'Seed Wars: Biotechnology, Intellectual Property, and the Quest for High Yield Seeds', *Boston College International and Comparative Law Review*, 23 (2000): 285–310

Fackelmann, Kathleen, 'Forecasting Alzheimer's Disease', *Science News*, 149 (1996) 312

Falk, Richard, 'The Interplay of Westphalia and Charter Conceptions of International Legal Order', in Cyril E. Black and Richard A. Falk (eds), *The Future of the International Legal Order* (Princeton: Princeton University Press, 1969)

Fears, J. Rufus, *Princeps a diis electus: the divine election of the emperor as a political concept at Rome* (Rome: American Academy in Rome, 1977)

Ferrari, Franco, '"Forum shopping" despite international uniform contract law conventions', *International and Comparative Law Quarterly*, 51 (2002): 689–707

Ficsor, Mihály, *The law of copyright and the Internet: the 1996 WIPO treaties, their interpretation and implementation* (Oxford: Oxford University Press, 2002)

Figgis, J.N., *The theory of the Divine Right of Kings* (2nd edn, Cambridge: Cambridge University Press, 1914)

Filmer, Sir Robert, *Patriarcha and other writings*, ed. J.P. Sommerville (London: Cambridge University Press, 1991)

Finer, S.E., *The history of government from the earliest times* (Oxford: Oxford University Press, 1997)

Finer, S.E., Vernon Bogdanor and Bernard Rudden, *Comparing Constitutions* (Oxford: Clarendon Press, 1995)

Finley, M.I., *Authority and legitimacy in the classical* city-state (København: Munksgaard, 1982)

Finnis, John, *Natural Law and natural rights* (Oxford: Claredon Press, 1980)

Firth, Alison (ed.), *The prehistory and development of intellectual property systems* (London: Sweet and Maxwell, 1997)

Fisher, Lane and Cheryl L. Mullin, 'Franchise laws in the age of electronic communication', *Franchise Law Journal*, 19 (1999): 47–51

Fishman, Renee M., Kara Josephberg, Jane Linn, Jane Pollack and Jena Victoriano, 'China issues rules on content enforcement', *Intellectual Property and Technology Law Journal*, 14(10) (2002): 24

——, 'Threat of international cyberterrorism on the rise', *Intellectual Property and Technology Law Journal*, 14 (2002): 23

Fleming, Robin, *Kings and Lords in Conquered England* (Cambridge: Cambridge University Press, 1991)

Floud, Roderick and Donald McCloskey, *The Economic History of Britain since 1700* (2nd edn, Cambridge: Cambridge University Press, 1994)

Foley, Michael, *The Silence of Constitutions: Gaps, 'Abeyances' and Political Temperament in the Maintenance of Government* (London: Routledge, 1989)

Fortescue, Sir John, *The Governance of England*, notes by Charles Plummer (Westport: Hyperion Press, 1979)

——, *In Praise of the Laws of England (De Laudibus Legum Angliæ)*, ed. Stanley Chrimes (Cambridge: Cambridge University Press, 1942)

van Fossen, Anthony, 'Financial frauds and pseudo-states in the Pacific Islands', *Crime, Law and Social Change*, 37 (2002): 357–78

Foucault, Michel, *Dispositive der Macht* (Berlin: Merve Verlag, 1978)

——, *The Foucault Effects: Studies in Governmentality*, ed. Graham Burchell, Colin Gordon and Peter Miller (London: Harvester Wheatsheaf, 1991)

——, 'Governmentality', in J.D. Faubion (ed.), *Michel Foucault, Power: The Essential Works* (London: Allen Lane Penguin Press, 2000)

——, 'Governmentality', *Ideology and Consciousness*, 6 (Summer 1986): 5–21

——, 'Omnes et Singulatim: Toward a Criticism of "Political Reason"', in *The Tanner Lectures of Human Values. II* (Salt Lake City: University of Utah Press/Cambridge University Press, 1981)

——, Power/Knowledge: Selected Inteeviews and Other Writings 1972–1977, ed. C. Gordon (New York: Pantheon, 1980)

——, *Resume des cours* (Paris: conferencs, essais et lecons du college de France/ Julliard, 1989): 190– 1982

——, 'Space, Knowledge and Power', in Paul Rabinow (ed.), *The Foucault Reader* (New York: Pantheon Books, 1984)

Fox, Gregory H. and Brad R. Roth (eds), *Democratic Governance and International Law* (Cambridge: Cambridge University Press, 2000)

Fox, Michael R., 'Nuclear regulation: the untold story; poor management? Yes, but lay the blame on too much regulation', *Public Utilities Fortnightly*, 133 (1994): 37–41

Frame, Robin, *The Political Development of the British Isles 1100–1400* (Oxford: Oxford University Press, 1990)

Franck, Thomas M., 'The Emerging Right to Democratic Governance', 86 *American Journal of International Law* (1992): 46–91

Friedman, David, 'Does technology require new law?', *Harvard Journal of Law and Public Policy*, 25 (2001): 71–85

Friedman, Thomas L., *The Lexus and the Olive Tree* (London: HarperCollins, 2000)

Friedmann, Wolfgang, *The Changing Structure of International Law* (New York: Columbia University Press, 1964)

Friedrich, Carl Joachim (ed.), *The Philosophy of Kant* (New York: Random House, 1949)

Fuller, Lon F., *The Morality of the Law* (New Haven: Yale University Press, 1964)

Furbach, Ulrich, 'Principles of Artificial Intelligence', *Artificial Intelligence*, 145 (2003): 245–52

Ganshof, Francois, *Feudalism*, trans. Philip Grierson (London: Longman, 1952, first published 1944)

Gardner, Peter J., 'United States Intellectual Property Law and the Biotech Challenge: Searching for an elusive balance', *Vermont Bar Journal*, 29 (2003): 24

Gaston, Kevin J. and John I. Spicer, *Biodiversity: an introduction* (2nd edn, London: Blackwell Publishing, 2004)

Geanakoplos, Deno John, *Constantinople and the West: essays on the late Byzantine (Palaeologan) and Italian Renaissances and the Byzantine and Roman churches* (Madison: University of Wisconsin Press, c.1989)

Geetter, Jennifer S., 'Coding for Change: The Power of the Human Genome to Transform the American Health Insurance System', *American Journal of Law and Medicine*, 28 (2001): 1–76

Gibbon, Edward, *The Decline and Fall of the Roman Empire* (London: David Campbell, 1994)

Gibney, Mark, 'Decommunization: Human Rights Lessons from the Past and Present, and Prospects for the Future', *Denver International Law and Policy*, 23 (1994): 87–133

Gibson, William, *Neuromancer* (New York: Ace Books, 1984)

Giles of Rome, *De regimine principum* (Rome: 1556, completed 1270s or 1280s)

Gillingham, John and J.C. Holt (eds), *War and Government in the Middle Ages* (Cambridge: Boydell Press, 1984)

Gillis, Anna Maria, 'The Patent Question of the Year', *BioScience*, 42 (1992): 336–40

Gimpel, Jean, *The Mediæval Machine: the industrial revolution of the Middle Ages* (London: Book Club Associates, 1977)

von Glahn, Gerhard, *Law Among Nations: An Introduction to Public International Law* (7th edn, Boston: Allyn and Bacon, 1996)

Gluckman, M., *Politics law and ritual in tribal society* (Oxford: Oxford University Press, 1977)

Goldenman, Gretta et al (eds), *Environmental liability and privatisation in Central and Eastern Europe* (London: Graham and Trotman, 1994)

Goldfinch, Shaun, 'The State', in Raymond Miller (ed.), *New Zealand Government and Politics* (Melbourne: Oxford University Press, 2001) 511 – 20

Goldsmith, Jack L., 'Against Cyberanarchy', *University of Chicago Law Review*, 65 (1998): 1199–250

——, 'Regulation of the Internet: Three Persistent Fallacies', *Chicago-Kent Law Review*, 73 (1998): 1119–31

Goldsworthy, Jeffrey, *The sovereignty of parliament: history and philosophy* (Oxford: Clarendon Press, 1999

Goldwin, Robert A., 'Locke's state of nature in political society', *Western Political Quarterly*, 31 (1976): 126–35

Gomez, Ivette P., 'Beyond the neighbourhood drugstore: United States regulation of online prescription drug sales by foreign businesses', *Rutgers Computer and Technology Law Journal*, 28 (2002): 431–62

Goncalves, Maria Eduarda, 'Technological change, Globalization and the Europeanization of rights', *International Review of Law, Computers and Technology*, 16 (2002): 301–16

Goody, Jack, *Technology, tradition and the state in Africa* (London: Hutchinson, 1980)

Gorski, Richard, *The fourteenth-century sheriff: English local administration in the late Middle Ages* (Woodbridge: Boydell Press, 2003)

Goss, Vladimir P. and Christine Verzair Bornstein (eds), *The meeting of two worlds: cultural exchange between East and West during the period of the Crusades* (Kalamazoo: Mediæval Institute Publications, Western Michigan University, 1986)

Goudie, Andrew, *The human impact on the natural environment* (4th edn, Oxford: Blackwell, 1990)

Grady, Mark F. and Michael T. McGuire, 'The Nature of Constitutions', *Journal of Bioeconomics*, 1 (1999): 227–40

——, 'A Theory of the Origin of Natural Law', *Journal of Contemporary Legal Issues*, 8 (1997): 87–129

Grady, Mark F., 'The state and the networked economy', *Harvard Journal of Law and Public Policy*, 25 (2001): 15–29

Grainger, John, *Nerva and the Roman succession crisis of AD 96–99* (London: Routledge, 2003)

Grant, Sir Francis, *A Manual of Heraldry* (Edinburgh: John Grant, 1924)

Grant, T., *The Recognition of States: Law and Practice in Debate and Evolution* (Westport: Praeger, 1999)

Gratian of Bologna, *Concordia discordantium canonum* (or *Decretum magistri Gratiani*) in A. Friedberg (ed.), *Corpus Iuris Canonici* (2 vols., Leipzig: Tauchnitz, 1879–81)

Gray, John, *The Two Faces of Liberalism* (Cambridge: Polity Press, 2000)

Green, Judith A., *English sheriffs to 1154* (London: HMSO, 1990)

Greene, Graham, *The Third Man* (London: William Heinemann, 1950)

Greenleaf, Graham, 'An Endnote on Regulating Cyberspace: Architecture vs Law?', *University of New South Wales Law Journal*, 21 (1998): 593–622

Gregory, J.D., 'The authentication of digital records', *EDI Law Review: Legal Aspects of Paperless Communication*, 6 (1999): 47–63

——, 'Solving legal issues in electronic commerce', *Canadian Business Law Journal*, 32 (1999): 84–131

Grewlich, Klaus W., Governance in 'Cyberspace' – Access and Public Interest in Global Telecommunications (The Hague: Kluwer Law International, 1999)

Griffin, Joseph P., 'Foreign Governmental Reactions to United States Assertion of Extraterritorial Jurisdiction', *George Mason Law Review*, 6 (1998): 505

Gross, Leo, 'The Peace of Westphalia, 1648–1948', *American Journal of International Law*, 42 (1948): 20–41

Grossman, Ilene K., 'The new Industrial Revolution: meeting the challenge', *Public Law Forum*, 4 (1985): 419–26

Grotius, Hugo, *De jure belli ac pacis*, ed. F.W. Kelsey (reprint of 1925 edn, New York: Oceana, 1964)

Guibernau, Montserrat, *Nationalisms: the nation-state and nationalism in the twentieth century* (Cambridge: Polity Press, 1996)

Gurney, O.R., *The Hittites* (2nd edn, Harmondsworth: Penguin, 1990)

Haddan, Arthur W., *Apostolic Succession in the Church of England* (rev. ed., London: Rivingtons, 1883, first published 1869)

El-Hadidy, Bahaa and Esther E. Horne (eds), *The infrastructure of an information society: proceedings of the First International Information Conference in Egypt, Cairo: 13–15 December, 1982* (Amsterdam: Egyptian Society for Information Technology/American Society for Information Science, 1982)

Halasz, Alexandra, *The marketplace of print: pamphlets and the public sphere in early modern England* (Cambridge: Cambridge University Press, 1997)

Hall, Clayton, *The Lords Baltimore and the Maryland Palatinate* (Baltimore: J. Murphy and Co., 1902)

Hall, Evelyn Beatrice (pseudonym S.G. Tallentyre), *The Friends of Voltaire* (London: Smith Elder & Co, 1906)

Hall, John, *The Grounds and Reasons of Monarchy* prefixed to *The Political Works of James Harrington*, ed. J.G.A. Pocock (Cambridge: Cambridge University Press, 1977)

Hall, Peter and Rosemary Taylor, 'Political Science and the Three New Institutionalisms', *Political Studies*, 44(4) (1996): 936–57

Hall, William E., *A Treatise on International Law*, ed. A. Pearce Higgins (8th edn, Oxford: Clarendon Press, 1924)

Hammond, Mason, *City-State* and world *state* in Greek and Roman political theory until Augustus (Cambridge: Harvard University Press, 1951)

Hanham, H.J., *The Nineteenth Century Constitution, 1815–1914* (Cambridge: Cambridge University Press, 1969)

Hannig, Mark, 'An examination of the possibility to secure intellectual property rights for plant genetic resources developed by indigenous peoples of the NAFTA states: Domestic legislation under the International Convention for Protection of New Plant Varieties', *Arizona Journal of International and Comparative Law*, 13 (1996): 175–252

Hardie, Frank, *The Political Influence of Queen Victoria, 1861–1901* (London: Oxford University Press, 1935)

Hardin, I. and N. Lewis, *The Noble Lie: The British Constitution and the Role of Law* (London: Hutchinson, 1987)

Hardin, Russel, 'Why a Constitution?' In Bernard Grofman, and Donald Wittman (eds), *The Federalist Papers and the New Institutionalism* (New York: Agathon Press, 1989)

Harding, Alan, *A Social History of English Law* (Harmondsworth: Penguin Books, 1966)

Hardt, Michael and Antonio Negri, *Empire* (Cambridge: Harvard University Press, 2000)

Hardy, Trotter, 'The Proper Legal Regime for "Cyberspace"', *University of Pittsburgh Law Review*, 55 (1994): 993–1055

Harlow, Carol, 'Power from the People?', in Patrick McAuslan and John McEldowney (ed.), *Law, Legitimacy and the Constitution: Essays marking the Centenary of Dicey's Law of the Constitution* (London: Sweet and Maxwell, 1985)

Harris, Bruce, 'Law-making powers of the New Zealand General Assembly', *Otago Law Review*, 5 (1984): 565–602

——, 'The "Third Source" of Authority for Government Action', *Law Quarterly Review*, 109 (1992): 626–51

Harrison, Roger, *Diagnosing organizational culture: trainer's manual* (San Diego: Pfeiffer, 1993)

Hart, H.L.A., *The Concept of Law* (Oxford: Clarendon Press, 1961)

Hart, Kathleen, 'Making Mythical Monsters', *The Progressive* (March 1990): 22

Hartley, Trevor C., *Constitutional Problems of the European Union* (Oxford: Hart Publishing, 1999)

Hartz, Louis, *The Liberal Tradition in America* (New York: Harcourt, Brace and Co, 1955)

Harvey, David, *The Condition of Postmodernity* (London: Blackwell, 1989)

Haskins, Charles, *The Renaissance in the twelfth century* (Cambridge: Harvard University Press, 1927)

Hastings Rashdall, *The Universities of Europe in the Middle Ages* new ed. Frederick M. Powicke and Alfred B. Emden (Oxford: Clarendon Press, 1936)

Hatschek, J., *An Outline of International Law*, trans. C. Manning (London: Bell and Sons, 1930)

Very Rev'd Rashdall Hastings, *The Universities of Europe in the Middle Ages*, ed. F.M. Powicke and A.B. Emden (new ed., Oxford: Clarendon Press, 1936, first published 1895)

Hearn, William, *The Government of England: Its Structure and its Development* (London: Longmans, Green, Reader and Dyer, 1867)

Hedieh, Nasheri, 'The Intersection of technology crimes and cyberspace in Europe: The Case of Hungary', *Information and Communications Technology Law*, 12 (2003): 25–48

Heere, W.P. and J.P.S. Offerhaus, *International Law in Historical Perspective* (The Hague: Martinus Nijhoff Publishers, 1998)

Held, David, *Political Theory and the Modern State* (Cambridge: Polity Press, 1989)

Heller, Hermann, 'The Decline of the Nation State and its Effect on Constitutional and International Economic Law', *Cardozo Law Review*, 18 (1996): 1139

Helman, G.B. and S.R. Ratner, 'Saving Failed States', *Foreign Policy*, 89 (1992–93): 3–20

van Hemel, Annemoon and Niki van der Wielen (eds), *Privatisation/desetatisation and culture. Conference reader for the Circle Round Table 1997* (Amsterdam: Boekman Foundation/Twente University, 1997)

Henderson, W.O., *Studies in German Colonial History* (Chicago: Quadrangle Books, 1962)

Henkin, Louis, 'That "S". Words: Sovereignty, and Globalization, and Human Rights, Et Cetera', *Ford Law Review*, 68 (1999): 1–14

Herbison, Elmore, *The Christian scholar in the age of the Reformation* (New York: Scribners, 1956)

Hermann, Thomas G., 'Is United States legal system an impediment to scientific progress?', *National Law Journal*, 19 (4 August 1997): C-15

Heuston, Robert, *Essays in Constitutional Law* (2nd edn, London: Stevens and Son, 1964)

Higgins, Dame Rosalyn, *The Development of International Law Through the Political Organs of the UN* (London: Oxford University Press, 1963)

Higham, Charles, *The civilization of Angkor* (London: Weidenfeld and Nicolson, 2001)

Hillgruber, C., 'The Admission of New States to the International Community', *European Journal of International Law*, 9 (1998): 491–509

Hinde, G.W., D.W. McMorland and P.B.A. Sim, *Land Law* (Wellington: Butterworths, 1978)

Hinsley, F., *Sovereignty* (2nd edn, Cambridge: Cambridge University Press, 1986)

Hobbes, Thomas, *The Cambridge companion to Locke's "Essay concerning human understanding"* ed. Lex Newman (Cambridge: Cambridge University Press, 2007)

——, *Leviathan*, ed. Edwin Curley (Indianapolis: Hackett Publishing Co., 1994, first published 1688)

Hobhouse, L.T., *Liberalism* (London: HUL, 1911)

Hogg, P.W., *Constitutional Law of Canada* (3rd edn., Scarborough, Ontario: Carswell, 1992)

——, Liability of the Crown in Australia, New Zealand and the United Kingdom (Sydney: The Law Book Co., 1971)

Holmes, Oliver Wendell, *The Common Law*, ed. Mark DeWolfe Howe (Cambridge: Belknap Press, 1963)

Holton, R.J., *Cities, capitalism, and civilization* (London: Allen and Unwin, 1986)

Honderich, Ted (ed.), *The Oxford Companion to Philosophy* (Oxford: Oxford University Press, 1995)

Hood, Leroy, 'Biology and Medicine in the Twenty-First Century', in Daniel J. Kevles and Leroy Hood (eds), *The Code of Codes, Scientific and social issues in the human genome project* (Harvard: Harvard University Press, 1992)

Hood, Miriam, *Gunboat diplomacy, 1895–1905: great power pressure in Venezuela* (London: Allen and Unwin, 1975)

Hood, Susan, *Royal Roots Republican Inheritance: The Survival of the Office of Arms* (Dublin: The Woodfield Press, 2002)

Horn, Lawrence A., 'To Be or Not to Be: The Republic of Minerva – Nation-founding by Individuals', *Columbia Journal of Transnational Law*, 12 (1973): 520

Hornby, Susan and Zoë Clarke (eds), *Challenge and change in the information society* (London: Facet, 2003)

Horowitz, Donald L., *A Democratic South Africa?: Constitutional Engineering in a Divided Society* (Berkeley: University of California Press, 1992)

Hovenkamp, Herbert, 'Technology, politics, and regulated monopoly: an American historical perspective', *Texas Law Review*, 62 (1984): 1263–312

Howard, J. Woodford, Jr., 'Constitution and society in comparative perspective', *Judicature*, 71 (1987): 211–15

Howard, Sir Michael, George J. Andreopoulos and Mark R. Shulman (eds), *The Laws of War: Constraints on Warfare in the Western World* (New Haven: Yale University Press, 1994)

Howard-Ellis, Charles, *The origin structure and working of the League of Nations* (Union: The Lawbook Exchange, 2003)
Howe, Paul, 'Nationality and Sovereignty Support in Quebec', *Canadian Journal of Political Science*, 31 (1998): 31–60
Hudson, John, *Land, law, and lordship in Anglo-Norman England* (Oxford: Clarendon Press, 1994)
Hudson, Kathy, 'The Human Genome Project, DNA Science and the Law: the American Legal System's Response to Breakthroughs in Genetic Science', *American University Law Review*, 51 (2002): 431–45
Hudson, Manley O. (ed.), *International Legislation* (Washington: Carnegie Endowment for International Peace, 1931–50)
Huff, Toby, *The rise of early modern science: Islam, China, and the West* (2nd edn., Cambridge: Cambridge University Press, 2003)
Hume Institute, *In search of new constitutions* (Edinburgh: Edinburgh University Press, 1994) vol. 2 no. 1 Hume Papers on Public Policy
Hunnisett, R.F., *The mediæval coroner* (Cambridge: Cambridge University Press, 1961)
Hunt, A. and G. Wickham, *Foucault and Law: Towards a Sociology of Law and Governance* (London: Pluto Press, 1994)
Huxley, Aldous, *Brave New World* (London: Chatto and Windus, 1932)
Ibusuki, Makoto (ed.), *Transnational Cyberspace Law* (Oxford: Hart, 2000)
Innis, Harold A., *The Bias of Communication* (Toronto: University of Toronto Press, 1951)
——, *Empire and Communication* (Oxford: Clarendon Press, 1950)
International Labour Organization, *World Labour Report* (London: International Labour Organization, 1995)
Jackson, Moana, 'Maori Law', in Ramari Young (ed.), *Mana Tiriti: The Art of Protest and Partnership* (Wellington: Haeata Project Waitangi/City Art Gallery/Daphne Brasell Associates Press, 1991) 15– 16
Jacob, Margaret C., *Scientific culture and the making of the industrial West* (New York: Oxford University Press, 1997)
Jacobs, Joseph, *The Republican Crown: Lawyers and the Making of the State in Twentieth Century Britain* (Aldershot: Dartmouth, 1996)
James I, HM King, *Basilikon Doron* (Menston: Scolar Press, 1969, first published 1599)
James, Colin (ed.), *Building the Constitution* (Wellington: Victoria University of Wellington Institute of Policy Studies, 2000)
Jennings, Sir Ivor, *The Law and the Constitution* (5th ed., London: University of London Press, 1959)
Jennings, Sir Robert and Sir Arthur Watts (eds), *Oppenheim's International Law* (9th edn., London: Longman, 1992)
Jessup, Philip, *A Modern Law of Nations* (New York: Macmillan, 1968)
John of Paris, *De potestate regia et papali, Johannes Quidort von Paris Über Königliche under päpstliche Gewalt*, ed. F. Bleienstein (Stuttgart: Klett, 1969)

Johnson, David R. and David G. Post, 'Law and Borders: The Rise of Law in Cyberspace', *Stanford Law Review*, 48 (1996): 1367–402

Johnston, W. Ross, *Sovereignty and protection: a study of British jurisdictional imperialism in the late nineteenth century* (Durham: Duke University Commonwealth Studies Centre, Duke University Press, 1973)

Jones, Eric L., *The European Miracle: Environments, Economies, and Geopolitics in the History of Europe and Asia* (2nd edn, Cambridge: Cambridge University Press, 1987)

——, *The Record of Global Economic Development* (Cheltenham: Edward Elgar, 2002)

Jones, Norman, *The English Reformation: religion and cultural adaptation* (Oxford: Blackwell, 2002)

Jones, Richard and Subhajit Basu, 'Taxation of electronic commerce: A developing problem', *International Review of Law, Computers and Technology*, 16 (2002): 35–52

Joseph, Gregory P., 'Internet and email evidence', *The Computer and Internet Lawyer*, 19 (2002): 17–22

Joseph, Philip, *Constitutional and Administrative Law in New Zealand* (Sydney: The Law Book Co., 1993)

——, 'Crown as a legal concept (I)', *New Zealand Law Journal* (1993): 126

——, 'The Crown as a legal concept (II)', *New Zealand Law Journal* (1993): 179

——, *Essays on the Constitution* (Wellington: Brookers, 1995)

——, 'Suspending Statutes Without Parliament's Consent', *New Zealand Universities Law Review*, 14 (1991): 282

Josephberg, Kara, Jane Pollack, Jenna Victoriano and Oriyan Gitig, 'Singapore free trade agreement addresses domain names', *Intellectual Property and Technology Law Journal*, 15 (2003): 20

Josselin, Jean-Michel and Alain Marciano, 'The Paradox of Leviathan: how to develop and contain the future European state', *European Journal of Law and Economics*, 4 (1997): 5–21

Judson, Horace F., 'A History of the Science and Technology Behind Gene Mapping and Sequencing', in Daniel J. Kevles and Leroy Hood (eds), *The Code of Codes, scientific and social issues in the human genome project* (Harvard: Harvard University Press, 1992)

Juenger, Friedrich, 'Judicial Jurisdiction in the United States and in the European Communities: A Comparison', *Michigan Law Review*, 82 (1984): 1195

Justice, Steven, *Writing and rebellion: England in 1381* (Berkeley: University of California Press, 1994)

Kagan, Richard L., *Students and society in early modern Spain* (Baltimore: Johns Hopkins University Press, 1974)

Kahin, Brian and Charles Nesson (eds), *Borders in cyberspace: information policy and the global information infrastructure* (Cambridge: MIT Press, 1997)

Kalir, Doron M., 'Taking Globalization Seriously: Towards General Jurisprudence', *Columbia Journal of Transnational Law*, 39 (2001): 785–821

Kanawati, Naguib, *The Egyptian administration in the Old Kingdom: evidence on its economic decline* (Warminster: Aris and Phillips, 1977)

Kantorowicz, Ernst, 'Kingship under the impact of scientific jurisprudence', in Marshall Clagett et al (eds), *Twelfth century Europe* (Madison: University of Wisconsin Press, 1961)

——, *The King's Two Bodies: A Study in Mediæval Political Theology* (Princeton: Princeton University Press, 1957)

Katyal, Sonia K., 'Ending the revolution', *Texas Law Review*, 80 (2002): 1465–86

Kay, Richard, 'Constitutional Chrononomy', *Ratio Juris*, 13 (2000): 31–48

Keen, Maurice H., *The Laws of War in the Late Middle Ages* (London: Routledge and Kegan Paul, 1965)

Keith, A.B., *Constitutional History of the First British Empire* (Oxford: Clarendon Press, 1930)

Kelsen, Hans, *General Theory of Law and State*, trans. Anders Wedberg (Cambridge: Harvard University Press, 1945)

Kelsey, Jane, 'Legal Imperialism and the Colonization of Aotearoa', in Paul Spoonley et al (eds), *Tauiwi*: *Racism and Ethnicity in New Zealand* (Palmerston North: Dunmore Press, 1984) 20–43

——, 'Restructuring the Nation', in Peter Fitzpatrick (ed.), *Nationalism, Racism and the Rule of Law* (Aldershot: Dartmouth, 1995) 177–94

——, *Rolling Back the State: Privatisation of Power in Aotearoa/New Zealand* (Wellington: Bridget Williams Books, 1993)

Kende, Mark S., 'Technology's future impact upon state constitutional law: the Montana example', *Montana Law Review*, 64 (2003): 273–94

Kevles, Daniel J. and Ari Berkowitz, 'The gene patenting controversy: A convergence of law, economic interests and ethics', *Brooklyn Law Review*, 67 (2001): 233–48

Kevles, Daniel J., 'Diamond v. Chakrabarty and Beyond: The Political Economy of Patenting Life', in Arnold Thackray (ed.), *Private Science: Biotechnology and the Rise of the Molecular Sciences* (Philadelphia: University of Pennsylvania Press, 1998)

——, 'Out of Eugenics: The Historical Politics of the Human Genome', in Daniel J. Kevles and Leroy Hood (eds), *The Code of Codes, scientific and social issues in the human genome project* (Harvard: Harvard University Press, 1992)

Khan, L. Ali, *The Extinction of Nation-States: A World without Borders* (The Hague: Kluwer Law International, 1996)

Khan, Mushtaq, 'State Failure in Weak States: a critique of new institutionalist explanations', in John Harris, Janet Hunter and Colin M. Lewis (eds), *The new institutional economics and Third World development* (London: Routledge, 1995)

Kim, Jae-Young, 'Deregulation reconsidered: Protecting Internet speech in the United States, Germany, and Japan', *Communications and the Law*, 24 (2002): 53–75

King, Robert G. and Ross Levine, 'Finance and Growth: Schumpeter Might Be Right', *Quarterly Journal of Economics*, 108 (1993): 717–37
Kirkaldy, Adam, *British shipping: its history, organization and importance, with a map of main routes and coaling stations and full appendices* (London: K. Paul, Trench and Trubner, 1914)
Kirkwood, Genevieve and Michael Purdue, 'High technology; role and status of central government policy', *Journal of Planning and Environmental Law* (1988): 111–18
Kleijn, Gerda de, *The Water Supply of Ancient Rome: City Area, Water, and Population* (Amsterdam: Gieben, 2001)
Klep, Paul and Eddy Van Cauwenberghe (eds), *Entrepreneurship and the transformation of the economy (10th–20th centuries): essays in honour of Herman Van der Wee* (Leuven: Leuven University Press, 1994)
Kloppenburg, Jack Ralph, Jr., *First the seed: The political economy of plant biotechnology 1492–2000* (Cambridge: Cambridge University Press, 1988)
——, 'No Hunting: Scientific Poaching and Global Biodiversity', *Z Magazine* (1990): 104–8
Kneale, William and Martha Kneale (eds), *The Development of Logic* (London: Oxford University Press, 1962)
Knoll, Arthur J. and Lewis H. Gann (eds), *Germans in the Tropics: Essays in German Colonial History* (New York: Greenwood Press, 1987)
Komesar, Neil, 'Taking Institutions seriously', *University of Chicago Law Review*, 51 (1984): 366
Kornberg, Allan and Harold Clarke, *Citizens and Community – Political Support in a Representative Democracy* (Cambridge: Cambridge University Press, 1992)
Koselleck, Reinhart, *Zeitschichten* (Frankfurt: Suhrkamp Verlap, 2000)
Koskenniemi, M., 'The Future of Statehood', *Harvard International Law Journal*, 32 (1991): 397
Kraemer, Kenneth L., 'Computers and the Constitution: A Helpful, Harmful or Harmless Relationship?', *Public Administration Review*, 47 (1987): 93–105
Krasner, Stephen, 'Sovereignty: an institutional perspective', *Comparative Political Studies*, 21 (1988): 66–94
Kreijen, Gerard, *State failure, sovereignty and effectiveness: Legal lessons from the decolonisation of Sub-Saharan Africa* (Leiden: Martinus Nijhoff, 2004)
Krimsky, Sheldon and Roger P. Wrubel, *Agricultural biotechnology and the environment* (Urbana: University of Illinois Press, 1996)
Krimsky, Sheldon, *Biotechnics and society: The rise of industrial genetics* (Westport: Praeger, 1991)
Krygier, Martin and Adam Czarnota (eds), *The Rule of Law After Communism: Problems and Prospects in East-Central Europe* (Brookfield: Ashgate, 1998)
Kuhn, Thomas, *The Structure of Scientific Revolutions* (Chicago: University of Chicago Press, 1962)

Kuran, Timur, 'The Islamic Commercial Crisis: Institutional Roots of Economic Underdevelopment in the Middle East', *The Journal of Economic History*, 63 (2003): 414–46

Kuznats, Simon, *Modern Economic Growth: Rate, Structure and Spread* (New Haven: Yale University Press, 1966)

Kynaston, David, *The Secretary of State* (Lavenham: Dalton, 1978)

Kyvig, David E., *Explicit and Authentic Acts: Amending the United States Constitution* (Lawrence: University of Kansas Press, 1996)

La Nauze, J.A., *The Making of the Australian Constitution* (Melbourne: Melbourne University Press, 1972)

Lal, Deepak, *Unintended consequences: the impact of factor endowments, culture, and politics on long run economic performance* (Cambridge, Massachusetts, MIT Press, 1998)

Lander, J.R., *The Limitations of English Monarchy in the Later Middle Ages* (Toronto: University of Toronto Press, 1989)

Landes, David S., *Revolution in Time – Clocks and the making of the Modern World* (New York: W.W. Norton, 1983)

——, *The Unbound Prometheus: Technological Change and Industrial Development in Western Europe from 1750 to the Present* (Cambridge: Cambridge University Press, 1969)

——, *The wealth and poverty of Nations: why some are so rich and some so poor* (New York: W.W. Norton, 1998)

Lang, Graeme, 'Structural factors in the origins of modern science: a comparison of China and Europe', in Steven Totosy de Zepetrek and Jennifer Jay, *East Asian Cultural and Historical Perspectives* (Edmonton: University of Alberta Research Institute for Comparative Literature and Cross-Cultural Studies, 1997)

Lash, W., 'The Decline of the Nation State in International Trade and Development', *Cardozo Law Review* (1996–97): 1001

Laski, Harold, *Authority in the Modern State* (New Haven: Yale University Press, 1919)

——, 'The Responsibility of the State in England', *Harvard Law Review*, 32 (1919): 447–72

——, 'The Theory of Popular Sovereignty', *Harvard Law Review*, 17 (1919): 201–15

Lasok, K.P.E., *The European Court of Justice: practice and procedure* (2nd edn, London: Butterworths, 1994)

Lassalle, Ferdinand, 'Uber Verfassungswesen', in E. Bernstein (ed.), *Gesammelte Reden und Schriften* (Berlin: P. Cassirer, 1919)

Latham, Richard, *The Law and the Commonwealth* (London: Greenwood Publishing Group, 1949) reprinted from W.K. Hancock (ed.), *Survey of British Commonwealth Affairs* (London: Oxford University Press, 1937)

——, 'What is an Act of Parliament?', *King's Council* (March 1939): 152–62

Lauterpacht, Sir Elihu, 'Sovereignty – Myth or Reality?', *International Affairs*, 73 (1997): 137–50

Lauterpacht, Sir Hersch, 'The Subjects of the Law of Nations', *Law Quarterly Review*, 63 (1947): 438–60

Law Commission of New Zealand, *Electronic Commerce Part One* (Wellington: Law Commission of New Zealand, 1998)

Law Commission of New Zealand, *Electronic Commerce Part Two: A Basic Legal Framework* (Wellington: Law Commission of New Zealand, 1999)

——, *Liability for loss resulting from the development, supply or use of genetically modified organisms* (Wellington: Law Commission of New Zealand, 2002)

Law Reform Commission of British Columbia, *Legal Position of the Crown* (Vancouver: The Law Reform Commission of British Columbia, 1972)

Law Reform Commission of Canada, *The Legal Status of the Federal Administration* (Ottawa: Law Reform Commission of Canada, 1985)

Lawrence, T.J., *The Principles of International Law* (7th edn, London: Macmillan, 1925)

Lawson, Michael, *Cnut: England's viking king* (2nd edn, Stroud: Tempus, 2004)

Lazare, Daniel, *The Frozen Republic: How the Constitution is Paralysing Democracy* (New York: Harcourt Brace and Co., 1996)

Lazer, David and Viktor Mayer-Schonberger, 'Governing networks: telecommunication deregulation in Europe and the United States', *Brooklyn Journal of International Law*, 27 (2002): 819–51

Legal Affairs Committee of the Parliamentary Assembly of the Council of Europe, *Legal Status of International Non-Governmental Organizations in Europe*, ed. D. Smith (Brussels: Legal Affairs Committee of the Parliamentary Assembly of the Council of Europe, 1986)

Leick, Gwendolyn, *Mesopotamia: the invention of the city* (London: Allen Lane, 2001)

Leoni, Bruno, *Freedom and the Law* (Princeton: D. Van Nostrand, 1961)

Lessig, Lawrence, *Code and other Laws of Cyberspace* (New York: Basic Books, 1999)

——, *The Future of Ideas: The Fate of the Commons in a Connected World* (New York: Random House, 2001)

Leventhal, Michael, 'The Golden Age of Wireless', *Intellectual Property and Technology Law Journal*, 14 (2002): 1

Levin, Nickolai G., 'Constitutional statutory synthesis', *Alabama Law Review*, 54 (2003): 1281–373

Levy-Ullmann, Henri, *The English Legal Tradition: Its Sources and History*, trans. M. Mitchell rev. and ed. Frederick Goadly (London: Macmillan, 1935)

Lewis, I.M., *A Modern History of Somalia: nation and state in the Horn of Africa* (4th edn, Oxford: James Currey, 1988)

——, *A Pastoral Democracy: a study of pastoralism and politics among the Northern Somali of the Horn of Africa* (Oxford: James Currey, 1982)

Lintott, Andrew, *Imperium Romanum: politics and administration* (London: Routledge, 1993)
Linz, Juan J. and Alfred Stepan, *Problems of Democratic Transition and Consolidation: Southern Europe, South Africa, and Post-Communist Europe* (Boston: Johns Hopkins University Press, 1996)
Lipset, Seymour Martin, *Political Man: The Social Bases of Politics* (New York: Doubleday, Garden City, 1960)
Little, Gavin, 'Scotland and Parliamentary Sovereignty', *Legal Studies*, 24(4) (2004): 540–67
Locke, John, 'Fundamental Constitutions for Carolina', in David Wootton (ed.), *Political Writings of John Locke* (London: Penguin, 1993)
——, *Two Treatises of Government*, ed. Peter Laslett (Cambridge: Cambridge University Press, 1988)
Locke, Robert R., *The end of the practical man: entrepreneurship and higher education in Germany, France, and Great Britain, 1880–1940* (Greenwich: Jai Press, 1984)
Loewenstein, Joseph, *The author's due: printing and the prehistory of copyright* (Chicago: University of Chicago Press, 2002)
von Loon, Richard and Michael Whittington, *The Canadian Political System: Environment, Structure and Process* (3rd edn, Toronto: McGraw-Hill Ryerson, 1981)
LoPatin, Nancy D., *Political unions, popular politics and the great Reform Act of 1832* (New York: St Martin's Press, 1999)
Lorenz, Joseph P., *Peace, power, and the United Nations: a security system for the twenty-first century* (Boulder: Westview Press, 1999)
Lot, Ferdinand, *The end of the ancient world and the beginnings of the Middle Ages* (London: Routledge and Kegan Paul, 1953)
Loughan, M. (ed.), *The Ten Tenets of Sovereignty* (Oxford: Hart Publishing, 2003)
Lowe, Cedric, *The reluctant imperialists: British foreign policy, 1878–1902* (London: Routledge and Kegan Paul, 1967)
Lowry, S. Todd, 'Lord Mansfield and the Law Merchant: Law and Economics in the Eighteenth Century', *Journal of Economic Issues*, 7 (1973): 605–22
Loyn, Henry, *The governance of Anglo-Saxon England, 500–1087* (London: Edward Arnold, 1984)
Lucy, R., *The Australian Form of Government* (Melbourne: Macmillan, 1985)
Lutz, Donald S., 'Toward a Theory of Constitutional Amendment', in Sanford Levinson (ed.), *Responding to Imperfection* (Princeton: Princeton University Press, 1995)
Lynch-Robinson, Bt, Sir Christopher and Adrian Lynch-Robinson, *Intelligible Heraldry. The application of a Mediæval System of Record and Identification to Modern Needs* (London: Macdonald & Co, 1948)
Lyons, Gene M. et al. (eds), *Beyond Westphalia? State Sovereignty and International Intervention* (Baltimore: Johns Hopkins University Press, 1995)

Mabry, Linda A., 'Multinational corporations and United States technology policy: rethinking the concept of corporate nationality', *Georgetown Law Journal*, 87 (1999): 563–673

Macartney Robbins, Helen, *Our First Ambassador to China: An Account of the Life of George, Earl of Macartney* (London: John Murray 1908)

MacCormick, N., 'Beyond the Sovereign States', *Modern Law Review*, 56 (1993): 1

MacDonald, W.A., *Documentary Source Book of American History* (New York: Macmillan, 1908)

McGinnis, John O. and Mark L. Movsesian, 'The World Trade Constitution', *Harvard Law Review*, 114 (2000): 511–605

McGinnis, John O., 'The Original Constitution and Our Origins', *Harvard Journal of Law and Public Policy*, 19 (1995): 251–61

——, 'The Symbiosis of Constitutionalism and Technology', *Harvard Journal of Law and Public Policy*, 25 (2001): 3–14

McGready, Steven, 'The Digital Reformation: Total Freedom, Risk, and Responsibility', *Harvard Journal of Law and Technology*, 10 (1996): 137–48

Machiavelli, Niccolo, *The Prince*, ed. Quentin Skinner and Russell Price (Cambridge: Cambridge University Press, 1988)

McHugh, P.G., 'Constitutional Myths and the Treaty of Waitangi', *New Zealand Law Journal* (1991): 316–20

——, 'Constitutional Theory and Maori Claims', in Sir Hugh Kawharu (ed.), *Waitangi*: *Maori and Pakeha Perspectives of the Treaty of Waitangi* (Auckland: Oxford University Press, 1989) 25–63

McKusick, Victor A., 'The Human Genome Project: Plans, Status, and Applications in Biology and Medicine', in George J. Annas and Sherman Elias (eds), *Gene Mapping: Using law and ethics as guides* (New York: Oxford University Press, 1992)

McLennan, Dan, 'The online revolution in government contracting', *Law Institute Journal*, 76 (2002): 78–81

MacLeod, Roy (ed.), *Government and expertise: specialists, administrators, and professionals, 1860–1919* (Cambridge: Cambridge University Press, 1988)

McManis, Charles, 'The Interface Between International Intellectual Property and Environmental Protection: Biodiversity and Biotechnology', *Washington University Law Quarterly*, 76 (1998): 255–79

McNeill, William, *The Rise of the West* (Chicago: University of Chicago Press, 1963)

Macridis, Roy, 'Major Characteristics of the Traditional Approach', in Bernard Susser (ed.), *Approaches to the Study of Politics* (New York: Macmillan Publishing, 1992) 16–49

Maddison, Angus, *The World Economy: a millennial perspective* (Paris: Development Centre of the Organisation for Economic Co-operation and Development)

Mahoney, Paul G., 'The Common Law and Economic Growth: Hayek might be right', *Journal of Legal Studies*, 30 (2001): 503–25

Maine, Sir Henry Sumner, *Early Law and Custom* (London: John Murray, 1890)

Mainwaring, Scott and Matthew Soberg Shugart (eds), *Presidentalism and Democracy in Latin America* (Cambridge: Cambridge University Press, 1997)

Maitland, Frederic and Sir Frederick Pollock, *History of English Law before the Times of Edward I* (2nd edn, Cambridge: Cambridge University Press, 1895)

Maitland, Frederic 'The Crown as a Corporation', *Law Quarterly Review*, 17 (1901): 131–46

——, *Domesday Book and Beyond – three essays on the early history of England* (New York: W.W. Norton, 1966, first published 1897)

Makower, Felix, *Constitutional History and Constitution of the Church of England* (London: S. Sonnenschein & Co., 1895)

Mallory, J.R., 'The Appointment of the Governor General', *Canadian Journal of Economics and Political Science* (1960): 96

Man, John, *The Gutenberg revolution: the story of a genius and an invention that changed the world* (London: Review, 2002)

Mancini, G.F., 'Europe: The Case for Statehood', *European Law Journal*, 4(1) (1998): 29–42

Mann, F.A., 'The Doctrine of Jurisdiction in International Law Revisited After Twenty Years', *Recueil des Cours*, 186 (1984): 9

——, 'The Doctrine of Jurisdiction in International Law', *Recueil des Cours*, 111 (1964): 9

Manning, Joseph G., *Land and power in Ptolemaic Egypt: the structure of land tenure* (Cambridge: Cambridge University Press, 2003)

Manolopoulos, Andreas, 'Raising "Cyber-Borders": The Interaction Between Law and Technology', *International Journal of Law and Information Technology*, 11 (2003): 40–58

Maravall, José María and Adam Przeworaski (eds), *Democracy and the Rule of Law* (Cambridge: Cambridge University Press, 2003)

Marden, Emily, 'Risk and regulation: U.S. regulatory policy on genetically modified food and agriculture', *Boston College Law Review*, 44 (2003): 733–87

Marsden, Christopher, *Regulating the Global Information Society* (London: Routledge, 2000)

Marshall, Geoffrey, *Constitutional Conventions – The Rules and Forms of Political Accountability* (Oxford: Oxford University Press, 1986)

——, *Parliamentary Sovereignty and the Commonwealth* (Oxford: Oxford University Press, 1957)

Marston, G., 'The British Acquisition of the Nicobar Islands, 1869: A Possible Example of Abandonment of Territorial Sovereignty', *British Yearbook of International Law*, 69 (1998) 245

Martin, L., H. Gutman and P. Hutton (eds), *Technologies of the Self: A Seminar with Michel Foucault* (London: Tavistock, 1998)

Marx, Karl, *Das Kapital: Kritik der politischen Ökonomie (Capital: A Critique of Political Economy)*, ed. Frederick Engels (New York: International Publishers, 1967)

Mathieson, D.L., 'Does the Crown have Human Powers?', *New Zealand Universities Law Review*, 15 (1992): 117–42

Matthews, J., 'Power Shift', *Foreign Affairs*, 76 (1997): 50–71

Maurice, Pearton, *The knowledge state: diplomacy, war, and technology since 1830* (London: Burnett Books, 1982)

Mayer, Franz C., 'The Internet and Public International Law – Worlds Apart?', *European Journal of International Law*, 12 (2001): 617–22

Melancon, G., 'Peaceful Intentions: The First British Trade Commission in China, 1833–5', *Historical Research*, 73(180) (2000): 33–47

Menefee, S.P., 'Republics of the Reefs: Nation-Building on the Continental Shelf and in the World's Oceans', *California Western International Law Journal*, 25 (1994): 81–111

Merelmen, Richard, 'Learning and Legitimacy', *American Political Science Review*, 60 (1966): 548–61

Merritt, Deborah Jones, 'The Constitution in a brave new world: a century of technological change and constitutional law', *Oregon Law Review*, 69 (1990): 1–45

Mikasa, HIH Prince Takahito (ed.), 'Monarchies and socio-religious traditions in the ancient Near East: papers read at the 31st International Congress of Human Sciences in Asia and North Africa' (Cairo: International Congress of Human Sciences in Asia and North Africa, 1984)

Miller, Chris (ed.), *Planning and environmental protection: a review of law and policy* (Oxford: Hart, 2001)

Miller, Henry J., 'Patenting Animals', *Issues of Science and Technology* (1988–89): 24

Miller, Michael B., 'The business trip: Maritime networks in the twentieth century', *Business History Review*, 77 (2003): 1–32

Miller, Raymond, *New Zealand Government and Politics* (3rd edn, Melbourne: Oxford University Press, 2003)

Mill, John Stuart, *Utilitarianism* (London: Everymans Edition, 1910)

Milliken, Jennifer (ed.), *State Failure, Collapse and Reconstruction* (Oxford: Blackwell Publishing, 2003)

Mirsky, Arthur, 'Influence of geologic factors on ancient Egyptian civilization', *Journal of Geoscience Education*, 45 (1997): 415

Mittels, Heinrich, *The state in the middle ages: a comparative constitutional history of feudal Europe*, trans. H.F. Orton (Amsterdam: North-Holland Publishing Co., 1975)

Modica, Joseph, 'The function and purpose of suffering, persecution, and martyrdom in Luke-Acts: An exegetical and theological inquiry', Drew University PhD thesis (1995)

Mokyr, Joel, *The Lever of Riches: Technological creativity and economic progress* (Oxford: Oxford University Press, 1990)
Molho, Anthony, Kurt Raaflaub and Julia Emlen, *City states in classical antiquity and Mediæval Italy* (Ann Arbor: University of Michigan Press, c.1991)
Moloney, Pat, 'Neo-Liberalism: A Pluralist Critique', in Raymond Miller (ed.), *New Zealand Government and Politics* (2nd edn, Melbourne: Oxford University Press, 2001): 533–43
——, 'Pluralist Theories of the State', in Raymond Miller (ed.), *New Zealand Politics in Transition* (Auckland: Oxford University Press, 1997): 317–28
Monahan, Arthur P., *Consent, coercion, and limit: the mediæval origins of parliamentary democracy* (Leiden: Brill, 1987)
Montesquieu, Charles de Secondat Baron de, 'The Spirit of the Laws', in Arend Lijphart (ed.), *Parliamentary versus Presidential Government* (Oxford: Oxford University Press, 1992): 48–51
Moore, Nick and Jane Steele, *Information-intensive Britain: an analysis of the policy issues* (London: Policy Studies Institute, 1991)
Moore, Sir William, 'Law and Government', *Commonwealth Law Review*, 3 (1905): 205
——, 'Liability for the Acts of Public Servants', *Law Quarterly Review*, 23 (1907): 112
Moorhouse, Geoffrey, *The diplomats: the Foreign Office today* (London: Jonathan Cape, 1977)
More, Charles, *Understanding the Industrial Revolution* (London: Routledge, 2000)
Morgan, G., *The Idea of a European Superstate: Public Justification and European Integration* (Princeton: Princeton University Press, 2005)
Morison, John, 'Modernising Government and the E-Government Revolution: Technologies of Government and Technologies of Democracy', in Nicholas Bamford and Peter Leyland (eds), *Public Law in a Multilayered Constitution* (Oxford: Hart Publishing, 2003)
Morrow, John, 'Neo-Liberalism', in Raymond Miller (ed.), *New Zealand Government and Politics* (2nd edn, Melbourne: Oxford University Press, 2001): 521–32
Morse, Edward A., 'State taxation of Internet commerce: something new under the sun?', *Creighton Law Review*, 30 (1997): 1113–67
Mozley and Whiteley's Law Dictionary, ed. E.R. Hardy Ivamy (10th edn, London: Butterworths, 1988)
Mulgan, Richard, 'Can the Treaty of Waitangi provide a constitutional basis for New Zealand's political future?', *Political Science*, 41 (1989): 51–68
——, *Democracy and Power in New Zealand: A study of New Zealand politics* (2nd edn, Auckland: Oxford University Press, 1989)
——, 'A pluralist analysis of the New Zealand State', in Brian Roper and Chris Rudd (eds), *State and Economy in New Zealand* (Auckland: Oxford University Press, 1993): 128–46

Mullett, Michael A., *The Catholic Reformation* (London: Routledge, 1999)
Munro, C., 'Laws and conventions distinguished', *Law Quarterly Review*, 91 (1975): 218–35
Murphy, Sean J., *Twilight of the Chiefs: The Mac Carthy Mór Hoax* (Bethesda: Academica Press, 2004)
Muschter, G., 'Kunstlerforderung in der Bundesrepublik Deutschland', in R. Strachwitz and S. Toepler (eds), *Kulturforderung: Mehr als Sponsoring* (Wiesbaden: Gabler, 1993)
Al Namlah, Saleh, 'Political legitimacy in Libya since 1969', Syracuse University PhD thesis (1992)
National Institutes of Health, U.S. Department of Health and Human Services, *Stem Cells: Scientific Progress and Future Research Directions* ES-2 (Washington: National Institutes of Health, 2001)
Naughton, John, *A brief history of the future: the origins of the Internet* (London: Phoenix, 2000)
Needham, Joseph, *The Great Titration: Science and Society in East and West* (George Allen & Unwin, London, 1969)
——, *Science and civilisation in China* (Cambridge University Press, Cambridge, 1954–95)
Nelson, Janet L., 'Kingship and empire', in J.H. Burns (ed.), *The Cambridge History of Mediæval Political Thought c.350–c.1450* (Cambridge: Cambridge University Press, 1988)
Nenner, Howard, The Right to be King – The Succession to the Crown of England, 1603–1714 (London: Macmillan, 1995)
Netanel, Neil Weinstock, 'Copyright and a democratic civil society', *Yale Law Journal*, 106 (1996): 283–387
Neumann, Peter G., 'Technology, laws, and society', *Association for Computing Machinery. Communications of the ACM*, 37 (1994): 138
Report of the Royal Commission on Newfoundland Finances (London: HMSO, 1933)
Nicoll, C.C., 'Electronic Commerce: a New Zealand perspective', *EDI Law Review: Legal Aspects of Paperless Communication*, 6 (1999): 5–20
Noll, R.G. and B.M. Owen, 'The Anticompetitive Use of Regulation: *United States v. AT&T*', in J.E. Kwoka and L.J. White (eds), *The Antitrust Revolution* (Glenview: Scott, Foresman and Co., 1989)
Norris, Pippa, *Digital Divide: Civic Engagement, Information Poverty, and the Internet Worldwide* (New York: Cambridge University Press, 2001)
North, Douglass C., *Institutions, institutional change and economic performance* (Cambridge: Cambridge University Press 1990)
——, *Structure and Change in Economic History* (London: W.W. Norton, 1981)
North, Sir Peter and J.J. Fawcett, *Cheshire and North's private international law* (13th edn., London: Butterworths, 1999)

Novotny, O., 'Key issues in the transformation of culture in the post-socialist countries: With particular reference to the Slovak Republic', *European Journal of Cultural Policy*, 1 (1995): 217–23

Nozick, Robert, *Anarchy, state, and Utopia* (Oxford: Blackwell, 1975)

Nwabueze, Remigius N., 'Ethnopharmacology, patents and the politics of plants' genetic resources', *Cardozo Journal of International and Comparative Law*, 11 (2003): 585–632

Ockham, William, *Quaestiones et decisiones in quattuor libros Sententiarum Petri Lombardi* ('Sentences of Peter Lombard') Editione Lugdunensi (Lyon: privately published, 1495)

O'Connell, D.P., *International Law* (2nd edn, London: Stevens, 1970)

O'Donnell, Guillermo, *Transitions from Authoritarian Rule: Tentative Conclusions about uncertain democracies* (Baltimore: Johns Hopkins University Press, 1986)

Office of Technology Assessment, Congress of the United States, *New developments in biotechnology: Ownership of human tissues and cells – Special Report* (Washington: Office of Technology Assessment, 1987) pub. no. OTA-BA-337

Olson, Mancur, 'Dictatorship, Democracy, and Development', *American Political Science Review*, 87 (1993): 567–76

Oresme, Nicole, *Le Livre des Politiques d'Aristote*, ed. Albert D. Menut, *Transactions of the American Philosophical Society*, 60 (1970): 1–380

Organization for Economic Co-operation and Development, *Bio technology and the changing role of government* (Paris, Organization for Economic Co-operation and Development, 1988)

Orwell, George, *Nineteen Eighty-Four, a Novel* (London: Secker and Warburg, 1949)

Ostry, Sylvia and Richard R. Nelson, *Techno-nationalism and techno-Globalism: conflict and cooperation* (Washington: Brookings Institution, c.1995)

Overby, A.B., 'Will cyberlaw be uniform?: an introduction to the UNCITRAL Model law on Electronic Commerce', *Tulane Journal of International and Comparative Law*, 7 (1999): 219–310

Paczolay, Peter, 'Constitutional Transition and Legal Continuity', *Connecticut Journal of International Law*, 8 (1993): 559–74

Palan, R., 'Tax Havens and the Commercialisation of State Sovereignty', *International Organization*, 56 (2002): 151–76

Papadakis, N., *The International Legal Regime of Artificial Islands* (Leiden: Sijthoff, 1977)

Partington, Martin, 'The Reform of Public Law in Britain', in Patrick McAuslan and John McEldowney (eds), *Law, Legitimacy and the Constitution: Essays marking the Centenary of Dicey's Law of the Constitution* (London: Sweet and Maxwell, 1985): 191–211

Passerin d'Entrèves, A., *The Notion of the State: An Introduction to Political Theory* (Oxford: Clarendon Press, 1967)

Patterson, Richard D., 'Wonders in the heavens and on the earth: Apocalyptic imagery in the Old Testament', *Journal of the Evangelical Theological Society*, 43 (2000): 385–403

Pauwelyn, Joost, *Conflict of norms in public international law: how WTO law relates to other rules of international law* (Cambridge: Cambridge University Press, 2003)

Peacock, Reginald, *The Donet of Reginald Peacock*, ed. Elsie Vaughan Hitchcock (London: Early English Text Society, 1921, repr 1971) EETS OS 156

Pearson, Heath, *Origins of Law and Economics* (Cambridge: Cambridge University Press, 1997)

Pearson, Hilary and Clifford Miller, *Commercial exploitation of intellectual property* (London: Blackstone, 1990)

Pennington, Kenneth, 'Law, Legislative authority and theories of government, 1150–1300', in J.H. Burns (ed.), *The Cambridge History of Mediæval Political Thought c.350–c.1450* (Cambridge: Cambridge University Press, 1988): 424–53

——, *The Prince and the Law, 1200–1600: Sovereignty and rights in the Western legal tradition* (Berkeley: University of California Press, 1993)

Perelman, Michael, *Classical political economy: primitive accumulation and the social division of labour* (Totowa: Rowman and Allanheld, 1984)

Perritt, Henry H., 'The Internet is Changing International Law', *Chicago-Kent Law Review*, 73 (1998): 997–1054

Perry, Paul and Alan Webster, *New Zealand Politics at the Turn of the Millennium: Attitudes and Values about Politics and Government* (Auckland: Alpha Publications, 1999)

Perry, Richard Warren and Bill Maurer (eds), *Globalization under construction: governmentality, law, and identity* (Minneapolis: University of Minnesota Press, c.2003)

Peters, Ronald M., Jr., *The Massachusetts constitution of 1780: a social compact* (Amherst: University of Massachusetts Press, 1978)

Peterson, D.J., *Troubled lands: the legacy of Soviet environmental destruction* (Boulder: Westview Press, 1993)

Petty, Sir William, *The Collected Works of William Petty*, ed. T.W. Hutchison (London:, Routldge, 1997)

Phillips, Jock, 'The Constitution and Independent Nationhood', in Colin James (ed.), *Building the Constitution* (Wellington: Victoria University of Wellington Institute of Policy Studies, 2000): 69–76

Philpott, Daniel, 'Sovereignty', *Journal of International Affairs*, 48 (1995): 353–68

Pierson, Paul and Theda Skocpol, 'Historical Institutionalism in Contemporary Political Science' in Ira Katznelson and Helen V. Milner (eds), *Political Science: State of the Discipline* (New York: Norton, 2002) 693–721

Pikirayi, Innocent, *The Zimbabwe culture: origins and decline of southern Zambezian states* (Walnut Creek: AltaMira Press, c.2001)

Pila, Justine, 'Bound Futures: Patent law and modern biotechnology', *Boston University Journal of Science and Technology Law*, 9 (2003): 326–78

Pine, L.G., *International Heraldry* (Rutland: Tuttle, 1970)

Plato, *The Republic*, ed. G.R.F. Ferrari trans. Tom Griffith (Cambridge: Cambridge University Press, 2000)

Pocock, John G.A., *The Ancient Constitution and the Feudal Law; A Study of English Historical Thought in the Seventeenth Century* (2nd edn, Cambridge: Cambridge University Press, 1987)

——, *The ancient constitution and the feudal law: a study of English historical thought in the seventeenth century* (Cambridge: Cambridge University Press, 1987)

Poggi, Gianfranco, *The Development of the Modern State: A Sociological Introduction* (London: Hutchinson, 1978)

Pollard, Sidney, *Essays on the industrial revolution in Britain*, ed. Colin Holmes (Aldershot: Ashgate, 2000)

Pomeranz, Kenneth, *The Great Divergence: Europe, China and the making of the modern World Economy* (Princeton: Princeton University Press, 2000)

Post, David G. and David R. Johnson, '"Chaos Prevailing on Every Continent": Towards a New Theory of Decentralised Decision-Making in Complex Systems', Social Science Research Network Electronic Library (14 June 1999), available at <http://papers.ssrn.com/sol3/delivery.cfm/-99032613.pdf?abstractid=157692> (as at 1 December 2003)

Postle, H.T., 'Commonwealth and Crown', *Australian Law Journal*, 3 (1929): 109

Potter, David, *Prophets and Emperors: Human and Divine Authority from Augustus to Theodosius* (Cambridge: Harvard University Press, 1994)

Puro, Steven, 'Technology, politics and the new Industrial Revolution', *Public Law Forum*, 4 (1985): 387–98

Putnam, George Haven, *The censorship of the Church of Rome and its influence upon the production and distribution of literature* (New York: B. Blom, 1967)

Puurunen, Tapio, 'The Legislative Jurisdiction of States over Transactions in International Electronic Commerce', *John Marshall Journal of Computer and Information Law*, 18 (2000): 689–754

Qiu, Jack Linchuan, 'Virtual Censorship in China: Keeping the Gate between the Cyberspaces', *International Journal of Communications Law and Policy*, 4 (1999–2000): 1–25

Rabinow, P. (ed.), *Michel Foucault: Ethics* (London: Penguin, 1997)

Rabkin, J.A., 'Is Sovereignty traded in trade agreements?', in J.A. Rabkin (ed.), *Law without Nations? Why Constitutional Government Requires Sovereign States* (Princeton: Princeton University Press, 2005)

Raines, Lisa J., 'The Mouse That Roared: Patent Protection for Genetically Engineered Animals Makes Legal, Moral, and Economic Sense', *Issues of Science and Technology* (1988): 65

Räisänen, Heikki, *Paul and the Law* (Tubingen: J.C.B. Mohr, 1983)

Rawls, John, *Political Liberalism* (New York: Columbia University Press, 1993)

——, *A Theory of Justice* (Cambridge: The Belknap Press, 1971)

Raz, Joseph, *The concept of a legal system; an introduction to the theory of legal system* (Oxford: Clarendon Press, 1970)

Rege, Vinod, 'Economies in transition and developing countries: prospects for greater co-operation in trade and economic fields', *Journal of World Trade (Law-Economics-Public Policy)*, 27 (1993): 83–115

Reidenberg, Joel R., 'Governing Networks and Rule-Making in Cyberspace', in Brian Kahin and Charles Nesson (eds), *Borders in Cyberspace* (Cambridge: MIT Press, 1997)

——, 'Governing Networks and Rule-making in Cyberspace', *Emory Law Journal*, 45 (1996): 911–30

——, 'Lex Informatica: The Formulation of Information Policy Rules Through Technology', *Texas Law Review*, 76 (1998): 553–94

Reinicke, W.H., 'Global Public Policy', *Foreign Affairs* (1997): 127–38

Reston, James, Jr., *Warriors of God: Richard the Lionheart and Saladin in the Third Crusade* (New York: Doubleday, 2001)

Reynolds, Glenn Harlan, 'Environmental Regulation of Nanotechnology: Some Preliminary Observations', *Environmental Law Reports*, 31 (2001): 10681–8

Reynolds, Susan, 'Law and Community in Western Christendom', *American Journal of Legal History* (1981): 206

Richardson, Martin (ed.), *Globalization and international trade* liberalisation: *continuity and change* (Cheltenham: Edward Elgar, 2000)

Rifkin, Jeremy, 'Creating the Efficient Gene', in Michael Ruse (ed.), *Philosophy of Biology* (Albany: State University of New York Press, 1989)

Riley, Patrick, *Will and political legitimacy: a critical exposition of social contract theory in Hobbes, Locke, Rousseau, Kant, and Hegel* (Cambridge: Harvard University Press, 1982)

Roberts, Adam and Richard Guellf (eds), *Laws of War* (Oxford: Oxford University Press, 2000)

Roberts, Leslie, 'Genome Patent Fight Erupts', *Science*, 254 (1991): 184–6

——, 'NIH Gene Patents, Round Two', *Science*, 255 (1992): 912–13

Robertson, A.J., *Laws of the Kings of England* (Cambridge: Cambridge University Press, 1925)

Rose, Gregory, 'International law of sustainable agriculture in the 21st century: The International Treaty on Plant Genetic Resources for Food and Agriculture', *Georgetown International Environmental Law Review*, 15 (2003): 583–632

Rose, Kenneth, Kings, Queens and Courtiers: Intimate Portraits of the Royal House of Windsor from its foundation to the Present Day (London: Weidenfeld and Nicolson, 1985)

Rose, Nicolas, 'Government and Control', *British Journal of Criminology*, 40 (2000): 321–39

——, *Powers of Freedom: Reframing Political Thought* (Cambridge: Cambridge University Press, 1999)

Rosenberg, Nathan, *Exploring the black box: technology, economics, and history* (Cambridge: Cambridge University Press, 1994)

Rosenberg, Nathan and E.E. Birdzell, *How the west grew rich: the economic transformation of the industrial world* (London: Tauris, 1986)

Rosenberg, Nathan and Walter G. Vincenti, *The Britannia Bridge: the generation and diffusion of technological knowledge* (Cambridge: MIT Press, 1978)

Ross, Alf, *On Law and Justice* (London: Stevens, 1958)

Rotberg, Robert I. (ed.), *State Failure and State Weakness in a Time of Terror* (Washington: Brookings Institute, 2003)

——, (ed.), *When States Fail: Causes and Consequences* (Princeton: Princeton University Press, 2003)

Rotberg, Robert I. and Theodore K. Rabb (eds), *The Origin and Prevention of Major Wars* (Cambridge: Cambridge University Press, 1988)

Rouseau, Jean-Jacques, *The Social Contract and other later political writings*, ed. and trans. Victor Goureatres (Cambridge: Cambridge University Press, 1997)

Royal Commission on the Electoral System, *Report of the Royal Commission on the Electoral System 'Towards a better democracy'* (Wellington: Government Printer, 1986)

Rudin, Thom W., 'State involvement in the "new Industrial Revolution"', *Public Law Forum*, 4 (1985): 411–17

Rushdoony, Rousas John, *The Institutes of Biblical Law* (Philadelphia: Presbyterian and Reformed Publishing, 1973)

Russell, Bertrand Earl, *Towards world government* (London: New Commonwealth, 1947)

Russell, Peter, *Constitutional Odyssey: Can Canadians become a Sovereign People*? (Toronto: University of Toronto Press, 1992)

Ryan, Chris, '"The Crown" and corporate bona vacantia', *Kingston Law Review*, 12 (1982): 75–87

Ryholt, K.S.B., *The Political Situation in Egypt during the Second Intermediate Period, c.1800–1550 BC* (Copenhagen: The Carsten Niebuhr Institute of Near Eastern Studies, 1997)

Safarian, A.E. and Gilles Y. Bertin (eds), *Multinationals, governments, and international technology transfer* (New York: St Martins, 1987)

Salter, Leonard M., 'Predictions for the Next Millennium', *Orange County Lawyer*, 42 (2000): 16–22

Sanford, B. and Michael J. Lorenger, 'Teaching an Old Dog New Tricks', *Connecticut Law Review*, 28 (1995–96): 1137–70

Sarcevíc, P. *Privatisation in Central and Eastern Europe* (London: Graham and Trotman, 1992)

Sardar, Ziauddin, *Science, Technology and Development in the Muslim World* (London: Croom Helm, 1977)

Sarnatar, A.I., 'Destruction of State and Society in Somalia: Beyond the Tribal Convention', *Journal of Modern African Studies*, 30 (1992): 625

Schaar, John, 'Legitimacy in the Modern State', in William Connolly (ed.), *Legitimacy and the State* (Oxford: Basil Blackwell, 1984)

Schedler, Andreas, Larry Diamond and Marc F. Plattner (eds), *The Self-Restraining State: Power and Accountability* (Boulder: Lynne Rienner Publishers, 1999)

Scheuerman, William E., 'Constitutionalism in an age of speed', *Constitutional Commentary*, 19 (2002): 353–90

Schreuer, Christopher, 'The Waning of the Sovereign State: Towards a New Paradigm for International Law', *European Journal of International Law*, 4 (1993): 447–71

Schroth, Peter W. and Preeti Sharma, 'Transnational law and technology as potential forces against corruption in Africa', *Management Decision*, 41 (2003): 296–303

Schultz, Cynthia B. and Tamara Raye Crockett, 'Economic development, democratization, and environmental protection in Eastern Europe', *Boston College Environmental Affairs Law Review*, 18 (1990): 53–84

Schulz, Regine and Matthias Seidel (eds), *Egypt: the world of the Pharaohs* (Köln: Könemann, 1998)

Schuster, J.M., 'Deconstructing a Tower of Babel: Privatisation, decentralisation and devolution as ideas in good currency in cultural policy', *Voluntas*, 8 (1997): 261–82

Schwartz, Paul M., 'Internet privacy and the State', *Connecticut Law Review*, 32 (2000): 815–59

Schwarzenberger, Georg and E.D. Brown, *A Manual of International Law* (6th edn, Milton: Professional Books, 1976)

Schwarzenberger, Georg, *A Manual of International Law* (1st edn., London: Stevens and Sons, 1947)

Scott, Jonathan, *Algernon Sidney and the Restoration Crisis, 1677–1683* (Cambridge: Cambridge University Press, 1991)

Seib, Philip, *Beyond the front lines: how the news media cover a world shaped by* war (New York: Palgrave Macmillan, 2004)

Serafini, Shirley and Michel Andrieu, *The Information Revolution and its Implications for Canada* (Ottawa: Minister of Supply and Services, 1981)

Shagan, Ethan H., *Popular politics and the English Reformation* (Cambridge: Cambridge University Press, 2003)

Shambaugh, David (ed.), *Greater China: the next superpower?* (Oxford: Oxford University Press, 1995)

Shapiro, Michael H., 'Thinking about biomedical advances: The role of ethics and law: On the possibility of "progress", in managing biomedical technologies: Markets, lotteries, and rational standards in organ transplantation', *Capital University Law Review*, 31 (2003): 13–127

Sharp, Andrew (ed.), 'Constitution', in Raymond Miller (ed.), *New Zealand Government and Politics* (2nd edn, Melbourne: Oxford University Press, 2001)

——, *Justice and the Maori: the philosophy and practice of Maori claims in New Zealand since the 1970s* (2nd edn, Auckland: Oxford University Press, 1997)

Sharp, Andrew (ed.), *Leap into the dark: the changing role of the state in New Zealand since 1984* (Auckland: Auckland University Press, 1994)

Sharpe, Kevin, *The Personal Rule of Charles I* (New Haven: Yale University Press, 1992)

Shelley, Mary Wollstonecraft, *Frankenstein, or The modern Prometheus*, ed. Marilyn Butler (Oxford: Oxford University Press, 1998, first published 1818)

Siedel, George J., *Using the Law to Gain Competitive Advantage* (San Francisco: Wiley, 2002)

Silberman, Bernard S., *Cages of reason: the rise of the rational state in France, Japan, the United States, and Great Britain* (Chicago: University of Chicago Press, 1993)

Silcock, Rachel, 'What is e-government?', *Parliamentary Affairs* (2001): 88–101

Silver, Lee M., *Remaking Eden: How Genetic Engineering and Cloning will Transform the American Family* (New York: Avon Books, 1998)

Simpson, Alan (ed.), *Constitutional Implications of MMP* (Wellington: School of Political Science and International Relations, Victoria University of Wellington: 1998)

Simpson, Gerry J., *Great powers and outlaw states unequal sovereigns in the international legal order* (Cambridge: Cambridge University Press, 2004)

Skinner, Quentin, 'Conquest and Consent: Thomas Hobbes and the Engagement Controversy', in G.E. Aylmer (ed.), *The Interregnum – The Quest for Settlement, 1640–1660* (Hamden: Archon Books, 1972)

Skocpol, Theda, *States and Social Revolution* (Cambridge: Cambridge University Press, 1979)

Slack, Paul, *The English poor law, 1531–1782* (New York: Economic History Society/Cambridge University Press, 1995)

Slaughter, A., 'The Real New World Order', *Foreign Affairs*, 76 (1997): 183–97

Slaughter, Anne-Marie and Alec Stone Sweet, 'Assessing the Effectiveness of International Adjudication', in *Structures of World Order: Proceedings of the 89th Annual Meeting*. Washington D.C.: American Society of International Law: 91–3

Smart, P.St.J. 'Revolution, Constitution and the Commonwealth: Grenada', *International and Comparative Law Quarterly*, 35 (1986): 950

Smith, David E., 'Bagehot, the Crown, and the Canadian Constitution', *Canadian Journal of Political Science*, 28 (1995): 619–37

——, 'Empire, Crown and Canadian Federalism', *Canadian Journal of Political Science*, 24 (1991): 451–73

——, The Invisible Crown: The First Principle of Canadian Government (Toronto: University of Toronto Press, 1995)

——, *The Republican Option in Canada, Past and Present* (Toronto: University of Toronto Press, 1999)

Smith, Sir Thomas, *De Republica Anglorum* (New York: Garland Publishing, 1979, first printed 1581)

Smith, Sir Thomas, 'Pretensions of English Law as "Imperial Law"', in *The Laws of Scotland* (Edinburgh: Law Society of Scotland/Butterworths, 1987)

Smith, Woodruff D., *European imperialism in the nineteenth and twentieth centuries* (Chicago: Nelson Hall, c.1982)

Snow, Alpheus H., *The administration of dependencies: a study of the evolution of the federal empire, with special reference to American colonial problems* (New York: G.P. Putnam's Sons, 1902)

Sobel, Dava, *Longitude: the true story of a lone genius who solved the greatest scientific problem of his time* (New York: Walker, 1995)

Sørensen, Georg, *Changes in Statehood: The Transformation of International Relations* (Basingstoke: Palgrave, 2001)

Spalding, James, *The Reformation of the Ecclesiastical Laws of England, 1552* (Kirksville: Sixteenth Century Journal Publishers, 1992), vol. XIX, Sixteenth Century Essays and Studies

Spitz, Lewis W., *The Reformation: education and history* (Aldershot: Variorum, 1997)

Squibb, George, *Doctors' Commons: a history of the College of Advocates and Doctors of Law* (Oxford: Clarendon Press, 1977)

——, 'Heraldic Authority in the British Commonwealth', *Coat of Arms*, 10 (no. 76) (1968): 125

Stadelmann, Rudolf, *Social and political history of the German 1848 revolution*, trans. J.G. Chastain (Athens: Ohio University Press, 1975)

Standage, Tom, *The Victorian Internet: the remarkable story of the telegraph and the nineteenth century's online pioneers* (London: Phoenix, 1999)

Stanford, J.S., 'The Application of the Sherman Act to Conduct Outside the United States: A View from Abroad', *Cornell International Law Journal*, 11 (1978): 195

Starek, Roscoe B., III and Lynda M. Rozell, 'The Federal Trade Commission's commitment to on-line consumer protection', *The John Marshall Journal of Computer and Information Law*, 15 (1997): 679–702

Stark, David M. et al, 'Regulation of the Amount of Starch in Plant Tissues by ADP Glucose Pyrophosphorylase', *Science*, 258 (1992): 287–92

Statutes of the Realm (Printed by command of His Majesty King George the Third in pursuance of an address of the House of Commons of Great Britain, London: HMSO, 1810–22)

Staunton, Sir George, *An account of Macartney's embassy to China* (London: W. Bulmer 1797)

Stefancic, Jean and Richard Delgado, 'Outsider jurisprudence and the electronic revolution: Will technology help or hinder the cause of law reform?', *Ohio State Law Journal*, 52 (1991): 847–58

Stenton, Frank M., *The first century of English feudalism* (Oxford: Clarendon Press, 1961)

Stern, Nicholas, *Transition: Private Sector Development and the Role of Financial Institutions* (London: European Bank for Reconstruction and Development, 1994), Working paper no. 13. XY/N-1

Stevens, Denise, 'Embryonic stem cell research: will President Bush's limitation on federal funding put the United States at a disadvantage? A comparison between United States and international law', *Houston Journal of International Law*, 25 (2003): 623–53

Stewart, Cecil, *Byzantine legacy* (London: Allen and Unwin, 1947)

Stiefel, Tina, *The Intellectual Revolution in Twelfth Century Europe* (New York: St Martin's Press, 1985)

Stock, Gregory, *Redesigning Humans, Our Inevitable Genetic Future* (Boston: Houghton Mifflin, 2002)

Stone, Peter, 'Internet consumer contracts and European private international law', *Information and Communications Technology Law*, 9 (2000): 5–15

Stoper, Emily and Emilia Ianeva, 'Democratization and women's employment policy in post-Communist Bulgaria', *Connecticut Journal of International Law*, 12 (1996): 9

Storey, Glenn R., 'The population of ancient Rome', *Antiquity*, 71 (1997): 966–78

Stover, William J., *Information technology in the Third World: Can I.T. lead to humane national development?* (Boulder: Westview Press, 1984)

Straus, J., 'Biodiversity and Intellectual Property', *AIPPI Yearbook*, 9 (1998): 99–128

Strayer, J.R., *On the Mediæval Origins of the Modern State* (Princeton: Princeton University Press, 1970)

Strickland, Matthew, 'Against the Lord's anointed', in George Garnett and John Hudson (eds), *Law and Government in Mediæval England and Normandy* (Cambridge: Cambridge University Press, 1994)

Strudwick, Nigel, *The administration of Egypt in the Old Kingdom: the highest titles and their holders* (London: Kegan Paul International, 1985)

Struve Catherine T. and R. Polk Wagner, 'Realspace sovereigns in cyberspace: Problems with the Anticybersquatting Consumer Protection Act', *Berkeley Technology Law Journal*, 17 (2002): 989–1041

Stubbs, William, *The Constitutional History of England* (4th edn., Oxford: Clarendon Press, 1906)

Suarez, Francisco, *Selections from three works: De legibus, ac deo legislators, 1612, Defensio fidei catholicae, et apostolicae adversus anglicanae sectae errores, 1613, De triplici virtute theologica, fide, spe, et charitate, 1621, trans. Gladys L. Williams, Ammi Brown and John Waldron* (Oxford: Clarendon Press, 1944)

Sundquist, James L., *Constitutional Reform and Effective Government* (Washington: The Brookings Institution, 1992)

Sung, Lawrence M., 'Collegiality and Collaboration in the Age of Exclusivity', *DePaul Journal of Health Care Law*, 3 (2000): 411–39

Sunkin, Maurice and Sebastian Payne, *The Nature of the Crown: A Legal and Political Analysis* (Oxford: Oxford University Press, 1999)

Sunstein, Cass R., *Republic.com* (Princeton: Princeton University Press, 2001)

Susser, Bernard (ed.), *Approaches to the Study of Politics* (New York: Macmillan Publishing, 1992)
Swanson, Matthew Lane, 'The social extract tradition and the question of political legitimacy', University of Missouri-Columbia PhD thesis (1995)
Sweet, A.S., *The Judicial Construction of Europe* (Oxford: Oxford University Press, 2004)
Swinburne, Richard, *Simplicity as Evidence for Truth* (Milwaukee: Marquette University Press, 1997)
Szoke, Helen, 'The nanny state or responsible government', *Journal of Law and Medicine*, 227 (2002): S–1
Taafahi, Tauassa, *Governance in the Pacific: the dismissal of Tuvalu's Governor-General* (Canberra: National Centre of Development Studies, Australian National University, 1996)
Talmon, S., 'Recognition of Governments: An Analysis of the New British Policy and Practice', *British Yearbook of International Law*, 58 (1992): 231–97
Tarifa, Fatos, 'Quest for legitimacy and the withering away of utopia', *Social Forces*, 76 (1997): 437–74
Tassé, Roger and Maxime Faille, 'Online Consumer Protection in Canada: The Problem of Regulatory Jurisdiction', *Internet and E-Commerce Law in Canada*, 2 (2000–2001): 41–8
Taylor, Arthur J., *Laissez-faire and state intervention in nineteenth-century Britain* (London: Economic History Society/Macmillan, 1972)
Taylor, Michael R. and Jody S. Tick, 'An incomplete picture. consideration of environmental laws to address problems that may arise from genetically engineered crops and food', *The Environmental Forum*, 20 (2003): 19
Teschke, Benno, *The myth of 1648: class, geopolitics, and the making of modern international relations* (London: Verso, 2003)
Tesón, Fernando, 'The Kantian Theory of International Law', 92 *Columbia Law Review* (1992): 53–102
——, *A Philosophy of International Law* (Boulder: Westview, 1998)
Thompson, Martyn P., *Ideas of contract in English political thought in the age of John Locke* (New York: Garland Publishing, 1987)
Tierney, Brian, *Church law and constitutional thought in the Middle Ages* (London: Variorum Reprints, 1979)
——, *Origins of Papal Infallibility, 1150–1350: a study on the concepts of infallibility, sovereignty and tradition in the Middle Ages* (Leiden: E.J. Brill, 1972)
——, *Religion, law, and the growth of constitutional thought, 1150–1650* (Cambridge: Cambridge University Press, 1982)
Tilly, Charles, *The Formation of National States in Western Europe* (Princeton: Princeton University Press, 1975)
Tizard, Dame Catherine, *Crown and Anchor; the present role of the Governor-General in New Zealand* (Wellington: Government House, 1993)

Toepler, Stefan, 'From Communism to civil society? the arts and the nonprofit sector in Central and Eastern Europe', *Journal of Arts Management, Law and Society*, 30 (2000): 7–18

Trakman, Leon, *The Law Merchant – The Evolution of Commercial Law* (Littleton: F.B. Rothman, 1983)

Traunmüller, R. and K. Lenk (eds), *Electronic Government: First International Conference*, EGOV 2002, Aix-en-Provence, France, September 2002 Proceedings (Berlin: Springer, 2002)

Trigger, Bruce G., *Early civilizations: ancient Egypt in context* (Cairo: American University in Cairo Press, 1993)

Tshuma, Lawrence, 'Hierarchies and Government versus Networks and Governance: Competing Regulatory Paradigms in Global Economic Regulation', Law, Social Justice and Global Development (1999) <http://elj.warwick.ac.uk/global/issue/2000-1/tshuma.html> (as at 22 January 2005)

Tsuji, Masatsugu, 'Transformation of the Japanese system towards a network economy', in Emanuele Giovannetti, Mitsuhiro Kagami and Masatsugu Tsuji (eds), *The Internet revolution: a global perspective* (Cambridge: Cambridge University Press, 2003)

Tucker, Robert C., *The Marx-Engels Reader* (New York: W.W. Norton and Co., 1972)

Tunstall, Ian, *Taxation and the Internet* (Pyrmont, Lawbook Co., 2003)

Twining, William, *Globalization and Legal Theory* (London: Butterworths, 1998)

Tyldesley, Joyce, *Hatchepsut: the female pharaoh* (London: Viking, 1996)

Ullmann, Walter, *The growth of papal government in the Middle Ages: a study in the ideological relation of clerical to lay power* (2nd edn, London: Methuen, 1965)

——, 'This Realm of England is an Empire', *Journal of Ecclesiastical History*, 30 (1979): 175–203

United Nations Conference on Trade and Development, *UNCTAD World Investment Report 2000: Cross-border mergers and acquisitions and development* (New York: United Nations Conference on Trade and Development, 2000)

Vagts, Detlev F., 'State Succession: The Codifiers View', *Virginia Journal of International Law*, 33 (1993): 275–97

Vaidhyanathan, Siva, *Copyright and copywrongs: The rise of intellectual property and how it threatens creativity* (New York: New York University, 2001)

Vallamsetty, Udaykiran, Krishna Kant and Prasant Mohapatra, 'Characterization of E-Commerce Traffic', *Electronic Commerce Research*, 3 (2003): 167–92

Varga, Csaba, 'Transformation to Rule of Law From No-Law: Societal Contexture of the Democratic Transition in Central and Eastern Europe', *Connecticut Journal of International Law*, 8 (1993): 487–505

van der Veen, Cornelius, 'Facts and figures on Rhine pollution', *International Business Lawyer*, 9 (1981): 41–52

Vile, John R., *The Constitutional Amending Process in American Political Thought* (New York: Praeger, 1992)

Vito, Christine C., 'State biotechnology oversight: the juncture of technology, law, and public policy', *Maine Law Review*, 45 (1993): 329–83
Volckart, Oliver and Antje Mangels, 'Are the roots of the modern lex mercatoria really mediæval?', *Southern Economic Journal*, 65 (1999): 427–50
Wade, Sir Henry, 'The Basis of Legal Sovereignty,', *Cambridge Law Journal* (1955): 172–97
Wade, Sir William, 'The Crown, Ministers and Officials: Legal Status and Liability', in Maurice Sunkin and Sebastian Payne (eds), *The Nature of the Crown: A Legal and Political Analysis* (Oxford: Oxford University Press, 1999)
Walbank, F.W., *The awful revolution: the decline of the Roman Empire in the West* (Liverpool: Liverpool University Press, 1969)
Walker, Clive, 'Review of the Prerogative', *Public Law* (1987): 62–84
Walker, Edward W., *Dissolution: sovereignty and the breakup of the Soviet Union* (Lanham: Rowman and Littlefield, 2003)
Walter, Bagehot, 'The English Constitution', in the *Collected Works of Walter Bagehot*, ed. Norman St John-Stevas (London: *The Economist*, 1974)
Walton, John K., *The Second Reform Act* (London: Methuen, 1987)
Walzer, Michael, *Just and Unjust Wars* (3rd edn, Plymouth: Plymbridge, 2000)
Warburton, David A., *Egypt and the Near East: politics in the Bronze Age* (Neuchâtel: Recherches et Publications, 2001)
——, *State and economy in ancient Egypt: fiscal vocabulary of the New Kingdom* (Göttingen: University Press, Fribourg/Vandenhoeck and Ruprecht, 1997)
Waskan, Jonathan, 'De facto legitimacy and popular will', *Social Theory and Practice*, 24 (1998): 25–56
Watson, Alan, *Society and Legal Change* (2nd edn, Philadelphia: Temple University Press, 2001)
Watson, James and Sir Francis Crick, 'Genetical Implications of the Structure of Deoxyribonucleic Acid', *Nature*, 171 (1953): 964–7
Weber, Maximilian, *The agrarian sociology of ancient civilizations*, trans. R.I. Frank (London: NLB, 1976)
——, *The Protestant Ethic and the Spirit of Capitalism*, trans. Talcott Parsons (London: Routledge, 1992, originally published 1905 as *Die Protestantische Ethik und der Geist des Kapitalismus*)
——, *Weber: Political Writings*, trans. Peter Lassman and Ronald Speirs (Cambridge: Cambridge University Press, 1994)
Wedgwood, Ruth, 'The Internet and Public International Law: Cyber-Nations', *Kentucky Law Journal*, 88 (2000): 957–65
Weingast, Barry, 'The Economic Role of Political Institutions: Market Preserving Federalism and Economic Development', *Journal of Law Economics and Organization*, 11 (1995): 24–8
Weinstein, Samuel Noah, 'United States v. Microsoft Corp', *Berkeley Technology Law Journal*, 17 (2002): 273

Weiser, Philip J., 'Internet governance, standard setting, and self-regulation', *Northern Kentucky Law Review*, 28 (2001): 822–46

Weiss, Daniel H. and Lisa Mahoney (eds), *France and the Holy Land: Frankish culture at the end of the crusades* (Baltimore: Johns Hopkins University Press, 2004)

Weller, M., 'The International Response to the Dissolution of the Socialist Federal Republic of Yugoslavia', *American Journal of International Law*, 86 (1992) 569

Western, J.R., *Monarchy and Revolution – the English State in the 1680's* (London: Blandford Press, 1972)

Whitman, R., 'No and After: Options for Europe', *International Affairs*, 81(4) (2005): 673–87

Whitten, Ralph U., 'United States conflict-of-laws doctrine and forum shopping, international and domestic (revisited)', *Texas International Law Journal*, 37 (2002): 559–89

Widner, Jennifer A., *Building the Rule of Law* (London: W.W. Norton & Co, 2001)

Wiener, J., *Globalisation and the Harmonisation of Law* (London: Pinter, 1999)

Wigram, W.A., *An introduction to the history of the Assyrian Church or the church of the Sassanid Persian Empire, 100–640 A.D.* (Piscataway: Gorgias Press, 2004)

Wilhelmsson, Thomas, Salla Tuominen and Heli Tuomola (eds), *Consumer law in the information society* (Boston: Kluwer Law International, 2001)

Wilkes, H. Garrison, 'Plant Genetic Resources over Ten Thousand Years: From a Handful of Seed to the Crop-Specific Mega-Gene Banks', in Jack R. Kloppenburg, Jr. (ed.), *Seeds and Sovereignty: The use and control of plant genetic resources* (Durham: Duke University Press, 1988)

Williams, David, 'The Constitutional Status of the Treaty of Waitangi: an historical perspective', *New Zealand Universities Law Review*, 14 (1990): 9–36

Williams, John C., 'The role of the United States government in encouraging technological innovation', *Canada-United States Law Journal*, 15 (1989): 219–28

Williams, Nigel, 'European Parliament Backs New Biopatent Guidelines', *Science*, 277 (1997): 472

Wilson, Margaret, 'The Reconfiguration of New Zealand Constitutional Institutions: the transformation of Tino Rangatiratanga into political reality?', *Waikato Law Review*, 5 (1997): 17

Winterton, George, 'The evolution of a separate Australian crown', *Monash University Law Review*, 19 (1993): 1–22

——, *Parliament, the executive and the Governor-General: A Constitutional Analysis* (Melbourne: Melbourne University Press, 1983)

Wittfogel, Karl A., *Oriental Despotism: A Comparative Study of Total Power* (New Haven: Yale University Press, 1957)

Wolf, Jonathan B., 'War games meets the Internet: Chasing 21st century cybercriminals with old laws and little money', *American Journal of Criminal Law*, 28 (2000): 95–117

Wolf, Martin, 'Will the nation-state survive Globalization?', *Foreign Affairs*, 80 (2001): 178–90

Wolfson, Joel Rothstein, 'Social and ethical issues in nanotechnology: Lessons from biotechnology and other high technologies', *Biotechnology Law Report*, 22 (2003): 376–96

Wolpe, Paul Root and Glenn McGee, '"Expert Bioethics" as Professional Discourse: The Case of Stem Cells', in Suzanne Holland, Karen Lebacqz and Laurie Zoloth (eds), *The Human Embryonic Stem Cell Debate: Science, Ethics, and Public Policy* (Cambridge: MIT Press, 2001)

Wonnell, Christopher T., 'The Noncompensation Thesis and its Critics: A Review of This Symposium's Challenges to the Argument for Not Compensating Victims of Legal Transitions', *Journal of Contemporary Legal Issues*, 13 (2003): 293–311

Woodward, Nicholas, *The management of the British economy, 1945–2001* (Manchester: Manchester University Press, 2004)

Woolliscroft, D.J., *Roman military signalling* (Stroud: Tempus, 2001)

Wriston, Walter B., *The Twilight of Sovereignty: How the information revolution is transforming our world* (New York: Scribner, 1992)

Wu, Timothy, 'Cyberspace Sovereignty? – The Internet and the International System', *Harvard Journal of Law and Technology*, 10 (1997): 647

Wulfstan of York, *An Werk Erzbischof Wulfstans von York – Die 'Institutes of Polity, Civil and Ecclesiastical*', ed. K. Jost (Tübingen: A. Francke, 1959)

Yavitz, Laura, 'The WTO and the environment: the Shrimp case that created a new world', *Journal of Natural Resources and Environmental Law*, 16 (2001): 203–55

Yen, Alfred C., 'Western frontier or feudal society?: Metaphors and Perceptions of cyberspace', *Berkeley Technology Law Journal*, 17 (2002): 1207–63

Zaret, David, *Origins of democratic culture: printing, petitions, and the public sphere in early-modern England* (Princeton: Princeton University Press, 2000)

Zekos, Georgios, 'Internet or Electronic Technology: A Threat to State Sovereignty', *Journal of Information, Law and Technology*, 3 (1999), available at <http://elj.warwick.ac.uk/jilt/99-3/zekos.html> (as at 28 November 2003)

Zeller, Eduard, *Outlines of the History of Greek Philosophy*, trans. L.R. Palmer (13th rev edn, London: Routledge, 1948)

Zinder, Norton D., 'Patenting cDNA 1993: Efforts and Happenings', *Gene*, 135 (1993): 295–8

Index